Workshop on Machine Reading for Question Answering 2019

Hong Kong, China
4 November 2019

ISBN: 978-1-7138-0084-2

Proceedings of the 2nd Workshop on Machine Reading for Question Answering

Nov 4, 2019
Hong Kong, China

facebook

NAVER

Introduction

Our workshop focuses on machine reading for question answering (MRQA), which has become an important testbed for evaluating how computer systems understand natural language, as well as a crucial technology for applications such as search engines and dialog systems. In recent years, research community has showed rapid progress on both datasets and models. Many large-scale datasets are proposed and the development of more accurate and more efficient question answering systems followed. Despite recent progress, yet there is much to be desired about these datasets and systems, such as model interpretability, ability to abstain from answering when there is no adequate answer, and adequate modeling of inference (e.g., entailment and multi-sentence reasoning).

This year, we focus on generalization of QA systems and present a new shared task on the topic. Our shared task addresses the following research question: how can one build a robust question answering system that can perform well questions from unseen domains? Train and test datasets may differ in passage distribution (from different sources (e.g., science, news, novels, medical abstracts, etc) with pronounced syntactic and lexical differences), question distribution (different styles (e.g., entity-centric, relational, other tasks reformulated as QA, etc) from different sources (e.g., crowdworkers, domain experts, exam writers, etc.)), as well as joint question-answering distribution (e.g., question collected independent vs. dependent of evidence).

For this task, we adapted and unified 18 distinct question answering datasets into the same format. We focus on extractive question answering. That is, given a question and context passage, systems must find a segment of text, or span in the document that best answers the question. While this format is somewhat restrictive, it allows us to leverage many existing datasets, and its simplicity helps us focus on out-of-domain generalization, instead of other important but orthogonal challenges. We released six larger datasets as training, and another six datasets for development. The rest six datasets were hidden from shared task participants until the final evaluation. Nine teams submitted to our shared task and the winning system achieved an average F1 score of 72.5 on the held-out datasets, 10.7 absolute points higher than our initial baseline based on BERT large.

This proceeding includes our report on the findings from this shared task as well as six system description papers from the shared task participants.

Similar to last year, we also sought research track submissions. We have received 39 paper submissions to the research track after the withdrawls, almost double the submission from last year. Out of this, twenty two papers are accepted and presented in this proceedings, and two papers are selected for the best paper award.

In the workshop program, we also include four cross submissions of work presented in other venues already.

The program features 22 new research track papers, six shared track papers and four cross-submissions from related areas, to be presented as either posters and talks. We are also excited to host remarkable invited speakers, including Mohit Bansal, Antoine Bordes, Jordan Boyd-Graber and Matt Gardner.

We thank the program committee, the EMNLP workshop chairs, the invited speakers, our sponsors Baidu, Facebook and NAVER and our steering committee: Jonathan Berant, Percy Liang, Luke Zettlemoyer.

Adam Fisch, Alon Talmor, Robin Jia, Minjoon Seo, Eunsol Choi, Danqi Chen

Steering Committee:

Jonathan Berant, Tel Aviv University
Percy Liang, Stanford University
Luke Zettlemoyer, University of Washington

Organizers:

Adam Fisch, MIT
Alon Talmor, Tel Aviv University
Robin Jia, Stanford University
Minjoon Seo, NAVER & University of Washington
Eunsol Choi, University of Washington & Google
Danqi Chen, Princeton University

Program Committee:

Alane Suhr, Cornell University
Chenguang Zhu, Microsoft
Christopher Clark, University of Washington
Daniel Khashabi, Allen Institute for AI
Danish Contractor, IBM
Dheeru Dua, UC Irvine
Gabriel Stanovsky, University of Washington/Allen Institute for AI
Hoifung Poon, Microsoft
Huan Sun, Ohio State University
Jiahua Liu, Tsinghua University
Jing Liu, Baidu
Jinhyuk Lee, Korea University
Johannes Welbl, University College London
Jonathan Herzig, Tel Aviv University
Kai Sun, Cornell University
Karthik Narasimhan, Princeton University
Kenton Lee, Google
Kevin Gimpel, TTIC
Li Dong, Microsoft
Luheng He, Google
Mandar Joshi, University of Washington
Matt Gardner, Allen Institute for AI
Matthew Richardson, Microsoft
Mausam, IIT
Minghao Hu, NUDT
Mohit Iyyer, UMass
Mor Geva, Tel Aviv University
Mrinmaya Sachan, Carnegie Mellon University
Nan Duan, Microsoft
Ni Lao, Mosaix
Nitish Gupta, University of Pennsylvania
Omer Levy, Facebook
Oyvind Tafjord, Allen Institute for AI
Panupong Pasupat, Google
Patrick Lewis, University College London

Peng Qi, Stanford University
Pradeep Dasigi, Allen Institute for AI
Quan Wang, Baidu
Rajarshi Das, UMass
Saizheng Zhang, University of Montreal
Sameer Singh, UC Irvine
Scott Wen-tau Yih, Facebook
Sebastian Riedel, University College London/Facebook
Semih Yagcioglu, Hacettepe University
Sewon Min, University of Washington
Siva Reddy, Stanford University
Todor Mihaylov, Heidelberg University
Tom Kwiatkowski, Google
Tushar Khot, Allen Institute for AI
Adams Wei Yu, Carnegie Mellon University
Wenhan Xiong, UC Santa Barbara
Xiaodong Liu, Microsoft
Yichen Jiang, UNC Chapel Hill
Zhilin Yang, Carnegie Mellon University

Invited Speaker:

Mohit Bansal, UNC Chapel Hill
Antoine Bordes, Facebook AI Research
Jordan Boyd-Graber, University of Maryland
Matt Gardner, Allen Institute for AI

Table of Contents

Conference Program

Monday, November 4, 2019

9:00–9:35   *Invited talk I: Antoine Bordes*

9:35–10:10   *Invited talk II: Matt Gardner*

10:10–10:30   *Best paper session I: Multi-step Entity-centric Information Retrieval for Multi-Hop Question Answering*

10:30–11:00   *Coffee break*

11:00–11:35   *Invited talk III: Jordan Boyd-Graber*

Shared task

11:35–12:10   *MRQA 2019 Shared Task: Evaluating Generalization in Reading Comprehension*
Adam Fisch, Alon Talmor, Robin Jia, Minjoon Seo, Eunsol Choi and Danqi Chen

12:10–12:30   *Shared task best system session: D-NET: A Pre-Training and Fine-Tuning Framework for Improving the Generalization of Machine Reading Comprehension*

12:30–14:00   *Lunch break*

14:00-14:20   *Best paper session II: Evaluating Question Answering Evaluation*

14:20–14:55   *Invited talk IV: Mohit Bansal*

Poster session

14:55–16:30 *Inspecting Unification of Encoding and Matching with Transformer: A Case Study of Machine Reading Comprehension*
Hangbo Bao, Li Dong, Furu Wei, Wenhui Wang, Nan Yang, Lei Cui, Songhao Piao and Ming Zhou

14:55–16:30 *CALOR-QUEST : generating a training corpus for Machine Reading Comprehension models from shallow semantic annotations*
FREDERIC BECHET, Cindy Aloui, Delphine Charlet, Geraldine Damnati, Johannes Heinecke, Alexis Nasr and Frederic Herledan

14:55–16:30 *Improving Subject-Area Question Answering with External Knowledge*
Xiaoman Pan, Kai Sun, Dian Yu, Jianshu Chen, Heng Ji, Claire Cardie and Dong Yu

14:55–16:30 *Answer-Supervised Question Reformulation for Enhancing Conversational Machine Comprehension*
Qian Li, Hui Su, CHENG NIU, Daling Wang, Zekang Li, Shi Feng and yifei zhang

14:55–16:30 *Simple yet Effective Bridge Reasoning for Open-Domain Multi-Hop Question Answering*
Wenhan Xiong, Mo Yu, Xiaoxiao Guo, Hong Wang, Shiyu Chang, Murray Campbell and William Yang Wang

14:55–16:30 *Improving the Robustness of Deep Reading Comprehension Models by Leveraging Syntax Prior*
Bowen Wu, Haoyang Huang, Zongsheng Wang, Qihang Feng, Jingsong Yu and Baoxun Wang

14:55–16:30 *Reasoning Over Paragraph Effects in Situations*
Kevin Lin, Oyvind Tafjord, Peter Clark and Matt Gardner

14:55–16:30 *Towards Answer-unaware Conversational Question Generation*
Mao Nakanishi, Tetsunori Kobayashi and Yoshihiko Hayashi

14:55–16:30 *Cross-Task Knowledge Transfer for Query-Based Text Summarization*
Elozino Egonmwan, Vittorio Castelli and Md Arafat Sultan

14:55–16:30 *Book QA: Stories of Challenges and Opportunities*
Stefanos Angelidis, Lea Frermann, Diego Marcheggiani, Roi Blanco and Lluís Màrquez

14:55–16:30 *FlowDelta: Modeling Flow Information Gain in Reasoning for Conversational Machine Comprehension*
Yi-Ting Yeh and Yun-Nung Chen

14:55–16:30   *Do Multi-hop Readers Dream of Reasoning Chains?*
Haoyu Wang, Mo Yu, Xiaoxiao Guo, Rajarshi Das, Wenhan Xiong and Tian Gao

14:55–16:30   *Machine Comprehension Improves Domain-Specific Japanese Predicate-Argument Structure Analysis*
Norio Takahashi, Tomohide Shibata, Daisuke Kawahara and Sadao Kurohashi

14:55–16:30   *On Making Reading Comprehension More Comprehensive*
Matt Gardner, Jonathan Berant, Hannaneh Hajishirzi, Alon Talmor and Sewon Min

14:55–16:30   *Multi-step Entity-centric Information Retrieval for Multi-Hop Question Answering*
Rajarshi Das, Ameya Godbole, Dilip Kavarthapu, Zhiyu Gong, Abhishek Singhal, Mo Yu, Xiaoxiao Guo, Tian Gao, Hamed Zamani, Manzil Zaheer and Andrew McCallum

14:55–16:30   *Evaluating Question Answering Evaluation*
Anthony Chen, Gabriel Stanovsky, Sameer Singh and Matt Gardner

14:55–16:30   *Bend but Don't Break? Multi-Challenge Stress Test for QA Models*
Hemant Pugaliya, James Route, Kaixin Ma, Yixuan Geng and Eric Nyberg

14:55–16:30   *ReQA: An Evaluation for End-to-End Answer Retrieval Models*
Amin Ahmad, Noah Constant, Yinfei Yang and Daniel Cer

14:55–16:30   *Comprehensive Multi-Dataset Evaluation of Reading Comprehension*
Dheeru Dua, Ananth Gottumukkala, Alon Talmor, Matt Gardner and Sameer Singh

14:55–16:30   *A Recurrent BERT-based Model for Question Generation*
Ying-Hong Chan and Yao-Chung Fan

14:55–16:30   *Let Me Know What to Ask: Interrogative-Word-Aware Question Generation*
Junmo Kang, Haritz Puerto San Roman and sung-hyon myaeng

14:55–16:30   *Extractive NarrativeQA with Heuristic Pre-Training*
Lea Frermann

14:55–16:30   *CLER: Cross-task Learning with Expert Representation to Generalize Reading and Understanding*
Takumi Takahashi, Motoki Taniguchi, Tomoki Taniguchi and Tomoko Ohkuma

MRQA 2019 Shared Task:
Evaluating Generalization in Reading Comprehension

Adam Fisch♦ **Alon Talmor**♠◇ **Robin Jia**♣ **Minjoon Seo**♥△ **Eunsol Choi**♥□ **Danqi Chen**♡

♦ Massachusetts Institute of Technology ♠ Tel Aviv University ♣ Stanford University
♥ University of Washington △ NAVER ♡ Princeton University
□ Google AI ◇ Allen Institute for Artificial Intelligence

Abstract

We present the results of the Machine Reading for Question Answering (MRQA) 2019 shared task on evaluating the generalization capabilities of reading comprehension systems.[1] In this task, we adapted and unified 18 distinct question answering datasets into the same format. Among them, six datasets were made available for training, six datasets were made available for development, and the final six were hidden for final evaluation. Ten teams submitted systems, which explored various ideas including data sampling, multi-task learning, adversarial training, and ensembling. The best system achieved an average F1 score of 72.5 on the 12 held-out datasets, 10.7 absolute points higher than our initial baseline based on BERT.

1 Introduction

Machine Reading for Question Answering (MRQA) has become an important testbed for evaluating how well computer systems understand human language. Interest in MRQA settings—in which a system must answer a question by reading one or more context documents—has grown rapidly in recent years, fueled especially by the creation of many large-scale datasets (Rajpurkar et al., 2016; Joshi et al., 2017; Kwiatkowski et al., 2019). MRQA datasets have been used to benchmark progress in general-purpose language understanding (Devlin et al., 2018; Yang et al., 2019). Interest in MRQA also stems from their use in industry applications, such as search engines (Kwiatkowski et al., 2019) and dialogue systems (Reddy et al., 2019; Choi et al., 2018).

While recent progress on benchmark datasets has been impressive, MRQA systems are still primarily evaluated on in-domain accuracy. It remains challenging to build MRQA systems that

generalize to new test distributions (Chen et al., 2017; Levy et al., 2017; Yogatama et al., 2019) and are robust to test-time perturbations (Jia and Liang, 2017; Ribeiro et al., 2018). A truly effective question answering system should do more than merely interpolate from the training set to answer test examples drawn from the same distribution: it should also be able to extrapolate to test examples drawn from different distributions.

In this work we introduce the MRQA 2019 Shared Task on Generalization, which tests extractive question answering models on their ability to generalize to data distributions different from the distribution on which they were trained. Ten teams submitted systems, many of which improved over our provided baseline systems. The top system, which took advantage of newer pre-trained language models (Yang et al., 2019; Zhang et al., 2019), achieved an average F1 score of 72.5 on our hidden test data, an improvement of 10.7 absolute points over our best baseline. Other submissions explored using adversarial training, multi-task learning, and better sampling methods to improve performance. In the following sections, we present our generalization-focused, extractive question-answering dataset, a review of the official baseline and participating shared task submissions, and a meta-analysis of system trends, successes, and failures.

2 Task Description

The MRQA 2019 Shared Task focuses on generalization to *out-of-domain* data. Participants trained models on a fixed training dataset containing examples from six QA datasets. We then evaluated their systems on examples from 12 held-out test datasets. For six of the test datasets, we provided participants with some development data; the other six datasets were entirely hidden—

---

[1]https://github.com/mrqa/MRQA-Shared-Task-2019.

Proceedings of the Second Workshop on Machine Reading for Question Answering, pages 1–13
Hong Kong, China, November 4, 2019. ©2019 Association for Computational Linguistics

participants did not know the identity of these datasets.

We restricted the shared task to English-language extractive question answering: systems were given a question and context passage, and were asked to find a segment of text in the context that answers the question. This format is used by several commonly-used reading comprehension datasets, including SQuAD (Rajpurkar et al., 2016) and TriviaQA (Joshi et al., 2017). We found that the extractive format is general enough that we could convert many other existing datasets into this format. The simplicity of this format allowed us to focus on out-of-domain generalization, instead of other important but orthogonal challenges.[2]

The datasets we used in our shared task are given in Table 1. The datasets differ in the following ways:

- **Passage distribution:** Context passages come from many different sources, including Wikipedia, news articles, Web snippets, and textbooks.

- **Question distribution:** Questions are of different styles (e.g., entity-centric, relational) and come from different sources, including crowdworkers, domain experts, and exam writers.

- **Joint distribution:** The relationship between the passage and question also varies. Some questions were written based on the passage, while other questions were written independently, with context passages retrieved afterwards. Some questions were constructed to require multi-hop reasoning on the passage.

Evaluation criteria Systems are evaluated using exact match score (EM) and word-level F1-score (F1), as is common in extractive question answering tasks (Rajpurkar et al., 2016; Joshi et al., 2017; Yang et al., 2018). EM only gives credit for predictions that exactly match (one of) the gold answer(s), whereas F1 gives a partial credit for partial word overlap with the gold answer(s). We follow the SQuAD evaluation normalization rules and ignore articles and punctuation when computing EM and F1 scores. While more strict evaluation (Kwiatkowski et al., 2019) computes scores based on the token indexes of the provided context, we compute scores based on answer string match (i.e., the prediction doesn't need to come from exact same annotated span as long as the predicted answer string matches the annotated answer string). We rank systems based on their macro-averaged test F1 scores across the 12 test datasets.

3 Dataset Curation

The MRQA 2019 Shared Task dataset is comprised of many sub-domains, each collected from a separate dataset. The dataset splits and sub-domains are detailed in Table 1. As part of the collection process, we adapted each dataset to conform to the following unified, extractive format:

1. The answer to each question must appear as a span of tokens in the passage.

2. Passages may span multiple paragraphs or documents, but they are concatenated and truncated to the first 800 tokens. This eases the computational requirements for processing large documents efficiently.

The first requirement is motivated by the following reasons:

- Extractive settings are easier to evaluate with stable metrics than abstractive settings.

- Unanswerable questions are hard to synthesize reliably on datasets without them. We investigated using distant supervision to automatically generate unanswerable questions, but found it would introduce a significant amount of noise.

- It is easier to convert multiple-choice datasets to extractive datasets than converting extractive datasets to multiple-choice, as it is difficult to generate challenging alternative answer options.

- Many of popular benchmark datasets are already extractive (or have extractive portions).

3.1 Sub-domain Splits

We partition the 18 sub-domains in the MRQA dataset into three splits:

Split I These sub-domains are available for model training and development, but are not included in evaluation.

	Dataset	Question (Q)	Context (C)	$|Q|$	$|C|$	$Q \perp C$	Train	Dev	Test
I	SQuAD	Crowdsourced	Wikipedia	11	137	✗	86,588	10,507	-
	NewsQA	Crowdsourced	News articles	8	599	✓	74,160	4,212	-
	TriviaQA♠	Trivia	Web snippets	16	784	✓	61,688	7,785	-
	SearchQA♠	Jeopardy	Web snippets	17	749	✓	117,384	16,980	-
	HotpotQA	Crowdsourced	Wikipedia	22	232	✗	72,928	5,904	-
	Natural Questions	Search logs	Wikipedia	9	153	✓	104,071	12,836	-
II	BioASQ♠	Domain experts	Science articles	11	248	✓	-	1,504	1,518
	DROP♢	Crowdsourced	Wikipedia	11	243	✗	-	1,503	1,501
	DuoRC♢	Crowdsourced	Movie plots	9	681	✓	-	1,501	1,503
	RACE♡	Domain experts	Examinations	12	349	✗	-	674	1,502
	RelationExtraction♠	Synthetic	Wikipedia	9	30	✓	-	2,948	1,500
	TextbookQA♡	Domain experts	Textbook	11	657	✗	-	1,503	1,508
III	BioProcess♡	Domain experts	Textbook	9	94	✗	-	-	219
	ComplexWebQ♠	Crowdsourced	Web snippets	14	583	✓	-	-	1,500
	MCTest♡	Crowdsourced	Crowdsourced	9	244	✗	-	-	1,501
	QAMR♢	Crowdsourced	Wikipedia	7	25	✗	-	-	1,524
	QAST	Domain experts	Transcriptions	10	298	✗	-	-	220
	TREC♠	Crowdsourced	Wikipedia	8	792	✓	-	-	1,021

Table 1: MRQA sub-domain datasets. The first block presents six domains used for training, the second block presents six given domains used for evaluation during model development and the last block presents six hidden domains used for evaluation. $| \cdot |$ denotes the average length in tokens of the quantity of interest. $Q \perp C$ is true if the question was written independently from the passage used for context. ♠-marked datasets used distant supervision to match questions and contexts, ♡-marked datasets were originally multiple-choice, and ♢-marked datasets are other datasets where only the answer string is given (rather than the exact answer span in the context).

Split II These sub-domains are not available for model training, but are available for model development. Their hidden test portions are included in the final evaluation.

Split III These sub-domains are not available for model training or development. They are completely hidden to the participants and only used for evaluation.

Additionally, we balance the testing portions of Splits II and III by re-partitioning the original sub-domain datasets so that we have 1,500 examples per sub-domain. We partition by context, so that no single context is shared across both development and testing portions of either Split II or Split III.[3]

3.2 Common Preprocessing

Datasets may contain contexts that are comprised of multiple documents or paragraphs. We concatenate all documents and paragraphs together. We separate documents with a `[DOC]` token, insert `[TLE]` tokens before each document title (if pro-

vided), and separate paragraphs within a document with a `[PAR]` token.

Many of the original datasets do not have labeled answer spans. For these datasets we provide all occurrences of the answer string in the context in the dataset. Additionally, several of the original datasets contain multiple-choice questions. For these datasets, we keep the correct answer if it is contained in the context, and discard the other options. We filter questions that depend on the specific options (e.g., questions of the form *"which of the following..."* or *"examples of... include"*). Removing multiple-choice options might introduce ambiguity (e.g., if multiple correct answers appear in the context but not in the original options). For these datasets, we attempt to control for quality by manually verifying random examples.

3.3 Sub-domain Datasets

In this section we describe the datasets used as sub-domains for MRQA. We focus on the modifications made to convert each dataset to the unified MRQA format. Please see Table 1 as well as the associated dataset papers for more details on each sub-domain's properties.

SQuAD (Rajpurkar et al., 2016) We used the SQuAD (Stanford **Q**uestion **A**nswering **D**ataset)

---

[3]We draw examples from each dataset's original test split until it is exhausted, and then augment if necessary from the train and dev splits. This preserves the integrity of the original datasets by ensuring that no original test data is leaked into non-hidden splits of the MRQA dataset.

dataset as the basis for the shared task format.[4] Crowdworkers are shown paragraphs from Wikipedia and are asked to write questions with extractive answers.

NewsQA (Trischler et al., 2017) Two sets of crowdworkers ask and answer questions based on CNN news articles. The "questioners" see only the article's headline and summary while the "answerers" see the full article. We discard questions that have no answer or are flagged in the dataset to be without annotator agreement.

TriviaQA (Joshi et al., 2017) Question and answer pairs are sourced from trivia and quiz-league websites. We use the web version of TriviaQA, where the contexts are retrieved from the results of a Bing search query.

SearchQA (Dunn et al., 2017) Question and answer pairs are sourced from the Jeopardy! TV show. The contexts are composed of retrieved snippets from a Google search query.

HotpotQA (Yang et al., 2018) Crowdworkers are shown two entity-linked paragraphs from Wikipedia and are asked to write and answer questions that require multi-hop reasoning to solve. In the original setting, these paragraphs are mixed with additional distractor paragraphs to make inference harder. We do not include the distractor paragraphs in our setting.

Natural Questions (Kwiatkowski et al., 2019) Questions are collected from information-seeking queries to the Google search engine by real users under natural conditions. Answers to the questions are annotated in a retrieved Wikipedia page by crowdworkers. Two types of annotations are collected: 1) the HTML bounding box containing enough information to completely infer the answer to the question (Long Answer), and 2) the sub-span or sub-spans within the bounding box that comprise the actual answer (Short Answer). We use only the examples that have short answers, and use the long answer as the context.

BioASQ (Tsatsaronis et al., 2015) BioASQ, a challenge on large-scale biomedical semantic indexing and question answering, contains question and answer pairs that are created by domain experts. They are then manually linked to multiple related science (PubMed) articles. We download the full abstract of each of the linked articles to use as individual contexts (e.g., a single question can be linked to multiple, independent articles to create multiple QA-context pairs). We discard abstracts that do not exactly contain the answer.

DROP (Dua et al., 2019) DROP (Discrete Reasoning Over the content of Paragraphs) examples were collected similarly to SQuAD, where crowdworkers are asked to create question-answer pairs from Wikipedia paragraphs. The questions focus on quantitative reasoning, and the original dataset contains non-extractive numeric answers as well as extractive text answers. We restrict ourselves to the set of questions that are extractive.

DuoRC (Saha et al., 2018) We use the ParaphraseRC split of the DuoRC dataset. In this setting, two different plot summaries of the same movie are collected—one from Wikipedia and the other from IMDb. Two different sets of crowdworkers ask and answer questions about the movie plot, where the "questioners" are shown only the Wikipedia page, and the "answerers" are shown only the IMDb page. We discard questions that are marked as unanswerable.

RACE (Lai et al., 2017) ReAding Comprehension Dataset From Examinations (RACE) is collected from English reading comprehension exams for middle and high school Chinese students. We use the high school split (which is more challenging) and also filter out the implicit "fill in the blank" style questions (which are unnatural for this task).

RelationExtraction (Levy et al., 2017) Given a slot-filling dataset,[5] relations among entities are systematically transformed into question-answer pairs using templates. For example, the $educated\_at(x, y)$ relationship between two entities x and y appearing in a sentence can be expressed as *"Where was x educated at?"* with answer y. Multiple templates for each type of relation are collected. We use the dataset's zero-shot benchmark split (generalization to unseen relations), and only keep the positive examples.

TextbookQA (Kembhavi et al., 2017) TextbookQA is collected from lessons from middle school Life Science, Earth Science, and Physical

---

[4] A few paragraphs are long, and we discard the QA pairs that do not align with the first 800 tokens (1.1% of examples).

[5] The authors use the WikiReading dataset (Hewlett et al., 2016) for the underlying slot-filling task.

Science textbooks. We do not include questions that are accompanied with a diagram, or that are "True or False" questions.

BioProcess (Berant et al., 2014) Paragraphs are sourced from a biology textbook, and question and answer pairs about those paragraphs are then created by domain experts.

ComplexWebQ (Talmor and Berant, 2018) ComplexWebQuestions is collected by crowdworkers who are shown compositional, formal queries against Freebase, and are asked to rephrase them in natural language. Thus, by design, questions require multi-hop reasoning. For the context, we use the default web snippets provided by the authors. We use only single-answer questions of type "composition" or "conjunction".

MCTest (Richardson et al., 2013) Passages accompanied with questions and answers are written by crowdworkers. The passages are fictional, elementary-level, children's stories.

QAMR (Michael et al., 2018) To construct the Question-Answer Meaning Representation (QAMR) dataset, crowdworkers are presented with an English sentence along with target non-stopwords from the sentence. They are then asked to create as many question-answer pairs as possible that contain at least one of the target words (and for which the answer is a span of the sentence). These questions combine to cover most of the predicate-argument structures present. We use only the filtered[6] subset of the Wikipedia portion of the dataset.

QAST (Lamel et al., 2008) We use Task 1 of the Question Answering on Speech Transcriptions (QAST) dataset, where contexts are taken from manual transcripts of spoken lectures on "speech and language processing." Questions about named entities found in the transcriptions are created by English native speakers. Each lecture contains around 1 hour of transcribed text. To reduce the length to meet our second requirement ($\leq$ 800 tokens), for each question we manually selected a sub-section of the lecture that contained the answer span, as well as sufficient surrounding context to answer it.

TREC (Baudiš and Šedivý, 2015) The Text REtrieval Conference (TREC) dataset is curated

from the TREC QA tasks (Voorhees and Tice, 2000) from 1999-2002. The questions are factoid. Accompanying passages are supplied using the Document Retriever from Chen et al. (2017), if the answer is found within the first 800 tokens of any of the top 5 retrieved Wikipedia documents (we take the highest ranked document if multiple documents meet this requirement).

4 Baseline Model

We implemented a simple, multi-task baseline model based on BERT (Devlin et al., 2018), following the MultiQA model (Talmor and Berant, 2019). Our method works as follows:

Modeling Given a question q consisting of m tokens $\{q_1, \ldots, q_m\}$ and a passage p of n tokens $\{p_1, \ldots, p_n\}$, we first concatenate q and p with special tokens to obtain a joint context $\{[\texttt{CLS}], q_1, \ldots, q_m, [\texttt{SEP}], p_1, \ldots, p_n, [\texttt{SEP}]\}$. We then encode the joint context with BERT to obtain contextualized passage representations $\{\mathbf{h}_1, \ldots, \mathbf{h}_n\}$. We train separate MLPs to predict start and end indices independently, and decode the final span using $\arg\max_{i,j}\{p_{start}(i) \times p_{end}(j)\}$.

Preprocessing Following Devlin et al. (2018), we create p and q by tokenizing every example using a vocabulary of 30,522 word pieces. As BERT accepts a maximum sequence length of 512, we generate multiple chunks $\{p^{(1)}, \ldots, p^{(k)}\}$ per example by sliding a 512 token window (of the joint context, including q) over the entire length of the original passage, with a stride of 128 tokens.

Training During training we select only the chunks that contain answers. We maximize the log-likelihood of the first occurrence of the gold answer in each of these chunks, and back-propagate into BERT's parameters (and the MLP parameters). At test time we output the span with the maximal logit across all chunks.

Multi-task Training We sample up to 75K examples from each training dataset, combine them, and create mixed batches of examples from all of the data. We then follow the same training procedure as before on all the composed training dataset batches.

---

[6]The questions that are valid and non-redundant.

5 Shared Task Submissions

Our shared task lasted for 3 months from May to August in 2019. All submissions were handled through the CodaLab platform.[7] In total, we received submissions from 10 different teams for the final evaluation (Table 2). Of these, 6 teams submitted their system description paper. We will describe each of them briefly below.

5.1 D-Net (Li et al., 2019)

The submission from Baidu adopts multiple pre-trained language models (LMs), including BERT (Devlin et al., 2018), XLNet (Yang et al., 2019), and ERNIE 2.0 (Zhang et al., 2019). Unlike other submissions which use only one pre-trained LM, they experiment with 1) training LMs with extra raw text data drawn from science questions and search snippets domains, and 2) multi-tasking with auxiliary tasks such as natural language inference and paragraph ranking (Williams et al., 2017). Ultimately, however, the final system is an ensemble of an XLNet-based model and an ERNIE-based model, without auxiliary multitask or augmented LM training.

5.2 Delphi (Longpre et al., 2019)

The submission from Apple investigates the effects of pre-trained language models (BERT vs XLNet), various data sampling strategies, and data augmentation techniques via back-translation. Their final submission uses XLNet (Yang et al., 2019) as the base model, with carefully sampled training instances from negative examples (hence augmenting the model with a no-answer option) and the six training datasets. The final submission does not include data augmentation, as it did not improve performance during development.

5.3 HLTC (Su et al., 2019)

The submission from HKUST studies different data-feeding schemes, namely shuffling instances from all datasets versus shuffling dataset-ordering only. Their submission is built on top of XLNet, with a multilayer perceptron layer for span prediction. They also attempted to substitute the MLP layer with a more complex attention-over-attention (AoA) (Cui et al., 2017) layer on top of XLNet, but did not find it to be helpful.

5.4 CLER (Takahashi et al., 2019)

The submission from Fuji Xerox adds a mixture-of-experts (MoE) (Jacobs et al., 1991) layer on top of a BERT-based architecture. They also use a multi-task learning framework trained together with natural language inference (NLI) tasks. Their final submission is an ensemble of three models trained with different random seeds.

5.5 Adv. Train (Lee et al., 2019)

The submission from 42Maru and Samsung Research proposes an adversarial training framework, where a domain discriminator predicts the underlying domain label from the QA model's hidden representations, while the QA model tries to learn to arrange its hidden representations such that the discriminator is thwarted. Through this process, they aim to learn domain (dataset) invariant features that can generalize to unseen domains. The submission is built based on the provided BERT baselines.

5.6 HierAtt (Osama et al., 2019)

The submission from Alexandria University uses the BERT-Base model to provide feature representations. Unlike other models which allowed fine-tuning of the language model parameters during training, this submission only trains model parameters associated with the question answering task, while keeping language model parameters frozen. The model consists of two attention mechanisms: one bidirectional attention layer used to model the interaction between the passage and the question, and one self-attention layer applied to both the question and the passage.

6 Results

6.1 Main Results

Table 3 lists the macro-averaged F1 scores of all the submissions on both the development and testing portions of the MRQA dataset. The teams are ranked by the F1 scores on the hidden testing portions of the 12 datasets (Split II and III in Section 3.1). As seen in Table 3, many of the submissions outperform our BERT-Large baseline significantly. The best-performing system, D-Net (Li et al., 2019), achieves an F1 score of 72.5, which is a 10.7 point absolute improvement over our baseline, and 11.5 and 10.0 point improvements, respectively, on Split II (with the development por-

---

[7]https://worksheets.codalab.org

Model	Affliation
D-Net (Li et al., 2019)	Baidu Inc.
Delphi (Longpre et al., 2019)	Apple Inc.
FT_XLNet	Harbin Institute of Technology
HLTC (Su et al., 2019)	Hong Kong University of Science & Technology
BERT-cased-whole-word	Aristo @ AI2
CLER (Takahashi et al., 2019)	Fuji Xerox Co., Ltd.
Adv. Train (Lee et al., 2019)	42Maru and Samsung Research
BERT-Multi-Finetune	Beijing Language and Culture University
PAL IN DOMAIN	University of California Irvine
HierAtt (Osama et al., 2019)	Alexandria University

Table 2: List of participants, ordered by the macro-averaged F1 score on the hidden evaluation set.

Model	Split I	Split II	Split II	Split III	Split II + III
Portion (# datasets)	Dev (6)	Dev (6)	Test (6)	Test (6)	Test (12)
D-Net (Li et al., 2019)	**84.1**	**69.7**	**68.9**	**76.1**	**72.5**
Delphi (Longpre et al., 2019)	82.3	68.5	66.9	74.6	70.8
FT_XLNet	82.9	68.0	66.7	74.4	70.5
HLTC (Su et al., 2019)	81.0	65.9	65.0	72.9	69.0
BERT-cased-whole-word	79.4	61.1	61.4	71.2	66.3
CLER (Takahashi et al., 2019)	80.2	62.7	62.5	69.7	66.1
Adv. Train (Lee et al., 2019)	76.8	57.1	57.9	66.5	62.2
Ours: BERT-Large	76.3	57.1	57.4	66.1	61.8
BERT-Multi-Finetune	74.2	53.3	56.0	64.7	60.3
Ours: BERT-Base	74.7	54.6	54.6	62.4	58.5
HierAtt (Osama et al., 2019)	71.1	48.7	50.5	61.7	56.1

Table 3: Performance as F1 score on the shared task. Each score is macro-averaged across individual datasets. The last column (test portion of Split II and III) is used for the final ranking. Our baselines are shaded in yellow, and the submissions which did not present system description papers are shaded in grey.

		#	Best	BERT Large	Impr.
Question Type	Crowdsourced	6	69.9	58.5	11.5
	Synthetic	1	88.9	84.7	4.2
	Domain experts	5	71.5	60.5	11.5
Context Type	Wikipedia	4	73.4	62.3	11.1
	Education	4	68.2	56.2	12.0
	Others	4	76.1	66.8	9.3
$Q \perp C$	✓	5	73.0	63.8	9.2
	✗	7	72.2	60.3	11.9

Table 4: Macro-averaged F1 scores based on the dataset characteristics as defined in Table 1. Best denotes the best shared task result and Base denotes our BERT-Large baseline.

tions provided) and Split III datasets (completely hidden to the participants).

We evaluate all the submissions on the in-domain datasets (Split I) in Table 3 and find that there is a very strong correlation between in-domain and out-of-domain performance. The top submissions on the out-of-domain datasets also obtain the highest scores on the six datasets that we provided for training.

We present per-dataset performances for 12 evaluation datasets in the appendix. Across the board, many submitted systems greatly outperform our baselines. Among the 12 datasets, performance on the DROP dataset has improved the most—from 43.5 F1 to 61.5 F1—while performance on the RelationExtraction dataset has improved the least (84.9 F1 vs. 89.0 F1). The models with higher average scores seemed to outperform in most datasets: the performance rankings of submissions are mostly preserved on individual datasets.

6.2 Summary of Findings

Improvements per data types We analyzed the average performance across the various types of datasets that are represented in Table 1. Table 4 summarizes our observations: (1) the datasets with naturally collected questions (either crowdsourced or curated by domain experts) all obtain large improvements; (2) The datasets collected from Wikipedia or education materials (textbooks and Science articles) receive bigger gains compared to those collected from Web snippets or transcriptions; and (3) There is a bigger improvement for datasets in which questions are posed dependent on the passages compared to those with independently collected questions (11.9 vs. 9.2 points).

Pre-trained language models The choice of pre-trained language model has a significant impact on the QA performance, as well as the generalization ability. Table 5 summarizes the pre-trained models each submission is based on, along with its evaluation F1 score. The top three performing systems all use XLNet instead of BERT-Large—this isolated change in pre-trained language model alone yields a significant gain in overall in- and out-of-domain performance. Li et al. (2019) argues that XLNet shows superior performances on datasets with discrete reasoning, such as DROP and RACE. Su et al. (2019), however, also use XLNet, but does not show strong gains on the DROP or RACE datasets.

The winning system ensembled two *different* pre-trained language models. Only one other submission (Takahashi et al., 2019) used an ensemble for their final submission, merging the same LM with different random seeds.

Model	Base Language Model	Eval F1 (II + III)
D-Net	XLNet-L + ERNIE 2.0	72.5
Delphi	XLNet-L	70.8
HLTC	XLNet-L	69.0
CLER	BERT-L	66.1
Adv. Train	BERT-L	62.2
BERT-Large	BERT-L	61.8
HierAtt	BERT-B	56.1

Table 5: Pretrained language models used in the shared task submissions. *-L and *-B denote large and base versions of the models.

Data sampling Our shared task required all participants to use our provided training data, compiled from six question answering datasets, and disallowed the use of any other question-answering data for training. Within these restrictions, we encouraged participants to explore *how* to best utilize the provided data.

Inspired by Talmor and Berant (2019), two submissions (Su et al., 2019; Longpre et al., 2019) analyzed similarities between datasets. Unsurprisingly, the performance improved significantly when fine-tuned on the training dataset most similar to the evaluation dataset of interest. Su et al. (2019) found each of the development (Split II) datasets resembles one or two training datasets (Split I)—and thus training with all datasets is crucial for generalization across the

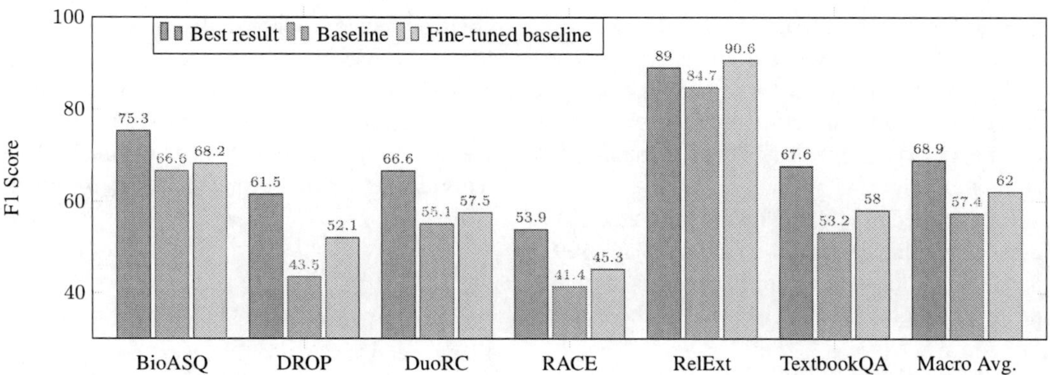

Figure 1: F1 scores on Split II sub-domains (test portions) comparing the best submitted system (D-Net) against our BERT-Large baseline. The third result for each dataset is from individually fine-tuning the BERT-Large baseline on the in-domain dev portion of the same dataset (i.e., Split II (dev)).

multiple domains. They experimented with data-feeding methodologies, and found that shuffling instances of all six training datasets is more effective than sequentially feeding all examples from each dataset, one dataset after another.

Additionally, Longpre et al. (2019) observed that the models fine-tuned on SearchQA and TriviaQA achieve relatively poor results across all the evaluation sets (they are both trivia-based, distantly supervised, and long-context datasets). Downsampling examples from these datasets increases the overall performance. They also found that, although our shared task focuses on answerable questions, sampling negative examples leads to significant improvements (up to +1.5 F1 on Split II and up to +4 F1 on Split I). Since most systems follow our baseline model (Section 4) by doing inference over *chunks* of tokens, not all examples fed to these models are actually guaranteed to contain an answer span.

Multi-task learning Two submissions attempted to learn the question answering model together with other auxiliary tasks, namely natural language inference (Takahashi et al., 2019; Li et al., 2019) or paragraph ranking (Li et al., 2019) (i.e., classifying whether given passages contains an answer to the question or not). This could improve the generalization performance on question answering for two reasons. First, the additional training simply exposes the model to more diverse domains, as the entailment dataset (Williams et al., 2017) contains multiple domains ranging from fiction to telephone conversations. Second, reasoning about textual entailment is often

necessary for question answering, while passage ranking (or classification) is an easier version of extractive question answering, where the model has to identify the passage containing the answer instead of exact span.

Both systems introduced task-specific fully connected layers while sharing lower level representations across different tasks. While Takahashi et al. (2019) showed a modest gain by multi-tasking with NLI tasks (+0.7 F1 score on the development portion of Split II), Li et al. (2019) reported that multitasking did not improve the performance of their best model.

Adversarial Training One submission (Lee et al., 2019) introduced an adversarial training framework for generalization. The goal is to learn domain-invariant features (i.e., features that can generalize to unseen test domains) by jointly training with a domain discriminator, which predicts the dataset (domain) for each example. According to Lee et al. (2019), this adversarial training helped on most of the datasets (9 out of 12), but also hurt performance on some of them. It finally led to +1.9 F1 gain over their BERT-Base baseline, although the gain was smaller (+0.4 F1) for their stronger BERT-Large baseline.

Ensembles Most extractive QA models, which output a logit for the start index and another for the end index, can be ensembled by adding the start and end logits from models trained with different random seeds. This has shown to improve performances across many model classes, as can be seen from most dataset leaderboards. The results from the shared task also show similar trends. A few submissions (Takahashi et al., 2019; Li et al., 2019) tried ensembling, and all reported modest gains. While ensembling is a quick recipe for a small gain in performance, it also comes at the cost of computational efficiency—both at training and at inference time.

Related to ensembling, Takahashi et al. (2019) uses a mixture of experts (Jacobs et al., 1991) layer, which learns a gating function to ensemble different weights, adaptively based on the input.

6.3 Comparison to In-domain Fine-tuning

Lastly, we report how the best shared task performance compares to in-domain fine-tuning performance of our baseline. Section 6.1 shows large improvements by the top shared task model, D-Net, over our baseline. We analyze to what extent the reduced performance on out-of-domain datasets can be overcome by exposing the baseline to only a few samples from the target distributions. As suggested by Liu et al. (2019), if the model can generalize with a few examples from the new domain, poor performance on that domain is an indicator of a lack of training data diversity, rather than of fundamental model generalization weaknesses.

Figure 1 presents our results on the six datasets from Split II, where we have individually fine-tuned the BERT-Large baseline on each of the Split II dev datasets and tested on the Split II test datasets. We see that while the gap to D-Net shrinks on all datasets (overall performance increases by 4.6 F1), surprisingly it is only completely bridged in one of the settings (RelationExtraction). This is potentially because this dataset covers only a limited number of relations, so having in-domain data helps significantly. This suggests that D-Net (and the others close to it in performance) is an overall stronger model—a conclusion also supported by its gain on in-domain data (Split I).

7 Conclusions

We have presented the MRQA 2019 Shared Task, which focused on testing whether reading comprehension systems can generalize to examples outside of their training domain. Many submissions improved significantly over our baseline, and investigated a wide range of techniques.

Going forward, we believe it will become increasingly important to build NLP systems that generalize across domains. As NLP models become more widely deployed, they must be able to handle diverse inputs, many of which may differ from those seen during training. By running this shared task and releasing our shared task datasets, we hope to shed more light how to build NLP systems that generalize beyond their training distribution.

Acknowledgements

We would like to thank Jonathan Berant, Percy Liang, and Luke Zettlemoyer for serving as our steering committee. We are grateful to Baidu, Facebook, and Naver for providing funding for our workshop. We thank Anastasios Nentidis and the entire BioASQ organizing committee for letting us use BioASQ shared task data for our task, and for hosting the data files. We also thank Valerie Mapelli and ELRA for providing us with the QAST data: CLEF QAST (2007-2009) – Evaluation Package, ELRA catalogue (http://catalog.elra.info), CLEF QAST (2007-2009) – Evaluation Package, ISLRN: 460-370-870-489-0, ELRA ID: ELRA-E0039. Finally, we thank the CodaLab Worksheets team for their help with running the shared task submissions.

References

Petr Baudiš and Jan Šedivý. 2015. Modeling of the question answering task in the yodaqa system. In *Proceedings of the 6th International Conference on Experimental IR Meets Multilinguality, Multimodality, and Interaction - Volume 9283*.

Jonathan Berant, Vivek Srikumar, Pei-Chun Chen, Abby Vander Linden, Brittany Harding, Brad Huang, Peter Clark, and Christopher D. Manning. 2014. Modeling biological processes for reading comprehension. In *EMNLP*.

Danqi Chen, Adam Fisch, Jason Weston, and Antoine Bordes. 2017. Reading Wikipedia to answer open-domain questions. In *ACL*.

Eunsol Choi, He He, Mohit Iyyer, Mark Yatskar, Wen-tau Yih, Yejin Choi, Percy Liang, and Luke Zettlemoyer. 2018. QuAC: Question answering in context. pages 2174–2184.

Yiming Cui, Zhipeng Chen, Si Wei, Ting Liu Shi-jin Wang, , and Guoping Hu. 2017. Attention-over-attention neural networks for reading comprehension. In *ACL*.

Jacob Devlin, Ming-Wei Chang, Kenton Lee, and Kristina Toutanova. 2018. BERT: Pre-training of deep bidirectional transformers for language understanding. In *NAACL*.

Dheeru Dua, Yizhong Wang, Pradeep Dasigi, Gabriel Stanovsky, Sameer Singh, and Matt Gardner. 2019. DROP: A reading comprehension benchmark requiring discrete reasoning over paragraphs. In *NAACL*.

Matthew Dunn, Levent Sagun, Mike Higgins, V. Ugur Güney, Volkan Cirik, and Kyunghyun Cho. 2017. SearchQA: A new Q&A dataset augmented with context from a search engine. *arXiv:1704.05179*.

Daniel Hewlett, Alexandre Lacoste, Llion Jones, Illia Polosukhin, Andrew Fandrianto, Jay Han, Matthew Kelcey, and David Berthelot. 2016. WikiReading: A novel large-scale language understanding task over wikipedia. In *ACL*.

Robert A. Jacobs, Michael I. Jordan, Steven J. Nowlan, and Geoffrey E. Hinton. 1991. Adaptive mixtures of local experts. *Neural Computation*, 3:79–87.

Robin Jia and Percy Liang. 2017. Adversarial examples for evaluating reading comprehension systems. In *EMNLP*.

Mandar Joshi, Eunsol Choi, Daniel Weld, and Luke Zettlemoyer. 2017. TriviaQA: A large scale distantly supervised challenge dataset for reading comprehension. In *ACL*.

Aniruddha Kembhavi, Minjoon Seo, Dustin Schwenk, Jonghyun Choi, Ali Farhadi, and Hannaneh Hajishirzi. 2017. Are you smarter than a sixth grader? textbook question answering for multimodal machine comprehension. In *CVPR*.

Tom Kwiatkowski, Jennimaria Palomaki, Olivia Redfield, Michael Collins, Ankur Parikh, Chris Alberti, Danielle Epstein, Illia Polosukhin, Matthew Kelcey, Jacob Devlin, Kenton Lee, Kristina N. Toutanova, Llion Jones, Ming-Wei Chang, Andrew Dai, Jakob Uszkoreit, Quoc Le, and Slav Petrov. 2019. Natural questions: a benchmark for question answering research. *TACL*.

Guokun Lai, Qizhe Xie, Hanxiao Liu, Yiming Yang, and Eduard Hovy. 2017. RACE: Large-scale reading comprehension dataset from examinations. In *EMNLP*.

Lori Lamel, Sophie Rosset, Christelle Ayache, Djamel Mostefa, Jordi Turmo, and Pere Comas. 2008. Question answering on speech transcriptions: the QAST evaluation in CLEF. In *LREC 2008*.

Seanie Lee, Donggyu Kim, and Jangwon Park. 2019. Domain-agnostic question-answering with adversarial training. In *Proceedings of 2nd Machine Reading for Reading Comprehension Workshop at EMNLP*.

Omer Levy, Minjoon Seo, Eunsol Choi, and Luke Zettlemoyer. 2017. Zero-shot relation extraction via reading comprehension. In *CoNLL*.

Hongyu Li, Xiyuan Zhang, Yibing Liu, Yiming Zhang, Quan Wang, Xiangyang Zhou, Jing Liu, Hua Wu, and Haifeng Wang. 2019. D-NET: A simple framework for improving the generalization of machine reading comprehension. In *Proceedings of 2nd Machine Reading for Reading Comprehension Workshop at EMNLP*.

Nelson F. Liu, Roy Schwartz, and Noah A. Smith. 2019. Inoculation by fine-tuning: A method for analyzing challenge datasets. In *Proceedings of the Conference of the North American Chapter of the Association for Computational Linguistics: Human Language Technologies*.

Shayne Longpre, Yi Lu, Zhucheng Tu, and Chris DuBois. 2019. MRQA 2019 shared task: Fine-tuned xlnet with negative sampling for multi-domain question answering. In *Proceedings of 2nd Machine Reading for Reading Comprehension Workshop at EMNLP*.

Julian Michael, Gabriel Stanovsky, Luheng He, Ido Dagan, and Luke Zettlemoyer. 2018. Crowdsourcing question-answer meaning representations. In *NAACL*.

Reham Osama, Nagwa El-Makky, and Marwan Torki. 2019. Question answering using hierarchical attention on top of bert features. In *Proceedings of 2nd Machine Reading for Reading Comprehension Workshop at EMNLP*.

Pranav Rajpurkar, Robin Jia, and Percy Liang. 2018. Know what you don't know: Unanswerable questions for SQuAD. In *ACL*.

Pranav Rajpurkar, Jian Zhang, Konstantin Lopyrev, and Percy Liang. 2016. SQuAD: 100,000+ questions for machine comprehension of text. In *EMNLP*.

Siva Reddy, Danqi Chen, and Christopher D. Manning. 2019. CoQA: A conversational question answering challenge. *TACL*.

Marco Tulio Ribeiro, Sameer Singh, and Carlos Guestrin. 2018. Semantically equivalent adversarial rules for debugging NLP models. In *ACL*.

Matthew Richardson, Christopher J. C. Burges, and Erin Renshaw. 2013. MCTest: A challenge dataset for the open-domain machine comprehension of text. In *EMNLP*.

Amrita Saha, Rahul Aralikatte, Mitesh M. Khapra, and Karthik Sankaranarayanan. 2018. DuoRC: Towards Complex Language Understanding with Paraphrased Reading Comprehension. In *ACL*.

Dan Su, Yan Xu, Genta Indra Winata, Peng Xu, Hyeondey Kim, Zihan Liu, and Pascale Fung. 2019. Generalizing question answering system with pretrained language model fine-tuning. In *Proceedings of 2nd Machine Reading for Reading Comprehension Workshop at EMNLP*.

Takumi Takahashi, Motoki Taniguchi, Tomoki Taniguchi, and Tomoko Ohkuma. 2019. CLER: Cross-task learning with expert representation to generalize reading and understanding. In *Proceedings of 2nd Machine Reading for Reading Comprehension Workshop at EMNLP*.

Alon Talmor and Jonathan Berant. 2018. The web as a knowledge-base for answering complex questions. In *NAACL*.

Alon Talmor and Jonathan Berant. 2019. Multiqa: An empirical investigation of generalization and transfer in reading comprehension. In *ACL*.

Adam Trischler, Tong Wang, Xingdi Yuan, Justin Harris, Alessandro Sordoni, Philip Bachman, and Kaheer Suleman. 2017. NewsQA: A machine comprehension dataset. In *Proceedings of the 2nd Workshop on Representation Learning for NLP*.

George Tsatsaronis, Georgios Balikas, Prodromos Malakasiotis, Ioannis Partalas, Matthias Zschunke, Michael R Alvers, Dirk Weissenborn, Anastasia Krithara, Sergios Petridis, Dimitris Polychronopoulos, et al. 2015. An overview of the bioasq large-scale biomedical semantic indexing and question answering competition. *BMC bioinformatics*, 16(1).

Ellen M. Voorhees and Dawn M. Tice. 2000. Building a question answering test collection. In *Proceedings of the 23rd Annual International ACM SIGIR Conference on Research and Development in Information Retrieval*.

Adina Williams, Nikita Nangia, and Samuel R. Bowman. 2017. A broad-coverage challenge corpus for sentence understanding through inference. In *NAACL-HLT*.

Zhilin Yang, Zihang Dai, Yiming Yang, Jaime G. Carbonell, Ruslan Salakhutdinov, and Quoc V. Le. 2019. XLNet: Generalized autoregressive pretraining for language understanding. In *NeurIPS*.

Zhilin Yang, Peng Qi, Saizheng Zhang, Yoshua Bengio, William W. Cohen, Ruslan Salakhutdinov, and Christopher D. Manning. 2018. HotpotQA: A dataset for diverse, explainable multi-hop question answering. In *EMNLP*.

Dani Yogatama, Cyprien de Masson d'Autume, Jerome Connor, Tomás Kociský, Mike Chrzanowski, Lingpeng Kong, Angeliki Lazaridou, Wang Ling, Lei Yu, Chris Dyer, and Phil Blunsom. 2019. Learning and evaluating general linguistic intelligence. *arXiv: 1901.11373*.

Zhengyan Zhang, Xu Han, Zhiyuan Liu, Xin Jiang, Maosong Sun, and Qun Liu. 2019. ERNIE: Enhanced language representation with informative entities. In *ACL*.

Appendix

We present the per-dataset performances in Table 6 and Table 7 for shared task submissions and our baselines.

Model	BioASQ		DROP		DuoRC		RACE		RelExt		TextbookQA	
	EM	F1	EM	F1	EM	F1	EM	F1	EM	F1	EM	F1
D-Net	**61.2**	**75.3**	**50.7**	**61.5**	**54.7**	**66.6**	**39.9**	53.5	**80.1**	**89.0**	**57.2**	**67.6**
Delphi	60.3	72.0	48.5	58.9	53.3	63.4	39.4	**53.9**	79.2	87.9	56.5	65.5
FT_XLNet	59.3	72.9	48.0	58.3	52.7	63.8	39.4	53.8	79.0	87.2	53.6	64.2
HLTC	59.6	74.0	41.0	51.1	51.7	63.1	37.2	50.5	76.5	86.2	55.5	65.2
BERT-cased-whole-word	57.8	72.9	43.1	53.2	42.3	53.5	35.0	48.7	78.5	87.9	43.9	51.9
CLER	53.2	68.8	37.7	47.5	51.6	62.9	31.9	45.0	78.6	87.7	53.5	62.9
Adv. Train	45.1	60.5	34.8	43.8	46.2	57.3	29.6	42.8	74.3	84.9	48.8	58.0
Ours: BERT-Large	49.7	66.6	33.9	43.5	43.4	55.1	29.0	41.4	72.5	84.7	45.6	53.2
BERT-Multi-Finetune	48.7	64.8	30.4	40.3	43.7	54.7	26.4	38.7	75.3	85.0	44.0	52.4
Ours: BERT-Base	46.4	60.8	28.3	37.9	42.8	53.3	28.2	39.5	73.3	83.9	44.3	52.0
HierAtt	43.0	59.1	24.4	34.8	38.5	49.6	24.6	37.4	67.9	81.3	32.1	40.5

Table 6: Performance on the six datasets of Split II (test portion). EM: exact match, F1: word-level F1-score.

Model	BioProcess		ComWebQ		MCTest		QAMR		QAST		TREC	
	EM	F1	EM	F1	EM	F1	EM	F1	EM	F1	EM	F1
D-NET	**61.3**	**75.6**	**67.8**	**68.3**	67.8	**80.8**	60.4	**76.1**	75.0	88.8	51.8	**66.8**
Delphi	58.9	74.2	55.1	62.3	**68.0**	80.2	**61.0**	75.3	**78.6**	**89.9**	**55.0**	65.8
FT_XLNet	62.6	75.2	54.8	62.7	66.0	79.6	56.5	73.4	76.8	90.0	51.8	65.5
HLTC	56.2	72.9	54.7	61.4	64.6	78.7	56.4	72.5	75.9	88.8	49.9	63.4
BERT-cased-whole-word	56.2	71.5	52.4	60.7	63.8	76.4	56.1	71.5	69.6	85.3	43.6	61.6
CLER	48.0	68.4	52.6	61.2	59.9	73.1	54.3	71.4	65.0	84.3	42.7	60.0
Adv. Train	46.1	62.9	48.7	56.9	57.2	70.9	56.8	71.7	56.8	77.8	42.6	58.8
Ours: BERT-Large	46.1	63.6	51.8	59.1	59.5	72.2	48.2	67.4	62.3	80.8	36.3	53.6
BERT-Multi-Finetune	43.4	58.8	49.6	57.7	59.2	72.2	48.6	67.0	60.0	80.1	34.6	52.3
Ours: BERT-Base	38.4	57.4	47.4	55.3	54.2	66.1	47.8	64.8	58.6	77.0	36.7	54.0
HierAtt	44.3	60.8	41.9	51.2	54.2	67.9	48.0	66.0	50.9	75.5	27.7	48.7

Table 7: Results on the six datasets of Split III. EM: exact match, F1: word-level F1-score.

Inspecting Unification of Encoding and Matching with Transformer: A Case Study of Machine Reading Comprehension

Hangbo Bao[†][*], **Li Dong**[‡], **Furu Wei**[‡], **Wenhui Wang**[‡],
Nan Yang[‡], **Lei Cui**[‡], **Songhao Piao**[†] and **Ming Zhou**[‡]
[†]School of Computer Science, Harbin Institute of Technology
[‡]Microsoft Research
hangbobao@gmail.com,piaosh@hit.edu.cn
lidong1,fuwei,wenwan,nanya,lecu,mingzhou@microsoft.com

Abstract

Most machine reading comprehension (MRC) models separately handle encoding and matching with different network architectures. In contrast, pretrained language models with Transformer layers, such as GPT (Radford et al., 2018) and BERT (Devlin et al., 2018), have achieved competitive performance on MRC. A research question that naturally arises is: apart from the benefits of pre-training, how many performance gain comes from the unified network architecture. In this work, we evaluate and analyze unifying encoding and matching components with Transformer for the MRC task. Experimental results on SQuAD show that the unified model outperforms previous networks that separately treat encoding and matching. We also introduce a metric to inspect whether a Transformer layer tends to perform encoding or matching. The analysis results show that the unified model learns different modeling strategies compared with previous manually-designed models.

1 Introduction

In spite of different neural network structures, encoding and matching components are two basic building blocks for many NLP tasks like machine reading comprehension (Rajpurkar et al., 2016; Joshi et al., 2017). A widely-used paradigm is that the input texts are encoded into vectors, and then these vectors are aggregated to model interactions between them by matching layers.

Figure 1(a) shows a typical machine reading comprehension model, encoding components separately encode question and passage to vector representations. Then, we obtain context-sensitive representations for input words by considering the interactions between question and passage. Finally, an output layer is used to predict the prob-

ability of each token being the start or end position of the answer span. The encoding layers are usually built upon recurrent neural networks (Hochreiter and Schmidhuber, 1997; Cho et al., 2014), and self-attention networks (Yu et al., 2018). For the matching component, various model components have been developed to fuse question and passage vector representations, such as match-LSTM (Wang and Jiang, 2016), co-attention (Seo et al., 2016; Xiong et al., 2016), and self-matching (Wang et al., 2017). Recently, Devlin et al. (2018) employ Transformer networks to pretrain a bidirectional language model (called BERT), and then fine-tune the layers on specific tasks, which obtains state-of-the-art results on MRC. A research question is: apart from the benefits of pretraining, how many performance gain comes from the unified network architecture.

In this paper, we evaluate and analyze unifying encoding and matching components with Transformer layers (Vaswani et al., 2017), using MRC as a case study. As shown in Figure 1(b), compared with previous specially-designed MRC networks, we do not explicitly distinguish encoding stages and matching stages. We directly concatenate input question and passage into one sequence at first, and append segment embeddings to word vectors in order to indicate whether each token is belong to question or passage. Next, the packed sequence is fed into a multi-layer Transformer network, which utilizes the self-attention mechanism to obtain contextualized representations for both question and passage. The first advantage is that the unified architecture enables the model to automatically learn the encoding and matching strategy, rather than empirically specifying layers one by one. Second, the proposed method is conceptually simpler than previous systems, which simplifies the model implementation.

We conduct experiments on the SQuAD v1.1

---

[*]Contribution during internship at Microsoft Research

Proceedings of the Second Workshop on Machine Reading for Question Answering, pages 14–18
Hong Kong, China, November 4, 2019. ©2019 Association for Computational Linguistics

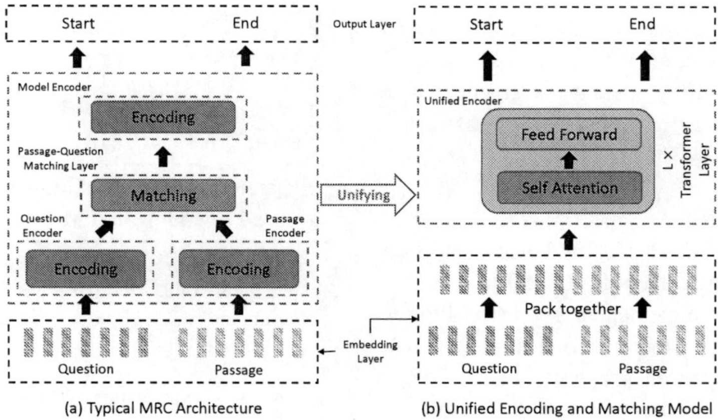

Figure 1: An illustration of a typical MRC architecture and the unified encoding and matching model.

dataset (Rajpurkar et al., 2016), which is an extractive reading comprehension benchmark. Experimental results show that the unified model outperforms previous state-of-the-art models that treat encoding and matching separately. The results indicate that part of improvements of BERT (Devlin et al., 2018) attribute to the architecture used for end tasks. Moreover, we introduce a metric to inspect the ratio of encoding and matching for each layer. The analysis illustrates that the unified model learns different strategies to handle questions and passages, which sheds lights on our future model design for MRC.

2 Unified Encoding and Matching Model

We focus on extractive reading comprehension in the work. Given input passage x^P and question x^Q, our goal is to predict the correct answer span $a = x_s^P \cdots x_e^P$ in the passage. The SQuAD v1.1 dataset assumes that the correct answer span is guaranteed to exist in the passage.

Figure 1(b) shows the overview of the unified model[1]. We first pack the question and passage into a single sequence. Then multiple Transformer (Vaswani et al., 2017) layers are employed to compute the vector representations of question and passage together. Finally, an output layer is used to predict the start and end positions of answer span. Compared with previous specially-designed networks illustrated in Figure 1(a), the model unifies encoding layers and matching layers by using multiple Transformer blocks. The self-attention mechanism is supposed to automatically

[1]The implementation and models are available at github.com/addf400/UnifiedModelForSQuAD.

learn question-to-question encoding, passage-to-passage encoding, question-to-passage matching, and passage-to-question matching.

2.1 Embedding Layer

For each word in questions and passages, the vector representation $\mathbf{x}$ is constructed by the word embedding $\mathbf{x}_w$, character embedding $\mathbf{x}_c$, and segment embedding $\mathbf{x}_s$. The character-level embeddings are computed in the similar way as (Yu et al., 2018). The segment embeddings are vectors used to indicate whether the word belongs to question or passage. The final representation is computed via $\mathbf{x} = \vartheta([\mathbf{x}_w; \mathbf{x}_c]) + \mathbf{x}_s$, where ϑ represents a Highway network (Srivastava et al., 2015).

2.2 Unified Encoder

Given question x^Q and passage x^P embeddings, we first pack them together into a single sequence $[\mathbf{x}_1^Q, \cdots, \mathbf{x}_{|Q|}^Q, \mathbf{x}_1^P, \cdots, \mathbf{x}_{|P|}^P]$, which also denoted as $\mathbf{h}_0$. Then an L-layer Transformer encoder is used to encode the packed representations:

$$\mathbf{h}_l = \text{Transformer}_l(\mathbf{h}_{l-1})$$

where $l \in [1, L]$ is the depth.

Transformer blocks use a self-attention mechanism to compute attention weights between each pair of tokens in the packed question and passage, which automatically learns the importance of encoding and matching. Specifically, for each token, the attention scores are normalized over the whole sequence. The weights between two question tokens can be regarded as question encoding. Similarly, the attention scores between two passage tokens can be viewed as passage encoding. The attention weights across the question segment and the passage segment can be considered as question-to-passage or passage-to-question matching.

2.3 Output Layer

Inspired by Yu et al. (2018), hidden vectors of different Transformer layers $\mathbf{h}_i, \mathbf{h}_j, \mathbf{h}_k$ ($i = 6, j = 9, k = 12$ in our implementation) are used to represent the input. Moreover, we employ a self-attentive method as in Wang et al. (2017) over question vectors to obtain a question attentive vector $\mathbf{v}^q$. Finally, we predict the probability of each token being the start (p^s) or end (p^e) position of the answer span:

$$p^s = \text{softmax}(\mathbf{W}_1[\mathbf{h}_i; \mathbf{h}_i \odot \mathbf{v}^q; \mathbf{h}_j; \mathbf{h}_j \odot \mathbf{v}^q])$$
$$p^e = \text{softmax}(\mathbf{W}_2[\mathbf{h}_i; \mathbf{h}_i \odot \mathbf{v}^q; \mathbf{h}_k; \mathbf{h}_k \odot \mathbf{v}^q])$$

where $\odot$ represents elementwise multiplication, and $\mathbf{W}_1, \mathbf{W}_2$ are parameters.

To train the model, we maximize the log likelihood of ground-truth start and end positions given input passage and question. At test time, we predict answer spans approximately by greedy search.

3 Experiments

3.1 Experimental Setup

Dataset Stanford Question Answering Dataset (SQuAD) (Rajpurkar et al., 2016) is composed of over 100,000 instances created by crowdworkers. Every answer is constrained to be a continuous sub-span of the passage.

Settings We employ the spaCy toolkit to preprocess data. We use 300-dimensional GloVe embeddings (Pennington et al., 2014) to initialize word vectors of both questions and passages, and keep them fixed during training. A special trainable token <UNK> is used to represent out-of-vocabulary words. We randomly mask some words in the passage to <UNK> with 0.2 probability while training. The dimension of character embedding and segment embedding is 64 and 128, respectively. The number of Transformer layers used in our model is 12. For each Transformer layer, we set the hidden size to 128, and use relative position embedding (Shaw et al., 2018) whose clipping distance is 16. The number of the attention heads is 8.

During training, the batch size is 32 and the number of the max training epochs is 80. We use

Model	EM / F1
BiDAF (Seo et al., 2016)	68.0 / 77.3
R-Net (Wang et al., 2017)	72.3 / 80.7
QAnet (Yu et al., 2018)	73.6 / 82.7
Separate Encoding and Matching	74.6 / 83.1
Unified Encoding and Matching	**75.7 / 84.2**

Table 1: Performance of different models on SQuAD development set.

Adam (Kingma and Ba, 2015) as the optimizer with $\beta_1 = 0.9$, $\beta_2 = 0.999$, $\epsilon = 10^{-6}$. We use warmup over the first $4,000$ steps, and keep the learning rate fixed for the remainder of training. The learning rate is set to 6×10^{-4}. We apply the exponential moving average on all trainable variables with decay rate of 0.9999. Layer dropout (Huang et al., 2016) is used in Transformer layers with 0.95 survival probability. We also apply dropout on word, character embeddings and each layers with dropout rate of 0.1, 0.05 and 0.1 respectively.

Comparison Models Apart from comparing with previous state-of-the-art models (Seo et al., 2016; Wang et al., 2017; Yu et al., 2018), we implement a baseline model that separately perform encoding and matching. The same settings as above are used. The first three Transformer layers are utilized to encode passage and question separately. Then we add a passage-question matching layer following Yu et al. (2018), with nine more Transformer layers used to compute the question-sensitive passage representations. To make a fair comparison, we only compare with the models that do not rely on pre-trained language models (Peters et al., 2018; Radford et al., 2018; Devlin et al., 2018).

3.2 Results

Exact match (EM) and F1 scores are two evaluation metrics for SQuAD. EM measures the percentage of the prediction that matches the ground-truth answer exactly, while F1 measures the overlap between the predicted answer answer and the ground-truth answer. The scores on the development set are evaluated by the official script.

As shown in Table 1, the unified model outperforms previous state-of-the-art models and the baseline model. We find that our unified model

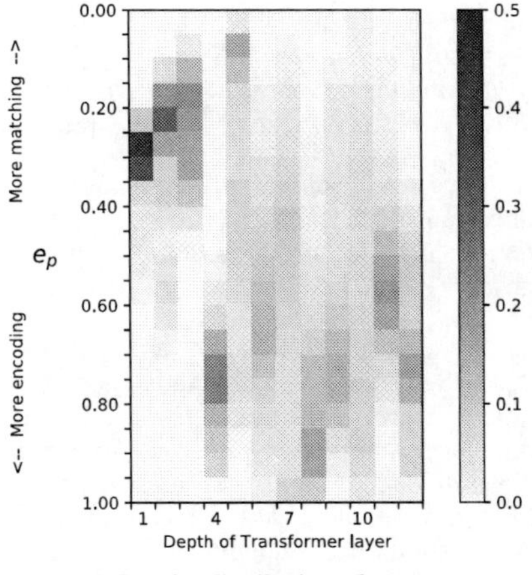
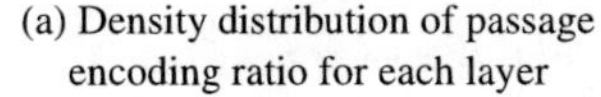
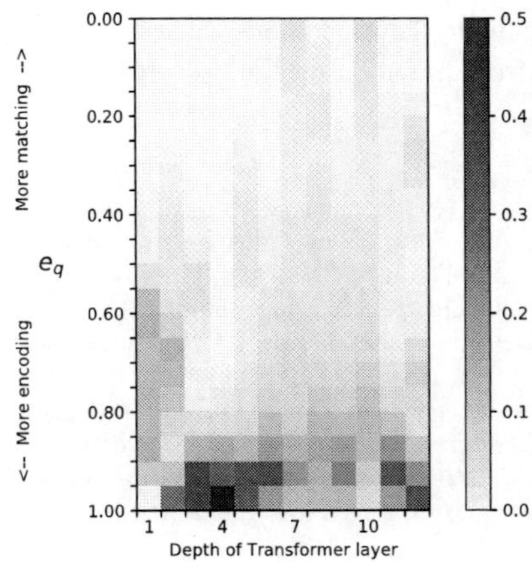

(a) Density distribution of passage
encoding ratio for each layer

(b) Density distribution of question
encoding ratio for each layer

Figure 2: Density distribution of passage encoding ratio e_p and question encoding ratio e_q for all attention heads in Transformer layers. Vertical axis represents encoding ratio. Larger encoding ratio means that the layer performs more encoding, while smaller ratio value indicates more matching. Darker color means higher density, i.e., more attention heads' encoding ratio values are within the range. The patterns show that the unified model learns different modeling strategies compared with previous manually-designed networks (see Section 3.3 for details).

brings 1.1/1.1 absolute improvement on EM/F1 over the baseline that separately conducts encoding and matching. The results indicate the unified model not only simplifies the model architecture, but also improves performance on SQuAD.

3.3   Analysis

We introduce passage encoding ratio e_p and question encoding ratio e_q to quantify the encoding and matching strategies for each layer of the unified encoder. Let us take the question encoding ratio of an attention head in the l-th Transformer layer for example. Given the attention head's self-attention weight matrix $\mathbf{A}$, the ratio e_q is computed via:

$$s_{q|q} = \mathrm{avg}_{i,j \in Q}\{\mathbf{A}_{i,j}\}$$
$$s_{q|p} = \mathrm{avg}_{i \in Q, j \in P}\{\mathbf{A}_{i,j}\}$$
$$e_q = s_{q|q}/(s_{q|q} + s_{q|p})$$

where $s_{q|q}$ is the average question-to-question attention weight, and $s_{q|p}$ is the average passage-to-question attention weight. To be specific, if e_q is close to 1, it means that the layer tends to perform question-to-question encoding. In contrast, if e_q is close to 0, it indicates the layer performs more passage-to-question matching. Similarly, we can compute passage encoding ratio e_p as above.

As shown in Figure 2, we compute passage encoding ratio e_p and question encoding ratio e_q for all the attention heads on the development set,

and plot their density distributions for each Transformer layer. We find that the unified model learns strategies that are clearly different from manually-designed architectures:

- Figure 2(a) shows that the first three layers perform question-to-passage matching and the fourth layer conducts passage-to-passage encoding, while most previous models perform passage encoding first.

- Figure 2(a) indicates that upper layers tend to conduct more encoding than matching.

- Figure 2(b) shows that all layers tend to perform question-to-question encoding than passage-to-question matching.

- Some layers are automatically learned to perform encoding and matching at the same time instead of separate modeling.

4   Conclusion

In this work, we evaluate and analyze unifying encoding and matching components with Transformer for the MRC task. Experimental results on the SQuAD dataset illustrate that the unified model outperforms previous networks that treat encoding and matching separately. We further introduce a metric to inspect whether a layer tends to act more like encoding or matching. The analysis results show that the unified Transformer layers automatically learn strategies that are clearly different from previous specially-designed models.

References

Kyunghyun Cho, Bart van Merrienboer, Çaglar Gülçehre, Dzmitry Bahdanau, Fethi Bougares, Holger Schwenk, and Yoshua Bengio. 2014. Learning phrase representations using RNN encoder-decoder for statistical machine translation. In *Proceedings of the 2014 Conference on Empirical Methods in Natural Language Processing, EMNLP 2014, October 25-29, 2014, Doha, Qatar, A meeting of SIGDAT, a Special Interest Group of the ACL*, pages 1724–1734.

Jacob Devlin, Ming-Wei Chang, Kenton Lee, and Kristina Toutanova. 2018. BERT: pre-training of deep bidirectional transformers for language understanding. *CoRR*, abs/1810.04805.

Sepp Hochreiter and Jürgen Schmidhuber. 1997. Long short-term memory. *Neural Computation*, 9(8):1735–1780.

Gao Huang, Yu Sun, Zhuang Liu, Daniel Sedra, and Kilian Q. Weinberger. 2016. Deep networks with stochastic depth. *CoRR*, abs/1603.09382.

Mandar Joshi, Eunsol Choi, Daniel Weld, and Luke Zettlemoyer. 2017. Triviaqa: A large scale distantly supervised challenge dataset for reading comprehension. In *Proceedings of the 55th Annual Meeting of the Association for Computational Linguistics (Volume 1: Long Papers)*, pages 1601–1611. Association for Computational Linguistics.

Diederik P Kingma and Jimmy Ba. 2015. Adam: A method for stochastic optimization. *In Proceedings of the International Conference on Learning Representations (ICLR)*.

Jeffrey Pennington, Richard Socher, and Christopher D. Manning. 2014. Glove: Global vectors for word representation. In *Empirical Methods in Natural Language Processing (EMNLP)*, pages 1532–1543.

Matthew E. Peters, Mark Neumann, Mohit Iyyer, Matt Gardner, Christopher Clark, Kenton Lee, and Luke Zettlemoyer. 2018. Deep contextualized word representations. In *Proceedings of the 2018 Conference of the North American Chapter of the Association for Computational Linguistics: Human Language Technologies, NAACL-HLT 2018, New Orleans, Louisiana, USA, June 1-6, 2018, Volume 1 (Long Papers)*, pages 2227–2237.

Alec Radford, Karthik Narasimhan, Tim Salimans, and Ilya Sutskever. 2018. Improving language understanding by generative pre-training.

Pranav Rajpurkar, Jian Zhang, Konstantin Lopyrev, and Percy Liang. 2016. Squad: 100, 000+ questions for machine comprehension of text. In *Proceedings of the 2016 Conference on Empirical Methods in Natural Language Processing, EMNLP 2016, Austin, Texas, USA, November 1-4, 2016*, pages 2383–2392.

Min Joon Seo, Aniruddha Kembhavi, Ali Farhadi, and Hannaneh Hajishirzi. 2016. Bidirectional attention flow for machine comprehension. *CoRR*, abs/1611.01603.

Peter Shaw, Jakob Uszkoreit, and Ashish Vaswani. 2018. Self-attention with relative position representations. In *Proceedings of the 2018 Conference of the North American Chapter of the Association for Computational Linguistics: Human Language Technologies, Volume 2 (Short Papers)*, pages 464–468. Association for Computational Linguistics.

Rupesh Kumar Srivastava, Klaus Greff, and Jürgen Schmidhuber. 2015. Highway networks. *CoRR*, abs/1505.00387.

Ashish Vaswani, Noam Shazeer, Niki Parmar, Jakob Uszkoreit, Llion Jones, Aidan N. Gomez, Lukasz Kaiser, and Illia Polosukhin. 2017. Attention is all you need. In *Advances in Neural Information Processing Systems 30: Annual Conference on Neural Information Processing Systems 2017, 4-9 December 2017, Long Beach, CA, USA*, pages 6000–6010.

Shuohang Wang and Jing Jiang. 2016. Machine comprehension using match-lstm and answer pointer. *CoRR*, abs/1608.07905.

Wenhui Wang, Nan Yang, Furu Wei, Baobao Chang, and Ming Zhou. 2017. Gated self-matching networks for reading comprehension and question answering. In *Proceedings of the 55th Annual Meeting of the Association for Computational Linguistics, ACL 2017, Vancouver, Canada, July 30 - August 4, Volume 1: Long Papers*, pages 189–198.

Caiming Xiong, Victor Zhong, and Richard Socher. 2016. Dynamic coattention networks for question answering. *CoRR*, abs/1611.01604.

Adams Wei Yu, David Dohan, Minh-Thang Luong, Rui Zhao, Kai Chen, Mohammad Norouzi, and Quoc V. Le. 2018. Qanet: Combining local convolution with global self-attention for reading comprehension. *CoRR*, abs/1804.09541.

CALOR-QUEST : generating a training corpus for Machine Reading Comprehension models from shallow semantic annotations

Frédéric Béchet[1]   Cindy Aloui[1]   Delphine Charlet[2]   Géraldine Damnati[2]
Johannes Heinecke[2]   Alexis Nasr[1]   Frédéric Herlédan[2]
(1) Aix-Marseille Univ, Université de Toulon, CNRS, LIS, Marseille, France
(2) Orange Labs, Lannion
(1) {first.last}@lis-lab.fr
(2) {first.last}@orange.com

Abstract

Machine reading comprehension is a task related to Question-Answering where questions are not generic in scope but are related to a particular document. Recently very large corpora (SQuAD, MS MARCO) containing triplets (document, question, answer) were made available to the scientific community to develop supervised methods based on deep neural networks with promising results. These methods need very large training corpus to be efficient, however such kind of data only exists for English and Chinese at the moment. The aim of this study is the development of such resources for other languages by proposing to generate in a semi-automatic way questions from the semantic Frame analysis of large corpora. The collect of *natural questions* is reduced to a validation/test set. We applied this method on the French CALOR-FRAME corpus to develop the CALOR-QUEST resource presented in this paper.

1 Introduction

Machine Reading Comprehension (MRC) is a *Natural Language Understanding* task consisting in retrieving text segments from a document thanks to a set of questions, each segment being an answer to a particular question. This task received a lot of attention in the past few years thanks to the availability of very large corpora of triplets *(document, question, answer)* such as **SQuAD** (Rajpurkar et al., 2016) or **MS MARCO** (Nguyen et al., 2016), each containing more than 100k triplets. In these corpora each question has been manually produced, either through crowd-sourcing or by collecting query logs from a search engine.

These large corpora opened the door to the development of supervised machine learning approaches for MRC, mostly based on Deep Neural Network (Wang and Jiang, 2016; Seo et al., 2016), improving greatly the state-of-the-art over previous methods based on linguistic analysis or similarity metrics between questions and segments (Hermann et al., 2015). Recently the use of contextual word embeddings such as **BERT** (Devlin et al., 2018) or **XLNet** (Yang et al., 2019) lead to obtain another great increase in performance, reaching human-level performance according to some benchmarks [1].

These large corpora are only available in English, and more recently Chinese (He et al., 2018) but for other languages, such as French, there is no comparable resources and the effort required to collect such a large amount of data is very important, limiting the use of these methods to other languages or other application frameworks.

To address this problem, several studies have proposed to *generate* automatically questions and answers directly from a text document such as Wikipedia pages (Du and Cardie, 2018) in order to build a training corpus for MRC models. One of the issues of such methods is the semantic errors that can occur between questions and answers due to the automatic generation process.

In order to try to overcome this problem, the method proposed in this paper makes use of a *FrameNet* semantic analysis of the documents in order to automatically generate questions. Semantic annotations are used to control the question generation process and the answer span identification.

We present in this study the **CALOR-QUEST** corpus which contains almost $100K$ triplets (text, question, answer) automatically obtained on French encyclopedic documents (Wikipedia, Vikidia, ClioTexte) with our semantically controlled question generation method. We report results on an MRC task similar to SQuAD obtained with the BERT SQuAD model (Devlin et al., 2018) fine-tuned on **CALOR-QUEST** and evaluated on a ma-

---

1. https ://rajpurkar.github.io/SQuAD-explorer/

Proceedings of the Second Workshop on Machine Reading for Question Answering, pages 19–26
Hong Kong, China, November 4, 2019. ©2019 Association for Computational Linguistics

nually collected corpus in French .

2 Related work

In addition to SQuAD and MS-MARCO already mentioned in the introduction, several corpora in English have been proposed for MRC tasks as presented in (Nguyen et al., 2016), such as **NewsQA** (Trischler et al., 2016), **SearchQA** (Dunn et al., 2017) including questions from the Jeopardy game paired to text segments collected through search queries, **NarrativeQA** (Kočiský et al., 2018) built from films and books abstract.

Developing such resources for a new language requires a lot of effort, as presented in (He et al., 2018) for Chinese. In this context, methods that can help reducing this cost have attracted a lot of attention and can be grouped into two categories : methods based on an automatic *translation* process between MRC resources in English and the target language ; methods based on an automatic *question generation* and *answer spans identification* process directly from documents in the target language.

In the first category, in addition to methods performing a full translation of English corpora into a target language, methods have been proposed to directly perform online translation with a multilingual alignment process (Asai et al., 2018) or to build a multilingual model with a GAN-based approach in which English and target language features can be joined (Lee and Lee, 2019). All these methods imply that the models or the resources created on the target language are on the same domains than the source language ones.

The second category of methods is more generic as it can be applied to any language or any domain, however it is more challenging since there is no human supervision used in the pairing of questions and answer spans.

Question generation from text has been the subject of many studies outside the scope of MRC, for example through evaluation programs such as (Boyer and Piwek, 2010). Traditionally two kinds of methods have been explored, whether through patterns built from the syntactic parsing of a sentence or from semantic analysis (Yao et al., 2012). Recent advances in these two fields have led to further advances in question generation (Mazidi and Nielsen, 2014). Recently, for example, (Pillai et al., 2018) and (Flor and Riordan, 2018) have proposed to generate factual questions from an analysis in PropBank semantic roles.

However these works often take place in an application context very different from MRC, namely the production of questions for language learning or quiz generation for education. In such contexts, the readability and grammaticality of the questions obtained is paramount and questions are usually evaluated by subjective tests or metrics like *BLEU* or *Meteor*.

Beyond knowledge-based pattern-based approaches, recent work consider question generation as a supervised machine learning task where questions or question patterns are generated by an end-to-end neural network directly from text (Dong et al., 2018; Yuan et al., 2017; Duan et al., 2017) conditioned by answer spans, even considering jointly question generation and answer span identification (Wang et al., 2017). In (Du and Cardie, 2018), the SQuAD corpus is used to train a question generation model that first extract candidate answers from Wikipedia documents, then generate answer-specific questions. This model takes co-reference into account, allowing to produce questions spanning over several sentences, a very important feature considering that nearly 30% of human-generated questions in SQuAD rely on information beyond a single sentence (Du and Cardie, 2017).

The question corpus generated by such approaches can then be used to train a MRC model, however there are two drawbacks with these methods : firstly the need for a large question/answer corpus in order to train question generation models, although such resource is not available for every language, especially for French which is the focus of this study ; secondly the fact that semantic errors can occur in the question/answer-span generation process, leading to introduce noise in the training corpus. One way to control this noise is to use an explicit semantic representation in order to relate questions and answers. This was done in (Serban et al., 2016) by using the *Freebase* (Bollacker et al., 2008) knowledge base combined to a question dataset (*SimpleQuestion* dataset (Bordes et al., 2015)) in order to generate a very large corpus of questions on the *Freebase* entities and relations.

The approach followed in this study is also based on an explicit semantic representation in order to generate pairs of question/answer-span. The main difference is that since we don't have a large corpus of question/answer pairs to train a question generation model, we will rely on simple patterns based on the semantic annotations of our target corpus. The main originality of this work is to use a large encyclopedic corpus in French annotated with a FrameNet semantic model, the **CALOR-FRAME** corpus (Marzinotto et al., 2018), in order to automatically produce a large amount of semantically-valid pairs of questions and answer-spans, the **CALOR-QUEST** corpus.

Using FrameNet annotations for generating an MRC training corpus has a major drawback : the human effort needed to build such resources is arguably bigger than building directly a question/answer corpus such as SQuAD. However we believe this method has several advantages :

— firstly corpora with frame-based annotations are available for many languages, even if often of limited sizes ;
— secondly frame-based annotation is not linked to a single task such as MRC, therefore data developed for other application frameworks can be reuse ;
— lastly the availability of *explicit* semantic annotations on which an end-to-end MRC model is trained and evaluated can give us insights about what is being learned by these models and on their generalization capabilities, as our first experiments will show in section 4.2.

3 Using shallow semantic annotations to obtain a question/answer corpus

The **CALOR-FRAME** corpus is made of 4 sub-corpora stemming from 3 encyclopedic sources : Wikipedia (WP), Vikidia (V) and ClioTexte (CT). Three themes are covered : World War I (WWI), archaeology (arch) and antiquity (antiq). This variety spans different genres ranging from historical documents for ClioTexte (speeches, declarations) to article for children in Vikidia. The corpus was hand-annotated with Semantic Frames, following the *Berkeley FrameNet* (Baker et al., 1998) annotation guidelines. Semantic Frames describe prototypical situations, such as *decide, lose, attack, win*. Every Frame has a *Lexical Unit (LU)*, which is a word or an expression that triggers the Frame and *Frame Elements (FE)* which are the participants to the situation denoted by the Frame. Every FE has a *label*, such as *Agent, Patient, Time, …* that denotes the relation that links the FE and the

Frame.

In the **CALOR-FRAME** corpus, 54 different Frames were used, that can be triggered by 145 lemmas (70 nouns and 75 verbs), as described in (Béchet et al., 2017). The annotation process of a sentence consists in first identifying the potential triggers, then the Frame triggered, and their FEs. A sequence of words can correspond to several FEs for sentences with several Frames occurrences. An example is given in Figure 1 for a sentence with two Frame occurrences : an occurrence of the Frame Losing triggered by the word lost and an occurrence of the Frame Attack triggered by the noun attacks [2].

When a FE is a pronoun (*e.g. they*) or a sub-specified noun phrase (*e.g. the troops*) the co-reference to the explicit mention (*e.g. German troops*) is annotated, therefore a Frame can span other several sentences in a document.

From such annotations, a *Question/Answer* corpus can be obtained. The method consists in producing, for every Frame occurrence f, a triplet (F, E, C) where F is the label of the Frame, E is one Frame Element of f and C (for Context) is the set of the other Frame Elements. Given a triplet (F, E, C), questions can be produced for which the answer is E.

In the case of the Losing Frame of Figure 1, which has three Frame Elements, three triplets (F, E, C) can be produced :

```
(Losing, Owner, {Time, Possession})
(Losing, Time, {Owner, Possession})
(Losing, Possession, {Owner, Time})
```

When a frame element is a co-reference to an explicit mention, it is the mention which is used, therefore a question can spread over several sentences in a document.

A triplet (F, E, C) yields a set of questions noted $Questions(F, E, C)$. The first triplet in the above list, for example, can produce the question *Who lost 80% of its number on 8 and 9 October.* or *Which troops were wiped out during the attacks of early October ?* Both questions have as an answer the same text segment : *the German troops*, but present very different forms : the first one is close to the original sentence and could be produced by a simple re-organization of the latter, without any lexical change while the second asks for a complete rewriting. Both types of questions have been produced using the Frame annotation of the

---

2. The original example is in French, it has been translated for readability reasons.

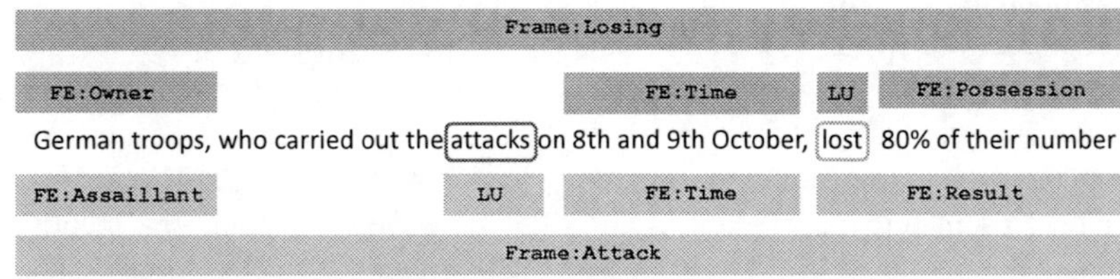

Figure 1: A sentence annotated with Frames defined in the Berkeley Framenet project

CALOR-FRAME corpus. The first type, called *automatic questions*, noted Q_A, has been produced automatically using rules applied on (F, E, C) triplets. The second type, called *natural questions*, noted Q_N, has been produced manually using a sub-part of the corpus, in a controlled setup. Both methods are described below.

In both cases, hand-produced Frame annotations have been used, as a proof of concept of the proposed method. Question production based on automatically predicted Frames is left for future work.

3.1 Rule-based question generation

The automatic production of questions is based on rules which are sentences with variables that correspond to FE. When applied on a triplet, the variables are instantiated with the corresponding FE. Some variables are optional, they can be omitted in the question. A single rule applied to a (F, E, C) triplet can therefore produce several questions.

Two rules are represented in Figure 2. Variables are prefixed with a $ sign, followed by an FE label. Optional parts are represented between square brackets.

	$F = \text{Leadership}\ E = \text{Time}$	
gen.	When lead [$Leader] [$Governed] [$Place] $Role] [$Duration] [$Activity]?	
spe.	When did $Leader lead $Governed [$Place]?	

Figure 2: Example of a generic and a specific rule for the Leadership Frame and the FE Time

Two types of rules has been used for generating questions : generic rules and specific rules.

Generic rules are produced automatically from a Frame description F, the indication of a specific FE E that corresponds to the answer of the question as well as the set of all possible verbs that can trigger F. The rules are built by selecting an interrogative pronoun that is compatible with E [3]

followed by a possible trigger for F and all possible combinations of FE excluding E which is the answer to the question. In the example of the generic rule of Figure 2, the pronoun is *When*, the trigger is *lead*, followed by all FE except the FE Time, which is the answer. Every FE is optional, which allows to exclude any subset of FE from the question. Such rules can lead to awkward questions, due either to lexico-syntactic reasons or to the choice of optional FE that are kept in the question produced.

Specific rules are built manually. They share the same format as generic rules but there is a manual control on the lexical and syntactic aspects of the question as well as the FE that are considered mandatory or optional.

Generic rules allow to produce a very large number of questions covering all possible questions a Frame could produce, without too much concern for the syntactic correctness of the questions produced. On the opposite, specific rules produce less questions but are closer to questions that one can naturally produce for a given Frame.

3.2 Collecting *real* questions from semantic annotations

To obtain *real* questions for our evaluation corpus we could have used the same protocol as for SQuAD and ask annotators to produce arbitrary questions directly from the **CALOR-FRAME** corpus. However, as discussed in section 2, one of the goals of this study is to provide insights about what is being learned by MRC end-to-end models by controlling semantic of both training and evaluation data. Therefore we decided to produce natural questions with annotators to whom (F, E, C) triplets were shown. The original sentence was not presented in order to leave more freedom for the annotator in her or his lexical ans syntactic choices. Besides, the annotator can select any elements of the context to include in the question. The

---

3. The list of compatible pairs of an interrogative pronoun and a FE has been built manually.

main advantage of this method is that it is possible to know, for each error made by an MRC system, which phenomenon was not well covered by the model.

The following example shows in the upper part the information that were given to the annotator and in the lower part, some questions produced.

```
Frame = Hiding_objects
    — Context
        — Agent : a Gallic militia leader
        — Hidden_object : a treasure
        — Hiding_place : in his Bassing farm
    — Answer
        — Place : Moselle

    — Questions produced :
        — In which region did the Gallic militia leader hide
          the treasure ?
        — Where is the location of the Bassing farm in
          which the Gallic militia leader hid the treasure ?
```

The natural questions produced with this protocol concerned only a sub-part of the **CALOR-QUEST** corpus but this sub-part has been selected in order to represent all the Frames used to annotate the corpus.

3.3 Collected corpus

With the proposed method, the resulting corpus CALOR-QUEST consists of about 300 documents in French, for which nearly 100 000 automatic question/answer pairs, and more than 1000 natural question/answer pairs are available. More detailed numbers per collection are given in table 1.

collection	#docs	#natural questions	#generated questions
V_antiq	61	274	4672
WP_arch	96	302	36259
CT_1GM	16	241	7502
WP_1GM	123	319	50971
total	**296**	**1136**	**99404**

Table 1: Description of CALOR-QUEST corpus

4 Evaluation

The main objective of our work is to create in a semi-automatic fashion a training corpus for reading comprehension model. Thus, for a given document annotated with frames, we want to generate automatically as many questions as possible, semantically valid, for which we have, by construction, the right answer span in the document. To validate this approach we perform an extrinsic evaluation of this corpus by using it for training a state-of-the-art Machine Reading Comprehension system publicly available, and by evaluating its performance on the set of natural questions collected.

4.1 Experiments with BERT-SQUAD

We use for our MRC system a fine-tuned version of BERT multilingual model : *multi_cased_L-12_H-768_A-12* (Devlin et al., 2018)[4], with default hyperparameters. To be in the same conditions as the SQuAD corpus, we cut the CALOR documents into paragraphs whose lengths are close to the average paragraph length of SQuAD (around 120 tokens) : starting at the beginning of each document, we look for the next end of sentence marker after 120 tokens. This constitutes the first paragraph on which the MRC system will be applied. Then the process is repeated on the text starting at the next sentence in the document.

The evaluation is done with SQuAD's evalution script (https://github.com/allenai/bi-att-flow/blob/master/squad/evaluate-v1.1.py), customized for French (removing french articles in the normalization process, instead of english articles). In this evaluation set-up, "*Exact Match*" represents the percentage of questions whose predicted answer matches exactly the ground-truth answer, and "*F1*" is the average F-measure per question, where for each question a precision/recall performance is measured between the predicted and ground-truth sets of tokens in answer spans.

The training is done on a randomly selected sample set of 14K generated questions (due to our computational storage limitation). In these experiments we first select automatic questions generated thanks to specific rules, then add questions produced by generic rules. The evaluation is done on the natural questions set. For the *SQUAD1.1* condition, all the questions are answerable in the given paragraphs. For the *SQUAD2.0* condition, the system is also able to detect if a question is answerable or not, in a given paragraph. For this set up, we build a specific test set, with 2/3 made of answerable questions for a given paragraph, and 1/3 made of answerable questions of another paragraph of the same document, thus assumed to be

---

4. https://github.com/google-research/bert/blob/master/run_squad.py)

unanswerable for the given paragraph (but dealing with the same topic).

Results are presented in table 2. As we can see the model find the correct answer with the correct span for about 60% of the natural questions of our test corpus, although it has been trained only on generated questions. F1 measure is satisfying for SQUAD1.1i (76.7), although it drops to 64.2 when introducing unanswerable questions in SQUAD2.0. However performance of unanswerable question detection are excellent (98.0). This validate our approach although there is a large margin of improvement considering the performance of current models on the English SQUAD corpus.

version	exact	F1	F1-HasAns	F1-NoAns
V1	59.4	76.7	76.7	-
V2	62.7	73.5	64.2	98.0

Table 2: Results obtained with BERT-SQUAD on CALOR-QUEST with two conditions : V1 correspond to SQUAD1.1 where all questions refer to an answer in the documents ; V2 correspond to SQUAD2.0 with unanswerable questions

4.2 Contrastive experiments

4.2.1 Generalization beyond the initial semantic model

In the following experiment, we evaluate how this framework generalizes to new semantic frames, and is able to answer questions related to semantic frames which were absent from the training set. To this purpose, we select 10 semantic frames for which we have the most numerous natural questions in the test set, and we discard from the training set the questions generated from these 10 semantic frames. In table 3, performances are reported for each subset of natural questions, including or not generated questions from the same semantic frame in the training. It can be seen that for most of these frames the decrease of performance observed when excluding them from the training set is not important, therefore we can conclude that our method allows to train models that can generalize beyond the set of semantic frames that was used to generate the training corpus.

However table 3 also shows that for 3 of these frames (*Departing, Appointing, Shoot-projectiles*) there is a loss of more than 10% F1 when using the

reduced training corpus, indicating that this generalization capabilities can be limited for some specific actions.

Frame	#quest	F1 (all)	F1 (w/o)
Death	49	89.2	78.78
Creating	38	81.0	85.0
Existence	38	83.0	79.2
Giving	65	80.9	73.8
Coming-up-with	27	86.4	82.9
Departing	64	86.3	71.8
Appointing	52	76.9	64.5
Buildings	62	77.5	73.6
Colonization	37	69.9	70.0
Shoot-projectiles	24	72.4	47.3

Table 3: F1 results on questions associated to 10 semantic frames of CALOR-QUEST with a model trained on the whole corpus (*all*) and one trained on a corpus where all the generated questions corresponding to these 10 frames have been removed (*w/o*)

4.2.2 Generalization to a new domain

We also evaluate our method on a different corpus to check how domain-depend are the models trained on **CALOR-QUEST** . (Asai et al., 2018) provides a French transcription of a subset of the development set of the original SQuAD corpus. They have extracted several paragraphs and their corresponding questions, resulting in 327 paragraph-question pairs over 48 articles. This subcorpus was manually translated into French by bilingual workers on Amazon Mechanical Turk and further corrected by bilingual experts. In this corpus of 327 questions, only 46 correspond to questions related to frames defined in CALOR, and themes are not restricted to historical knowledge as in CALOR. Thus, we have a semantic shift but also a lexical shift between the training set of CALOR and the testing set of french_squad.

We test this corpus on the model trained on **CALOR-QUEST** . For sake of comparison, we report baseline performance obtained in (Asai et al., 2018) with a back-translation approach : the French evaluation corpus is first translated to English with an automatic French-to-English translation service, then the BERT system with English model is applied to this automatic translation, finally the outputs of the system are automatically back-translated to French for evaluation.

Results are presented in table 4. Although we observe an important decrease in performance, in comparison with the results obtained on CALOR, performance is still much better than the one obtained with a back-translation baseline of the well-trained BERT-model in English.

Model	exact	F1
CALOR-QUEST	38.5	53.6
BERT-SQUAD (auto trans.) (Asai et al., 2018)	23.5	44.0

Table 4: Results obtained on the French SQuAD test corpus with a model trained on CALOR-QUEST and the original BERT-SQUAD model for English with back-translation

5 Conclusion

In this work, we have proposed a semi-automatic method to generate question/answer pairs from a corpus of documents annotated in semantic frames, with the purpose of building a large training corpus for machine reading comprehension in French. Based on simple rules applied on shallow semantic annotations, the produced questions are valid semantically, but their syntactic validity is not guaranteed. Additionally, a set of more than 1000 question/answer pairs has been collected manually, to be used as a test corpus. We validate the usefulness of the corpus of automatic questions, by training a state of the art, publicly available, machine reading comprehension system, based on fine-tuning multilingual BERT features on this corpus. We then test the resulting model on the set of real questions, and on a french translation of a subset of the SQuAD corpus, and promising results have been obtained. Further work will focus on extending this approach to semantic annotations obtained automatically. The extension to another semantic annotation scheme such as PropBank will also be studied. The **CALOR-QUEST** corpus of automatic and natural questions will be made publicly available, to foster machine reading comprehension for French language.

References

Akari Asai, Akiko Eriguchi, Kazuma Hashimoto, and Yoshimasa Tsuruoka. 2018. Multilingual extractive reading comprehension by runtime machine translation. *CoRR*, abs/1809.03275.

Collin F Baker, Charles J Fillmore, and John B Lowe. 1998. The berkeley framenet project. In *Proceedings of the 36th Annual Meeting of the Association for Computational Linguistics and 17th International Conference on Computational Linguistics-Volume 1*, pages 86–90. Association for Computational Linguistics.

Frédéric Béchet, Géraldine Damnati, Johannes Heinecke, Gabriel Marzinotto, and Alexis Nasr. 2017. CALOR-Frame : un corpus de textes encyclopédiques annoté en cadres sémantiques. In *ACor4French – Les corpus annotés du français - Atelier TALN*, Orléans, France.

Kurt Bollacker, Colin Evans, Praveen Paritosh, Tim Sturge, and Jamie Taylor. 2008. Freebase : a collaboratively created graph database for structuring human knowledge. In *Proceedings of the 2008 ACM SIGMOD international conference on Management of data*, pages 1247–1250. AcM.

Antoine Bordes, Nicolas Usunier, Sumit Chopra, and Jason Weston. 2015. Large-scale simple question answering with memory networks. *arXiv preprint arXiv :1506.02075*.

Kristy Elizabeth Boyer and Paul Piwek. 2010. *Proceedings of QG2010 : The Third Workshop on Question Generation*. questiongeneration. org.

Jacob Devlin, Ming-Wei Chang, Kenton Lee, and Kristina Toutanova. 2018. Bert : Pre-training of deep bidirectional transformers for language understanding. *arXiv preprint arXiv :1810.04805*.

Xiaozheng Dong, Yu Hong, Xin Chen, Weikang Li, Min Zhang, and Qiaoming Zhu. 2018. Neural question generation with semantics of question type. In *CCF International Conference on Natural Language Processing and Chinese Computing*, pages 213–223. Springer.

Xinya Du and Claire Cardie. 2017. Identifying where to focus in reading comprehension for neural question generation. In *Proceedings of the 2017 Conference on Empirical Methods in Natural Language Processing*, pages 2067–2073.

Xinya Du and Claire Cardie. 2018. Harvesting paragraph-level question-answer pairs from wikipedia. In *Proceedings of the 56th Annual Meeting of the Association for Computational Linguistics (Volume 1 : Long Papers)*, pages 1907–1917.

Nan Duan, Duyu Tang, Peng Chen, and Ming Zhou. 2017. Question generation for question answering. In *Proceedings of the 2017 Conference on Empirical Methods in Natural Language Processing*, pages 866–874, Copenhagen, Denmark. Association for Computational Linguistics.

Matthew Dunn, Levent Sagun, Mike Higgins, V Ugur Guney, Volkan Cirik, and Kyunghyun Cho. 2017. Searchqa : A new q&a dataset augmented with context from a search engine. *arXiv preprint arXiv :1704.05179*.

Michael Flor and Brian Riordan. 2018. A semantic role-based approach to open-domain automatic question generation. In *Proceedings of the Thirteenth Workshop on Innovative Use of NLP for Building Educational Applications*, pages 254–263.

Wei He, Kai Liu, Jing Liu, Yajuan Lyu, Shiqi Zhao, Xinyan Xiao, Yuan Liu, Yizhong Wang, Hua Wu, Qiaoqiao She, et al. 2018. Dureader : a chinese machine reading comprehension dataset from real-world applications. *ACL 2018*, page 37.

Karl Moritz Hermann, Tomáš Kočiský, Edward Grefenstette, Lasse Espeholt, Will Kay, Mustafa Suleyman, and Phil Blunsom. 2015. Teaching machines to read and comprehend. In *Proceedings of the 28th International Conference on Neural Information Processing Systems - Volume 1*, NIPS'15, pages 1693–1701, Cambridge, MA, USA. MIT Press.

Tomáš Kočiský, Jonathan Schwarz, Phil Blunsom, Chris Dyer, Karl Moritz Hermann, Gáabor Melis, and Edward Grefenstette. 2018. The narrative qa reading comprehension challenge. *Transactions of the Association of Computational Linguistics*, 6 :317–328.

Chia-Hsuan Lee and Hung-Yi Lee. 2019. Cross-lingual transfer learning for question answering. *arXiv preprint arXiv :1907.06042*.

Gabriel Marzinotto, Jeremy Auguste, Frederic Bechet, Géraldine Damnati, and Alexis Nasr. 2018. Semantic frame parsing for information extraction : the calor corpus. In *Proceedings of the Eleventh International Conference on Language Resources and Evaluation (LREC-2018)*. European Language Resource Association.

Karen Mazidi and Rodney D. Nielsen. 2014. Linguistic considerations in automatic question generation. In *ACL*.

Tri Nguyen, Mir Rosenberg, Xia Song, Jianfeng Gao, Saurabh Tiwary, Rangan Majumder, and Li Deng. 2016. Ms marco : A human generated machine reading comprehension dataset. *arXiv preprint arXiv :1611.09268*.

Lekshmi R Pillai, G Veena, and Deepa Gupta. 2018. A combined approach using semantic role labelling and word sense disambiguation for question generation and answer extraction. In *2018 Second International Conference on Advances in Electronics, Computers and Communications (ICAECC)*, pages 1–6. IEEE.

Pranav Rajpurkar, Jian Zhang, Konstantin Lopyrev, and Percy Liang. 2016. Squad: 100,000+ questions for machine comprehension of text. In *Proceedings of the 2016 Conference on Empirical Methods in Natural Language Processing*, pages 2383–2392. Association for Computational Linguistics.

Minjoon Seo, Aniruddha Kembhavi, Ali Farhadi, and Hannaneh Hajishirzi. 2016. Bidirectional attention flow for machine comprehension. *arXiv preprint arXiv :1611.01603*.

Iulian Vlad Serban, Alberto García-Durán, Caglar Gulcehre, Sungjin Ahn, Sarath Chandar, Aaron Courville, and Yoshua Bengio. 2016. Generating factoid questions with recurrent neural networks : The 30m factoid question-answer corpus. In *Proceedings of the 54th Annual Meeting of the Association for Computational Linguistics (Volume 1 : Long Papers)*, pages 588–598.

Adam Trischler, Tong Wang, Xingdi Yuan, Justin Harris, Alessandro Sordoni, Philip Bachman, and Kaheer Suleman. 2016. Newsqa : A machine comprehension dataset. *arXiv preprint arXiv :1611.09830*.

Shuohang Wang and Jing Jiang. 2016. Machine comprehension using match-lstm and answer pointer. *arXiv preprint arXiv :1608.07905*.

Tong Wang, Xingdi Yuan, and Adam Trischler. 2017. A joint model for question answering and question generation. *CoRR*, abs/1706.01450.

Zhilin Yang, Zihang Dai, Yiming Yang, Jaime G. Carbonell, Ruslan Salakhutdinov, and Quoc V. Le. 2019. Xlnet: Generalized autoregressive pretraining for language understanding. *CoRR*, abs/1906.08237.

Xuchen Yao, Gosse Bouma, and Yi Zhang. 2012. Semantics-based question generation and implementation. *Dialogue & Discourse*, 3(2) :11–42.

Xingdi Yuan, Tong Wang, Caglar Gulcehre, Alessandro Sordoni, Philip Bachman, Saizheng Zhang, Sandeep Subramanian, and Adam Trischler. 2017. Machine comprehension by text-to-text neural question generation. In *Proceedings of the 2nd Workshop on Representation Learning for NLP*, pages 15–25. Association for Computational Linguistics.

Improving Question Answering with External Knowledge

Xiaoman Pan[1]*   Kai Sun[2]*   Dian Yu[3]   Jianshu Chen[3]
Heng Ji[1]   Claire Cardie[2]   Dong Yu[3]
[1]University of Illinois at Urbana-Champaign, Champaign, IL, USA
[2]Cornell University, Ithaca, NY, USA
[3]Tencent AI Lab, Bellevue, WA, USA

Abstract

We focus on multiple-choice question answering (QA) tasks in subject areas such as science, where we require both broad background knowledge and the facts from the given subject-area reference corpus. In this work, we explore simple yet effective methods for exploiting two sources of external knowledge for subject-area QA. The first enriches the original subject-area reference corpus with relevant text snippets extracted from an open-domain resource (i.e., Wikipedia) that cover potentially ambiguous concepts in the question and answer options. As in other QA research, the second method simply increases the amount of training data by appending additional in-domain subject-area instances.

Experiments on three challenging multiple-choice science QA tasks (i.e., ARC-Easy, ARC-Challenge, and OpenBookQA) demonstrate the effectiveness of our methods: in comparison to the previous state-of-the-art, we obtain absolute gains in accuracy of up to 8.1%, 13.0%, and 12.8%, respectively. While we observe consistent gains when we introduce knowledge from Wikipedia, we find that employing additional QA training instances is not uniformly helpful: performance degrades when the added instances exhibit a higher level of difficulty than the original training data. As one of the first studies on exploiting unstructured external knowledge for subject-area QA, we hope our methods, observations, and discussion of the exposed limitations may shed light on further developments in the area.

1   Introduction

To answer questions relevant to a given text (e.g., a document or a book), human readers often rely on a certain amount of broad background knowledge obtained from sources outside of the text (McNamara et al., 2004; Salmerón et al., 2006). It is perhaps not surprising then, that machine readers also require knowledge external to the text itself to perform well on question answering (QA) tasks.

We focus on multiple-choice QA tasks in subject areas such as science, in which facts from the given reference corpus (e.g., a textbook) need to be combined with broadly applicable external knowledge to select the correct answer from the available options (Clark et al., 2016, 2018; Mihaylov et al., 2018). For convenience, we call these **subject-area QA** tasks.

Question: a magnet will stick to __?
A.	a belt buckle. ✓	**B.**	a wooden table.
C.	a plastic cup.	**D.**	a paper plate.

Table 1: A sample problem from a multiple-choice QA task OpenBookQA (Mihaylov et al., 2018) in a scientific domain (✓: correct answer option).

To correctly answer the question in Table 1, for example, scientific facts[1] from the provided reference corpus — { *"a magnet attracts magnetic metals through magnetism"* and *"iron is always magnetic"*}, as well as general world knowledge extracted from an external source such as { *"a belt buckle is often made of iron"* and *"iron is metal"*} are required. Thus, these QA tasks provide suitable testbeds for evaluating external knowledge exploitation and intergration.

Previous subject-area QA methods (e.g., (Khot et al., 2017; Zhang et al., 2018; Zhong et al., 2018)) explore many ways of exploiting structured knowledge. Recently, we have seen that the framework of fine-tuning a pre-trained language model (e.g., GPT (Radford et al., 2018) and BERT (Devlin et al., 2019)) outperforms previous state-of-

---

* Equal contribution. This work was conducted when the two authors were at Tencent AI Lab, Bellevue, WA.

[1]Ground truth facts are usually not provided in this kind of question answering tasks.

Proceedings of the Second Workshop on Machine Reading for Question Answering, pages 27–37
Hong Kong, China, November 4, 2019. ©2019 Association for Computational Linguistics

the-art methods (Mihaylov et al., 2018; Ni et al., 2019). However, it is still not clear how to incorporate different sources of external knowledge, especially unstructured knowledge, into this powerful framework to further improve subject-area QA.

We investigate two sources of external knowledge (i.e., **open-domain** and **in-domain**), which have proven effective for other types of QA tasks, by incorporating them into a pre-trained language model during the **fine-tuning** stage. First, we identify concepts in question and answer options and link these potentially ambiguous concepts to an **open-domain** resource that provides unstructured background information relevant to the concepts and used to enrich the original reference corpus (Section 2.2). In comparison to previous work (e.g., (Yadav et al., 2019)), we perform information retrieval based on the enriched corpus instead of the original one to form a document for answering a question. Second, we increase the amount of training data by appending additional **in-domain** subject-area QA datasets (Section 2.3).

We conduct experiments on three challenging multiple-choice science QA tasks where existing methods stubbornly continue to exhibit performance gaps in comparison with humans: ARC-Easy, ARC-Challenge (Clark et al., 2016, 2018), and OpenBookQA (Mihaylov et al., 2018), which are collected from real-world science exams or carefully checked by experts. We fine-tune BERT (Devlin et al., 2019) in a two-step fashion (Section 2.1). We treat entire Wikipedia as the **open-domain** external resource (Section 2.2) and all the evaluated science QA datasets (question-answer pairs and reference corpora) except the target one as **in-domain** external resources (Section 2.3). Experimental results show that we can obtain absolute gains in accuracy of up to 8.1%, 13.0%, and 12.8%, respectively, in comparison to the previous published state-of-the-art, demonstrating the effectiveness of our methods. We also analyze the gains and exposed limitations. While we observe consistent gains by introducing knowledge from Wikipedia, employing additional in-domain training data is not uniformly helpful: performance degrades when the added data exhibit a higher level of difficulty than the original training data (Section 3).

To the best of our knowledge, this is the first work to incorporate external knowledge into a pre-trained model for improving subject-area QA. Be-sides, our promising results emphasize the importance of external unstructured knowledge for subject-area QA. We expect there is still much scope for further improvements by exploiting more sources of external knowledge, and we hope the present empirical study can serve as a new starting point for researchers to identify the remaining challenges in this area.

2 Method

In this section, we first introduce our BERT-based QA baseline (Section 2.1). Then, we present how we incorporate external open-domain (Section 2.2) and in-domain (Section 2.3) sources of knowledge into the baseline.

2.1 Baseline Framework

Given a question q, an answer option o_i, and a reference document d_i, we concatenate them with @ and # as the input sequence $@d_i\#q\#o_i\#$ to BERT (Devlin et al., 2019), where @ and # stand for the classifier token [CLS] and sentence separator token [SEP] in BERT, respectively. A segmentation A embedding is added to every token before q (exclusive) and a segmentation B embedding to every other token, where A and B are learned during the language model pretraining of BERT. For each instance in the ARC (Easy and Challenge) and OpenBookQA tasks, we use Lucene (McCandless et al., 2010) to retrieve up to top K sentences using the non-stop words in q and o_i as the query and then concatenate the retrieved sentences to form d_i (Sun et al., 2019). The final prediction for each question is obtained by a linear plus softmax layer over the output of the final hidden state of the first token in each input sequence.

By default, we employ the following **two-step** fine-tuning approach unless explicitly specified. Following previous work (Sun et al., 2019) based on GPT (Radford et al., 2018), we first fine-tune BERT (Devlin et al., 2019) on a large-scale multiple-choice machine reading comprehension dataset RACE (Lai et al., 2017) collected from English-as-a-foreign-language exams, which provides a ground truth reference document instead of a reference corpus for each question. Then, we further fine-tune the model on the target multiple-choice science QA datasets. For convenience, we call the model obtained after the first fine-tuning phase as a **pre-fine-tuned model**.

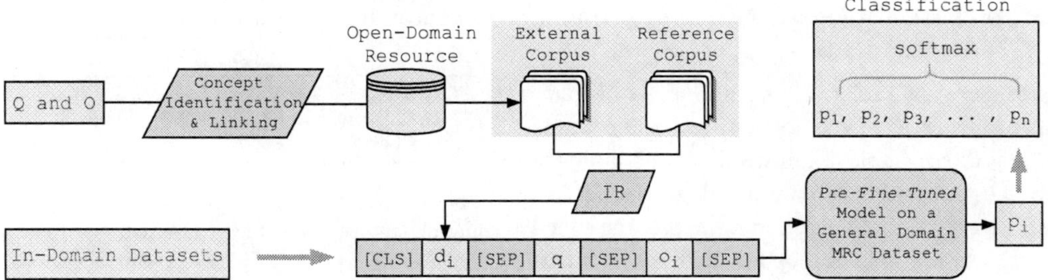

Figure 1: Overview of our framework (IR: information retrieval; MRC: machine reading comprehension). Q, O, q, o_i, d_i, and n denote the set of all questions, the set of all answer options, a question, one of the answer options associated with question q, the document (formed by retrieved sentences) associated with the (q, o_i) pair, and the number of answer options of q, respectively.

Question: Mercury, the planet nearest to the Sun, has extreme surface temperatures, ranging from $465°C$ in sunlight to $-180°C$ in darkness. Why is there such a large range of temperatures on Mercury?

A. The planet is too small to hold heat.
B. The planet is heated on only one side.
C. The planet reflects heat from its dark side.
D. The planet lacks an atmosphere to hold heat. ✓

Table 2: A sample problem from the ARC-Challenge dataset (Clark et al., 2018) (✓: correct answer option).

2.2 Utilization of External Knowledge from an Open-Domain Resource

Just as human readers activate their background knowledge related to the text materials (Kendeou and Van Den Broek, 2007), we link concepts identified in questions and answer options to an open-domain resource (i.e., Wikipedia) and provide machine readers with unstructured background information relevant to these concepts, used to enrich the original reference corpus.

Concept Identification and Linking: We first extract concept mentions from texts. Most mention extraction systems (e.g., Manning et al. (2014)) are trained using pre-defined classes in general domain such as PERSON, LOCATION, and ORGANIZATION. However, in ARC and OpenBookQA, the vast majority of mentions are from scientific domains (e.g., *"rotation"*, *"revolution"*, *"magnet"*, and *"iron"*). Therefore, we simply consider all noun phrases as candidate concept mentions, which are extracted by a noun phrase chunker. For example, in the sample problem in Table 2, we extract concept mentions such as *"Mercury"*.

Then each concept mention is disambiguated and linked to its corresponding concept (page) in

Wikipedia. For example, the ambiguous concept mention *"Mercury"* in Table 2 should be linked to the concept `Mercury_(planet)` rather than `Mercury_(element)` in Wikipedia. For concept disambiguation and linking, we simply adopt an existing unsupervised approach (Pan et al., 2015) that first selects high quality sets of concept *collaborators* to feed a simple similarity measure (i.e., Jaccard) to link concept mentions.

Reference Corpus Enrichment: We apply concept identification and linking to the text of all questions and answer options. Then, for each linked concept, we extract Wikipedia sentences that contain this concept and all sentences from the Wikipedia article of this concept without removing redundant information. For example, the following sentence in the Wikipedia article of `Mercury_(planet)` is extracted: *"Having almost no **atmosphere** to retain **heat**, it has surface temperatures that vary diurnally more than on any other planet in the Solar System."*, which can serve as a reliable piece of evidence to infer the correct answer option D for the question in Table 2.

Most previous methods (Khashabi et al., 2017; Musa et al., 2018; Ni et al., 2019; Yadav et al., 2019) perform information retrieval on the reference corpus to retrieve relevant sentences to form reference documents. In contrast, we retrieve relevant sentences from the **combination** of an open-domain resource and the original reference corpus to generate a reference document for each (question, answer option) pair. We still keep **up to top** K sentences for each reference document (Section 2.1). See the framework overview in Figure 1.

2.3 Utilization of External Knowledge from In-Domain Data

Since there are a relatively small number of training instances available for a single subject-area QA task (see Table 3), instead of fine-tuning a pre-fine-tuned model on a single target dataset, we also investigate into fine-tuning a pre-fine-tuned model on multiple in-domain datasets simultaneously. For example, when we train a model for ARC-Challenge, we use the training set of ARC-Challenge together with the training, development, and test sets of ARC-Easy and Open-BookQA. We also explore two settings with and without merging the reference corpora from different tasks. We introduce more details and discussions in Section 3.2 and Section 3.6.

3 Experiments and Discussions

3.1 Datasets

In our experiment, we use RACE (Lai et al., 2017) — the largest existing multiple-choice machine reading comprehension dataset collected from real and practical **language** exams — in the pre-fine-tuning stage. Questions in RACE focus on evaluating linguistic knowledge acquisition of participants and are commonly used in previous methods (Wang et al., 2018a; Sun et al., 2019).

We evaluate the performance of our methods on three multiple-choice **science** QA datasets: ARC-Easy, ARC-Challenge, and OpenBookQA. ARC-Challenge and ARC-easy originate from the same set of exam problems collected from multiple sources. ARC-Challenge contains questions answered incorrectly by both a retrieval-based method and a word co-occurrence method, and the remaining questions form ARC-Easy. Questions in OpenBookQA are crowdsourced by turkers and then carefully filtered and modified by experts. See the statistics of these datasets in Table 3. Note that for OpenBookQA, we do not utilize the accompanying auxiliary reference knowledge bases to ensure a fair comparison with previous work.

3.2 Experimental Settings

For the two-step fine-tuning framework, we use the uncased BERT$_{\text{LARGE}}$ released by Devlin et al. (2019) as the pre-trained language model. We set the batch size to 24, learning rate to 2×10^{-5}, and the maximal sequence length to 512. When the input sequence length exceeds 512, we truncate the longest sequence among q, o_i, and d_i (defined

Dataset	Train	Dev	Test	Total
RACE	87,866	4,887	4,934	97,687
ARC-Easy	2,251	570	2,376	5,197
ARC-Challenge	1,119	299	1,172	2,590
OpenBookQA	4,957	500	500	5,957

Table 3: The number of questions in RACE and the multiple-choice subject-area QA datasets for evaluation: ARC-Easy, ARC-Challenge, and OpenBookQA.

Dataset	Dev	Test
RACE-M	76.7	76.6
RACE-H	71.0	70.1
RACE-M + RACE-H	72.7	72.0

Table 4: Accuracy (%) of the pre-fine-tuned model on the RACE dataset, which contains two subsets: RACE-M and RACE-H, representing problems collected from **m**iddle and **h**igh school language exams, respectively.

in Section 2.1). We first fine-tune BERT$_{\text{LARGE}}$ for five epochs on RACE to get the pre-fine-tuned model and then further fine-tune the model for eight epochs on the target QA datasets in scientific domains. We show the accuracy of the pre-fine-tuned model on RACE in Table 4.

We use the noun phrase chunker in spaCy[2] to extract concept mentions. For information retrieval, we use the version 7.4.0 of Lucene (Mc-Candless et al., 2010) and set the maximum number of the retrieved sentences K to 50. We use the stop word list from NLTK (Bird and Loper, 2004).

In addition, we design two slightly different settings for information retrieval. In **setting 1**, the original reference corpus of each dataset is independent. Formally, for each dataset $x \in D$, we perform information retrieval based on the corresponding original reference corpus of x and/or the external corpus generated based on problems in x, where $D = \{$ARC-Easy, ARC-Challenge, OpenBookQA$\}$. In **setting 2**, all original reference corpora are integrated to further leverage external in-domain knowledge. Formally, for each dataset $x \in D$, we conduct information retrieval based on the given reference corpus of D and/or the external corpus generated based on problems in D instead of x.[3]

3.3 Baselines

Here we only briefly introduce three baselines (i.e., GPT^{II}, RS^{II}, and BERT^{II}) that all fine-tune a

---

[2] https://spacy.io/.
[3] https://github.com/nlpdata/external.

Method	ARC-E	ARC-C	OBQA
IR (Clark et al., 2018)	62.6	20.3	–
Odd-One-Out (Mihaylov et al., 2018)	–	–	50.2
DGEM (Khot et al., 2018)	59.0	27.1	24.4
KG^2 (Zhang et al., 2018)	–	31.7	–
AIR (Yadav et al., 2018)	58.4	26.6	–
NCRF++ (Musa et al., 2018)	52.2	33.2	–
TriAN++ (Zhong et al., 2018)	–	33.4	–
Two Stage Inference (Pirtoaca et al., 2019)	61.1	26.9	–
ET-RR (Ni et al., 2019)	–	36.6	–
GPT^{II} (Radford et al., 2018; Sun et al., 2019)	57.0	38.2	52.0
RS^{II} (Sun et al., 2019)	66.6	40.7	55.2
Our BERT-Based Implementations			
Setting 1			
Reference Corpus (RC) (i.e., BERT^{II})	71.9	44.1	64.8
External Corpus (EC)	65.0	39.4	62.2
RC + EC	73.3	45.0	65.2
Setting 2			
Integrated Reference Corpus (IRC)	73.2	44.8	65.0
Integrated External Corpus (IEC)	68.9	40.1	63.0
IRC + IEC	**74.7**	46.1	67.0
IRC + MD	69.4	50.7	67.4
IRC + IEC + MD	72.3	**53.7**	**68.0**
Human Performance	–	–	91.7

Table 5: Accuracy (%) on the test sets of ARC-Easy, ARC-Challenge, and OpenBookQA datasets. RACE is used in the pre-fine-tuning stage for all the tasks (Section 2.1). MD stands for fine-tuning on **m**ultiple target **d**atasets simultaneously (Section 2.3). All results are single-model performance. GPT^{II}, RS^{II}, and BERT^{II} are baselines that use two-step fine-tuning (Section 3.3). ARC-E: ARC-Easy; ARC-C: ARC-Challenge; OBQA: OpenBookQA.

pre-trained language model on downstream tasks without substantial modifications to model architectures, which achieve remarkable success on many question answering tasks. Following the two-step fine-tuning framework (Section 2.1), **all** three strong baselines use RACE in the first fine-tuning stage for a fair comparison. We will discuss the impacts of pre-fine-tuning on baseline model performance in Section 3.8, noting that pre-fine-tuning is not the contribution of this work.

GPT^{II}: This baseline is based on fine-tuning a generative pre-trained transformer (GPT) language model (Radford et al., 2018) instead of BERT (Devlin et al., 2019).

RS^{II}: Based on GPT, general reading strategies (RS) (Sun et al., 2019) are applied during the fine-tuning stage such as adding a trainable embedding into the text embedding of tokens relevant to the question and candidate answer options.

BERT^{II}: Based on BERT, this baseline is an exact implementation described in Section 2.1.

3.4 Main Results

We see consistent improvements in accuracy across all tasks after we enrich the reference corpus with relevant texts from Wikipedia to form new reference documents (i.e., RC + EC and

IRC + IEC in Table 5). Moreover, using only the extracted external corpus to perform information retrieval for reference document generation can achieve reasonable performance compared to using the original reference corpus, especially on the OpenBookQA dataset (62.2% vs. 64.8% under setting 1 and 63.0% vs. 65.0% under setting 2). This indicates that we can extract reliable and relevant texts from external open-domain resources such as Wikipedia via linked concepts mentioned in Section 2.2. Moreover, using the integrated corpus (i.e., setting 2) consistently boosts the performance. Since the performance in setting 2 (integrated corpus) is better than that in setting 1 (independent corpus) based on our experiments, we take **setting 2** by default for discussions unless explicitly specified.

We see further improvements on ARC-Challenge and OpenBookQA, by fine-tuning the pre-fine-tuned model on multiple target datasets (i.e., ARC-Easy, ARC-Challenge, and OpenBookQA). However, we do not see a similar gain on ARC-Easy by increasing the number of in-domain training instances. We will further discuss it in Section 3.6.

Our best models (i.e., IRC + IEC for ARC-

Question	Answer Options	Sentence(s) From Wikipedia
What boils at the boiling point?	A. *Kool-Aid*. ✓ B. Cotton. C. Paper Towel. D. Hair.	*Kool-Aid* is known as Nebraska's official soft drink. Common types of drinks include plain drinking *water*, milk, coffee, tea, hot chocolate, juice and *soft drinks*.
Forest fires occur in many areas due to *drought conditions*. If the drought conditions continue for a long period of time, which might cause the repopulation of trees to be threatened?	A. a decrease in the *thickness of soil*. ✓ B. a decrease in the amount of erosion. C. an increase in the bacterium population. D. an increase in the production of oxygen and fire.	It is highly resistant to *drought conditions*, and provides excellent fodder; and has also been used in controlling *soil erosion*, and as revegetator, often after *forest fires*.
Juan and LaKeisha roll a few objects down a ramp. They want to see which object rolls the farthest. What should they do so they can repeat their *investigation?*	A. Put the objects in groups. B. Change the height of the ramp. C. Choose different objects to roll. D. *Record* the details of the *investigation*. ✓	The use of measurement developed to allow *recording* and comparison of *observations* made at different times and places, by different people.
Which statement best explains why the sun appears to *move across the sky* each day?	A. The sun revolves around Earth. B. Earth rotates around the sun. C. The sun revolves on its axis. D. *Earth rotates* on its *axis*. ✓	*Earth's rotation* about its *axis* causes the fixed stars to apparently *move across the sky* in a way that depends on the observer's latitude.

Table 6: Examples of corrected errors using the reference corpus enriched by the sentences from Wikipedia.

Easy and IRC + IEC + MD for ARC-Challenge and OpenBookQA) outperform the strong baseline BERT[II] introduced in Section 2.1 (74.7% vs. 71.9% on ARC-Easy, 53.7% vs. 44.1% on ARC-Challenge, and 68.0% vs. 64.8% on OpenBookQA), which already beats the previous state-of-the-art model RS[II]. In the remaining sections, we analyze our models and discuss the impacts of external knowledge from various aspects.

3.5 Impact of External Knowledge from an Open-Domain Resource

Table 6 shows some examples of errors produced by IRC (Table 5) that do not leverage external knowledge from open-domain resources. These errors can be corrected by enriching the reference corpus with external sentences extracted from Wikipedia (IRC + IEC in Table 5). In the first example, the correct answer option *"Kool-Aid"* never appears in the original reference corpus. As a result, without external background knowledge, it is less likely to infer that *"Kool-Aid"* refers to liquid (can boil) here.

In addition to performing information retrieval on the enriched reference *corpus*, we investigate an alternative approach that uses concept identification and linking to directly enrich the reference *document* for each (question, answer option) pair. More specifically, we apply concept identification and linking to each (question, answer option) pair (q, o_i) and extract sentences from Wikipedia based

Task	Wiki	OBQA	ARC	Total
ARC-E	20.8	0.4	78.7	1,039,059
ARC-C	21.5	0.4	78.2	517,846
OBQA	20.6	1.1	78.3	1,191,347

Table 7: Percentage (%) of retrieved sentences from each source. Wiki: Wikipedia; Total: total number of retrieved sentences for all (question, answer option) pairs in a single task. ARC-Easy and ARC-Challenge share the same original reference corpus.

on the linked concepts. These extracted sentences are appended to the reference documents d_i of (q, o_i) directly. We still keep up to K (i.e., 50) sentences per document. We observe that this direct appending approach generally cannot outperform the reference corpus enrichment approach described in Section 2.2.

We report the statistics of the sentences (without redundancy removal) extracted from each source in Table 7, used as inputs to our methods IRC + IEC and IRC + IEC + MD in Table 5. As the original reference corpus of OpenBookQA is made up of 1,326 sentences, fewer retrieved sentences are extracted from its reference corpus for all tasks compared to other sources.

3.6 Impact of External Knowledge from In-Domain Data

Compared to fine-tuning the pre-fine-tuned model on a single multiple-choice subject-area QA

First 4	Last 4	Accuracy	# Epochs
ARC-C	ARC-E	69.4	8
OBQA	ARC-E	70.9	8
ARC-C + OBQA	ARC-E	72.6	8
ARC-E	-	72.9	4
ARC-E	ARC-E	74.7	8

Table 8: Accuracy (%) on the ARC-Easy test set. The first four epochs are fine-tuned using the dataset(s) in the first column. The last four epochs are fine-tuned using the dataset in the second column. # Epochs: the total number of epochs.

Question Type	ARC-E		ARC-C	
	BERT[II]	Ours	BERT[II]	Ours
Word Matching	81.3	**85.4**	30.4	**73.9**
Paraphrasing	90.9	90.9	46.7	**66.7**
Knowledge	58.3	**83.3**	44.4	**55.6**
Math/Logic	100.0	100.0	33.3	33.3
Valid	80.0	**86.0**	36.1	**66.7**
Invalid	50.0	**80.0**	41.7	41.7
Easy	80.0	**90.0**	33.3	**53.3**
Hard	70.0	**80.0**	43.3	**60.0**

Table 9: Accuracy (%) by different categories on the annotated test sets of ARC-Easy and ARC-Challenge, which are released by Sugawara et al. (2018).

dataset, we observe improvements in accuracy by fine-tuning on multiple in-domain datasets (MD) simultaneously (Section 2.3) for ARC-Challenge and OpenBookQA. In particular, we see a dramatic gain on the ARC-Challenge dataset (from 46.1% to 53.7%) as shown in Table 5.

However, MD leads to a performance drop on ARC-Easy. We hypothesize that other commonly adopted approaches may also lead to performance drops. To verify that, we explore another way of utilizing external knowledge for ARC-Easy by first fine-tuning the pre-fine-tuned model for four epochs on external in-domain data (i.e., ARC-Challenge, OpenBookQA, or ARC-Challenge + OpenBookQA) and then further fine-tuning for four epochs on ARC-Easy. As shown in Table 8, we also observe that compared to only fine-tuning on ARC-Easy, fine-turning on external in-domain data hurts the performance. The consistent performance drops across the two methods of using MD on ARC-Easy are perhaps due to an intrinsic property of the tasks themselves – the question-answer instances in ARC-Easy are relatively simpler than those in ARC-Challenge and OpenBookQA. Introducing relatively complex problems from ARC-Challenge and OpenBookQA may hurt the final performance on ARC-Easy. As mentioned earlier, compared to questions in ARC-Easy, questions in ARC-Challenge are less likely to be answered correctly by retrieval-based or word co-occurrence methods. We argue that questions in the ARC-Challenge tend to require more external knowledge for reasoning, similar to the observation of Sugawara et al. (2018) (30.0% vs. 20.0%).

3.7 Discussions about Question Types and Remaining Challenges

We use the human annotations such as required reasoning skills (i.e., *word matching, paraphras-ing, knowledge, meta/whole*, and *math/whole*) and validity of questions in ARC-Easy and ARC-Challenge released by Sugawara et al. (2018) to analyze the impacts of external knowledge on instances in various categories. Sixty instances are annotated for each dataset. We refer readers to Sugawara et al. (2018) for detailed definitions of each category. We do not report the accuracy for *math/whole* as no annotated question in ARC belongs to this category.

We compare the BERT[II] baseline in Table 5 that only uses the original reference corpus of a given end task with our best model. As shown in Table 9, by leveraging external knowledge from in-domain datasets (instances and reference corpora) and open-domain texts, we observe consistent improvements on most of the categories. Based on these experimental results on the annotated subset, we may assume it could be a promising direction to further improve challenging multiple-choice subject-area QA tasks through exploiting high-quality external knowledge besides designing task-specific models for different types of questions (Clark et al., 2016).

We also analyze the instances that our approach fails to answer correctly in the OpenBookQA development set to study the remaining challenges. It might be promising to identify the relations among concepts within an answer option. For example, our current model mistakenly selects the answer option *"the sun orbits the earth"* associated with the question *"Revolution happens when ?"* probably because *"sun"*, *"orbits"*, and *"earth"* frequently co-occur in our generated reference document, though these concepts such as *"revolution"* are successfully linked to their corresponding Wikipedia pages in the astronomy field.

Besides, we might also need to identify causal

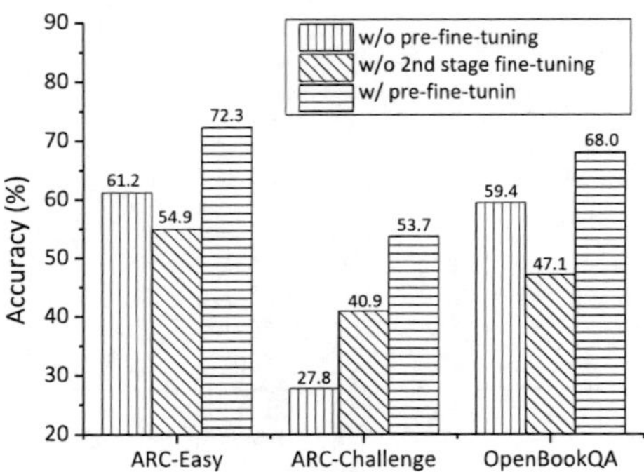

Figure 2: Accuracy (%) on the test sets of evaluation tasks with and without the pre-fine-tuning stage (2nd stage fine-tuning: fine-tune the pre-fine-tuned model on target science question answering datasets).

relations between events. For example, given the question *"The type of climate change known as anthropogenic is caused by this"*, our model mistakenly predicts another answer option *"forest fires"* with its associated contexts *"climate change has caused the island to suffer more frequent severe droughts, leading to large forest fires"*, instead of the real cause *"humanity"* supported by *"the problem now is with anthropogenic climate change—that is, climate change caused by human activity, which is making the climate change a lot faster than it normally would"*.

3.8 Discussions about Pre-Fine-Tuning

Previous work (Devlin et al., 2019) has shown that fine-tuning $BERT_{LARGE}$ on small datasets can be sometimes unstable. Additionally, Sun et al. (2019) show that fine-tuning GPT (Radford et al., 2018) that is pre-fine-tuned on RACE can dramatically improve the performance of relatively small multiple-choice tasks. Here we only use the $BERT^{II}$ baseline for a brief discussion. We have a similar observation: we can obtain more stable performance on the target datasets by first fine-tuning BERT on RACE (language exams), and we see consistent performance improvements on all the evaluated science QA datasets. As shown in Figure 2, we see that the performance drops dramatically without using pre-fine-tuning on the RACE dataset.

4 Related Work

4.1 Subject-Area QA Tasks and Methods

As there is not a clear distinction between QA and machine reading comprehension (**MRC**) tasks,

for convenience we call a task in which there is no reference document provided for each instance as a QA task. In this paper, we focus on multiple-choice subject-area QA tasks, where the in-domain reference corpus does not provide sufficient relevant content on its own to answer a significant portion of the questions (Clark et al., 2016; Kobayashi et al., 2017; Welbl et al., 2017; Clark et al., 2018; Mihaylov et al., 2018). In contrast to other types of QA scenarios (Nguyen et al., 2016; Dhingra et al., 2017; Joshi et al., 2017; Dunn et al., 2017; Kwiatkowski et al., 2019), in this setting: (1) the reference corpus does not reliably contain text spans from which the answers can be drawn, and (2) it does not provide sufficient information on its own to answer a significant portion of the questions. Thus they are suitable for us to study how to exploit external knowledge for QA.

Our work follows the general framework of discriminatively fine-tuning a pre-trained language model such as GPT (Radford et al., 2018) and BERT (Devlin et al., 2019) on QA tasks (Radford et al., 2018; Devlin et al., 2019; Hu et al., 2019; Yang et al., 2019). As shown in Table 5, the baseline based on BERT already outperforms previous state-of-the-art methods designed for subject-area QA tasks (Yadav et al., 2018; Pirtoaca et al., 2019; Ni et al., 2019; Sun et al., 2019).

4.2 Utilization of External Knowledge for Subject-Area QA

Previous studies have explored many ways to leverage structured knowledge to solve questions in subject areas such as science exams. Many researchers investigate how to directly or indirectly use automatically constructed knowledge bases/graphs from reference corpora (Khot et al., 2017; Kwon et al., 2018; Khashabi et al., 2018; Zhang et al., 2018) or existing external general knowledge graphs (Li and Clark, 2015; Sachan et al., 2016; Wang et al., 2018a,c; Zhong et al., 2018; Musa et al., 2018) such as ConceptNet (Speer et al., 2017). However, for subject-area QA, unstructured knowledge is seldom considered in previous studies, and it is still not clear the usefulness of this kind of knowledge.

As far as we know, for subject-area QA tasks, this is the first attempt to impart sources of external unstructured knowledge into one state-of-the-art pre-trained language model, and we are among the first to investigate the effectiveness of the external unstructured texts in Wikipedia (Pirtoaca et al., 2019) and additional in-domain QA data.

4.3 Utilization of External Knowledge for Other Types of QA and MRC

For both QA and MRC tasks in which the majority of answers are extractive such as SQuAD (Rajpurkar et al., 2016) and TriviaQA (Joshi et al., 2017), previous work has shown that it is useful to introduce external open-domain QA instances and textual information from Wikipedia by first retrieving relevant documents in Wikipedia and then running a MRC model to extract a text span from the documents based on the question (Chen et al., 2017; Wang et al., 2018b; Kratzwald and Feuerriegel, 2018; Lee et al., 2018; Lin et al., 2018).

Based on Wikipedia, we apply concept identification and linking to enrich QA reference corpora, which has not been explored before. Compared to previous data argumentation studies for other types of QA tasks (Yu et al., 2018), differences exist in: 1) we focus on in-domain data and discuss the impacts of the difficulties of additional in-domain instances on a target task; 2) we are the first to show it is useful to merge reference corpora from different in-domain subject-area QA tasks.

5 Conclusion and Future Work

We focus on how to incorporate external knowledge into a pre-trained model to improve subject-area QA tasks that require background knowledge. We exploit two sources of external knowledge through: enriching the original reference corpus with relevant texts from open-domain Wikipedia and using additional in-domain QA datasets (instances and reference corpora) for training. Experimental results on ARC-Easy, ARC-Challenge, and OpenBookQA show the effectiveness of our simple method. The promising results also demonstrate the importance of unstructured external knowledge for subject-area QA. In the future, we plan to jointly exploit various types of external unstructured and structured knowledge.

Acknowledgments

We thank the anonymous reviewers for their constructive and helpful feedback.

References

Steven Bird and Edward Loper. 2004. NLTK: the natural language toolkit. In *Proceedings of the ACL (Demonstrations)*, Barcelona, Spain.

Danqi Chen, Adam Fisch, Jason Weston, and Antoine Bordes. 2017. Reading Wikipedia to answer open-domain questions. In *Proceedings of the ACL*, Vancouver, Canada.

Peter Clark, Isaac Cowhey, Oren Etzioni, Tushar Khot, Ashish Sabharwal, Carissa Schoenick, and Oyvind Tafjord. 2018. Think you have solved question answering? Try ARC, the AI2 reasoning challenge. *arXiv preprint*, cs.CL/1803.05457v1.

Peter Clark, Oren Etzioni, Tushar Khot, Ashish Sabharwal, Oyvind Tafjord, Peter D Turney, and Daniel Khashabi. 2016. Combining retrieval, statistics, and inference to answer elementary science questions. In *Proceedings of the AAAI*, Phoenix, AZ.

Jacob Devlin, Ming-Wei Chang, Kenton Lee, and Kristina Toutanova. 2019. BERT: Pre-training of deep bidirectional transformers for language understanding. In *Proeedings of the NAACL-HLT*, Minneapolis, MN.

Bhuwan Dhingra, Kathryn Mazaitis, and William W Cohen. 2017. Quasar: Datasets for question answering by search and reading. *arXiv preprint*, cs.CL/1707.03904v2.

Matthew Dunn, Levent Sagun, Mike Higgins, V Ugur Guney, Volkan Cirik, and Kyunghyun Cho. 2017. SearchQA: A new Q&A dataset augmented with context from a search engine. *arXiv preprint*, cs.CL/1704.05179v3.

Minghao Hu, Yuxing Peng, Zhen Huang, Nan Yang, Ming Zhou, et al. 2019. Read+Verify: Machine reading comprehension with unanswerable questions. In *Proceedings of the AAAI*, Honolulu, HI.

Mandar Joshi, Eunsol Choi, Daniel S. Weld, and Luke Zettlemoyer. 2017. TriviaQA: A large scale distantly supervised challenge dataset for reading comprehension. *arXiv preprint*, cs.CL/1705.03551v2.

Panayiota Kendeou and Paul Van Den Broek. 2007. The effects of prior knowledge and text structure on comprehension processes during reading of scientific texts. *Memory & cognition*, 35(7).

Daniel Khashabi, Tushar Khot, Ashish Sabharwal, and Dan Roth. 2017. Learning what is essential in questions. In *Proceedings of the CoNLL 2017*.

Daniel Khashabi, Tushar Khot, Ashish Sabharwal, and Dan Roth. 2018. Question answering as global reasoning over semantic abstractions. In *Proceedings of the AAAI*, New Orleans, LA.

Tushar Khot, Ashish Sabharwal, and Peter Clark. 2017. Answering complex questions using open information extraction. In *Proceedings of the ACL*, Vancouver, Canada.

Tushar Khot, Ashish Sabharwal, and Peter Clark. 2018. SciTail: A textual entailment dataset from science question answering. In *Proceedings of the AAAI*, New Orleans, LA.

Mio Kobayashi, Ai Ishii, Chikara Hoshino, Hiroshi Miyashita, and Takuya Matsuzaki. 2017. Automated historical fact-checking by passage retrieval, word statistics, and virtual question-answering. In *Proceedings of the IJCNLP*, Taipei, Taiwan.

Bernhard Kratzwald and Stefan Feuerriegel. 2018. Adaptive document retrieval for deep question answering. In *Proceedings of the EMNLP*, Brussels, Belgium.

Tom Kwiatkowski, Jennimaria Palomaki, Olivia Redfield, Michael Collins, Ankur Parikh, Chris Alberti, Danielle Epstein, Illia Polosukhin, Matthew Kelcey, Jacob Devlin, Kenton Lee, Kristina N. Toutanova, Llion Jones, Ming-Wei Chang, Andrew Dai, Jakob Uszkoreit, Quoc Le, and Slav Petrov. 2019. Natural Questions: A benchmark for question answering research. *TACL*.

Heeyoung Kwon, Harsh Trivedi, Peter Jansen, Mihai Surdeanu, and Niranjan Balasubramanian. 2018. Controlling information aggregation for complex question answering. In *Proceedings of the ECIR*, Grenoble, France.

Guokun Lai, Qizhe Xie, Hanxiao Liu, Yiming Yang, and Eduard Hovy. 2017. RACE: Large-scale reading comprehension dataset from examinations. In *Proceedings of the EMNLP*, Copenhagen, Denmark.

Jinhyuk Lee, Seongjun Yun, Hyunjae Kim, Miyoung Ko, and Jaewoo Kang. 2018. Ranking paragraphs for improving answer recall in open-domain question answering. In *Proceedings of the EMNLP*, Brussels, Belgium.

Yang Li and Peter Clark. 2015. Answering elementary science questions by constructing coherent scenes using background knowledge. In *Proceedings of the EMNLP*, Lisbon, Portugal.

Yankai Lin, Haozhe Ji, Zhiyuan Liu, and Maosong Sun. 2018. Denoising distantly supervised open-domain question answering. In *Proceedings of the ACL*, Melbourne, Australia.

Christopher D. Manning, Mihai Surdeanu, John Bauer, Jenny Finkel, Steven J. Bethard, and David McClosky. 2014. The Stanford CoreNLP natural language processing toolkit. In *Proceedings of the ACL (Demonstrations)*, Baltimore, MD.

Michael McCandless, Erik Hatcher, and Otis Gospodnetic. 2010. *Lucene in Action, Second Edition: Covers Apache Lucene 3.0*. Manning Publications Co., Greenwich, CT.

Danielle S McNamara, Irwin B Levinstein, and Chutima Boonthum. 2004. iSTART: Interactive strategy training for active reading and thinking. *Behavior Research Methods, Instruments, & Computers*, 36(2).

Todor Mihaylov, Peter Clark, Tushar Khot, and Ashish Sabharwal. 2018. Can a suit of armor conduct electricity? a new dataset for open book question answering. In *Proceedings of the EMNLP*, Brussels, Belgium.

Ryan Musa, Xiaoyan Wang, Achille Fokoue, Nicholas Mattei, Maria Chang, Pavan Kapanipathi, Bassem Makni, Kartik Talamadupula, and Michael Witbrock. 2018. Answering science exam questions using query rewriting with background knowledge. *arXiv preprint*, cs.AI/1809.05726v1.

Tri Nguyen, Mir Rosenberg, Xia Song, Jianfeng Gao, Saurabh Tiwary, Rangan Majumder, and Li Deng. 2016. MS MARCO: A human generated machine reading comprehension dataset. *arXiv preprint*, cs.CL/1611.09268v2.

Jianmo Ni, Chenguang Zhu, Weizhu Chen, and Julian McAuley. 2019. Learning to attend on essential terms: An enhanced retriever-reader model for open-domain question answering. In *Proceedings of the NAACL-HLT*, Minneapolis, MN.

Xiaoman Pan, Taylor Cassidy, Ulf Hermjakob, Heng Ji, and Kevin Knight. 2015. Unsupervised entity linking with abstract meaning representation. In *Proceedings of the NAACL-HLT*, Denver, CO.

George-Sebastian Pirtoaca, Traian Rebedea, and Stefan Ruseti. 2019. Improving retrieval-based question answering with deep inference models. *arXiv preprint*, cs.CL/1812.02971v2.

Alec Radford, Karthik Narasimhan, Tim Salimans, and Ilya Sutskever. 2018. Improving language understanding by generative pre-training. In *Preprint*.

Pranav Rajpurkar, Jian Zhang, Konstantin Lopyrev, and Percy Liang. 2016. SQuAD: 100,000+ questions for machine comprehension of text. In *Proceedings of the EMNLP*, Austin, TX.

Mrinmaya Sachan, Avinava Dubey, and Eric P Xing. 2016. Science question answering using instructional materials. In *Proceedings of the ACL*, Berlin, Germany.

Ladislao Salmerón, Walter Kintsch, and José J Caãs. 2006. Reading strategies and prior knowledge in learning from hypertext. *Memory & Cognition*, 34(5).

Robyn Speer, Joshua Chin, and Catherine Havasi. 2017. ConceptNet 5.5: An open multilingual graph of general knowledge. In *Proceedings of the AAAI*, San Francisco, CA.

Saku Sugawara, Kentaro Inui, Satoshi Sekine, and Akiko Aizawa. 2018. What makes reading comprehension questions easier? In *Proceedings of the EMNLP*, Brussels, Belgium.

Kai Sun, Dian Yu, Dong Yu, and Claire Cardie. 2019. Improving machine reading comprehension with general reading strategies. In *Proceedings of the NAACL-HLT*, Minneapolis, MN.

Liang Wang, Meng Sun, Wei Zhao, Kewei Shen, and Jingming Liu. 2018a. Yuanfudao at SemEval-2018 Task 11: Three-way attention and relational knowledge for commonsense machine comprehension. In *Proceedings of the SemEval*, New Orleans, LA.

Shuohang Wang, Mo Yu, Xiaoxiao Guo, Zhiguo Wang, Tim Klinger, Wei Zhang, Shiyu Chang, Gerald Tesauro, Bowen Zhou, and Jing Jiang. 2018b. R^3: Reinforced reader-ranker for open-domain question answering. In *Proceedings of the AAAI*, New Orleans, LA.

Xiaoyan Wang, Pavan Kapanipathi, Ryan Musa, Mo Yu, Kartik Talamadupula, Ibrahim Abdelaziz, Maria Chang, Achille Fokoue, Bassem Makni, Nicholas Mattei, et al. 2018c. Improving natural language inference using external knowledge in the science questions domain. *arXiv preprint*, cs.CL/1809.05724v2.

Johannes Welbl, Nelson F Liu, and Matt Gardner. 2017. Crowdsourcing multiple choice science questions. In *Proceedings of the W-NUT*, Copenhagen, Denmark.

Vikas Yadav, Steven Bethard, and Mihai Surdeanu. 2019. Alignment over heterogeneous embeddings for question answering. In *Proceedings of the NAACL-HLT*, Minneapolis, MN.

Vikas Yadav, Rebecca Sharp, and Mihai Surdeanu. 2018. Sanity check: A strong alignment and information retrieval baseline for question answering. In *Proceedings of the ACM SIGIR*, Ann Arbor, MI.

Wei Yang, Yuqing Xie, Aileen Lin, Xingyu Li, Luchen Tan, Kun Xiong, Ming Li, and Jimmy Lin. 2019. End-to-end open-domain question answering with bertserini. *arXiv preprint*, cs.CL/1902.01718v1.

Adams Wei Yu, David Dohan, Minh-Thang Luong, Rui Zhao, Kai Chen, Mohammad Norouzi, and Quoc V Le. 2018. QANet: Combining local convolution with global self-attention for reading comprehension. In *Proceedings of the ICLR*, Vancouver, Canada.

Yuyu Zhang, Hanjun Dai, Kamil Toraman, and Le Song. 2018. KG^2: Learning to reason science exam questions with contextual knowledge graph embeddings. *arXiv preprint*, cs.LG/1805.12393v1.

Wanjun Zhong, Duyu Tang, Nan Duan, Ming Zhou, Jiahai Wang, and Jian Yin. 2018. Improving question answering by commonsense-based pre-training. *arXiv preprint*, cs.CL/1809.03568v1.

Answer-Supervised Question Reformulation for Enhancing Conversational Machine Comprehension

Qian Li[◇*], **Hui Su**[‡], **Cheng Niu**[‡], **Daling Wang**[◇], **Zekang Li**[♠], **Shi Feng**[◇], **Yifei Zhang**[◇]

[◇]School of Computer Science and Engineering, Northeastern University, Shenyang, China
[‡]Pattern Recognition Center, WeChat AI, Tencent Inc, China
[♠]Key Laboratory of Intelligent Information Processing
Institute of Computing Technology, Chinese Academy of Sciences
qianli@stumail.neu.edu.cn, {wangdaling,fengshi,zhangyifei}@cse.neu.edu.cn,
{aaronsu,chengniu}@tencent.com, lizekang19g@ict.ac.cn

Abstract

In conversational machine comprehension, it has become one of the research hotspots integrating conversational history information through question reformulation for obtaining better answers. However, the existing question reformulation models are trained only using supervised question labels annotated by annotators without considering any feedback information from answers. In this paper, we propose a novel **A**nswer-**S**upervised **Q**uestion **R**eformulation (ASQR) model for enhancing conversational machine comprehension with reinforcement learning technology. ASQR utilizes a pointer-copy-based question reformulation model as an **agent**, takes an **action** to predict the next word, and observes a **reward** for the whole sentence **state** after generating the end-of-sequence token. The experimental results on QuAC dataset prove that our ASQR model is more effective in conversational machine comprehension. Moreover, pretraining is essential in reinforcement learning models, so we provide a high-quality annotated dataset for question reformulation by sampling a part of QuAC dataset.

1 Introduction

The performance of the single-turn machine comprehension models has been greatly improved, even close to human-level recently (Wang et al., 2018; Devlin et al., 2018; Sun et al., 2018; Hu et al., 2018; Liu et al., 2017), while the conversational machine comprehension models are far from satisfactory (Choi et al., 2018; Huang et al., 2018; Zhu et al., 2018). In single-turn machine comprehension, different questions for the same paragraph have no connection. However, the questions omitting a great of key information in conversational machine comprehension are only

meaningful by considering the previous questions and answers history (Table 1). Therefore, the major difficulty of solving conversational machine comprehension lies in how to integrate the conversational history when answering the questions.

Sentence reformulation aims to get more fluent and meaningful sentences based on supplementary information (Liu et al., 2018; Rastogi et al., 2019), and has been adopted in abstract extraction (Nallapati et al., 2016; See et al., 2017), query reformulation (Riezler and Liu, 2010; Rastogi et al., 2019), and translation reformulation (Niehues et al., 2016; Junczys-Dowmunt and Grundkiewicz, 2017). Question reformulation (Buck et al., 2017; Nogueira and Cho, 2017; Rastogi et al., 2019), as an important branch of sentence reformulation, aims to reformulate question according to conversational history.

However, the existing question reformulation models are trained with annotated labels via a training mechanism as *teacher forcing* (Bengio et al., 2015). The annotated labels-supervised training approaches have some drawbacks: **(1) Minority**: Due to the limitation of human resources and funds, annotated data only accounts for a small part of all data. **(2) Errors**: Some fatal errors that adversely affect model training may exist in annotated data inadvertently. **(3) Unmet requirements**: What deserves attention is that the training mechanism for the existing question reformulation models do not consider any feedback information from subsequent functions, while the feedback information is always important. Particularly, the question reformulation model in conversational machine comprehension aims to get better answers, so the quality of the reformulated questions should depend on gold answers but not question labels. To our best knowledge, there are some preliminary attempts to reformulate question with downstream feedback in question answering

---

*This work was done when Qian Li was interning at Pattern Recognition Center, WeChat AI, Tencent.

Proceedings of the Second Workshop on Machine Reading for Question Answering, pages 38–47
Hong Kong, China, November 4, 2019. ©2019 Association for Computational Linguistics

Title: Skid Row	
Paragraph: Skid Row, released in January 1989, was an instant success. The record went 5x platinum on the strength of the Top 10 singles. Skid Row supported the album by opening for Bon Jovi on their New Jersey tour. As part of the six-month tour, Skid Row played its first ever UK gig supporting Bon Jovi's outdoor show at Milton Keynes Bowl on August 19, 1989. ... CANNOTANSWER.	
Q1: Did they release any albums	A1: <u>Skid Row</u>, released in January 1989
Q2: How did it do **Q2': How did Skid Row do**	A2: instant success
Q3: Did it go on tour **Q3': Did Skid Row go on tour**	A3: first supporting Bon Jovi's <u>outdoor show</u>
Q4: Did the Tour have a name **Q4': Did the outdoor show have a name**	A4: <u>New Jersey tour</u>
Q5: How long did the tour last **Q5': How long did the New Jersey tour last**	A5: CANNOTANSWER

Table 1: An example of conversational machine comprehension from QuAC dataset (Choi et al., 2018). Giving a paragraph title, the student asks teacher questions according to the conversational history. The teacher answers the question by choosing a text span from the paragraph context or CANNOTANSWER. **Qi'** is the reformulated question for Qi by annotators.

tasks (Buck et al., 2017; Nogueira and Cho, 2017), while no work in conversational machine comprehension tasks. How to train the question reformulation models with supervised information from answers in conversational machine comprehension is still a major challenge.

In this paper, we present ASQR, an Answer-Supervised Question Reformulation model for conversational machine comprehension with reinforcement learning technology (Figure 1). At our ASQR model, the agent, a novel pointer-copy-based question reformulation model proposed in Section 2, takes an action to predict the next word. The state for the whole sentence is composed of continuous actions and end with the end-of-sequence (EOS) signal. The agent only observes a reward for the whole sentence state after generating the EOS token, which is quite different from the teacher forcing models. The reward is the similarity score between the gold answer and the predicted answer obtained by feeding the whole sentence state to a single-turn machine comprehension model.

We validate the effectiveness of our ASQR model on QuAC dataset (Choi et al., 2018). Pretraining is essential in deep reinforcement learning models (Yin et al., 2018; Xiong et al., 2018), so we sample a part of QuAC dataset, and reformulate the questions according to the conversational history by several professional annotators. The major contributions of this paper are as follows:

- We present a novel answer-supervised question reformulation model for conversational machine comprehension with reinforcement learning technology, which could be a new study direction for conversational problems.

- We provide a high-quality annotated dataset for question reformulation in conversational comprehension, which could be of great help to future related research.

- The experimental results outperforming the baseline models on the benchmark dataset prove that our model is more effective in conversational machine comprehension.

In Section 2, we will present a new pointer-copy-based question reformulation model which is as an agent in the ASQR model. The overall ASQR model with reinforcement learning technology is presented in Section 3. Then in Section 4, we introduce our annotated dataset and the experiments. The related work and some conclusions are drawn in Section 5 and 6.

2 Question Reformulation Model

In this section, we present a novel question reformulation model based on the pointer copy mechanism, which is the agent of our ASQR model in Section 3. The question reformulation model is an encoder-decoder framework shown in the left of Figure 1. The encoder is to encode the questions and their conversational history separately with the recurrent neural network. The decoder,

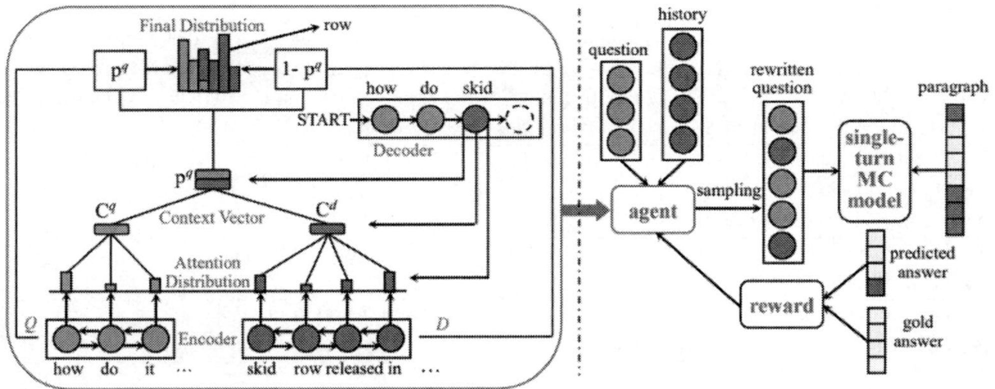

Figure 1: Our proposed ASQR Model. The left is our pointer-copy-based question reformulation model. The right is the overall perspective of the ASQR model with the left model as an agent.

a copy mechanism, copies a word from questions or conversational history according to a gate network at each time step. For simplicity, we denote each training sample as (D, Q, R), therein $D = \{Q_1, A_1, ..., Q_{n-1}, A_{n-1}\}$ represents the conversational history, (Q_i, A_i) represents the question and answer in the ith turn of the conversation, $Q = Q_n$ is the question in nth turn of the conversation. R is the reformulated question carrying important conversational information for the question Q.

2.1 Encoder

The role of the Encoder is to get the representation for the input sentence. There are two types of the input sentence: question $Q = \{x_1^q, ..., x_{m_q}^q\}$ and its conversational history $D = \{x_1^d, ..., x_{m_d}^d\}$, m_q, m_d are the number of words in question and conversational history. Here we employ bidirectional LSTM (BiLSTM) to encode each word in the sentence(Lee et al., 2017), where the BiLSTM is defined as:

$$h_t^q = BiLSTM(x_t^q) \tag{1}$$

$$h_t^d = BiLSTM(x_t^d) \tag{2}$$

where h_t^q is the representation for the word x_t^q in the question sentence, h_t^d is the representation for the word x_t^d in the conversational history sentence.

2.2 Decoder

The Decoder is to generate the reformulated questions based on the representation of questions and conversational history sentence in the Encoder. The essence of the Decoder is a copy mechanism.

Decoder copies words from the input question Q or the input conversational history D. For each training sample, we should retain the original key information from the input question, and replace pronouns with entities in the conversational history, and get complete information from the conversational history if the question is incomplete.

At each time step t, let s_t be the decoder hidden state, the context vector of question be c_t^q, the context vector of conversational history be c_t^d, and the output word be y_t. The hidden state s_t can be constructed by the LSTM function as follows:

$$s_t = LSTM(s_{t-1}, c_{t-1}^q, c_{t-1}^d, y_{t-1}) \tag{3}$$

$$s_0 = tanh(W_0^q h_1^q + W_0^d h_1^d + b) \tag{4}$$

where the initial state s_0 is obtained by an activation function, W_0^q, W_0^d, b are learnable parameters.

The context vector c_t^q, c_t^d for the time step t can be computed by the attention mechanism(Luong et al., 2015; Zhou et al., 2018). We use the decoder hidden state s_t and the representation of input sentence from the encoder to get an importance score. Especially, the context vector c_t^q of question is:

$$e_{t,i} = v^T tanh(W s_t + U h_i^q) \tag{5}$$

$$a_{t,i} = \frac{exp(e_{t,i})}{\sum_{i=1}^{m_q} exp(e_{t,i})} \tag{6}$$

$$c_t^q = \sum_{i=1}^{m_q} a_{t,i} h_i^q \tag{7}$$

where v, W, U are all learnable parameters. For simplicity, we define the above attention as $c_t^q = Atten(s_t, h_i^q)$. When computing the context vector c_t^d of conversational history, it is necessary to consider the context vector of question. Therefore, the context vector c_t^d of conversational history is:

$$c_t^d = Atten((s_t, c_t^q), h_i^d) \qquad (8)$$

Next, we present a switch gate network to decide to copy words from questions or conversational history. The switch gate network can be obtained based on the embedding of the previous output word y_{t-1}, the current hidden state s_t and the current context vector c_t^q, c_t^d (Zhou et al., 2018).

$$p_t^q = \sigma(w_t^y y_{t-1} + w_t^s s_t + w_t^q c_t^q + w_t^d c_t^d + b) \qquad (9)$$

$$p_t^d = 1 - p_t^q \qquad (10)$$

where σ is a sigmoid activation function, p_t^q is the probability of copying a word from the questions, and p_t^d is the probability of copying a word from the conversational history at the time step t.

After determining the source (input question or conversational history) of the copying words, we need to design the location of each copying word. Here, we use the pointer network (PtrN) (Vinyals et al., 2015; Zhou et al., 2018) to get the attention distribution of the words in the input questions and conversation history separately.

$$k_{i,t}^q = PtrN(s_t, h_i^q) \qquad (11)$$

$$k_{i,t}^d = PtrN(s_t, h_i^d) \qquad (12)$$

Therefore, we can get the probability of a word ν copying from the input question P_q and from the conversational history P_d:

$$P_q(y_t = \nu) = p_t^q * k_{\nu,t}^q \qquad (13)$$

$$P_d(y_t = \nu) = p_t^d * k_{\nu,t}^d = (1 - p_t^q) * k_{\nu,t}^d \qquad (14)$$

$$P(y_t = \nu) = P_q(y_t = \nu) + P_d(y_t = \nu) \qquad (15)$$
$$= p_t^q * k_{\nu,t}^q + (1 - p_t^q) * k_{\nu,t}^d$$

2.3 Pretrained Question Reformulation

Pretraining is essential in deep reinforcement learning(Yin et al., 2018; Xiong et al., 2018), so we pretrain the question reformulation model with the annotated data. The objective of the question reformulation model is to minimize the negative log-likelihood loss $L(\theta)$:

$$L(\theta) = -\frac{1}{N} \sum_{i=1}^{N} \sum_{t=1}^{T} \log P(y_t) \qquad (16)$$

where N is the number of the training dataset, y be the annotated question for the input question Q, and T is the number of the words in y.

3 Overall ASQR Model

In this section, we introduce our proposed answer-supervised question reformulation model ASQR for conversational machine comprehension as shown in Figure 1. The architecture of our ASQR model is a reinforcement learning framework with the question reformulation model in Section 2 as an agent. In a conversational machine comprehension example, ASQR first reformulates the input questions by question reformulation model, then feeds the reformulated questions to a single-turn machine comprehension model and gets the predicted answers. The similarity scores between predicted answers and gold answers are as the reward to optimize the question reformulation model. The details are as follows:

Agent: The question reformulation model in Section 2 is defined as the agent. The reinforcement learning agent is a policy network $\pi_\theta(state, action) = p_\theta(action|state)$, where θ represents the model's parameters.

Action: The action is to predict the next word y_t by the agent. The word y_t is sampled from the input question, or from the input conversational history according to the probability distribution of vocabulary.

State: After each action, the state is updated by the agent. The state of the whole sentence is defined as $S_T = (y_1, ..., y_T)$, where y_t is the action in the time step t, T is the number of words in the sentence, and the last action y_T is an end-of-sequence token.

Reward: For each state S_T, the agent observes a reward. At this, we feed the state S_T to a pretrained single-turn machine comprehension model. The pretrained single-turn machine comprehension model predicts the answer for the state S_T, and computes the similarity score between the predicted answer and the gold answer. The similarity score is as the reward $R(S_T)$.

The goal of our reinforcement learning is to train the parameters of the agent. At this, we use the REINFORCE policy gradient algorithm (Williams, 1992; Keneshloo et al., 2018) to minimize the negative expected reward.

$$J(\theta) = -E_{S_T \sim p_\theta} R(S_T) \qquad (17)$$

Because the expectation is exponential in the length of the action sequence, it always gets an unbiased estimate of the gradient instead of the full gradient. The expected gradient can be estimated with a single sample $S_T \sim p_\theta$. So the expected gradient of a non-differentiable reward function is as follows:

$$\nabla_\theta J(\theta) = -\nabla_\theta E_{S_T \sim p_\theta} R(S_T)$$

$$= -E_{S_T \sim p_\theta} \nabla_\theta \log p_\theta(S_T) R(S_T) \quad (18)$$

$$\approx -\nabla_\theta \log p_\theta(S_T) R(S_T)$$

But the variance for estimation of the gradient may be very high, which makes the results difficult to observe. Steven et al. (Rennie et al., 2016) prove that subtracting a baseline value from the reward $R(S_T)$ does not change the expected gradient if the baseline value does not depend on the action. Therefore, we can subtract a baseline value to reduce the variance, and the baseline can be an arbitrary action-independent function. If the reward for an action is greater than baseline, the action will be encouraged, otherwise discouraged. Here, the baseline $R(S_T^g)$ we used is the output sentence of our question reformulation model by a greedy search(Rennie et al., 2016). The expected gradient of the reward function is:

$$\nabla_\theta J(\theta) \approx -\nabla_\theta \log p_\theta(S_T)(R(S_T) - R(S_T^g)) \quad (19)$$

Using the chain rule, the above equation can be reformulated as:

$$\nabla_\theta J(\theta) = \sum_{t=1}^{T} \frac{\partial J(\theta)}{\partial o_t} \frac{\partial o_t}{\theta} \quad (20)$$

where o_t is the input to the softmax function. The gradient of $\frac{\partial J(\theta)}{\partial o_t}$ is given by (Rennie et al., 2016; Keneshloo et al., 2018):

$$\frac{\partial J(\theta)}{\partial o_t} \approx (p_\theta(y_t|h_t) - 1(y_t))(R(S_T) - R(S_T^g)) \quad (21)$$

Pretrained Single-turn MC Model In our model, the agent observes a reward for each sentence state S_T, so we need a pretrained single-turn machine comprehension model to return a reward. The single turn machine comprehension model we used is the Bert model with one additional output layer(Devlin et al., 2018), which has been proved to do well on the single-turn SQuAD dataset (Rajpurkar et al., 2018).

Type	dataPretrain			QuAC		
	train	val	test	train	val	test
questions	20k	5k	3k	81k	7k	7k
dialogs	3k	600	400	11k	1k	1k

Table 2: data statistics.

4 Experiments

In the following work, we evaluate our model on QuAC dataset(Choi et al., 2018). To prove the performance of the model, we will conduct experiments from two perspectives: (1) Quality of the question reformulation model: How our question reformulation model in Section 2 can reformulate question accurately. (2) Effectiveness of the ASQR model: whether the reformulated questions by our ASQR model are more effective in conversational machine comprehension.

4.1 Dataset

We use the QuAC dataset (Choi et al., 2018) to evaluate our model. Table 1 gives an example of conversational machine comprehension in QuAC dataset. In this conversational machine comprehension data, students ask teachers questions based on the conversational history, teachers answer the questions by intercepting fragments from the context or cannot answer. For experiments, there are two types of dataset: (1) **dataPretrain**: Our annotated dataset to pretrain the question reformulation model in section 2. (2) **QuAC**: The all official QuAC dataset to train our ASQR model.

Our annotated data **dataPretrain** with 28k questions and 4k dialogs have been sampled from QuAC dataset randomly and annotated through a formal annotation platform. Annotators reformulate question earnestly according to the conversational history if at least one of coreference and omission occurs in current question. In the case of sentence fluency, annotators only copy words, but can not introduce extra words. To ensure the annotation quality, 15% of annotated questions are daily examined by a manager, and considered acceptable when the accuracy surpasses 90%. Some annotated questions can be seen in Table 1.

The investigation on our annotated dataset shows that there are 51.7%-coreference and 10.1%-omission questions, only 38.2% questions don't need to reformulated, which proves that

Model	BLEU1	BLEU2	BLEU3	BLEU4	EM	ROUGE_L	F1
Generate	56.18	47.38	37.01	27.43	11.09	62.65	66.36
Ptr-Generate	76.02	71.83	66.53	61.64	45.93	81.97	83.73
Ptr-Net	76.75	72.72	67.83	62.15	47.20	82.47	84.12
Ptr-Copy(4-qa)	78.13	73.84	68.20	62.52	47.20	83.49	85.22
Ptr-Copy(all-qa)	**78.74**	**74.80**	**69.67**	**64.20**	**49.85**	**84.15**	**85.75**

Table 3: BLEU-1,2,3,4, EM, ROUGE_L and F1 scores on the test dataset in the dataPretrain.

question reformulation is necessary and important for downstream tasks. We divide the dataPretrain dataset into a training dataset (7/10), a validation dataset (2/10), a test dataset (1/10). Table 2 describes the data statistics.

4.2 Settings

Question Reformulation Model We train the question reformulation model with the loss in Section 2.3 and the annotated **dataPretrain**. We built our vocabulary based on the nltk word tokenizer for all QuAC dataset. The vocabulary size we used is 10697. We set the word embedding as 128. The dimension of hidden states for both encoder and decoder is 256. The batch size is 64. The max encoder step is 400, the max decoder step is 30, and the minimum decoder steps is 5. We use Adagrad to train our model, wherein the learning rate is 0.1 and the initial accumulator value is 0.1. In the test stage, we generate reformulated question by the beam search strategy, the beam size is 4.

Pretrained Single turn MC Model We use the Bert model with one additional output layer (Devlin et al., 2018) as our single-turn machine comprehension model, which has a good performance on SQuAD2.0 dataset. The pretrained model of Bert we used is *BERT-Base, Uncased* with 12 layers, 768 hidden states, 12 heads and 110M parameters. The batch size is 24. The maximum length of an answer that can be generated is 30. The initial single-turn machine comprehension model is fine-tuned with all official QuAC data. If the reformulated questions are more meaningful than official questions, we will fine-tune the single-turn machine comprehension model with the reformulated data. The parameters of the single-turn machine comprehension model are fixed when training our ASQR model.

ASQR Model Our ASQR model can be trained based on above pretrained question reformulation model and single-turn machine comprehension model. We use the Adam optimizer with 1e-5 learning rate to update the trainable parameters in our ASQR model. The F1 score is used to evaluate the similarity between the predicted answer and the golden answer.

4.3 Quality of Question Reformulation

We first evaluate the accuracy of our question reformulation model in Section 2 leveraging the annotation dataset **dataPretrain**.

Compared Models The compared models of our question reformulation model are as follows:

(1) **Generate**: Attention generator model in (Nallapati et al., 2016). In this model, the words are only generated from a fixed vocabulary.

(2) **Ptr-Generate**: Pointer Generator model in (See et al., 2017). In this model, the word can be copied from the input sentence or generated from the vocabulary. Here, we concatenate the conversational history information and the current question as the input sentence.

(3) **Ptr-Net**: Pure pointer-based copy model with an encoder and a decoder, the input of encoder can be the concatenation of question and conversation history, the decoder only copies words from the input sentences.

(4) **Ptr-Copy**: Pointer copy model is our question reformulation model in Section 2. The word can be either copied from the input questions or copied from the input conversational history.

Results Each question in the annotated dataset has its label reformulated by annotators, so the similarity score between question and its label can be used to evaluate the quality of question reformulation model. The metrics of the similarity scores are BLEU-1,2,3,4, EM (the exact match score), ROUGE_L and F1 scores. The current question may be strongly related to the previous several questions/answers but not all questions/answers history occasionally since topic switching may occur during a conversation. At the same time, sentences containing all history information are longer, which may be not conducive to learning

Model	F1	HEQ-Q	HEQ-D
Pretrained InferSent	20.8	10.0	0.0
Logistic regression	33.9	22.2	0.2
BiDAF++(no-ctx)	50.2	43.3	2.2
ASQR	**53.7**	**48.1**	**2.9**
human	80.8	100	100

Table 4: F1, HEQ-Q and HEQ-D scores on the test dataset of QuAC dataset.

Model	F1	HEQ-Q	HEQ-D
Bert	51.6	46.6	2.9
Ptr-Copy-Bert(4-qa)	52.5	46.9	2.7
Ptr-Copy-Bert(all-qa)	53.1	47.8	2.9
ASQR	**54.2**	**48.5**	**2.9**

Table 5: Model performance on the validation dataset of QuAC dataset.

key information. To verify the above conjecture, we encode previous N questions/answers as conversational history, $N = \{4, all\}$. The results are listed in Table 3. Several conclusions can be drawn from the results:

(1) The Generate model performs poorly since all words in the annotated questions are from the question Q or the conversational history D.

(2) The inferior effect of the Ptr-Generate and Ptr-Net models over our Ptr-Copy model shows that separately encoding the question Q and the conversational history D are better than concatenating them. Because most words in reformulated questions are copied from Q, only referential and missing information needs to be copied from D.

(3) Our Ptr-Copy model with previous all question/answers history performing well proves that our question reformulation model can identify key information accurately in the case of topic switching and longer sentences.

4.4 Effectiveness of ASQR Model

We validate the reformulated data by our ASQR model are more effective for conversational machine comprehension in all **QuAC** dataset.

Compared Models The compared models of our ASQR model are as follows:

(1) **Pretrained InferSent**: Lexical matching baseline model outputting the sentence in paragraph whose pretrained InferSent representation has the highest cosine for the question.

(2) **Logistic regression**: Logistic regression model trained by Vowpal Wabbit dataset (Langford et al., 2007) with simple matching features, bias features and contextual features.

(3) **BiDAF++(no-ctx)**: Single-turn machine comprehension model based on BiDAF (Seo et al., 2016) with self-attention and contextualized embeddings (Peters et al., 2018).

The above three models are baseline models proposed in (Choi et al., 2018). The following models are used in our model.

(4) **Bert**: The pretrained single-turn machine comprehension model with Bert model and one additional output layer trained by official QuAC data.

(5) **Ptr-Copy-Bert**: Get reformulated QuAC data by Ptr-Copy model in Section 2, and train Bert model with the reformulated QuAC data.

(6) **ASQR**: Our ASQR model, an answer-supervised question reformulation model for conversational machine comprehension with reinforcement learning technology. We use the reformulated data by ASQR model to train the Bert model.

Results It is worth noting that the questions in official QuAC dataset do not have labels. The quality of reformulated questions only can be evaluated by their answers. A model is better if the reformulated questions by this model are more beneficial to get better answers. Therefore, we use the similarity scores between predicted answers from single-turn machine comprehension model and the gold answers as the evaluation parameters. The metrics of similarity scores are F1 and HEQ (Human Equivalence score, HEQ-Q for question, HEQ-D for dialog), wherein HEQ-Q is true when the F1 score of the question is higher than the average human F1 score, and HEQ-D is true when the HEQ-Q score of all the questions in the dialog are true.

Table 4 shows the scores on the test dataset of QuAC dataset compared with some baseline models. Our ASQR model has the best F1 (53.7), HEQ-Q (48.1) and HEQ-D (2.9) scores over the baseline models, indicating that the question reformulation model can be beneficial to conversational machine comprehension.

At the same time, some ablation studies have developed on the validation dataset (Table 5). Compared with the Bert trained with original official QuAC dataset, we observe 2.6-improvement on F1 score. The model Ptr-Copy-Bert(all-qa) with the all question/answers history over the model Ptr-Copy-Bert(4-qa) with the part of conversational history has good performance, which is consistent with the result in Section 4.3. The best performance on F1 and HEQ-Q score of our ASQR model compared with the Ptr-Copy-Bert models prove that our answer-supervised training method is more effective than traditional question label-supervised method. Some examples of reformulation data by ASQR over Ptr-Copy model are mentioned in the supplementary section.

Analysis We should point out that the aim of our paper is to prove the effectiveness of answer-supervised question reformulation model. But only question reformulation cannot reach the best performance for conversational machine comprehension problems, because question turns, scenario transformation, answer lapse, et al. are all important factors. The models in Leaderboard such as FlowQA, BiDAF++ w/2 have considered the above import factors, other models such as TransBERT, BertMT use a large amount of data for other tasks. Therefore, it is unfair to compare our model with those models.

Besides, the feedback mechanism of the ASQR model is not good enough because single-turn machine comprehension model does not give appropriate answers occasionally trained by the original QuAC dataset, which severely limits the performance improvement of ASQR model. Some similar question answering models (Buck et al., 2017; Nogueira and Cho, 2017) get feedback by utilizing sophisticated QA system or Search Engine which do not depend on the distribution of input data, while the existing machine comprehension models are strongly dependent on data's distribution. In the future, we will study how to get correct and appropriate feedback, and combine question reformulation with implicit conversational models to better integrate conversational information.

5   Related Work

Recently, several approaches have been proposed for conversational machine comprehension. BiDAF++ w/ k-ctx (Choi et al., 2018) integrates the conversation history by encoding turn number to the question embedding and previous N answer locations to the context embedding. FlowQA (Huang et al., 2018) provides a FLOW mechanism that encodes the intermediate representation of the previous questions to the context embedding when processing the current question. SDnet (Zhu et al., 2018) prepends previous questions and answers to the current question and leverages the contextual embedding of BERT to obtain an understanding of conversation history. The existing models always integrate the conversational history implicitly and can not understand the history effectively.

It is worth noting that much work has introduced question reformulation models into machine comprehension tasks (Feldman and El-Yaniv, 2019; Das et al., 2019). Many question reformulation models can integrate the conversational history explicitly by making coreference resolution and completion for the current question. Rastogi et al. (Rastogi et al., 2019) prove that can get a better answer when inputting a reformulated question to the single-turn question answering models. Nogueira et al. (Nogueira and Cho, 2017) introduce a query reformulation reinforcement learning system with relevant documents recall as a reward. Buck et al. (Buck et al., 2017) propose an active question answering model with reinforcement learning, and learn to reformulate questions to elicit the best possible answers with an agent that sits between the user and a QA system. However, the above work is still in the preliminary exploratory stage, and there is no work to reformulate questions with feedback from downstream tasks in conversational machine comprehension tasks. How to train the reformulation models with feedback from subsequent functions is still a major challenge.

6   Conclusion

In this paper, we present an answer-supervised question reformulation model for conversational machine comprehension with reinforcement learning technology. We provide a high-quality dataset for question reformulation in conversational machine comprehension. The experimental results on a benchmark dataset prove that our model can be more beneficial to improve the performance of conversational machine comprehension.

Acknowledgements

The work was supported by the National Key R&D Program of China under grant 2018YFB1004700, and National Natural Science Foundation of China (61772122, 61872074). We sincerely thank the anonymous reviewers for their thorough reviewing and valuable suggestions.

References

Samy Bengio, Oriol Vinyals, Navdeep Jaitly, and Noam Shazeer. 2015. Scheduled sampling for sequence prediction with recurrent neural networks. In *International Conference on Neural Information Processing Systems*.

Christian Buck, Jannis Bulian, Massimiliano Ciaramita, Wojciech Gajewski, Andrea Gesmundo, Neil Houlsby, and Wei Wang. 2017. Ask the right questions: Active question reformulation with reinforcement learning. *arXiv preprint arXiv:1705.07830*.

Eunsol Choi, He He, Mohit Iyyer, Mark Yatskar, Wentau Yih, Yejin Choi, Percy Liang, and Luke Zettlemoyer. 2018. Quac: Question answering in context. *arXiv preprint arXiv:1808.07036*.

Rajarshi Das, Shehzaad Dhuliawala, Manzil Zaheer, and Andrew McCallum. 2019. Multi-step retriever-reader interaction for scalable open-domain question answering. *arXiv preprint arXiv:1905.05733*.

Jacob Devlin, Ming Wei Chang, Kenton Lee, and Kristina Toutanova. 2018. Bert: Pre-training of deep bidirectional transformers for language understanding.

Yair Feldman and Ran El-Yaniv. 2019. Multi-hop paragraph retrieval for open-domain question answering. *arXiv preprint arXiv:1906.06606*.

Minghao Hu, Yuxing Peng, Zhen Huang, Nan Yang, Ming Zhou, et al. 2018. Read+ verify: Machine reading comprehension with unanswerable questions. *arXiv preprint arXiv:1808.05759*.

Hsin-Yuan Huang, Eunsol Choi, and Wen-tau Yih. 2018. Flowqa: Grasping flow in history for conversational machine comprehension. *arXiv preprint arXiv:1810.06683*.

Marcin Junczys-Dowmunt and Roman Grundkiewicz. 2017. An exploration of neural sequence-to-sequence architectures for automatic post-editing. *arXiv preprint arXiv:1706.04138*.

Yaser Keneshloo, Tian Shi, Chandan K Reddy, and Naren Ramakrishnan. 2018. Deep reinforcement learning for sequence to sequence models. *arXiv preprint arXiv:1805.09461*.

John Langford, Lihong Li, and Alex Strehl. 2007. Vowpal wabbit online learning project.

Kenton Lee, Luheng He, Mike Lewis, and Luke Zettlemoyer. 2017. End-to-end neural coreference resolution.

Hengrui Liu, Wenge Rong, Libin Shi, Yuanxin Ouyang, and Zhang Xiong. 2018. Question rewrite based dialogue response generation. In *International Conference on Neural Information Processing*, pages 169–180. Springer.

Xiaodong Liu, Yelong Shen, Kevin Duh, and Jianfeng Gao. 2017. Stochastic answer networks for machine reading comprehension. *arXiv preprint arXiv:1712.03556*.

Minh Thang Luong, Hieu Pham, and Christopher D. Manning. 2015. Effective approaches to attention-based neural machine translation. *Computer Science*.

Ramesh Nallapati, Bowen Zhou, Caglar Gulcehre, Bing Xiang, et al. 2016. Abstractive text summarization using sequence-to-sequence rnns and beyond. *arXiv preprint arXiv:1602.06023*.

Jan Niehues, Eunah Cho, Thanh-Le Ha, and Alex Waibel. 2016. Pre-translation for neural machine translation. *arXiv preprint arXiv:1610.05243*.

Rodrigo Nogueira and Kyunghyun Cho. 2017. Task-oriented query reformulation with reinforcement learning. *arXiv preprint arXiv:1704.04572*.

Matthew E Peters, Mark Neumann, Mohit Iyyer, Matt Gardner, Christopher Clark, Kenton Lee, and Luke Zettlemoyer. 2018. Deep contextualized word representations. *arXiv preprint arXiv:1802.05365*.

Pranav Rajpurkar, Robin Jia, and Percy Liang. 2018. Know what you don't know: Unanswerable questions for squad.

Pushpendre Rastogi, Arpit Gupta, Tongfei Chen, and Lambert Mathias. 2019. Scaling multi-domain dialogue state tracking via query reformulation. *arXiv preprint arXiv:1903.05164*.

Steven J. Rennie, Etienne Marcheret, Youssef Mroueh, Jarret Ross, and Vaibhava Goel. 2016. Self-critical sequence training for image captioning.

Stefan Riezler and Yi Liu. 2010. Query rewriting using monolingual statistical machine translation. *Computational Linguistics*, 36(3):569–582.

Abigail See, Peter J. Liu, and Christopher D. Manning. 2017. Get to the point: Summarization with pointer-generator networks.

Minjoon Seo, Aniruddha Kembhavi, Ali Farhadi, and Hannaneh Hajishirzi. 2016. Bidirectional attention flow for machine comprehension. *arXiv preprint arXiv:1611.01603*.

Fu Sun, Linyang Li, Xipeng Qiu, and Yang Liu. 2018. U-net: Machine reading comprehension with unanswerable questions. *arXiv preprint arXiv:1810.06638*.

Oriol Vinyals, Meire Fortunato, and Navdeep Jaitly. 2015. Pointer networks. In *Advances in Neural Information Processing Systems*, pages 2692–2700.

Wei Wang, Ming Yan, and Chen Wu. 2018. Multi-granularity hierarchical attention fusion networks for reading comprehension and question answering. *arXiv preprint arXiv:1811.11934*.

Ronald J. Williams. 1992. Simple statistical gradient-following algorithms for connectionist reinforcement learning. *Machine Learning*, 8(3-4):229–256.

Wenhan Xiong, Thien Hoang, and William Yang Wang. 2018. Deeppath: A reinforcement learning method for knowledge graph reasoning.

Qingyu Yin, Zhang Yu, Weinan Zhang, Ting Liu, and William Yang Wang. 2018. Deep reinforcement learning for chinese zero pronoun resolution.

Qingyu Zhou, Yang Nan, Furu Wei, and Zhou Ming. 2018. Sequential copying networks.

Chenguang Zhu, Michael Zeng, and Xuedong Huang. 2018. Sdnet: Contextualized attention-based deep network for conversational question answering. *arXiv preprint arXiv:1812.03593*.

Simple yet Effective Bridge Reasoning
for Open-Domain Multi-Hop Question Answering

Wenhan Xiong[†], Mo Yu[‡], Xiaoxiao Guo[‡], Hong Wang[†], Shiyu Chang[‡],
Murray Campbell[‡], William Yang Wang[†]
[†] University of California, Santa Barbara
[‡] IBM Research
{xwhan, william}@cs.ucsb.edu, {yum,mcam}@us.ibm.com, {shiyu.chang, xiaoxiao.guo}@ibm.com

Abstract

A key challenge of multi-hop question answering (QA) in the open-domain setting is to accurately retrieve the supporting passages from a large corpus. Existing work on open-domain QA typically relies on off-the-shelf information retrieval (IR) techniques to retrieve **answer passages**, i.e., the passages containing the groundtruth answers. However, IR-based approaches are insufficient for multi-hop questions, as the topic of the second or further hops is not explicitly covered by the question. To resolve this issue, we introduce a new subproblem of open-domain multi-hop QA, which aims to recognize the bridge (*i.e.*, the anchor that links to the answer passage) from the context of a set of start passages with a reading comprehension model. This model, the **bridge reasoner**, is trained with a weakly supervised signal and produces the candidate answer passages for the **passage reader** to extract the answer. On the full-wiki HotpotQA benchmark, we significantly improve the baseline method by 14 point F1. Without using any memory-inefficient contextual embeddings, our result is also competitive with the state-of-the-art that applies BERT in multiple modules.

1 Introduction

As machines have achieved super-human performance (Devlin et al., 2018) for single-passage question answering on the standard SQuAD dataset (Rajpurkar et al., 2016), building QA systems with human-like reasoning ability has attracted broad attention recently. In this challenge, the QA system is required to reason with distributed piece of information from multiple passages to derive the answer. Several multi-hop QA benchmarks include WIKIHOP (Welbl et al., 2018), ComplexWebQuestions (Talmor and Berant, 2018) and HotpotQA (Yang et al., 2018) have been released recently to advance this line of research. In this paper, we focus on the practical open-domain HotpotQA benchmark where the questions are asked upon natural language passages instead of knowledge bases and the supporting passages are not known beforehand.

The typical pipeline of open-domain QA systems (Chen et al., 2017; Wang et al., 2018; Htut et al., 2018) is to first use an IR system to retrieve a compact set of paragraphs and then run a machine reading model over the concatenated or reranked paragraphs. While IR works reasonably well for simple questions[1], it often fails to retrieve the correct answer paragraph for multi-hop questions. This is due to the fact that the question often cannot fully cover the information for the second or further hops. Consider the question *"What government position was held by the woman who portrayed Corliss Archer in the film Kiss and Tell?"* from the HotpotQA (Yang et al., 2018) dataset. Since the name of the person (*Shirley Temple*) is not directly mentioned in the question and the answer is about another aspect of the person other than film acting, traditional IR heuristics based on n-gram matching might fail to retrieve the answer passage. In fact, the correct answer passage of *Shirley Temple* never appears in the top passages ranked by the default IR method of HotpotQA.

Instead of predicting the answer passage with text matching between passages and questions, we claim that the answer passage can be better inferred based on the context-level information. Noticing that the IR retrieved passages can usually successfully cover the first hop evidence of the questions (i.e. **start passages**), we propose to use a reading comprehension model to infer the entities linking to the answer passage from the start passages. Our experiments show that this simple approach can tremendously increase the an-

---

[1]As shown in Table 3 of Chen et al. (2017), a simple IR method can achieve 77.8% recall on the SQuAD dataset.

Proceedings of the Second Workshop on Machine Reading for Question Answering, pages 48–52
Hong Kong, China, November 4, 2019. ©2019 Association for Computational Linguistics

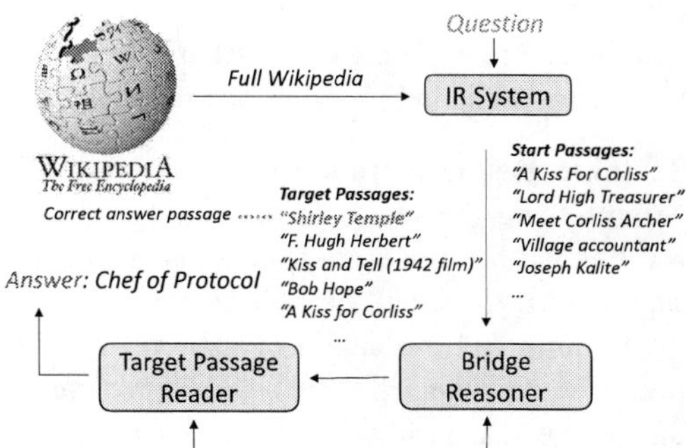

Figure 1: The overview of our QA system. The **bridge reasoner** reads the start passages retrieved by an IR system and predicts a set of candidate bridges (anchor links) that lead to the answer passages, which is further processed by the **passage reader** to return the answer.

swer coverage of the top-ranked passages and thus increase the final QA performance by 14 point F1. Despite that our bridge reasoner and passage reader only learn above GloVe embeddings (Pennington et al., 2014), we achieve competitive performance with methods that use BERT (Devlin et al., 2018) in multiple modules.

2 Problem Definition and Motivation

An open-domain multi-hop QA system aims to answer complex questions by retrieving evidence from a large open-domain passage corpus, such as Wikipedia. Usually the evidence scatters in a distributed set of supporting passages $p_1, p_2, ..., p_n$ that forms an ordered chain. Each p_i provides evidence that partially fulfills the information required to answer the question, as well as provides clues (usually concepts or entities) that lead to the next supporting passage p_{i+1}. The last passage p_n of the chain contains the answer and is referred to as the **answer passage**. Although the supervision of the complete supporting chains could be beneficial for training and diagnosing the QA system, predicting these complete reasoning sequences at evaluation time is usually quite challenging.

This work builds on an important observation that the prediction of the entire chain is not necessary for the QA performance. As a matter of fact, we conduct a preliminary experiment that compares a QA model that has full access to the supporting passages, versus a model that only has access to the answer passage. This experiment was conducted on the distractor version of HotpotQA (Yang et al., 2018), which has groundtruth supporting passage annotations. We use the baseline QA model from Yang et al. (2018). The result shows that the full access only gives marginal improvements[2], even this model uses the supporting passage labels as additional supervision signals. The above result confirms that the multi-hop QA performance largely depends on the accurate retrieval of the answer passages.

Definition of Bridge Reasoning The key idea of our approach is to reformulate the problem of answer passage retrieval as a reading comprehension task. The reading model predicts an entity that points to the answer passage. Such entities serve as the bridges connecting the supporting passages, therefore we refer them as bridge entities. When working with passages from Wikipedia, we consider the anchor links in each article as the candidate set of bridge entities. Thus each bridge candidate is a title of another passage and we use **bridge entity** and **answer passage** interchangably.

Note that our definition of bridge reasoning here can be easily extended beyond anchor links, as long as we have entity linking tools to connect the same entities in different passages and build links between them. The main goal of this paper is to demonstrate that the bridge reasoning task can be effectively formulated as a reading comprehension task, and we leave the investigation of the broader definition of bridge reasoning to future work.

Remark on Distant Supervision It is also worthy to note that obtaining the supervision of the answer passages is much easier – as long as there are question-answer pairs, we can use distant supervision to obtain answer passage annotations. Therefore the proposed bridge reasoning task is rather general and is easy to be extend to more datasets without support passage supervision.

3 The Proposed Approach

Our QA system is illustrated in Figure 1. We first use the **bridge reasoner** to get the answer passages and then feed the top candidate answer passages into a standard **passage reader** to predict the final answer to the multi-hop question.

3.1 The Base Span Prediction Model

Both the bridge reasoner and the passage reader use a model that predicts a relevant span given a

---

[2]66.07 F1 and 49.43 EM with full support access versus 64.77 F1 and 50.96 EM with only answer passage access.

question. We use the same model architecture for both tasks and the architecture is base on the document QA model from (Clark and Gardner, 2018), which is used by Yang et al. (2018) as the baseline for HotpotQA. The model uses a shared bidirectional GRU (Cho et al., 2014) to encode the question and the passages. The encoded questions and passages are then passed to a bidirectional attention layer (Seo et al., 2017) to get the question-aware passage states. The state vectors are enhanced by a self-attention layer (Wang et al., 2017) and are finally fed into linear layers to predict the start and end span scores at every word position.

3.2 Bridge Reasoner

Our bridge reasoner integrates multiple types of evidence to predict the bridge entities that link to potential answer passages.

Local Context Evidence The most critical evidence we use is the local context of the start passages. These passages usually cover the first hop of the question and provide clues about the bridges. Our bridge reasoner therefore employs the span prediction model to predict the spans of bridge entities from the context of the start passages. Unlike typical span prediction models that consider all possible spans, the bridge reasoner here only needs to rank all the entities that have anchor links. We take the final representation of each token from the span prediction model and use each anchor's start token representation $h_{a_s}^c$ to represent the anchor's local context evidence.

Passage Content Evidence Each bridge entity in our setting is associated with a Wikipedia article, so the relevance of each bridge can be computed by matching the article content with the question. Here we use a bi-LSTM to encode the abstract passages and use max-pooling on the output states to get the passage content representation h_a^p.

Both the local context evidence $h_{a_s}^c$ and passage content evidence h_a^p are integrated into our final bridge reasoner by a linear layer. The supervision for training the bridge reasoner is derived from the distractor version of HotpotQA: we take the title of the support passage that contains the groundtruth answer as the groundtruth bridge entity. When there are multiple passages that contain the answer, we randomly pick one of the passages.

3.3 Target Passage Reader

Our passage reader has the same neural architecture as the bridge reasoner and the goal here is to extract the correct answer span. We run the target passage reader on the top 10 answer passage candidates predicted by the bridge reasoner.

Training Passages from Cross-validation As we are using the same set of training questions for training the bridge reasoner and the target passage reader, there will be a discrepancy between the training and evaluation of QA: at evaluation time, the reader sees the passages predicted by the bridge reasoner, while at training time, the groundtruth answer passage is known. On the other hand, we also cannot use the predicted passages for training the reader, as the bridge reasoner itself is trained on the training set so the top predicted passages on training set are already overfitted. To make the training match the evaluation, we use the bridge reasoner model to perform two-fold cross-validation on training questions and use the cross-predicted passages for training the reader.

Auxiliary Training Objective of Bridge Prediction We introduce an auxiliary objective to encourage the reader to utilize the answer passage supervision during training. This is done by adding a span loss for predicting the answer passage title[3]. This simple auxiliary loss introduces implicit regularization for the reader and turns to be beneficial for the final QA performance.

4 Experiments

Setup Our experiments mainly focus on the "*bridge*" questions of which the supporting passages can form a reasoning chain and the answers can be found in the last passage. For the "*comparison*" questions in the dataset, the topics for comparison are often explicitly mentioned in the questions, so IR methods are often sufficient and we keep the IR retrieved passages for comparison answer prediction. Because HotpotQA does not provide training passages for the open-domain setting, we use a hybrid tf-idf and bm25 approach to retrieve 10 start passages for each training question. For the dev and test questions, we directly run the trained bridge reasoner on the start passages retrieved by HotpotQA's default IR approach. To further expand the coverage of the start passages, we find a useful external entity linking tool[4] and we append the abstracts of the Top2

---

[3]The passage titles are included as part of the context for QA.

[4]https://tagme.d4science.org/tagme/

Approach	Hits@10
HotpotQA IR	48.4
Our Methods	
Bridge Reasoner	76.6
w/o local context evidence	75.4
w/o passage content evidence	65.7
Bridge Reasoner + entity linking	**80.6**

Table 1: Answer passage prediction performance, measured by Hits@10 on dev bridge questions.

Model	Dev		Test	
	EM	F1	EM	F1
Methods w/o BERT				
HotpotQA Baseline	24.68	34.36	23.95	32.89
GRN	-	-	27.34	36.48
Ours	36.81	48.48	36.04	47.43
w/o EL	35.00	46.16	-	-
Methods with BERT				
GRN + BERT	-	-	29.87	39.14
CogQA	37.6	49.4	37.12	48.87
w/o EL	34.6	46.2	-	-
w/o re-scoring	33.6	45.0	-	-
Methods with Unknown Usage of BERT				
DecompRC	-	-	30.00	40.65
MUPPET	-	-	30.61	40.26

Table 2: QA performance on HotpotQA. The underline methods use the same resource, but our method does not use any pre-trained contextual embeddings like BERT.

returned Wikipedia articles for both bridge reasoning and answer prediction.

Answer Passage Prediction The performance of the bridge reasoner on answer passage predictions is shown in Table 1. Overall, the bridge reasoner retrieves the answer passage with significantly higher accuracy than HotpotQA's IR method. We also see that the local context evidence is more effective than the passage content evidence for answer passage prediction. Since conventional IR methods also use passage content for ranking, the results here validate our assumption that the bridges can be better inferred by reading the context of the start passages.

Question Answering Results Table 2 shows the final multi-hop QA performance. We compare several concurrent systems on the leaderboard, including the newly published CogQA (Ding et al., 2019) and a few anonymous results that are released at the same period as CogQA, *e.g.*, MUPPET, GRN, and DecompRC. Most of the top systems on the leaderboard benefit from the pretrained contextual embedding BERT, while our method is trained from scratch. We categorize all

Model	Bridge Only		Full Dev	
	EM	F1	EM	F1
Our approach	34.19	47.16	36.81	48.48
w/o EL	32.91	45.42	35.00	46.16
w/o Multi-Task	32.91	46.13	35.80	47.14
w/o Bridge Reasoner	22.52	32.78	27.05	36.67

Table 3: QA performance ablation on the development set.

the systems according to their usages of BERT. Among all the results without BERT, our approach shows a huge advantage and is about 10% higher in terms of both EM and F1 compared to the current known best system w/o BERT (GRN). Since our reader has the same architecture as the HotpotQA baseline, this shows the great potential of our bridge reasoner. When compared to models w/ BERT, *i.e.*, the CogQA, our result is still competitive. Similarly to CogQA, we also investigate the passage initialization with question entity linking, and observed significant performance boost. Note that the CogQA paper does not provide details of the entity linker, so the results with our entity linker may not be the same to the one used by CogQA. Furthermore, when entity linking is not used, our method and CogQA start with the same initial passages. This gives an apple-to-apple comparison except that ours does not use BERT. According to the dev results, our method is on par with CogQA (35.0 v.s. 34.6 for EM and both 46.2 for F1). This proves that our bridge reasoning method is superior to the cognitive graph generator in CogQA.

Ablation Study Table 3 gives ablation results on the dev set, where both entity linking and the auxiliary objective slightly improve the performance. As the focus of the paper is to improve the coverage of answer passages for "bridge" questions, we also report the "bridge" question portion where the improvement is more significant.

5   Conclusion

This paper introduces an important sub-problem of bridge reasoning for the task of multi-hop QA in the open-domain setting. We propose a bridge reasoner that utilizes multiple types of evidence to derive the passages that cover the answers. The reasoner significantly improves the coverage of answer passages than IR methods. With the predicted passages, we show that a standard reading comprehension model is able to achieve similar performance as the state-of-the-art method that requires BERT in multiple modules.

References

Danqi Chen, Adam Fisch, Jason Weston, and Antoine Bordes. 2017. Reading Wikipedia to answer open-domain questions. In *Proceedings of the 55th Annual Meeting of the Association for Computational Linguistics (Volume 1: Long Papers)*, pages 1870–1879, Vancouver, Canada. Association for Computational Linguistics.

Kyunghyun Cho, Bart van Merrienboer, Caglar Gulcehre, Dzmitry Bahdanau, Fethi Bougares, Holger Schwenk, and Yoshua Bengio. 2014. Learning phrase representations using RNN encoder–decoder for statistical machine translation. In *Proceedings of the 2014 Conference on Empirical Methods in Natural Language Processing (EMNLP)*, pages 1724–1734, Doha, Qatar. Association for Computational Linguistics.

Christopher Clark and Matt Gardner. 2018. Simple and effective multi-paragraph reading comprehension. In *Proceedings of the 56th Annual Meeting of the Association for Computational Linguistics (Volume 1: Long Papers)*, pages 845–855, Melbourne, Australia. Association for Computational Linguistics.

Jacob Devlin, Ming-Wei Chang, Kenton Lee, and Kristina Toutanova. 2018. Bert: Pre-training of deep bidirectional transformers for language understanding. *arXiv preprint arXiv:1810.04805*.

Ming Ding, Chang Zhou, Qibin Chen, Hongxia Yang, and Jie Tang. 2019. Cognitive graph for multi-hop reading comprehension at scale. *arXiv preprint arXiv:1905.05460*.

Phu Mon Htut, Samuel Bowman, and Kyunghyun Cho. 2018. Training a ranking function for open-domain question answering. In *Proceedings of the 2018 Conference of the North American Chapter of the Association for Computational Linguistics: Student Research Workshop*, pages 120–127, New Orleans, Louisiana, USA. Association for Computational Linguistics.

Jeffrey Pennington, Richard Socher, and Christopher Manning. 2014. Glove: Global vectors for word representation. In *Proceedings of the 2014 Conference on Empirical Methods in Natural Language Processing (EMNLP)*, pages 1532–1543, Doha, Qatar. Association for Computational Linguistics.

Pranav Rajpurkar, Jian Zhang, Konstantin Lopyrev, and Percy Liang. 2016. SQuAD: 100,000+ questions for machine comprehension of text. In *Proceedings of the 2016 Conference on Empirical Methods in Natural Language Processing*, pages 2383–2392, Austin, Texas. Association for Computational Linguistics.

Min Joon Seo, Aniruddha Kembhavi, Ali Farhadi, and Hannaneh Hajishirzi. 2017. Bidirectional attention flow for machine comprehension. In *5th International Conference on Learning Representations, ICLR 2017, Toulon, France, April 24-26, 2017, Conference Track Proceedings*. OpenReview.net.

Alon Talmor and Jonathan Berant. 2018. The web as a knowledge-base for answering complex questions. In *Proceedings of the 2018 Conference of the North American Chapter of the Association for Computational Linguistics: Human Language Technologies, Volume 1 (Long Papers)*, pages 641–651, New Orleans, Louisiana. Association for Computational Linguistics.

Shuohang Wang, Mo Yu, Xiaoxiao Guo, Zhiguo Wang, Tim Klinger, Wei Zhang, Shiyu Chang, Gerry Tesauro, Bowen Zhou, and Jing Jiang. 2018. R^3: Reinforced ranker-reader for open-domain question answering. In *Proceedings of the Thirty-Second AAAI Conference on Artificial Intelligence, (AAAI-18), the 30th innovative Applications of Artificial Intelligence (IAAI-18), and the 8th AAAI Symposium on Educational Advances in Artificial Intelligence (EAAI-18), New Orleans, Louisiana, USA, February 2-7, 2018*, pages 5981–5988. AAAI Press.

Wenhui Wang, Nan Yang, Furu Wei, Baobao Chang, and Ming Zhou. 2017. Gated self-matching networks for reading comprehension and question answering. In *Proceedings of the 55th Annual Meeting of the Association for Computational Linguistics, ACL 2017, Vancouver, Canada, July 30 - August 4, Volume 1: Long Papers*, pages 189–198. Association for Computational Linguistics.

Johannes Welbl, Pontus Stenetorp, and Sebastian Riedel. 2018. Constructing datasets for multi-hop reading comprehension across documents. *TACL*, 6:287–302.

Zhilin Yang, Peng Qi, Saizheng Zhang, Yoshua Bengio, William Cohen, Ruslan Salakhutdinov, and Christopher D. Manning. 2018. HotpotQA: A dataset for diverse, explainable multi-hop question answering. In *Proceedings of the 2018 Conference on Empirical Methods in Natural Language Processing*, pages 2369–2380, Brussels, Belgium. Association for Computational Linguistics.

Improving the Robustness of Deep Reading Comprehension Models by Leveraging Syntax Prior

Bowen Wu[1], Haoyang Huang[2], Zongsheng Wang[1], Qihang Feng[1],
Jingsong Yu[2], Baoxun Wang[1]
[1]Platform and Content Group, Tencent
[2]School of Software & Microelectronics, Peking University, Beijing, China
`jasonbwwu, jasoawang, careyfeng, asulewang@tencent.com`
`huanghaoyang@pku.edu.cn, yjs@ss.pku.edu.cn`

Abstract

Despite the remarkable progress on Machine Reading Comprehension (MRC) with the help of open-source datasets, recent studies indicate that most of the current MRC systems unfortunately suffer from weak robustness against adversarial samples. To address this issue, we attempt to take sentence syntax as the leverage in the answer predicting process which previously only takes account of phrase-level semantics. Furthermore, to better utilize the sentence syntax and improve the robustness, we propose a Syntactic Leveraging Network, which is designed to deal with adversarial samples by exploiting the syntactic elements of a question. The experiment results indicate that our method is promising for improving the generalization and robustness of MRC models against the influence of adversarial samples, with performance well-maintained.

1 Introduction

As one of the ultimate goals of natural language processing, Machine Reading Comprehension (MRC) has been attracting much attention from both the academical and industrial institutions (Richardson et al., 2013; Hermann et al., 2015). Recently, most of the outstanding studies have benefited from the rapid development of machine reading competitions with shared datasets, such as SQuAD (Rajpurkar et al., 2016), MS MARCO (Nguyen et al., 2017). According to the competition results, the Deep Learning based approaches have shown significant strength on MRC tasks and achieved most of the top-ranked positions (Wang et al., 2017; Yu et al., 2018).

Nevertheless, the very recent research in MRC indicates that simply chasing the performance improvement on given datasets is unwise, since the generalization and robustness might be weakened due to the great fitting capability of DL models trained on a specific corpus. Especially, the research on adversarial reading comprehension samples conducted by Jia and Liang (2017) has shown that the performances of most of the DL based MRC models decrease significantly on the adversarial samples. These adversarial samples are constructed by simply appending one sentence similar to the question into the paragraph, without changing the original answer. This work indicates that, apparently, there exists quite a gap between the current MRC approaches and the methodologies that really comprehend natural language passages.

In this paper, we attempt to face the challenge brought by the RC adversarial samples and aim at proposing a reading comprehension system with better generalization and robustness. For this purpose, this paper presents a method to improve the answer inferencing process of MRC, by leveraging the probability function for estimating answer using the information related to sentence-question matching. Moreover, to further improve the robustness of the MRC system, we propose a novel model named syntactic leveraging network which exploits the syntax of the question as the prior information to match the answer-contained sentence and question more precisely.

2 Methodology

Most existent MRC methods predict answers by calculating probabilities of answer spans (i, j). For an answer a starts at position i, ends at j and locates in sentence k, we denote it as $a = \{i, j, k\}$. Given a question $\mathbf{q}$ and a paragraph $\mathbf{p}$, the probability of a is computed by:

$$p(a|\mathbf{q}, \mathbf{p}) = p_s(i|\mathbf{q}, \mathbf{p}) \cdot p_e(j|\mathbf{q}, \mathbf{p}) \tag{1}$$

and:

$$\begin{aligned} p_s(i|\mathbf{q}, \mathbf{p}) &= f_s(i|\mathbf{q}, \mathbf{p}) \\ p_e(j|\mathbf{q}, \mathbf{p}) &= f_e(j|\mathbf{q}, \mathbf{p}) \end{aligned} \tag{2}$$

Proceedings of the Second Workshop on Machine Reading for Question Answering, pages 53–57
Hong Kong, China, November 4, 2019. ©2019 Association for Computational Linguistics

Here functions f_s and f_e are usually implemented by neural networks to predict the probabilities.

In most non-inferencing machine reading comprehension datasets such as SQuAD, all information needed to identify answers can be found inside one single sentence (Raiman and Miller, 2017). In such datasets, given one question and one phrase inside a sentence, overall whether this phrase is the answer depends on two conditions: 1) if the phrase itself generally matches with the question; 2) if the syntactic elements in the sentence are precisely consistent with the syntactic elements in the question.

However, the experiment results in Jia and Liang (2017) have shown that the current MRC systems pay less attention to the second condition, thus can be easily attacked by question-related sentences as adversarial samples. We attribute this deficiency to the fact that the current models solely takes the phrase-level information into account when predicting the probability $p(a|\mathbf{q}, \mathbf{p})$, but fails to exploit the sentence-level matching between the answer-contained sentence and the question, which is of importance on evaluating the second condition. Consequently, we propose a new probability function for estimating answers by considering the sentence level matching degree:

$$p^*(a|\mathbf{q}, \mathbf{p}) = p_s(i|\mathbf{q}, \mathbf{p}) \cdot p_e(j|\mathbf{q}, \mathbf{p}) \cdot p_{sent}(k|\mathbf{q}, \mathbf{p})^\alpha$$
$$p_{sent}(k|\mathbf{q}, \mathbf{p}) = f_{sent}(\mathbf{q}, s_k)$$
$$(3)$$

where s_k is the $k - th$ sentence in p. In general, p_{sent} predicts if the answer a presents in the $k - th$ sentence from the paragraph, it captures the matching between sentence and question as a leverage to improve the system robustness. α is the leveraging factor for $p_{sent}(k|\mathbf{q}, \mathbf{p})$.

2.1 Syntactic Leveraging Network

Although theoretically f_{sent} can be implemented by any model aiming at evaluating the matching between two sentences, to correctly identify real answer-contained sentences from semantically-closed adversarial sentences, it is necessary to come up with a model which is capable of precisely extracting and comparing the syntactic elements within sentences and questions. Therefore Syntactic Leveraging Network (SLN) is proposed to predict $p_{sent}(k|\mathbf{q}, \mathbf{p})$, so as to improve the robustness of MRC models. The structure of SLN is shown in Figure 1, which consists of the **SRL (Semantic role labeling) extractor**, the **CNN encoder**, the **Matching operator** performing optimal transport (Tam et al., 2019) and a classifier.

2.1.1 SRL Extractor

We utilize SRL (Gildea and Jurafsky, 2002; Khashabi et al., 2018) to analyze the syntax of sentences as prior information. In brief, it automatically produces syntactic analyses by exploiting generalizations from syntax-semantics links and assigns labels to phrases in a sentence based on their syntactic roles.

Given a question $\mathbf{q}$, the SRL extractor separates $\mathbf{q}$ into a sequence of phrases Q, specifically:

$$Q = \text{SRL}(\mathbf{q}) = [q_1, q_2, \ldots, q_n] \qquad (4)$$

with corresponding lengths $L = [l_1, l_2, \ldots, l_n]$. Here each q_i represents one syntactic element within the $\mathbf{q}$, and each can also be considered as a condition that answer-contained sentences must satisfy. The SLN model takes such sequence of n-grams as inputs to represent the question.

2.1.2 CNN Encoder

The encoder projects the syntactic elements in Q and s into real-valued vectors. Assuming CNN's filter windows range from w_{min} to w_{max} with each kernel size of k. For q_i in Q, it is only transferred into the filter window of size l_i in CNN:

$$q_i^v = CNN_{l_i}(q_i) \qquad i \in [1, n] \qquad (5)$$

This CNN is performed following Kim (2014), so that the size of each q_i^v equals to the kernel size k.

For sentence s of length L, it is first split into m^1 separate phrases $[s_1, s_2, \ldots, s_m]$, which contains all n-grams ($w_{min} \leq n < w_{max}$) in the sentence. Then, each s_i is transferred into s_j^v of size k through CNN filters, such that:

$$\mathbf{s}^v = [s_1^v, s_2^v, \ldots, s_m^v] \qquad (6)$$

where s_j^v and q_i^v represent pieces of semantics in the sentence and question.

2.1.3 Matching Operator

The matching operator is designed to evaluate if the sentence generally matches with the syntactic elements of the question. It first computes the cosine-similarity between each q_i^v and s_j^v, which gives a similarity matrix $\mathbf{S} \in \mathbb{R}^{n \times m}$. Then we implement the max pooling across the row of $\mathbf{S}$ to obtain $\mathbf{q}^{sim}$:

$$\mathbf{q}^{sim} = max_{row}(\mathbf{S}) = [q_1^{sim}, q_2^{sim}, \ldots, q_n^{sim}] \qquad (7)$$

$^1 m = (w_{max} - w_{min} + 1) * L - \sum_{i=min}^{max}(w_i - 1)$

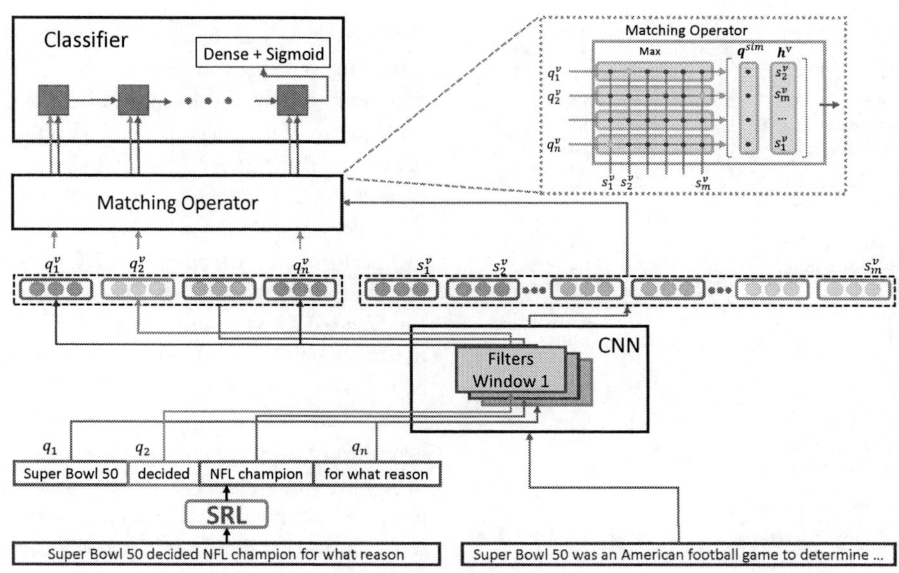

Figure 1: The Architecture of Syntactic Leveraging Network

The value of each q_i^{sim} varies from 0 to 1, which indicates the degree of similarity of each syntactic element q_i in s. Meanwhile, q_i^{sim} equals to 1 if the syntactic element q_i exist exactly in the s, which is a significant signal for the element matching.

Furthermore, given $\mathbf{S}$, for each q_i^v we compute its corresponding h_i^v. Specifically:

$$h_i^v = [s_{\arg\max_j S_{ij}}^v; q_i^{sim}]$$
$$\mathbf{h}^v = [h_1^v, h_2^v, \ldots, h_n^v] \tag{8}$$

where $s_{\arg\max_j S_{ij}}^v$ is the vector representation of the most semantically-similar phase in the sentence given q_i^v, and q_i^{sim} represents the degree of similarity. Overall, h_i^v represents the most matched phase in the sentence for one syntactic element in the question and its corresponding degree of matching. Finally, $\mathbf{h}^v$ is transferred from the Matching Operator as the output.

2.1.4 Classifier

The final classifier of SLN is designed to predict if the sentence matches with the question. It first concatenates the outputs h_i^v from the matching operator with q_i^v as the LSTM inputs, such that:

$$c_i = LSTM(c_{i-1}, [h_i; q_i]) \tag{9}$$

The last LSTM hidden states c_n is then transferred into a dense layer followed by a sigmoid activation function, and binary cross-entropy is adopted as the loss function.

3 Experiments

3.1 Experimental Setups

Data Description. We implement our method on several end-to-end MRC models trained by SQuAD dataset, and evaluate their robustness before and after considering $p_{sent}(k|\mathbf{q}, \mathbf{p})$ using the AddSent adversarial dataset (Jia and Liang, 2017). The training and test sets for MRC models are generated from SQuAD. To compute $p_{sent}(k|\mathbf{q}, \mathbf{p})$, we set those answer-contained sentences in SQuAD as positive samples. For each positive sample, three sentences inside the same paragraph which do not contain answer are randomly chosen as negative samples, so that the positive/negative ratio is 1:3. All sentence-level matching models are trained on above samples as a binary-classification task using cross-entropy loss.

Baselines. Besides of SLN, we use relevance-LSTM and Inner-Attention (Liu et al., 2016) as baselines to compute $f_{sent}(\mathbf{q}, s_k)$. Relevance-LSTM simply takes the last hidden states of the sentence and question for similarity computation, which is also used in the MRC model of Raiman and Miller (2017); while Inner-Attention is the abbreviation for the Bidirectional LSTM encoders with intra-attention, it utilizes the sentence's representation to attend words appearing in itself. BiDAF (Seo et al., 2017) and MneReader (Hu et al., 2017) are chosen as the back-end MRC models, and the results are obtained by our Keras

	SQuAD		AddSent	
	EM	F1	EM	F1
BiDAF				
original	67.7	77.4	26.4	34.2
+Relevance-LSTM	67.8	77.6	26.4	34.2
+Inner-Attention	**68.0**	**77.9**	27.4	35.4
+SLN	67.7	77.5	**28.4**	**36.4**
MneReader				
original	71.1	80.6	36.3	44.7
+Relevance-LSTM	70.8	80.1	36.1	44.3
+Inner-Attention	**71.2**	**80.7**	37.4	46.0
+SLN	70.9	80.3	**37.9**	**46.7**

Table 1: Results on the MRC datasets

	Accuracy	P@1
Random Guess	75.0%	25.0%
Relevance-LSTM	83.2%	80.1%
Inner-Attention	**87.8%**	**86.2%**
SLN	85.6%	82.7%

Table 2: Results on Sentence Matching

implementation (Chollet et al., 2015).

Parameter Settings. For SLN, we utilize the AllenNLP to perform SRL (Gardner et al., 2017), the filter windows are set from 1 to 8, with each kernel size of 128. The hidden size of LSTM is set as 128, while the size of the dense layer is set as 64. Adam (Kingma and Ba, 2014) with learning rate 0.001 is used to optimize SLN, the batch size is set as 8 and the models are trained for 50 epochs, with the early stop when the loss on validation set starts to drop. Dropout rate is set to 0.2 to prevent overfitting (Srivastava et al., 2014). We utilize the pretrained 100-dim GloVe embeddings for all the models and set it as untrainable during training (Pennington et al., 2014). The leveraging factor α are all set as 0.25 for relevance-LSTM, Inner-Attention, and SLN.

For BiDAF and MneReader as back-end MRC models, we follow the exact hyperparameter settings of (Seo et al., 2017; Hu et al., 2017).

3.2 Results of the MRC Task

Table 1 details the performances of models on MRC datasets. The results show that both the performances of BiDAF and MneReader drop significantly on the adversarial dataset, which indicates that current MRC models are not robust enough to distinguish the semantically similar candidates from answers. Concerning robustness, both Inner-Attention and SLN improve the EM and F1 of BiDAF and MneReader on AddSent dataset. This shows evidence that the robustness of MRC models can be improved by properly exploiting the

sentence-level matching information. It can be also observed that introducing the sentence-level matching into the models overall is not detrimental to the performances of models on the regular dataset, and the Inner-Attention even slightly increases the EM and F1 on regular SQuAD.

By contrary, Relevance-LSTM fails to improve the performance of current MRC models. We attribute this phenomenon to two reasons: 1) Relevance-LSTM mainly focuses on the semantics of the whole sentence to evaluate the relevance of two sentences, but current MRC models have already captured this information; 2) The word-level or phrase-level correspondence is important in identifying whether two sentences are talking about the same thing, which is also omitted in current End-to-End metric-oriented MRC models.

3.3 Analysis on Sentence Matching

The results of the sentence matching are shown in Table 2. It can be observed that Inner-Attention achieves the best performance. We attribute its high performance to the fact that its attention mechanism helps to capture the semantics clues on detecting answer-related sentences given the question. However, although the Inner-Attention outperforms SLN significantly on sentence matching, the results on Adversarial dataset show that SLN is more effective on robustness-promoting, reflected by the highest EM and F1 achieved by SLN on AddSent. Since most current MRC models have already modeled the high-level semantics in the sentences sufficiently, the attention mechanism in inner-attention might be redundant thus less effective in identifying the adversarial samples. The performance of SLN on robustness-promotion further verifies our hypothesis that introducing the syntax information as leverage on answer prediction is a feasible way to enhance the robustness of MRC systems.

4 Conclusions

In this paper, we exploit the usage of sentence-level information, especially sentence syntax as leverage, on machine reading comprehension task. The experiment results show such approach is capable of improving the robustness of MRC systems against adversarial samples, with the performance on regular datasets well maintained, although currently, the improvements on robustness are relatively moderate.

References

François Chollet et al. 2015. Keras.

Matthew Gardner, Joel Grus, Mark Neumann, Oyvind Tafjord, Pradeep Dasigi, Nelson F. Liu, Matthew E. Peters, Michael Schmitz, and Luke S. Zettlemoyer. 2017. Allennlp: A deep semantic natural language processing platform. *CoRR*, abs/1803.07640.

Daniel Gildea and Daniel Jurafsky. 2002. Automatic labeling of semantic roles. *Computational Linguistics*, 28(3):245–288.

Karl Moritz Hermann, Tomas Kocisky, Edward Grefenstette, Lasse Espeholt, Will Kay, Mustafa Suleyman, and Phil Blunsom. 2015. Teaching machines to read and comprehend. In *Advances in neural information processing systems*, pages 1693–1701.

Minghao Hu, Yuxing Peng, and Xipeng Qiu. 2017. Reinforced mnemonic reader for machine comprehension. *arXiv preprint arXiv:1705.02798*.

Robin Jia and Percy Liang. 2017. Adversarial examples for evaluating reading comprehension systems. In *Proceedings of the 2017 Conference on Empirical Methods in Natural Language Processing*, pages 2021–2031.

Daniel Khashabi, Ashish Sabharwal, Tushar Khot, and Dan Roth. 2018. Question answering as global reasoning over semantic abstractions. In *AAAI-18 AAAI Conference on Artificial Intelligence*.

Yoon Kim. 2014. Convolutional neural networks for sentence classification. In *Proceedings of the 2014 Conference on Empirical Methods in Natural Language Processing (EMNLP)*, pages 1746–1751.

Diederik P Kingma and Jimmy Ba. 2014. Adam: A method for stochastic optimization. *arXiv preprint arXiv:1412.6980*.

Yang Liu, Chengjie Sun, Lei Lin, and Xiaolong Wang. 2016. Learning natural language inference using bidirectional lstm model and inner-attention. *arXiv preprint arXiv:1605.09090*.

Tri Nguyen, Mir Rosenberg, Xia Song, Jianfeng Gao, Saurabh Tiwary, Rangan Majumder, and Li Deng. 2017. Ms marco: A human-generated machine reading comprehension dataset. *neural information processing systems*.

Jeffrey Pennington, Richard Socher, and Christopher D. Manning. 2014. Glove: Global vectors for word representation. In *Proceedings of the 2014 Conference on Empirical Methods in Natural Language Processing (EMNLP)*, pages 1532–1543.

Jonathan Raiman and John Miller. 2017. Globally normalized reader. In *Proceedings of the 2017 Conference on Empirical Methods in Natural Language Processing*, pages 1059–1069.

Pranav Rajpurkar, Jian Zhang, Konstantin Lopyrev, and Percy Liang. 2016. Squad: 100, 000+ questions for machine comprehension of text. In *Proceedings of the 2016 Conference on Empirical Methods in Natural Language Processing*, pages 2383–2392.

Matthew Richardson, Christopher JC Burges, and Erin Renshaw. 2013. Mctest: A challenge dataset for the open-domain machine comprehension of text. In *Proceedings of the 2013 Conference on Empirical Methods in Natural Language Processing*, pages 193–203.

Min Joon Seo, Aniruddha Kembhavi, Ali Farhadi, and Hannaneh Hajishirzi. 2017. Bidirectional attention flow for machine comprehension. *international conference on learning representations*.

Nitish Srivastava, Geoffrey E. Hinton, Alex Krizhevsky, Ilya Sutskever, and Ruslan Salakhutdinov. 2014. Dropout: a simple way to prevent neural networks from overfitting. *Journal of Machine Learning Research*, 15(1):1929–1958.

Derek Tam, Nicholas Monath, Ari Kobren, Aaron Traylor, Rajarshi Das, and Andrew McCallum. 2019. Optimal transport-based alignment of learned character representations for string similarity. In *Proceedings of the 57th Annual Meeting of the Association for Computational Linguistics*, pages 5907–5917.

Wenhui Wang, Nan Yang, Furu Wei, Baobao Chang, and Ming Zhou. 2017. Gated self-matching networks for reading comprehension and question answering. In *Proceedings of the 55th Annual Meeting of the Association for Computational Linguistics (Volume 1: Long Papers)*, pages 189–198. Association for Computational Linguistics.

Adams Wei Yu, David Dohan, Minh-Thang Luong, Rui Zhao, Kai Chen, Mohammad Norouzi, and Quoc V Le. 2018. Qanet: Combining local convolution with global self-attention for reading comprehension. *arXiv preprint arXiv:1804.09541*.

Reasoning Over Paragraph Effects in Situations

Kevin Lin, Oyvind Tafjord, Peter Clark, and **Matt Gardner**
Allen Institute for Artificial Intelligence
`{kevinl,oyvindt,peterc,mattg}@allenai.org`

Abstract

A key component of successfully reading a passage of text is the ability to apply knowledge gained from the passage to a new situation. In order to facilitate progress on this kind of reading, we present **ROPES**, a challenging benchmark for reading comprehension targeting **R**easoning **O**ver **P**aragraph **E**ffects in **S**ituations. We target expository language describing causes and effects (e.g., "animal pollinators increase efficiency of fertilization in flowers"), as they have clear implications for new situations. A system is presented a background passage containing at least one of these relations, a novel situation that uses this background, and questions that require reasoning about effects of the relationships in the background passage in the context of the situation. We collect background passages from science textbooks and Wikipedia that contain such phenomena, and ask crowd workers to author situations, questions, and answers, resulting in a 14,322 question dataset. We analyze the challenges of this task and evaluate the performance of state-of-the-art reading comprehension models. The best model performs only slightly better than randomly guessing an answer of the correct type, at 61.6% F1, well below the human performance of 89.0%.

1 Introduction

Comprehending a passage of text requires being able to understand the implications of the passage on other text that is read. For example, after reading a background passage about how animal pollinators increase the efficiency of fertilization in flowers, a human can easily deduce that given two types of flowers, one that attracts animal pollinators and one that does not, the former is likely to have a higher efficiency in fertilization (Figure 1). This kind of reasoning however, is still challenging for state-of-the-art reading comprehension models.

Recent work in reading comprehension has seen impressive results, with models reaching human performance on well-established datasets (Devlin et al., 2019; Wang et al., 2017; Chen et al., 2016), but so far has mostly focused on extracting local predicate-argument structure, without the need to apply what was read to outside context.

We introduce **ROPES**[1], a reading comprehension challenge that focuses on understanding causes and effects in an expository paragraph, requiring systems to apply this understanding to

---

Background: Scientists think that the earliest flowers attracted insects and other animals, which spread pollen from flower to flower. This greatly increased the efficiency of fertilization over wind-spread pollen, which might or might not actually land on another flower. To take better advantage of this animal labor, plants evolved traits such as brightly colored petals to attract pollinators. In exchange for pollination, flowers gave the pollinators nectar.

Situation: Last week, John visited the national park near his city. He saw many flowers. His guide explained him that there are two categories of flowers, category A and category B. Category A flowers spread pollen via wind, and category B flowers spread pollen via animals.

Question: Would category B flower have more or less efficient fertilization than category A flower?
Answer: more

Question: Would category A flower have more or less efficient fertilization than category B flower?
Answer: less

Question: Which category of flowers would be more likely to have **brightly colored petals**?
Answer: Category B

Question: Which category of flowers would be less likely to have **brightly colored petals**?
Answer: Category A

Figure 1: Example questions in **ROPES**.

---

[1] https://allennlp.org/ropes

Proceedings of the Second Workshop on Machine Reading for Question Answering, pages 58–62
Hong Kong, China, November 4, 2019. ©2019 Association for Computational Linguistics

novel situations. If a new situation describes an occurrence of the cause, then the system should be able to reason over the effects if it has properly understood the background passage.

We constructed **ROPES** by first collecting background passages from science textbooks and Wikipedia articles that describe causal relationships. We showed these paragraphs to crowd workers and asked them to write situations that involve the relationships found in the background passage, and questions that connect the situation and the background using the causal relationships. The answers are spans from either the situation or the question. The dataset consists of 14,322 questions from various domains, mostly in science and economics.

In analyzing the data, we find (1) that there are a variety of cause / effect relationship types described; (2) that there is a wide range of difficulties in matching the descriptions of these phenomena between the background, situation, and question; and (3) that there are several distinct kinds of reasoning over causes and effects that appear.

To establish baseline performance on this dataset, we use a reading comprehension model based on RoBERTa (Liu et al., 2019), reaching an accuracy of 61.6% F_1. Most questions are designed to have two sensible answer choices (eg. "more" vs. "less"), so this performance is little better than randomly picking one of the choices. Expert humans achieved an average of 89.0% F_1 on a random sample.

2 Related Work

Reading comprehension There are many reading comprehension datasets (Richardson et al., 2013; Rajpurkar et al., 2016; Kwiatkowski et al., 2019; Dua et al., 2019), the majority of which principally require understanding local predicate-argument structure in a passage of text. The success of recent models suggests that machines are becoming capable of this level of understanding. **ROPES** challenges reading comprehension models to handle more difficult phenomena: understanding the *implications* of a passage of text. **ROPES** is also particularly related to datasets focusing on "multi-hop reasoning" (Yang et al., 2018; Khashabi et al., 2018), as by construction answering questions in **ROPES** requires connecting information from multiple parts of a given passage.

The most closely related datasets to **ROPES** are

ShARC (Saeidi et al., 2018), OpenBookQA (Mihaylov et al., 2018), and QuaRel (Tafjord et al., 2019). ShARC shares the same goal of understanding causes and effects (in terms of specified rules), but frames it as a dialogue where the system has to also generate questions to gain complete information. OpenBookQA, similar to **ROPES**, requires reading scientific facts, but it is focused on a *retrieval* problem where a system must find the right fact for a question (and some additional common sense fact), whereas **ROPES** targets *reading* a given, complex passage of text, with no retrieval involved. QuaRel is also focused on reasoning about situational effects in a question-answering setting, but the "causes" are all pre-specified, not read from a background passage, so the setting is limited.

Recognizing textual entailment The application of causes and effects to new situations has a strong connection to notions of entailment— **ROPES** tries to get systems to understand what is entailed by an expository paragraph. The setup is fundamentally different, however: instead of giving systems pairs of sentences to classify as entailed or not, as in the traditional formulation (Dagan et al., 2006; Bowman et al., 2015, *inter alia*), we give systems questions whose answers require understanding the entailment.

3 Data Collection

Background passages: We automatically scraped passages from science textbooks[2] and Wikipedia that contained causal connectives eg. "causes," "leads to," and keywords that signal qualitative relations, e.g. "increases," "decreases."[3]. We then manually filtered out the passages that do not have at least one relation. The passages can be categorized into physical science (49%), life science (45%), economics (5%) and other (1%). In total, we collected over 1,000 background passages.

Crowdsourcing questions We used Amazon Mechanical Turk (AMT) to generate the situations, questions, and answers. The AMT workers were given background passages and asked to write situations that involved the relation(s) in the background passage. The AMT workers then authored questions about the situation that required both the

---

[2]We used life science and physical science concepts from www.ck12.org, and biology, chemistry, physics, earth science, anatomy and physiology textbooks from openstax.org

[3]We scraped Wikipedia online in March and April 2019

Statistic	Train	Dev	Test
# of annotators	7	2	2
# of situations	1411	203	300
# of questions	10924	1688	1710
avg. background length	121.6	90.7	123.1
avg. situation length	49.1	63.4	55.6
avg. question length	10.9	12.4	10.6
avg. answer length	1.3	1.4	1.4
background vocabulary size	8616	2008	3988
situation vocabulary size	6949	1077	2736
question vocabulary size	1457	1411	1885

Table 1: Key statistics of **ROPES**. In total there were 588 background passages selected by the workers.

Type	Background
C (70%)	Scientists think that the earliest flowers attracted insects and other animals, which spread pollen from flower to flower. This greatly increased the efficiency of fertilization over wind-spread pollen ...
Q (4%)	... As **decibel levels get higher**, **sound waves have greater intensity** and sounds **are louder**. ...
C&Q (26%)	... Predators can be keystone species . These are species that can have a large effect on the balance of organisms in an ecosystem. For example, if all of the wolves are removed from a population, then the population of deer or rabbits may increase...

Table 2: Types of relations in the background passages. **C** refers to causal relations and **Q** refers to qualitative relations.

background and the situation to answer. In each human intelligence task (HIT), AMT workers are given 5 background passages to select from and are asked to create a total of 10 questions. To mitigate the potential for easy lexical shortcuts in the dataset, the workers were encouraged via instructions to write questions in *minimal pairs*, where a very small change in the question results in a different answer. Two examples of these pairs are given in Figure 1: switching "more" to "less" results in the opposite flower being the correct answer to the question.

4 Dataset Analysis

We qualitatively and quantitatively analyze the phenomena that occur in **ROPES**. Table 1 shows the key statistics of the dataset. We randomly sample 100 questions and analyze the type of relation in the background, grounding in the situation, and reasoning required to answer the question.

Type	Background	Situation
Explicit (67%)	As decibel levels get higher, sound waves have greater intensity and sounds are louder.	...First, he went to stage one, where the music was playing in high decibel.
Common sense (13%)	... if we want to convert a substance from a gas to a liquid or from a liquid to a solid, we remove energy from the system	... She remembered they would be needing ice so she grabbed and empty ice tray and filled it...
Lexical gap (20%)	... Continued exercise is necessary to maintain bigger, stronger muscles...	... Mathew goes to the gym ... does very intensive workouts.

Table 3: Types of grounding found in **ROPES**.

Background passages We manually annotate whether the relation in the background passage being asked about is causal (a clear cause and effect in the background), qualitative (e.g., as X increases, Y decreases), or both. Table 2 shows the breakdown of the kinds of relations in the dataset.

Grounding To successfully apply the relation in the background to a situation, the system needs to be able to ground the relation to parts of the situation. To do this, the model has to either find an *explicit* mention of the cause/effect from the background and associate it with some property, use a *common sense fact*, or overcome a large *lexical gap* to connect them. Table 3 shows examples and breakdown of these three phenomena.

Question reasoning Table 4 shows the breakdown and examples of the main types of questions by the types of reasoning required to answer them. In an *effect comparison*, two entities are each associated with an occurrence or absence of the cause described in the background and the question asks to compare the effects on the two entities. Similarly, in a *cause comparison*, two entities are each associated with an occurrence or absence of the effect described in the background and the question compares the causes of the occurrence or absence. In an *effect prediction*, the question asks to directly predict the effect on an occurrence of the cause on an entity in the situation. Finally, in *cause prediction*, the question asks to predict the cause of an occurrence of the effect on an entity in the situation. The majority of the examples are effect or cause comparison questions; these are challenging, as they require the model to ground two occurrences of causes or effects.

Reasoning	Background	Situation	Question	Answer
Effect comparison (71%)	... gas atoms change to ions that can carry an electric current. The current causes the Geiger counter to click. The faster the clicks occur, the higher the level of radiation.	... Location A had very high radiation; location B had low radiation	Would location A have faster or slower clicks than location B?	faster
Effect prediction (5%)	... Continued exercise is necessary to maintain bigger, stronger muscles. ...	... Mathew goes to the gym 5 times a week and does very intensive workouts. Damen on the other hand does not go to the gym at all and lives a mostly sedentary lifestyle.	Given Mathew suffers an injury while working out and cannot go to the gym for 3 months, will Mathews strength increase or decrease?	decrease
Cause comparison (15%)	... This carbon dioxide is then absorbed by the oceans, which lowers the pH of the water...	The biologists found out that the Indian Ocean had a lower water pH than it did a decade ago, and it became acidic. The water in the Arctic ocean still had a neutral to basic pH.	Which ocean has a lower content of carbon dioxide in its waters?	Arctic
Cause prediction (1%)	... Conversely, if we want to convert a substance from a gas to a liquid or from a liquid to a solid, we remove energy from the system and decrease the temperature. ...	... she grabbed and empty ice tray and filled it. As she walked over to the freezer ... When she checked the tray later that day the ice was ready.	Did the freezer add or remove energy from the water?	remove
Other (8%)	... Charging an object by touching it with another charged object is called charging by conduction. ... induction allows a change in charge without actually touching the charged and uncharged objects to each other.	... In case A he used conduction, and in case B he used induction. In both cases he used same two objects. Finally, John tried to charge his phone remotely. He called this test as case C.	Which experiment would be less appropriate for case C, case A or case B?	case A

Table 4: Example questions and answers from **ROPES**, showing the relevant parts of the associated passage and the reasoning required to answer the question. In the last example, the situation grounds the desired outcome and asks which of two cases would achieve the desired outcome.

Dataset split In initial experiments, we found splitting the dataset based on the situations resulted in high scores due to annotator bias from prolific workers generating many examples (Geva et al., 2019). We follow their proposal and separate training set annotators from test set annotators, and find that models have difficulty generalizing to new workers.

5 Baseline performance

We use the RoBERTa question answering model proposed by Liu et al. (2019) as our baseline and concatenate the background and situation to form the passage, following their setup for SQuAD. To estimate the presence of annotation artifacts in our dataset (and as a potentially interesting future task where background reading is done up front), we also run the baseline without the background passage. Table 5 presents the results for the baselines,

	Development		Test	
	EM	F1	EM	F1
RoBERTa $_{BASE}$	38.0	53.5	35.8	45.5
- background	40.7	59.3	33.7	46.1
RoBERTa $_{LARGE}$	59.7	70.2	55.4	61.1
- background	48.7	55.2	53.6	60.4
+ RACE	60.1	73.5	55.5	61.6
Human	-	-	82.7	89.0

Table 5: Performance of baselines and human performance on the dev and test set.

which are significantly lower than human performance. We also experiment with first fine-tuning on RACE (Lai et al., 2017) before fine-tuning on **ROPES**.

Human performance is estimated by expert human annotation on 400 random questions with the same metrics as the baselines. None of the ques-

61

tions share the sample background or situation to ensure that the humans do not have an unfair advantage over the model by using knowledge of how the dataset is constructed, e.g. the fact that pairs of questions like in Table 1 will have opposite answers.

6 Conclusion

We present **ROPES**, a new reading comprehension benchmark containing 14,322 questions, which aims to test the ability of systems to apply knowledge from reading text in a new setting. We hope that **ROPES** will aide efforts in tying language and reasoning together for more comprehensive understanding of text.

7 Acknowledgements

We thank the anonymous reviewers for their feedback. We also thank Dheeru Dua and Nelson Liu for their assistance with the crowdsourcing setup, and Kaj Bostrom for the human evaluation. We are grateful for discussion with other AllenNLP and Aristo team members and the infrastructure provided by the Beaker team. Computations on beaker.org were supported in part by credits from Google Cloud.

References

Samuel R. Bowman, Gabor Angeli, Christopher Potts, and Christopher D. Manning. 2015. A large annotated corpus for learning natural language inference. In *EMNLP*.

Danqi Chen, Jason Bolton, and Christopher D Manning. 2016. A thorough examination of the cnn/daily mail reading comprehension task. *arXiv preprint arXiv:1606.02858*.

Ido Dagan, Oren Glickman, and Bernardo Magnini. 2006. The pascal recognising textual entailment challenge. *Lecture Notes in Computer Science*, pages 177–190.

Jacob Devlin, Ming-Wei Chang, Kenton Lee, and Kristina Toutanova. 2019. Bert: Pre-training of deep bidirectional transformers for language understanding. In *NAACL*.

Dheeru Dua, Yizhong Wang, Pradeep Dasigi, Gabriel Stanovsky, Sameer Singh, and Matt Gardner. 2019. DROP: A reading comprehension benchmark requiring discrete reasoning over paragraphs. In *NAACL*.

Mor Geva, Yoav Goldberg, and Jonathan Berant. 2019. Are we modeling the task or the annotator? an investigation of annotator bias in natural language understanding datasets. *EMNLP*.

Daniel Khashabi, Snigdha Chaturvedi, Michael A. Roth, Shyam Upadhyay, and Dan Roth. 2018. Looking beyond the surface: A challenge set for reading comprehension over multiple sentences. In *NAACL-HLT*.

Tom Kwiatkowski, Jennimaria Palomaki, Olivia Redfield, Michael Collins, Ankur Parikh, Chris Alberti, Danielle Epstein, Illia Polosukhin, Jacob Devlin, Kenton Lee, Kristina Toutanova, Llion Jones, Matthew Kelcey, Ming-Wei Chang, Andrew M. Dai, Jakob Uszkoreit, Quoc Le, and Slav Petrov. 2019. Natural questions: a benchmark for question answering research. In *TACL*.

Guokun Lai, Qizhe Xie, Hanxiao Liu, Yiming Yang, and Eduard Hovy. 2017. Race: Large-scale reading comprehension dataset from examinations. *arXiv preprint arXiv:1704.04683*.

Yinhan Liu, Myle Ott, Naman Goyal, Jingfei Du, Mandar Joshi, Danqi Chen, Omer Levy, Mike Lewis, Luke Zettlemoyer, and Veselin Stoyanov. 2019. Roberta: A robustly optimized bert pretraining approach. *arXiv preprint arXiv:1907.11692*.

Todor Mihaylov, Peter Clark, Tushar Khot, and Ashish Sabharwal. 2018. Can a suit of armor conduct electricity? a new dataset for open book question answering. In *Proceedings of the 2018 Conference on Empirical Methods in Natural Language Processing*, pages 2381–2391.

Pranav Rajpurkar, Jian Zhang, Konstantin Lopyrev, and Percy Liang. 2016. Squad: 100,000+ questions for machine comprehension of text. In *EMNLP*.

Matthew Richardson, Christopher J. C. Burges, and Erin Renshaw. 2013. Mctest: A challenge dataset for the open-domain machine comprehension of text. In *EMNLP*.

Marzieh Saeidi, Max Bartolo, Patrick Lewis, Sameer Singh, Tim Rocktäschel, Mike Sheldon, Guillaume Bouchard, and Sebastian Riedel. 2018. Interpretation of natural language rules in conversational machine reading. *arXiv preprint arXiv:1809.01494*.

Oyvind Tafjord, Peter Clark, Matt Gardner, Wen-tau Yih, and Ashish Sabharwal. 2019. Quarel: A dataset and models for answering questions about qualitative relationships. In *AAAI*.

Wenhui Wang, Nan Yang, Furu Wei, Baobao Chang, and Ming Zhou. 2017. Gated self-matching networks for reading comprehension and question answering. In *Proceedings of the 55th Annual Meeting of the Association for Computational Linguistics (Volume 1: Long Papers)*, pages 189–198.

Zhilin Yang, Peng Qi, Saizheng Zhang, Yoshua Bengio, William W. Cohen, Ruslan R. Salakhutdinov, and Christopher D. Manning. 2018. Hotpotqa: A dataset for diverse, explainable multi-hop question answering. In *EMNLP*.

Towards Answer-unaware Conversational Question Generation

Mao Nakanishi   **Tetsunori Kobayashi**   **Yoshihiko Hayashi**
School of Science and Engineering, Waseda University
Waseda-machi 27, Shinjuku, Tokyo 1690042, Japan

`nakanishi@pcl.cs.waseda.ac.jp`   `koba@waseda.jp`   `yshk.hayashi@aoni.waseda.jp`

Abstract

Conversational question generation is a novel area of NLP research which has a range of potential applications. This paper is first to present a framework for conversational question generation that is *unaware* of the corresponding answers. To properly generate a question coherent to the grounding text and the current conversation history, the proposed framework first locates the focus of a question in the text passage, and then identifies the question pattern that leads the sequential generation of the words in a question. The experiments using the CoQA dataset demonstrate that the quality of generated questions greatly improves if the question foci and the question patterns are correctly identified. In addition, it was shown that the question foci, even estimated with a reasonable accuracy, could contribute to the quality improvement. These results established that our research direction may be promising, but at the same time revealed that the identification of question patterns is a challenging issue, and it has to be largely refined to achieve a better quality in the end-to-end automatic question generation.

1   Introduction

Research on question generation has attracted considerable attention from NLP community, and several neural network-based methods have been proposed (Pan et al., 2019). Many of these methods are developed for text-based question answering (QA) with stand-alone interactions. That is, QA pairs is basically independent each other. Besides, they are generally *answer-aware*: a question generation system presumes that the corresponding answer to a to-be-generated question is being supplied.

One of the recently emerging directions in QA is conversational QA, in which a series of interrelated QA turns is performed. Within this trend,

Gao et al. (2019) recently proposed a framework for conversational question generation. The proposed work is reported effective, but still answer-aware, which may prevent the proposed framework to be applied to practical applications such as chatbots and dialogue systems: answers are usually not provided in the usage scenarios.

Being motivated by this situation, the present work is first to propose a framework for *answer-unaware* conversation question generation, by assuming that questions coherent to the target text and the current conversation history can be generated, provided the question focus and the question type are properly identified. To confirm this assumption, we have developed a deep neural architecture for answer-unaware question generation, which first tries to locate the focus of a question in the grounding text passage, and then identify the question type that leads the sequential generation of the words in a question.

The experiments using the CoQA dataset (Reddy et al., 2019) demonstrate that the quality of generated questions greatly improves if the question foci and the question patterns are correctly identified. Besides, it was shown that the question foci can be estimated with a certain degree of accuracy, and the quality of the generated questions referring the question foci are superior to that generated from the whole text passage, suggesting that the proper narrowing down of the source of question is essential. These results established that our research direction may be promising. However, it was also proved that it difficult to correctly estimate the question pattern, and the wrongly-identified question patterns severely affect the quality of generated questions. This result may highlight the necessity of incorporating additional clues, such as entities in the text, and developing a refined model to better consume the enriched input information.

Proceedings of the Second Workshop on Machine Reading for Question Answering, pages 63–71
Hong Kong, China, November 4, 2019. ©2019 Association for Computational Linguistics

2 Related Work

Given a range of application areas, such as intelligent tutoring systems, dialogue systems and question answering systems, question generation has attracted larger research attention in NLP community. The major trend in question generation has shifted from template-based generation systems to neural network-based end-to-end methods (Pan et al., 2019), which generally employs encoder-decoder models. Succeeding the pioneering work (Du et al., 2017), several proposals (Zhou et al., 2017; Du and Cardie, 2018; Yuan et al., 2017; Tang et al., 2017) have been made to chiefly improve the quality of generated questions. These methods all deal with text-based question answering, which relies on datasets, such as SQuAD (Rajpurkar et al., 2018), which was originally developed for the machine reading for question answering (MRQA) research. In the context of the present work, however, it should be noted that the majority of these methods are *answer-aware*, which means that a generation system requires the corresponding answer to a to-be-generated question is supplied.

Recently, research interests in MRQA have been extended to conversational-style QA, in which a series of inter-related QA turns is performed in the expectation that it would simulate more natural interactions involving a human. Datasets such as CoQA (Reddy et al., 2019) and QuAC (Choi et al., 2018) have been developed to facilitate the relevant research efforts (Yatskar, 2019). Given this trend, Gao et al. (2019) was first to propose a framework for conversational question generation (CQG). Their proposal has initiated the dedicated field of CQG by particularly considering coreferences and conversion flows, both may be essential elements in conversational QA. Their proposal, however, remained answer-aware, which may somehow restrict its application areas, in particular such as dialogue systems. Thus **answer-unaware conversational question generation** first to offered by the present work would be a natural research direction to go.

3 Framework for Conversational Question Generation

3.1 Overview

Figure 1 overviews our proposed framework for CQG, where the following assumptions are made.

- A question coherent to the current conversational context can be generated primarily by knowing the current focus of interrogation, even without knowing the pre-defined corresponding answer. We herein expect that a **question focus** can be properly estimated as a textual region in the given passage by exploiting **conversation history**.

- The quality of a question can be further improved, if the type of a question is identified ahead of time. We consider that the **question pattern** that linguistically realizes a question type could be identified by using the estimated question focus.

3.2 Problem Formulation

The generation of a conversational question $\bar{Q}_i$ at the current (i-th) QA turn is formulated as follows.

$$\bar{Q}_i = \arg\max_{Q_i} Prob(Q_i | P, H_i) \qquad (1)$$

Here, P denotes the whole text passage provided for the QA session, and H_i dictates the current conversation history, which can be formulated as $H_i = ((Q_1, A_1), \cdots , (Q_{i-1}, A_{i-1}))$. Notice that the answer A_i corresponding to the to-be-generated question $\bar{Q}_i$ is *not* included in our problem formulation.

Question Focus Estimation: We assume that a question focus F_i can be located at a textual region in the grounding text passage P, meaning that the answer of a to-be-generated question can be found in this textual region. Given the conversation history H_i, the estimation of a question focus is formulated as a classification problem which identifies the most probable text chunk $\bar{P}_i$ from the N_c-divided passages $P = (P_1, \cdots , P_{N_C})$.

Question Pattern Identification: We expect by additionally knowing the type of a question, such as *When*, *Who*, *Where*, and *Did*, the quality of a generated question may further improve. As detailed in the next section, we cast the identification of a question type as the classification from an inventory of question patterns, or as the actual generation of a question-leading linguistic expression. As discussed in the later section, we experimentally compare these two methods. We denote a question pattern T_i as an element defined in the set of question patterns $T_Q = \{T_1, \cdots , T_{N_T}\}$. T_Q has been mined, in the present work, from the target dataset.

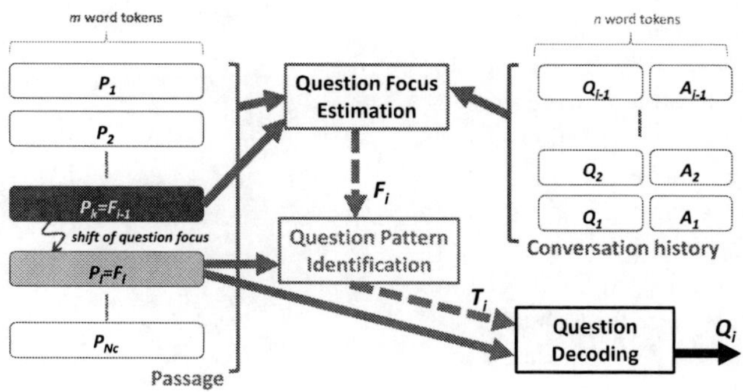

Figure 1: Overview of the proposed framework.

Question Decoding: The conversational question generation as formulated in Eq.1 can be further conditioned by incorporating the estimated question focus F_i, and the identified question pattern T_i. We employ a conventional encoder-decoder model for this process.

$$\bar{Q}_i = \arg\max_{Q_i} Prob(Q_i|P, H_i, F_i, T_i) \qquad (2)$$

4 Model Description

This section details the components in the proposed framework, which are (1) Question focus estimation, (2) Question pattern identification, and (3) Question decoding.

Let us assume that the current time step is $t = i$ in the following descriptions. The input to the entire question generation system is the target text passage P and the current conversation history H_i.

The passage P is segmented into a sequence of N_c chunks $(P_1, \cdots, P_{N_C})$, where the c-th chunk $P_c = (w_1^{p_c}, \cdots, w_m^{p_c})$ is a sequence of m word tokens.

Although the conversation history H_i at the i-th QA turn is conceptually defined as $H_i = ((Q_1, A_1), \cdots, (Q_{i-1}, A_{i-1}))$, we implement it as the sequence of words taken from the question and the answer, separated by a separator: $H_i = (\cdots, w_{q_1}^t \cdots w_{q_{|Q|}}^t, \langle sep \rangle, w_{a_1}^t, \cdots, w_{a_{|A|}}^t, \cdots)$. We henceforth abbreviated it as $H_i = (w_1^{H_i} \cdots w_n^{H_i})$.

The question focus F_i for the i-th QA turn is estimated as one of the chunks. It is hence denoted as a sequence of m-word tokens: $F_i = (w_1^F, \cdots, w_m^F)$.

The question pattern T_i that is identified for a to-be-generated question is chosen from the pre-

defined set T_Q of linguistic expressions, or generated on-the-fly. It is formulated as a sequence of l word tokens: $T_i = (w_1^{T_i}, \cdots, w_l^{T_i})$.

4.1 Question Focus Estimation

Figure 2 models the deep architecture for estimating a question focus, which consists of embedding layer, contextual layers, attention layer, modeling layer, and output layer.

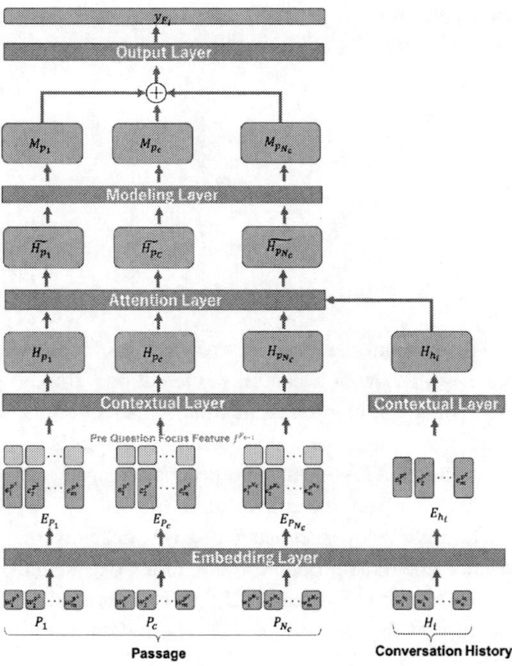

Figure 2: Question focus estimation model.

The embedding layer maps each chunk P_c in the passage to a vector sequence $\boldsymbol{E}^{p_c} = (e_1^{p_c} \cdots e_m^{p_c}) \in \mathbb{R}^{m \times d}$. Here $e_i^{p_c}$ denotes the d-

dimensional embedding vector for the i-th word token in E^{p_c}. We employ GloVe (Pennington et al., 2014) vectors ($d = 300$) as word embeddings. Similarly we map a conversation history H_i to $\boldsymbol{E}^{H_i} = (\boldsymbol{e}_1^{H_i} \cdots \boldsymbol{e}_n^{H_i}) \in \mathbb{R}^{n \times d}$.

Two contextual layers, one is for passage chunks and the other is for conversation history, are both implemented by using Bi-GRU. The input to the passage context layer for a chunk P_c is the concatenation of $\boldsymbol{E}^{p_c}$ and $\boldsymbol{f}_{i-1}^{QF}$. The latter vector $\boldsymbol{f}_{i-1}^{QF}$ carries important information in the sense that it specifies the question focus at the previous time step ($t = i - 1$). The elements of $\boldsymbol{f}_{i-1}^{QF}$ are all one if $F_{i-1} = P_c$, otherwise they are all zero. The representation of the current conversation history $\boldsymbol{E}^{H_i}$ is also fed into the contextual layer. The resulting contextual representations $\boldsymbol{H}^{P_c} \in \mathbb{R}^{m \times 2v}$ and $\boldsymbol{H}^{H_i} \in \mathbb{R}^{n \times 2v}$ are fed into the attention layer. Here v represents the dimensionality of the hidden layers: $v = 128$ in our experiments.

The attention layer captures the relative importance of each chunk seeing from the current conversation history as an attentional weight, and hence yields history-augmented contextual representations for the chunks, as formulated below. Here, W_e and W_h are trainable parameters.

$$e_{t,j}^f = tanh(\boldsymbol{W}_e^f [h_t^{c_i}; h_j^{H_i}]) \tag{3}$$

$$\alpha_{t,j}^f = \frac{exp(e_{t,j}^f)}{\sum_{k=1}^n exp(e_{t,k}^f)} \tag{4}$$

$$c_t^f = \sum_j \alpha_{t,j}^f h_j^{c_i} \tag{5}$$

$$\tilde{h}_t^{c_i} = tanh(\boldsymbol{W}_h^f [c_t^f; h_t^{c_i}]) \tag{6}$$

The modeling layer is also realized by employing Bi-GRU, which captures interactions among the history-augmented contextual representations. That is, we expect that the resulting representation for a chunk $\boldsymbol{M}^{c_i} \in \mathbb{R}^{m \times 2v}$ incorporates relevant information from the conversation history.

The output layer, consists of two linear layers, predicts the most probable chunk index y_{F_i}, which means that the designated chunk is estimated as the current question focus F_i. The inputs to this layer is $[\boldsymbol{M}^{c_1}; \boldsymbol{M}^{c_2}, \cdots, ; \boldsymbol{M}^{c_N}] \in \mathbb{R}^{(N_c m) \times 2v}$, which is the concatenation of the chunk representations yielded by the modeling layer.

4.2 Question Pattern Identification

The proper identification of a question pattern help improve the quality of a generated question. We

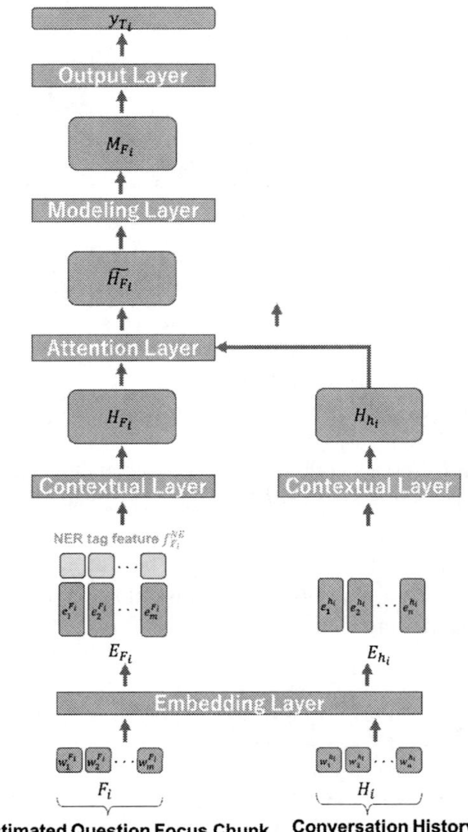

Figure 3: Question pattern classification model.

approach this task by either of classification or generation, and experimentally compare them.

4.2.1 Question Pattern Classification

As displayed in Figure 3, the whole structure of the classification model is similar to that of the question focus estimation model. This model however only considers the chunk that is estimated as the current question focus. More specifically, the question focus is represented as $[\boldsymbol{E}^{F_i}; \boldsymbol{f}_{F_i}^{NE}]$. That is, the original representation for question focus $\boldsymbol{E}^{F_i}$ is enhanced by the named-entity (NE) tag features $\boldsymbol{f}_{F_i}^{NE} \in \mathbb{R}^{m \times 18}$. We assign to each word token in F_i an NE tag with the BIO format. We use spaCy[1] as the NE recogniizer, which maintains 18 NE types[2].

The history-augmented representation of the question focus $\bar{H}^F$, yielded by the attention and

---

[1] https://spacy.io
[2] https://spacy.io/api/annotation# named-entities.

vant parts in the question focus chunk.

$$s_t = GRU(w_{t-1}^{P_i}, c_{t-1}, s_{t-1}) \qquad (7)$$

$$e_{t,j}^q = tanh(\boldsymbol{W}_e^q s_{t-1} + \boldsymbol{U}_e^q h_{t-1}^E) \qquad (8)$$

$$\alpha_{t,j}^q = \frac{exp(e_{t,j}^q)}{\sum_{k=1}^n exp(e_{t,k}^q)} \qquad (9)$$

$$c_t^q = \sum_j \alpha_{t,j}^q h_t^E \qquad (10)$$

$$\tilde{h}_t^q = tanh(W_h^q[c_t^q; h_t^E]) \qquad (11)$$

$$p(w_t^{P_i}|w_{<t}^{P_i}, h_i) = softmax(\boldsymbol{W}_d \tilde{h}_t^q) \qquad (12)$$

4.3 Question Decoding

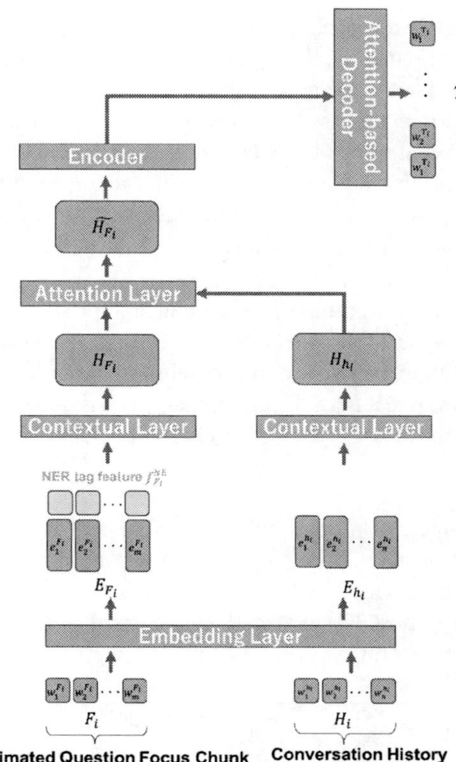

Figure 4: Question pattern generation model.

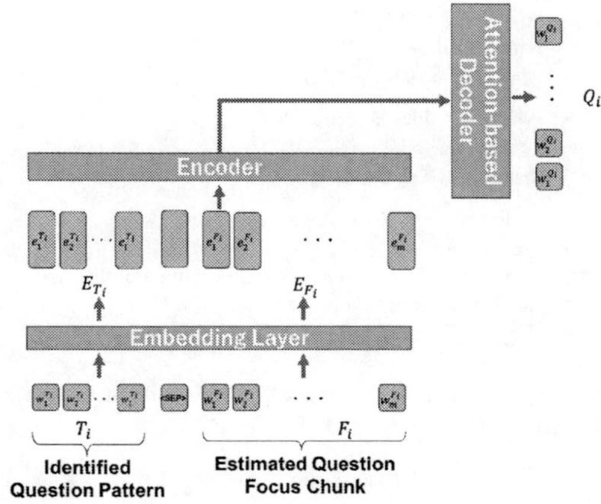

Figure 5: Question decoding model.

the modeling layers, is then fed into the output layer, and the index of the most probable question pattern $y_{T_i} \in \mathbb{R}^{N_P}$ is finally obtained, where N_P represents the number of pre-defined question patterns.

4.2.2 Question Pattern Generation

As illustrated in Figure 4, the generation model only differs from the classification model at the output layer: instead of the classification layer, this model naturally employs a conventional encoder-decoder layers for generating a question pattern.

The encoder takes the question focus $\tilde{H}^F$ as the input, and encodes its word token sequence by employing Bi-GRU. The decoder generates the most probable question pattern P_i as a sequence of word tokens $(w_1^{P_i}...w_l^{P_i})$, while attending to rele-

The question decoding model also employs a conventional encoder-decoder model with attention. Its behavior depends on whether a predicted/generated question pattern is employed. That is, when a question pattern is not used, the input to the encoder is only the representations for a question focus F_i. On the other hand, in the latter case, the input to the encoder is the concatenation of the representation for the predicted/generated question pattern $T_i = (w_1^{T_i}, \cdots, w_l^{T_i})$ and the question focus chunk $F_i = (w_1^{F_i}, \cdots, w_m^{F_i})$, delimited by the separator $\langle sep \rangle$.

5 Experiments

5.1 Dataset

The present work relies on the CoQA dataset (Reddy et al., 2019) in the evaluation as well as the model training, which enables us to compare our results with the most relevant related

The Virginia governor's race, billed as the marquee battle of an otherwise anticlimactic 2013 election cycle, is shaping up to be a foregone conclusion. Democrat Terry McAuliffe, the longtime political fixer and moneyman, hasn't trailed in a poll since May. Barring a political miracle, Republican Ken Cuccinelli will be delivering a concession speech on Tuesday evening in Richmond. In recent ...

Q_1: What are the candidates **running** for?
A_1: Governor
R_1: The Virginia governor's race

Q_2: **Where?**
A_2: Virginia
R_2: The Virginia governor's race

Q_3: Who is the democratic candidate?
A_3: **Terry McAuliffe**
R_3: Democrat Terry McAuliffe

Q_4: Who is **his** opponent?
A_4: **Ken Cuccinelli**
R_4 Republican Ken Cuccinelli

Q_5: What party does **he** belong to?
A_5: Republican
R_5: Republican Ken Cuccinelli

Q_6: Which of **them** is winning?
A_6: Terry McAuliffe
R_6: Democrat Terry McAuliffe, the longtime political fixer and moneyman, hasn't trailed in a poll since May

Figure 6: Example of a QA conversation in CoQA; adopted from (Reddy et al., 2019).

work (Gao et al., 2019). The dataset collects 8k text-grounded QA conversations, where 127k QA pairs are maintained.

An example conversation is given in Figure 6, where an answers is given in free-text, but its corresponding textual region in the text passage is explicitly annotated as *R: rationale*. We identify each of the ground-truth question foci as a region in the passage that overlaps with a rationale given in the dataset.

As exemplified in this example, this dataset exhibits several conversational phenomena, including ellipsis, co-reference by pronouns. Naturally, a question is posed by reflecting the current conversational situation. As pointed out by (Reddy et al., 2019; Yatskar, 2019), the question foci gradually shift through regions in the text passage as the QA session proceeds.

5.2 Experimental Settings

Passage chunks: The target text passage of a QA session is divided into N_c chunks of same number of sentences. Our framework identifies the most probable chunk as a question focus, implying that the division of a passage would affect the identification of a question focus, and hence the final results also. Thus we compare the experimental results while altering N_c among 5 and 10. Note that the average length of a rationale in the CoQA dataset is 10.3 words, and only a small portion of them ($< 5\%$) exceed a sentence boundary.

Question patterns: We defined a question pattern set by collecting N^t frequent sentence-leading n-grams from the training portion of the CoQA dataset. In preliminary experiments, we confirmed that the best results were achieved when we set $n = \{1, 2, 3\}$ and $N^t = 200$. We thus only report the experimental results with this setting. Table 1 displays some question patterns and their frequencies. We train the question pattern identification models by limiting the number of examples to at most 300 to avoid the data imbalance across the patterns.

Pattern	Raw count	Frequency (%)
what	32098	29.5
who	15692	14.4
. . .	. . .	. . .
what did	5636	5.19
what did he	1801	1.66
. . .	. . .	. . .
UNKOWN	2898	2.67

Table 1: Question patterns ($n = \{1, 2, 3\}$, $N = 200$).

Comparing baselines: Two baseline question generation systems are employed.

- NQG (Du et al., 2017) is used to assess the efficacy of question focus prediction and question pattern identification. We consider the whole passage as a single chunk when using this system. This means that a question focus is not narrowed down to some textual regiosn, rather it spreads to the whole passage.

- CFNet (Gao et al., 2019), the only known CQG system, is adopted to chiefly evaluate the impact of answer-unawareness. This system still requires the corresponding answer to be supplied to generate a question, although it may be superior to our system in that it is equipped with explicit mechanisms to deal with coreference and conversation flow.

6 Results and Discussions

6.1 Quality of the Generated Questions

The results shown in Table 2 establish our primary assumption, which states that a question coherent to the current conversational context can be generated primarily by knowing the current focus of interrogation. As shown in the table, the qualities of generated questions (as measured by BLEU 1-4), when a question focus is estimated ($N_c > 1$), were better than that from the case where the whole text passage was simply considered as a question focus ($N_c = 1$). These results indeed dictate that the notion of question focus is effective.

N_c	B1	B2	B3	B4
1 (whole passage)	30.19	12.85	0.32	0.13
5 (random)	33.83	16.08	0.59	0.13
5 (predicted)	34.64	16.65	0.70	0.18
10 (predicted)	34.71	16.68	0.70	0.17
5 (GT)	34.19	16.30	0.71	0.21
10 (GT)	34.71	16.67	0.73	0.21

Table 2: Qualities (BLEU scores) of generated questions (without considering question patterns).

The table further shows that the qualities of generated questions were slightly better than that from the random choice of a chunk as question focus, suggesting that the incorporation of even an estimated question focus is effective. The displayed results, on the other hand, shows that the quality of generated questions (B1 around 34.6) is still not suffice by only knowing the question foci, suggesting the necessity of additional information.

Given these discussions, Table 3 displays the qualities of generated questions under several conditions, and it confirms the above mentioned prospect may be probable. The major outcomes provided in the table are: (1) the generation quality could be largely improved if the focus and the pattern of the to-be-generated question are correctly identified, and (2) the current question pattern identification models severely suffer from the low accuracies, even with classification or generation, and they are comparable or only slightly better than the Random baseline, largely affecting the final generation results.

Table 4 presents the comparison with the baseline systems. It clearly shows that our method with ground-truth question foci and question patterns largely outperformed the comparing systems, suggesting that our primary direction is promising. On the other hand, as our results with the pre-

N_c	Focus	Pattern	B1	B2	B3	B4
5	P	Gen	24.15	9.80	0.14	0.02
5	P	Class	27.62	13.67	0.13	0.04
5	P	Random	27.35	13.70	0.17	0.03
10	P	Gen	32.36	16.06	0.37	0.04
10	P	Class	26.87	13.00	0.16	0.04
10	P	Random	28.45	14.43	0.20	0.04
5	GT	GT	56.22	38.84	18.69	7.10
10	GT	GT	53.05	34.17	14.23	5.25

Table 3: Qualities (BLEU scores) of generated questions. P and GT in Focus column respectively indicate predicted and ground-truth foci. Gen and Class in Pattern column are generated and classified.

dicted question foci and question patterns were worse than that with the comparing systems, insisting that the current deficiency of our methods for question focus estimation and question pattern identification is obvious.

model	B1	B2	B3	B4
NQG (GT)	33.3	16.1	0.85	0.22
CFNet	37.38	22.81	16.25	-
Ours (P)	27.62	13.67	0.13	0.04
Ours (GT)	56.22	38.84	18.69	7.10

Table 4: Comparison of the qualities (BLEU scores) with the baseline systems: NQG (Zhou et al., 2017) and CFNet (Gao et al., 2019).

6.2 Accuracy of Question Focus Estimation

Table 5 measures the accuracy of query focus estimation with varying N_c. The accuracy figures presented in the table may be reasonable, if not satisfactory. The longer chunks achieve apparently higher classification accuracies, but there may be a trade-off between the quality of generated questions. A bigger textual region may not well constrain the content of a to-be-generated question.

N_c	Ave. Chunk Length	Accuracy (%)
5	120	59.78
10	60	48.17

Table 5: Accuracy of question focus estimation.

6.3 Accuracy of Question Pattern Identification

On the other hand, Table 6 and Table 7 show embarrassingly unsatisfactory results of question pattern identification. In the tables, P and GT in the Focus column indicate the cases where the predicted question foci and ground-truth are respectively used. As already discussed, these low performances obviously affected the quality of generated questions.

N_c	Focus	n	N	Accuracy (%)
5	P	1, 2, 3	200	0.45
10	P	1, 2, 3	200	0.80
5	GT	1, 2, 3	200	0.73
10	GT	1, 2, 3	200	0.62

Table 6: Accuracy of question pattern classification.

N_c	Focus	B1	B2	B3
5	P	20.00	3.39	0.000
10	P	18.68	3.47	0.14
5	GT	17.38	3.26	0.11
10	GT	18.28	3.79	0.17

Table 7: Accuracy (BLEU scores) of question pattern generation.

Besides, the accuracies of generated question patterns are almost comparable across the predicted and the ground-truth question foci. This insists that the identification of question patterns is almost impossible by only relying on the current inputs (question focus and conversation history) and/or with the present models. This turns out that the process of question pattern identification has higher degree of freedom and should be more constrained with additional information such as entities appeared in the text passage.

6.4 Generated Question Examples

Figure 7 showcases generated examples.

In the top (good) example, both of question focus estimation and question pattern identification were correct, leading to the generation of a question that completely matched with the ground-truth question.

The second example exhibits a mixed case. As the generated question is largely different from the ground-truth question, the BLEU score is quite low. However the generated question may be acceptable, given the QA conversation situation. This example suggests that we need to devise a better metrics for properly evaluating conversationally adequate questions.

The third and fourth examples present failed question generation cases. The former example shows failed question pattern identification and the latter example further exemplifies a fail in question pattern identification. As a result, the generated questions made no senses to the current question foci.

good	F (GT=P): (CNN) -- Dennis Farina, the dapper, mustachioed cop-turned-actor best known for his tough-as-nails work in such tv series as "law & order, " "crime story," and "Miami Vice," has died. He was 69.485 pred "we are deeply saddened by the loss of a great actor and a wonderful man," said his publicist, Lori De Waal, in a statement Monday. "Dennis Farina was always warmhearted and professional, with a great sense of humor and passion for his profession. P (GT=P): what did he Q(GT): What did he do? Q(P): What did he do?
good?	F (GT=P): The dog, called prince, was an intelligent animal and a slave to Williams. From morning till night, he had a number of clear duties, for which Williams had patiently trained him and, like a good pupil, prince lived for the chance to prove his abilities. When Williams wanted to put on his boots, he would murmur. P (GT): what is the P (P): what did the Q(GT): What is the dog 's name? Q(P): What did the man do to the animal?
bad	F (GT=P): Just then, thunder was all-around them. The moment he turned the flashlight on. The house lights went off. A second later, the kitchen windows were broken. Eppes and Danielle ran to their boys who were still sleeping in their bedroom. "get up, get up, r.j.!" Eppes shouted, waving his flashlight. P (GT): did the P (P): what time Q(GT): Did the house lights go out? Q(P): What time of day was it?
bad	F (GT): Las Vegas (Spanish for "the meadows"), officially the city of las Vegas and often known simply as Vegas, is the 28th-most populated city in the united states, the most populated city in the state of Nevada, and the county seat of Clark county. F (P): The city anchors the las vegas valley metropolitan area and is the largest city within the greater Mojave desert. P (GT): is it P (P): what's Q(GT): Is it a small city? Q(P): What's his name?

Figure 7: Good and bad examples of generated questions.

7 Conclusions

Conversational question generation (CQG) is a recently emerging area of NLP research initiated by (Gao et al., 2019). Given a range of potential practical applications, a question coherent to the current QA situation should be generated even without the corresponding answer provided. This study is first to propose a framework for answer-unaware CQG by assuming that the quality of questions can be improved by knowing the question focus and the question pattern. That is, the former contributes to choose a question topic (what-to-ask), and the later could lead the proper generation of the words in a question (how-to-ask). The experimental results confirmed that our research direction would be promising, but highlighted that further effort has to be made: in particular, the question pattern identification process should be greatly improved by enhancing the model and its ingredients.

To further push forward this new area of research, it would be necessary to establish a better evaluation metrics that could more adequately reflect the conversational natures of natural QA dialogues.

References

Eunsol Choi, He He, Mohit Iyyer, Mark Yatskar, Wentau Yih, Yejin Choi, Percy Liang, and Luke Zettlemoyer. 2018. QuAC: Question answering in context. In *Proceedings of the 2018 Conference on Empirical Methods in Natural Language Processing*.

Xinya Du and Claire Cardie. 2018. Harvesting paragraph-level question-answer pairs from Wikipedia. In *Proceedings of the 56th Annual Meeting of the Association for Computational Linguistics*.

Xinya Du, Junru Shao, and Claire Cardie. 2017. Learning to ask: Neural question generation for reading comprehension. In *Proceedings of the 55th Annual Meeting of the Association for Computational Linguistics*.

Yifan Gao, Piji Li, Irwin King, and Michael R. Lyu. 2019. Interconnected question generation with coreference alignment and conversation flow modeling. In *Proceedings of the 57th Annual Meeting of the Association for Computational Linguistics*.

Liangming Pan, Wenqiang Lei, Tat-Seng Chua, and Min-Yen Kan. 2019. Recent advances in neural question generation. arXiv preprint arXiv:1905.08949.

Jeffrey Pennington, Richard Socher, and Christopher D. Manning. 2014. Glove: Global vectors for word representation. In *Proceedings of the 2014 Conference on Empirical Methods in Natural Language Processing*.

Pranav Rajpurkar, Robin Jia, and Percy Liang. 2018. Know what you don't know: Unanswerable questions for squad. In *Proceedings of the 56th Annual Meeting of the Association for Computational Linguistics*.

Siva Reddy, Danqi Chen, and Christopher D. Manning. 2019. CoQA: A conversational question answering challenge. *Transactions of the Association for Computational Linguistics*, 7:249–266.

Duyu Tang, Nan Duan, Tao Qin, Zhao Yan, and Ming Zhou. 2017. Question answering and question generation as dual tasks. arXiv preprint arXiv:1706.02027.

Mark Yatskar. 2019. A qualitative comparison of CoQA, SQuAD 2.0 and QuAC. In *Proceedings of the 2019 Conference of the North American Chapter of the Association for Computational Linguistics: Human Language Technologies*.

Xingdi Yuan, Tong Wang, Caglar Gulcehre, Alessandro Sordoni, Philip Bachman, Saizheng Zhang, Sandeep Subramanian, and Adam Trischler. 2017. Machine comprehension by text-to-text neural question generation. *In Proceedings of the 2nd Workshop on Representation Learning for NLP*.

Qingyu Zhou, Nan Yang, Furu Wei, Chuanqi Tan, Hangbo Bao, and Ming Zhou. 2017. Neural question generation from text: A preliminary study. arXiv preprint arXiv:1704.01792.

Cross-Task Knowledge Transfer for Query-Based Text Summarization

Elozino Egonmwan †*   **Vittorio Castelli** ‡   **Md Arafat Sultan** ‡

† University of Lethbridge, Lethbridge, AB, Canada
‡ IBM Research AI

elozino.egonmwan@uleth.ca, vittorio@us.ibm.com, arafat.sultan@ibm.com

Abstract

We demonstrate the viability of knowledge transfer between two related tasks: machine reading comprehension (MRC) and query-based text summarization. Using an MRC model trained on the SQuAD1.1 dataset as a core system component, we first build an *extractive* query-based summarizer. For better precision, this summarizer also compresses the output of the MRC model using a novel sentence compression technique. We further leverage pre-trained machine translation systems to *abstract* our extracted summaries. Our models achieve state-of-the-art results on the publicly available CNN/Daily Mail and Debatepedia datasets, and can serve as simple yet powerful baselines for future systems. We also hope that these results will encourage research on transfer learning from large MRC corpora to query-based summarization.

1 Introduction

Query-based single-document text summarization is the process of selecting the most relevant points in a document for a given query and arranging them into a concise and coherent snippet of text. The query can range from an individual word to a fully formed natural language question. *Extractive* summarizers select verbatim the most relevant span of text in the source, while *abstractive* summarizers further paraphrase the selected content for better clarity and brevity.

By and large, existing approaches train models using summarization data corpora (Nema et al., 2017; Hasselqvist et al., 2017), which are of moderate size. At the same time, large corpora are available for related tasks, specifically machine reading comprehension (MRC) and machine translation (MT). To find out if such corpora have utility for summarizers, we propose methods to di-

rectly produce extractive and abstractive query-based summaries from pretrained MRC and MT modules, requiring no further adaptation or transfer learning steps.

In our experiments, this approach outperforms existing methods, suggesting a novel route to query-based summarization: pre-training systems on such related tasks, where an abundance of training data is enabling extremely rapid progress (Wang et al., 2018; Sun et al., 2018; Vaswani et al., 2017), and using summarization-specific corpora for transfer learning.

The main contributions of this work are:

- We show how existing off-the-shelf components for tasks other than query-based summarization are competitive with the state-of-the-art in the field, even without model adaptation or transfer learning – we hope to encourage researchers to more closely examine transfer learning among these tasks.

- Specifically, we show how processing the output of an MRC system (trained on the SQuAD1.1 dataset (Rajpurkar et al., 2016)) with a simple rule-based sentence compression module that operates on the dependency parse (de Marneffe and Manning, 2008) of the answer sentence yields results that are better than those of query-based extractive summarizers trained for the specific dataset.

- We demonstrate how a sequence-to-sequence model (Sutskever et al., 2014) that uses two machine translation engines—from and to English, respectively—applied to the output of the above, yields results that are better than query-based abstractive summarizers trained for the specific dataset.

---

*Work done at IBM.

Proceedings of the Second Workshop on Machine Reading for Question Answering, pages 72–77
Hong Kong, China, November 4, 2019. ©2019 Association for Computational Linguistics

Passage: people whether overweight or not are still people. you can not compare a person with a suitcase. suitcases don't live and breathe. this rule is the same with weight. excess weight in a suitcase is not comparable with a fat person .
Query: is it necessary to charge fat passengers extra when flying?
Reference Summary: there is no comparison between a person and a suitcase.
Our method (abstractive) : The overweight in the bag can't be compared with the fat guy. **Diversity driven attention model:** beings are definitely by the <unk> to illegal illegal.

Table 1: Example/comparison of our *abstractive* summary on a Debatepedia sample with the output of the diversity driven attention model of Nema et al. (2017). Our generated summary is relevant to the query.

2   Task Definition

Given a document $D = (S_1, ..., S_n)$ with n sentences comprising of a set of words $D_W = \{d_1, ..., d_w\}$, and a query $Q = (q_1, ..., q_m)$ with m words, one desires to produce an *extractive* (S_E) or *abstractive* (S_A) summary that provides information about the answer to Q, where $S_E \subseteq D_W$ and $S_A = \{w_1, ..., w_s\} \mid \exists w_i \notin D_W$. Tables 1 and 2 show examples of abstractive and extractive summaries, respectively.

3   Method

Our proposed system comprises of three modules for extractive summarization: retrieval of candidate answer phrases using a reading comprehension system, sentence extraction, and sentence compression. Additionally we utilize two MT modules (English to Spanish and back) to paraphrase for abstractive summarization.

3.1   Machine Reading Comprehension

MRC requires the identification of a contiguous span of words in a passage that answers a given query (Rajpurkar et al., 2016; Wang et al., 2018; Hu et al., 2017). We use the MRC model by Wang et al. (2016b) trained on the SQuAD1.1 dataset (Rajpurkar et al., 2016) to identify the top n (empirically: n=5) possibly overlapping candidate answer phrases, or *chunks*, for the given query. The chunks are typically short, 3.2 words on average in the training set. Obviously, chunks from MRC are

Passage (truncated): [...] offensive italian football expert and author john foot explained how paulo berlusconi 's words were offensive on several levels . " it is an insult , " foot told cnn [...]
Query: john foot
Reference Summary: italian football expert and author john foot says paulo berlusconi 's words are offensive on several levels .
Our method (extractive) : offensive italian football expert and author john foot explained how paulo berlusconi 's words were offensive on several levels .

Table 2: Example of our *extractive* summary on an example from the query-based version of CNN/Daily Mail (Hermann et al., 2015).

not meant to be summaries, but in our system they help the summarizer focus on the regions of the input document that appear related to the query.

3.2   Sentence Extraction

Sentence extraction consists of selecting the sentences containing the top n chunks produced by MRC. This is in contrast to methods based on sentence ranking algorithms such as those used in (Boudin et al., 2015; Parveen and Strube, 2015; Nallapati et al., 2017; Cheng and Lapata, 2016). For our experiments, we impose the constraint that the candidate answer chunks for each query be contained in a single sentence. Hence, starting from $n = 5$, we iteratively reduce n until the top n candidate chunks are all contained in one sentence.

3.3   Sentence Compression

Sentence extraction often produces results that are much longer than those in the reference summaries—the training data (Table 4) suggests that 20 words is a good upper limit for the length of the summaries. We address this problem by introducing a novel sentence compression framework based on pruning the dependency parses of the sentences. Our approach is partially inspired by the work of Wang et al. (2016a), which performs sentence compression based on constituency parses. The intuition is that dependency parses better capture the semantic relations between words than constituents, which actually model syntactic structure.

	CNN.	Deb.
Test	14,725	979
Avg. #words/psg.	776	70
Avg. #words/query	2	11
Avg. #words/summ.	14	10

Table 4: Statistics of the dataset test samples after processing by the Wang et al. (2016b) MRC system's preprocessing module. Note that the preprocessor fails to parse 2-3% of the test samples in each dataset.

Input Sentence: it is ridiculous to suggest governments should restrict their own ability to help their economies.   **Paraphrase (with MT):** It is **absurd** to suggest that governments **impose limits** on their ability to help their economies.
Input Sentence: this favoritism would only increase that of which the laws are trying to suppress .   **Paraphrase (with MT):** These **nepotism** will only increase the laws that you try to suppress.

Table 3: Examples of some of our paraphrased sentences using an MT system. Bolded words are novel.

Given a summary with length ≥ 20, we obtain the dependency parses of its sentences using the IBM Watson NLU toolkit. Next, we remove words in the sentences (starting from the rear) that are not in a dependency relationship with any of the candidate phrases, until the summary length limit is reached.

3.4 Back Translation

Recent research has shown gains in leveraging on the enormous corpora in machine translation (MT) for paraphrasing (Mallinson et al., 2017; Wieting and Gimpel, 2017). Inspired by such research and our fundamental goal of investigating the viability of cross-task knowledge transfer for query-based summarization, we paraphrase our extracts using an off-the-shelf MT system[1]. The final English paraphrase of the input sentence is obtained by translating it into Spanish and back-translating the translation into English. We experimented with English-French-English and English-Italian-English as well as with multi-hops approaches before settling on the English-Spanish pair, based on subjective analysis of the results. Table 3 shows examples of paraphrased sentences using back-translation.

4 Experiments

We test our approach on two publicly available datasets—Debatepedia (Nema et al., 2017) for abstractive summarization, and the version of CNN/Daily Mail that was adapted in (Hermann et al., 2015) for both extractive and abstractive summarization. No training was involved; the test sets were simply passed through the modules discussed in section 3.

4.1 Datasets

We processed the CNN/DM[2] and Debatepedia[3] datasets using the respective official Python scripts to yield the corpora with passages, queries and summaries tailored to the queries (Table 4). CNN/DM is much larger in terms of both the number of samples and the lengths of passages, with short queries consisting of few words, mostly entity names. Debatepedia is a smaller dataset, but the queries are fully-formed natural language questions. Interestingly, although our MRC system was originally designed to answer full-length questions, as our results show later in this section, it identifies key regions of the document remarkably well in both test sets.

4.2 Evaluation

As customary in summarization tasks, we evaluate our system using ROUGE (Lin, 2004)—a family of metrics that compute the textual overlap between the output and the reference summary. The publicly available `ROUGE 2.0 toolkit`[4] was used as the implementation.

4.3 Results

Tables 5 and 6 summarize the performances of our model and other published models on Debatepedia and CNN/Daily Mail, respectively. Our models, both extractive and abstractive, outperform the published results on both test sets.

The extractive performance on CNN/DM indicates that the combination of a reading compre-

---

[1] The MT engine is used in the IBM Watson Language Translator service.

[2] `https://github.com/helmertz/query-sum-data/`

[3] `https://github.com/PrekshaNema25/DiverstiyBasedAttentionMechanism`

[4] `https://rxnlp.com/rouge-2-0/`

Abstractive	R-1	R-2	R-L
Diversity (Nema et al., 2017)	41.26	18.75	40.43
RSA (Baumel et al., 2018)	53.09	16.10	46.18
Ours	**64.43**	**18.93**	**46.80**

Table 5: ROUGE (%) performances of our model and competing models on the Debatepedia dataset. Our model outpeforms both baselines on all metrics.

Extractive	R-1	R-2	R-L	R-SU4
QSum (Hasselqvist et al., 2017)	33.81	18.19	29.22	17.49
Ours	**65.45**	**30.07**	**60.40**	**36.62**
Abstractive				
QSum (Hasselqvist et al., 2017)	18.25	5.04	16.17	6.13
Ours	**58.46**	**25.12**	**54.32**	**32.06**

Table 6: ROUGE (%) scores of our models and the competing model on the CNN/Daily Mail dataset. Our proposed approach yields the best system for both extractive and abstractive summarization.

hension system and a syntax-driven compression module can be highly effective in identifying regions in a document that contain key information with respect to a given query. Moreover, the abstractive performances on both test sets show the effectiveness of machine translation as a paraphrasing component for abstractive summarization. In particular, in the CNN/DM test set the improvement over the baseline is greater in the abstractive than in the extractive case, again suggesting that both text selection and MT-based paraphrasing contribute to the gain.

5 Related Work

Text summarization has long been an active area of research and query-based summarization has gained momentum more recently. Classical summarization models usually identify salient parts of a text by encapsulating manually crafted rules into linear functions (Lin and Bilmes, 2011) which are solved using integer linear programming (ILP) (Nayeem and Chali, 2017; Boudin et al., 2015), conditional random fields (CRF) (Shen et al., 2007), or graph algorithms (Parveen and Strube, 2015; Erkan and Radev, 2004). More recently, neural networks, mostly with an encoder-decoder framework (Bahdanau et al., 2014), have been used to learn the underlying features (Jadhav and Rajan, 2018; Nallapati et al., 2016) trained by minimizing the cross-entropy loss (Nallapati et al., 2017) or reinforcement learning (Narayan et al., 2018; Paulus et al., 2017).

Our baseline models for query-based summa-

rization (Nema et al., 2017; Hasselqvist et al., 2017) are both implemented on the encoder-decoder framework with the former incorporating a diversity function in their model aimed at minimizing the problem of repetitive word generation inherent in encoder-decoder models. However our approach is similar to neither, as our goal is not to train a query-based summarizer from scratch but rather to investigate the competitiveness of using pre-trained models for closely related tasks—i.e., MRC and MT—on query-based summarization.

6 Conclusions

We described an approach to extractive and abstractive summarization that relies on components designed for different tasks: MRC, sentence compression, and MT. We have shown that retrieving the top n answer chunks from a passage with an MRC system and trimming the corresponding sentences using their dependency trees yields an extractive summarizer that outperforms published results on a publicly available dataset. We also showed that using MT to produce a paraphrase of the answers yields a high-performance abstractive summarization method.

This work lays the foundations for transfer learning based approaches that use summarization data to adapt MRC models for summarization. We also envision: i) using summarization data to learn how to re-rank top n candidates from back-translation; ii) replacing the pruning system with a trained sequence-to-sequence model with an objective function that incorporates readability; and

iii) computing the AMR parse (Banarescu et al., 2013) of the candidate answers followed by text generation (Song et al., 2018) instead of using MT.

Acknowledgments

We thank the reviewers for their valuable comments and suggestions. We also thank Zhiguo Wang and Preksha Nema for clarification of their work.

References

Dzmitry Bahdanau, Kyunghyun Cho, and Yoshua Bengio. 2014. Neural machine translation by jointly learning to align and translate. *arXiv preprint arXiv:1409.0473*.

Laura Banarescu, Claire Bonial, Shu Cai, Madalina Georgescu, Kira Griffitt, Ulf Hermjakob, Kevin Knight, Philipp Koehn, Martha Palmer, and Nathan Schneider. 2013. Abstract meaning representation for sembanking. In *Proceedings of the 7th Linguistic Annotation Workshop and Interoperability with Discourse*, pages 178–186. Association for Computational Linguistics.

Tal Baumel, Matan Eyal, and Michael Elhadad. 2018. Query focused abstractive summarization: Incorporating query relevance, multi-document coverage, and summary length constraints into seq2seq models. *arXiv preprint arXiv:1801.07704*.

Florian Boudin, Hugo Mougard, and Benoit Favre. 2015. Concept-based summarization using integer linear programming: From concept pruning to multiple optimal solutions. In *Conference on Empirical Methods in Natural Language Processing (EMNLP) 2015*.

Jianpeng Cheng and Mirella Lapata. 2016. Neural summarization by extracting sentences and words. *arXiv preprint arXiv:1603.07252*.

Günes Erkan and Dragomir R Radev. 2004. Lexrank: Graph-based lexical centrality as salience in text summarization. *Journal of artificial intelligence research*, 22:457–479.

Johan Hasselqvist, Niklas Helmertz, and Mikael Kågebäck. 2017. Query-based abstractive summarization using neural networks. *arXiv preprint arXiv:1712.06100*.

Karl Moritz Hermann, Tomas Kocisky, Edward Grefenstette, Lasse Espeholt, Will Kay, Mustafa Suleyman, and Phil Blunsom. 2015. Teaching machines to read and comprehend. In *Advances in Neural Information Processing Systems*, pages 1693–1701.

Minghao Hu, Yuxing Peng, Zhen Huang, Xipeng Qiu, Furu Wei, and Ming Zhou. 2017. Reinforced mnemonic reader for machine reading comprehension. *arXiv preprint arXiv:1705.02798*.

Aishwarya Jadhav and Vaibhav Rajan. 2018. Extractive summarization with swap-net: Sentences and words from alternating pointer networks. In *Proceedings of the 56th Annual Meeting of the Association for Computational Linguistics (Volume 1: Long Papers)*, volume 1, pages 142–151.

Chin-Yew Lin. 2004. Rouge: A package for automatic evaluation of summaries. *Text Summarization Branches Out*.

Hui Lin and Jeff Bilmes. 2011. A class of submodular functions for document summarization. In *Proceedings of the 49th Annual Meeting of the Association for Computational Linguistics: Human Language Technologies-Volume 1*, pages 510–520. Association for Computational Linguistics.

Jonathan Mallinson, Rico Sennrich, and Mirella Lapata. 2017. Paraphrasing revisited with neural machine translation. In *Proceedings of the 15th Conference of the European Chapter of the Association for Computational Linguistics: Volume 1, Long Papers*, volume 1, pages 881–893.

Marie-Catherine de Marneffe and Christopher D. Manning. 2008. *Stanford typed dependencies manual*. Stanford.

Ramesh Nallapati, Feifei Zhai, and Bowen Zhou. 2017. Summarunner: A recurrent neural network based sequence model for extractive summarization of documents. In *AAAI*, pages 3075–3081.

Ramesh Nallapati, Bowen Zhou, Cicero dos Santos, Ça glar Gulçehre, and Bing Xiang. 2016. Abstractive text summarization using sequence-to-sequence rnns and beyond. *CoNLL 2016*, page 280.

Shashi Narayan, Shay B Cohen, and Mirella Lapata. 2018. Ranking sentences for extractive summarization with reinforcement learning. In *Proceedings of the 2018 Conference of the North American Chapter of the Association for Computational Linguistics: Human Language Technologies, Volume 1 (Long Papers)*, volume 1, pages 1747–1759.

Mir Tafseer Nayeem and Yllias Chali. 2017. Extract with order for coherent multi-document summarization. In *Proceedings of TextGraphs-11: the Workshop on Graph-based Methods for Natural Language Processing*, pages 51–56.

Preksha Nema, Mitesh M Khapra, Anirban Laha, and Balaraman Ravindran. 2017. Diversity driven attention model for query-based abstractive summarization. In *Proceedings of the 55th Annual Meeting of the Association for Computational Linguistics (Volume 1: Long Papers)*, volume 1, pages 1063–1072.

Daraksha Parveen and Michael Strube. 2015. Integrating importance, non-redundancy and coherence in graph-based extractive summarization. In *IJCAI*, pages 1298–1304.

Romain Paulus, Caiming Xiong, and Richard Socher. 2017. A deep reinforced model for abstractive summarization. *arXiv preprint arXiv:1705.04304*.

Pranav Rajpurkar, Jian Zhang, Konstantin Lopyrev, and Percy Liang. 2016. Squad: 100,000+ questions for machine comprehension of text. *arXiv preprint arXiv:1606.05250*.

Dou Shen, Jian-Tao Sun, Hua Li, Qiang Yang, and Zheng Chen. 2007. Document summarization using conditional random fields. In *IJCAI*, volume 7, pages 2862–2867.

Linfeng Song, Yue Zhang, Zhiguo Wang, and Daniel Gildea. 2018. A graph-to-sequence model for amr-to-text generation. In *Proceedings of the 56th Annual Meeting of the Association for Computational Linguistics (Volume 1: Long Papers)*, pages 1616–1626. Association for Computational Linguistics.

Fu Sun, Linyang Li, Xipeng Qiu, and Yang Liu. 2018. U-net: Machine reading comprehension with unanswerable questions. *arXiv preprint arXiv:1810.06638*.

Ilya Sutskever, Oriol Vinyals, and Quoc V Le. 2014. Sequence to sequence learning with neural networks. In *Advances in neural information processing systems*, pages 3104–3112.

Ashish Vaswani, Noam Shazeer, Niki Parmar, Jakob Uszkoreit, Llion Jones, Aidan N Gomez, Ł ukasz Kaiser, and Illia Polosukhin. 2017. Attention is all you need. In I. Guyon, U. V. Luxburg, S. Bengio, H. Wallach, R. Fergus, S. Vishwanathan, and R. Garnett, editors, *Advances in Neural Information Processing Systems 30*, pages 5998–6008. Curran Associates, Inc.

Lu Wang, Hema Raghavan, Vittorio Castelli, Radu Florian, and Claire Cardie. 2016a. A sentence compression based framework to query-focused multi-document summarization. *arXiv preprint arXiv:1606.07548*.

Wei Wang, Ming Yan, and Chen Wu. 2018. Multi-granularity hierarchical attention fusion networks for reading comprehension and question answering. In *Proceedings of the 56th Annual Meeting of the Association for Computational Linguistics (Volume 1: Long Papers)*, volume 1, pages 1705–1714.

Zhiguo Wang, Haitao Mi, Wael Hamza, and Radu Florian. 2016b. Multi-perspective context matching for machine comprehension. *arXiv preprint arXiv:1612.04211*.

John Wieting and Kevin Gimpel. 2017. Pushing the limits of paraphrastic sentence embeddings with millions of machine translations. *arXiv preprint arXiv:1711.05732*.

BookQA: Stories of Challenges and Opportunities

Stefanos Angelidis[1*]   **Lea Frermann**[2]   **Diego Marcheggiani**[3]   **Roi Blanco**[3]   **Lluís Màrquez**[3]

[1]Institute for Language, Cognition and Computation, School of Informatics, University of Edinburgh
[2]School of Computing and Information Systems, The University of Melbourne
[3]Amazon Research

`s.angelidis@ed.ac.uk`   `lea.frermann@unimelb.edu.au`
`{marchegg,roiblan,lluismv}@amazon.com`

Abstract

We present a system for answering questions based on the full text of books (BookQA), which first selects book passages given a question at hand, and then uses a memory network to reason and predict an answer. To improve generalization, we pretrain our memory network using artificial questions generated from book sentences. We experiment with the recently published NarrativeQA corpus, on the subset of *Who* questions, which expect book characters as answers. We experimentally show that BERT-based retrieval and pretraining improve over baseline results significantly. At the same time, we confirm that NarrativeQA is a highly challenging data set, and that there is need for novel research in order to achieve high-precision BookQA results. We analyze some of the bottlenecks of the current approach, and we argue that more research is needed on text representation, retrieval of relevant passages, and reasoning, including commonsense knowledge.

1 Introduction

Considerable volume of research work has looked into various Question Answering (QA) settings, ranging from retrieval-based QA (Voorhees, 2001) to recent neural approaches that reason over Knowledge Bases (KB) (Bordes et al., 2014), or raw text (Shen et al., 2017; Deng and Tam, 2018; Min et al., 2018). In this paper we use the NarrativeQA corpus (Kocisky et al., 2018) as a starting point and focus on the task of answering questions from the full text of books, which we call BookQA. BookQA has unique characteristics which prohibit the direct application of current QA methods. For instance, (a) books are usually orders of magnitude longer than the short texts (e.g.,

Wikipedia articles) used in neural QA architectures; (b) many facts about a book story are never made explicit, and require external or common-sense knowledge to infer them; (c) the QA system cannot rely on pre-existing KBs; (d) traditional retrieval techniques are less effective in selecting relevant passages from self-contained book stories (Kocisky et al., 2018); (e) collecting human-annotated BookQA data is a significant challenge; (f) stylistic disparities in the language used among different books may hinder generalization.

Additionally, the style of book questions may vary significantly, with different approaches being potentially useful for different question types: from queries about story facts that have entities as answers (e.g., *Who* and *Where* questions); to open-ended questions that require the extraction or generation of longer answers (e.g., *Why* or *How* questions). The difference in reasoning required for different question types can make it very hard to draw meaningful conclusions.

For this reason, we concentrate on the task of answering *Who* questions, which expect book characters as answers (e.g., *"Who is Harry Potter's best friend?"*). This task allows to simplify the output and evaluation (we look for entities, and we can apply precision-based and ranking evaluation metrics), but still retains the important elements of the original NarrativeQA task, i.e., the need to explore over the full content of the book and to reason over a deep understanding of the narrative. Table 1 exemplifies the diversity and complexity of *Who* questions in the data, by listing a set of questions from a single book, which require increasingly complex types of reasoning.

NarrativeQA (Kocisky et al., 2018) is the first publicly available dataset for QA over long narratives, namely the full text of books and movie scripts. The full-text task has only been addressed

---

*Work done while first author was interning at Amazon.

Proceedings of the Second Workshop on Machine Reading for Question Answering, pages 78–85
Hong Kong, China, November 4, 2019. ©2019 Association for Computational Linguistics

Table 1: *Who* questions from NarrativeQA for the book *The Mysteries of Udolpho*, by Ann Radcliffe. The diversity and complexity of questions in the corpus remains high, even when considering only the subset of *Who* questions that expect characters as answers.

by Tay et al. (2019), who proposed a curriculum learning-based two-phase approach (*context selection* and *neural inference*). More papers have looked into answering NarrativeQA's questions from only book/movie *summaries* (Indurthi et al., 2018; Bauer et al., 2018; Tay et al., 2018a,b; Nishida et al., 2019). This is a fundamentally simpler task, because: i) the systems need to reason over a much shorter context, i.e., the summary; and ii) there is the certainty that the answer can be found in the summary. This paper is another step in the exploration of the full NarrativeQA task, and embraces the goal of finding an answer in the complete book text. We propose a system that first selects a small subset of relevant book passages, and then uses a memory network to reason and extract the answer from them. The network is specifically adapted for generalization across books. We analyze different options for selecting relevant contexts, and for pretraining the memory network with artificially created question–answer pairs. Our key contributions are: i) this is the first systematic exploration of the challenges in full-text BookQA, ii) we present a full pipeline framework for the task, iii) we publish a dataset of *Who* questions which expect book characters as an answer, and iv) we include a critical discussion on the shortcomings of the current QA approach, and we discuss potential avenues for future research.

2 Book Character Questions

NarrativeQA was created using a large annotation effort, where participants were shown a human-curated *summary* of a book/script and were asked to produce question-answer pairs *without referring to the full story*. The main task of interest is to answer the questions by looking at the *full story* and not at the summary, thus ensuring that answers cannot be simply copied from the story. The full corpus contains 1,567 stories (split equally between books and movies) and 46,765 questions.

We restrict our study to *Who* questions about *books*, which have *book characters* as answers (e.g., *"Who is charged with attempted murder?"*). Using the book preprocessing system, book-nlp (see Section 3.1), and a combination of automatic and crowdsourced efforts, we obtained a total of 3,427 QA pairs, spanning 614 books.[1]

3 BookQA Framework

The length of books and limited annotated data prohibit the application of end-to-end neural QA models that reason over the full text of a book. Instead, we opted for a pipeline approach, whose components are described below.

3.1 Book & Question Preprocessing

Books and questions are preprocessed in advance using the book-nlp parser (Bamman et al., 2014), a system for character detection and shallow parsing in books (Iyyer et al., 2016; Frermann and Szarvas, 2017) which provides, among others: sentence segmentation, POS tagging, dependency parsing, named entity recognition, and coreference resolution. The parser identifies and clusters character mentions, so that all coreferent (direct or pronominal) character mentions are associated with the same unique character identifier.

3.2 Context Selection

In order to make inference over book text tractable and give our model a better chance at predicting the correct answer, we must restrict the context to only a small number of book sentences. We developed two context selection methods to retrieve relevant book passages, which we define as windows of 5 consecutive sentences:

IR-style selection (BM25F): We constructed a searchable *book index* to store individual book sentences. We replace every book character mention, including pronoun references, with the character's unique identifier. At retrieval time, we similarly replace character mentions in each question, and rank passages from the corresponding book using BM25F (Zaragoza et al., 2004).

BERT-based selection: We developed a neural context selection method, based on the BERT language representation model (Devlin et al., 2019). A pretrained BERT model is fine-tuned to predict

---

[1]To obtain the BookQA data, follow the instructions at: https://github.com/stangelid/bookqa-who.

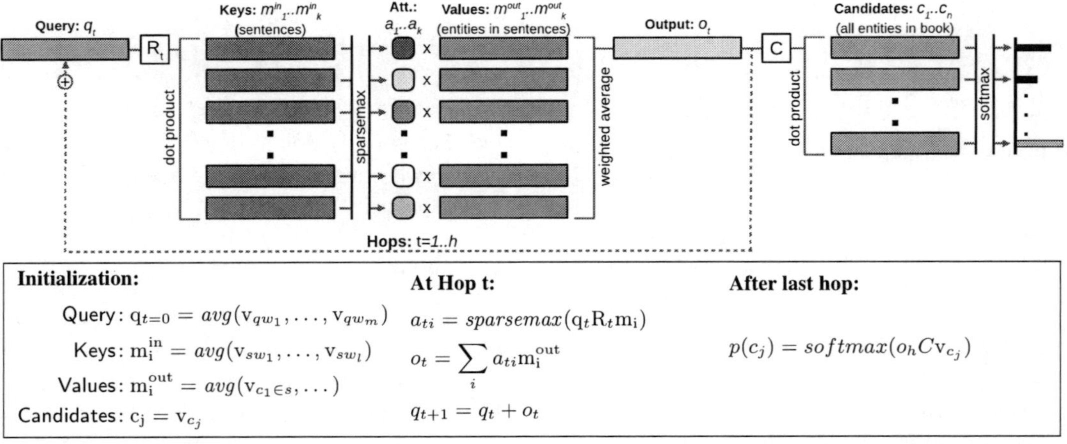

$$\text{Initialization:} \qquad\qquad \text{At Hop } t: \qquad\qquad\qquad \text{After last hop:}$$

Initialization:

Query: $q_{t=0} = avg(v_{qw_1}, \ldots, v_{qw_m})$

Keys: $m_i^{in} = avg(v_{sw_1}, \ldots, v_{sw_l})$

Values: $m_i^{out} = avg(v_{c_1 \in s}, \ldots)$

Candidates: $c_j = v_{c_j}$

At Hop t:

$a_{ti} = sparsemax(q_t R_t m_i)$

$o_t = \sum_i a_{ti} m_i^{out}$

$q_{t+1} = q_t + o_t$

After last hop:

$p(c_j) = softmax(o_h C v_{c_j})$

Figure 1: Overview of our Key-Value Memory Network for BookQA. Encodings of questions, keys (selected sentences), and values (characters mentioned in those sentences) are loaded. After multiple hops of inference, the model's output is compared against the candidate answers' encodings to make a prediction.

if a sentence is relevant to a question, using positive (*questions, summary sentence*) training pairs which have been heuristically matched. Randomly sampled negative pairs were also used. At retrieval time, a question is used to retrieve relevant passages from the full text of a book.

3.3 Neural Inference

Having replaced character mentions in questions and books with character identifiers, we first pretrain word2vec embeddings (Mikolov et al., 2013) for all words and book characters in our corpus.[2] Our neural inference model is a variant of the Key-Value Memory Network (KV-MemNet) (Miller et al., 2016), which has been previously applied to QA tasks over KBs and short texts. The original model was designed to handle a fixed set of potential answers across all QA examples, as do most neural QA architectures. This comes in contrast with our task, where the pool of candidate characters is different for each book. Our KV-MemNet variant, illustrated in Figure 1, uses a dynamic output layer where different candidate answers are made available for different books, while the remaining model parameters are shared.

A question is initially represented as q_0, i.e., the average of its word embeddings[3] (gray vector). The *Key* memories $m_1^{in} \ldots m_k^{in}$ (purple vectors) are filled with the k most relevant sentences, as retrieved from the context selection step, us-

ing the average of their word embeddings. *Value* memories $m_1^{out} \ldots m_k^{out}$ (green vectors) contain the average embedding of all characters mentioned in the respective sentence, or a padding vector if no character is mentioned. Candidate embeddings $c_1 \ldots c_n$ (orange vectors) hold the embeddings of every character in the current book. The model makes multiple reasoning hops $t = 1 \ldots h$ over the memories. At each hop, q_t is passed through linear layer R_t and is then compared against all key memories. The *sparsemax*-normalized (Martins and Astudillo, 2016) attention weights $a_1 \ldots a_k$ are then used for obtaining output vector o_t, as the weighted average of value memories. The process is repeated h times, and the final output is passed through linear layer C, before being compared against all candidate vectors via dotproduct, to obtain the final prediction. The model is trained using negative log-likelihood.

3.4 Pretraining

A significant obstacle towards effective BookQA is the limited amount of data available for supervised training. A potential avenue for overcoming this is pretraining the neural inference model on an auxiliary task, for which we can generate orders of magnitude more training examples. To this end, we generated 688,228 artificial questions from the book text using a set of simple pruning rules over the dependency trees of book sentences. We used all book sentences where a character mention is the agent or the patient of an active voice verb, or the patient of a passive voice verb. Two examples

---

[2]Character identifiers are treated like all other tokens.

[3]Experiments with more sophisticated question/sentence representation variants showed no significant improvements.

| Metric → | **P@1** | | **P@5** | | **MRR** | |
Context selection →	BM25F	BERT	BM25F	BERT	BM25F	BERT
Baselines:						
Book frequency	15.73		56.29		0.337	
Context frequency	10.53	13.80	51.42	53.02	0.276	0.305
KV-MemNet:						
No pretraining	15.57±0.97	15.89±0.95	58.18±1.57	58.77±1.29	0.339±0.006	0.343±0.008
Pretrain w/ Artif. Qs	15.92±0.73	**18.73**±1.07	61.25±0.74	**62.81**±1.07	0.351±0.005	**0.376**±0.006

Table 2: Precision scores (P@1, P@5), and Mean Reciprocal Rank (MRR) for frequency-based baselines and our system, with and without pretraining. We report average and standard deviation over 50 runs.

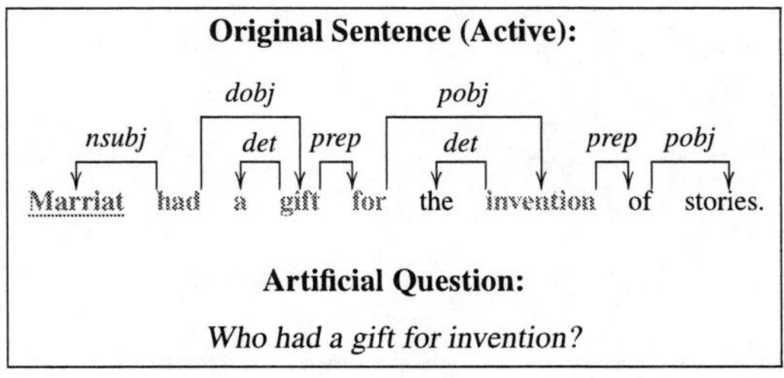

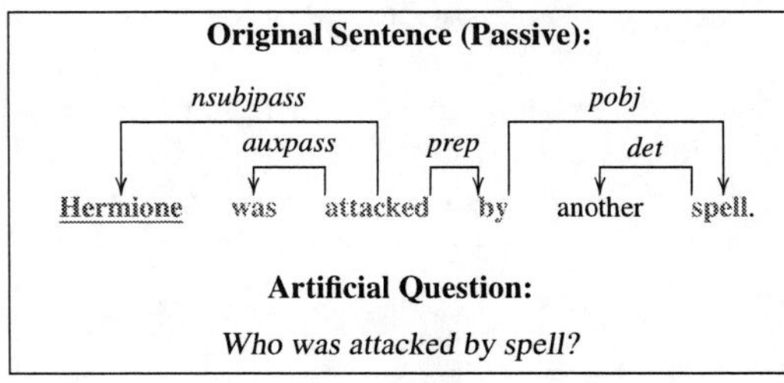

Figure 2: Examples of artificial questions generated from the dependency trees of an active voice (top) and a passive voice (bottom) sentence. The correct answer (*verb's subject*) is marked with blue, whereas the yellow words are used in the question. The remaining words are discarded by pruning the dependency tree.

are illustrated in Figure 2: at the top, the active voice sentence *"Marriat had a gift for the invention of stories."* is transformed into the question *"Who had a gift for invention?"* and, at the bottom, the passive voice sentence *"Hermione was attacked by another spell."* is transformed into the question *"Who was attacked by a spell?"*. The previous 20 book sentences, including the source sentence, are used as context during pretraining.

4 Experimental Setup

For every question, 100 sentences (top 20 passages of five sentences) were selected as contexts using our retrieval methods. We used word and book character embeddings of 100 dimensions. The number of reasoning hops was set to 3. When no pretraining was performed, we trained on the real QA examples for 60 epochs, using Adam with initial learning rate of 10^{-3}, which we reduced by 10% every two epochs. Word and character embeddings were fixed during training. When using pretraining, we trained the memory network for one epoch on the auxiliary task, including the embeddings. Then, the model was fine-tuned as described above on the real QA examples where, again, embeddings were fixed. We use Precision at the 1st and 5th rank (P@1 and P@5) and Mean Reciprocal Rank (MRR) as evaluation metrics. We adopted a 10-fold cross validation approach and performed 5 trials for each cross validation split, for a total of 50 experiments.

Baselines: We implemented a random baseline and two frequency-based baselines, where the most frequent character in the entire book (*Book* frequency) or the selected context (*Context* frequency) was selected as the answer.

5 Results

Our main results are presented in Table 2. Firstly, we observe one of the dataset's biases, as the book's most frequent character is the correct answer in more than 15% of examples, whereas selecting a character at random would only yield the correct answer 2.5% of the time.

With regards to our BookQA pipeline, the results confirm that BookQA is a very challenging task. Without pretraining, our KV-MemNet which uses IR contexts achieves 15.57% P@1, and it is slightly outperformed by its BERT-based counterpart.[4] When pretraining the memory network with artificial questions, the BERT-based model achieves 18.73% P@1. The same trend is observed with the other metrics.

Number of hops: We also calculated the impact of the number of hops with respect to the P@1 for a pretrained model fine-tuned with BERT-selected

---

[4]Despite the similar performance to the Book frequency baseline, we *did not* observe that our model was systematically selecting the most frequent character as the answer.

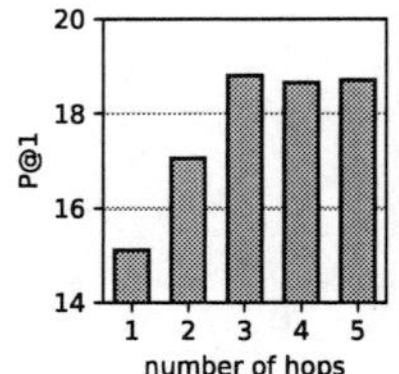 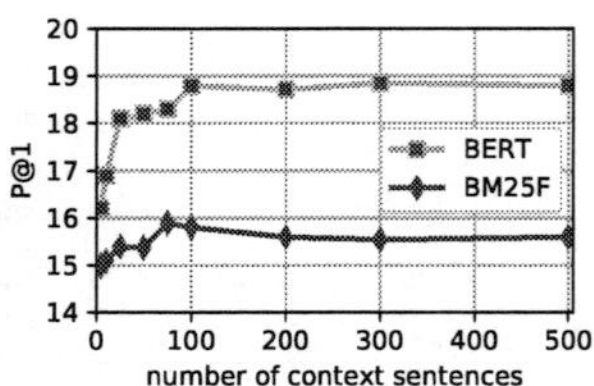

Figure 3: P@1 for different number of hops.

Figure 4: P@1 for varying context sizes from BM25F and BERT.

correct character mentioned in context	BM25F	69.7%
	BERT	74.7%
full evidence found in context		27%
partial evidence found in context	BM25F	47%
no evidence found in context		26%

Table 3: Percentage of contexts where the correct character is mentioned (top). Percentage of contexts where full/partial/no evidence for the answer was found according to crowd-workers who examined a sample of 100 cases (bottom).

contexts. Figure 3 shows that performance increases up to 3 hops and then it stabilizes.

Context size: We expected the context size (i.e., the number of retrieved sentences that we store in the memory slots of our KV-MemNet) to significantly affect performance. Smaller contexts, obtained by only retrieving the topmost relevant passages, might miss important evidence for answering a question at hand. Conversely, larger contexts might introduce noise in the form of irrelevant sentences that hinder inference. Figure 4 shows the performance of our method when varying the number of context sentences (or, equivalently, memory slots). The neural inference model struggles for very small context sizes and achieves its best performance for 75 and 100 context sentences obtained by BM25F and BERT, respectively. For both alternatives, we observe no further improvements for larger contexts.

Pretraining size & epochs: A key component of our BookQA framework is the pretraining of our neural inference model with artificially generated questions. Although it helped achieve the highest percentage of correctly answered questions, the performance gains were relatively small given the number of artificial questions used to pretrain the model. We further investigated the effect of pretraining by varying the number of artificial questions used during training and the number of pretraining epochs. Figure 5 shows the QA performance achieved on the real BookQA questions (using BM25F or BERT contexts) after pretraining on a randomly sampled subset of the artificial questions. For our BERT-based variant, the percentage of correctly answered questions increases steadily, but flattens out when reaching 75% of pretraining set usage. On the contrary, when using BM25F contexts we achieved insignificant gains, with performance appearing constrained by the quality of retrieved passages. In Figure 6 we show

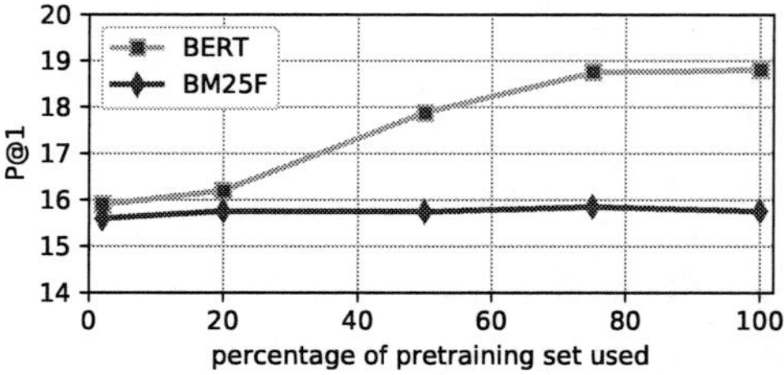

Figure 5: P@1 for varying percentage of pretraining questions used (BM25F and BERT contexts).

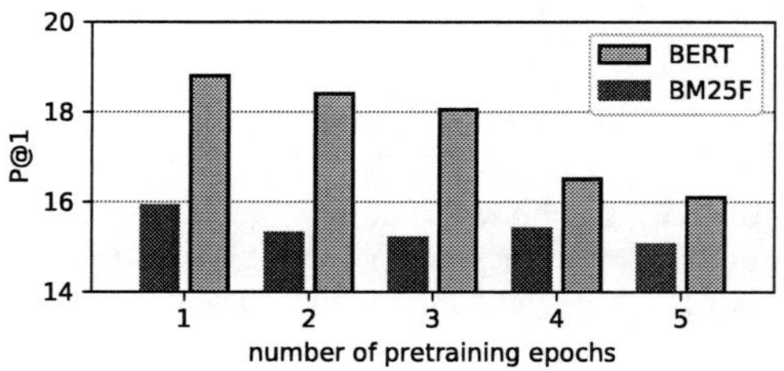

Figure 6: P@1 as a function of pretraining epochs for BM25F and BERT contexts.

P@1 scores as a function of the number of pretraining epochs. Best performance is achieved after only one epoch for both variants, indicating that further pretraining might cause the model to overfit to the simpler type of reasoning required for answering artificial questions.

5.1 Further Discussion

Despite the limitation to *Who* questions, the employment of strong models for context selection and neural inference, and our pretraining efforts, the overall BookQA accuracy remains modest, as our best-performing system achieves a P@1 score below 20%. Even when we only allowed our system to answer if it was very confident (according to the probability difference between top-ranked candidate answers), it answered correctly 35% of times.

We have identified a number of reasons which inhibit better performance. Firstly, the passage selection process constrains the answers that can be logically inferred. We provide our findings in regards to this claim in Table 3. We calculated that the correct answer appears in the IR-selected contexts in 69.7% of cases. For BERT-selected contexts it appears in 74.7% of cases. In practice, however, these upper-bounds are not achievable; even when the correct answer appears in the context, there is no guarantee that enough evidence exists to infer it. To further investigate this, we ran a survey on Amazon Mechanichal Turk, where participants were asked to indicate if the selected context (IR-retrieved) contained partial or full evidence for answering a question. For a set of 100 randomly sampled questions, participants found full evidence for answering a question in just 27% of cases. Only partial evidence was found in 47% of cases, and no evidence in the remaining 26%.

Manual inspection of context sentences indicated that a common reason for the absence of full evidence is the inherent vagueness of literary language. Repeated expressions or direct references to character names are often avoided by authors, thus requiring very accurate paraphrase detection and coreference resolution. We believe that commonsense knowledge is particularly crucial for improving BookQA. When exploring the output of our system, we repeatedly found cases where the model failed to arrive at the correct answer due to key information being left implicit. Common examples we identified were: i) character relationships which were clear to the reader, but never explicitly described (e.g., *"Who did Mark's best friend marry?"*); ii) the attitude of a character towards an event or situation (e.g., *"Who was angry at the school's policy?"*); iii) the relative succession of events (e.g., *"Who did Marriat talk to after the big fight?"*). The injection of commonsense knowledge into a QA system is an open problem for general and, consequently, BookQA.

In regards to pretraining, the lack of further improvements is likely related to the difference in the type of reasoning required for answering the artificial questions and the real book questions. By construction, the artificial questions will only require that the model accurately matches the source sentence, without the need for complex or multi-hop reasoning steps. In contrast, real book questions require inference over information spread across many parts of a book. We believe that our proposed auxiliary task mainly helps the model by improving the quality of word and book character representations. It is, however, clear from our results that pretraining is an important avenue for improving BookQA accuracy, as it can increase the number of training instances by many orders of magnitude with limited human involvement. Future work should look into automatically constructing auxiliary questions that better approximate the types of reasoning required for realistic questions on the content of books.

We argue that the shortcomings discussed in previous paragraphs, i.e., the lack of evidence in retrieved passages, the difficulty of long-term reasoning, the need for paraphrase detection and commonsense knowledge, and the challenge of useful pretraining, are not specific to *Who* questions. On the contrary, we expect that the requirement for novel research in these areas will generalize or, potentially, increase in the case of more general questions (e.g., open-ended questions).

6 Conclusions

We presented a pipeline BookQA system to answer character-based questions on NarrativeQA, from the full book text. By constraining our study to *Who* questions, we simplified the task's output space, while largely retaining the reasoning challenges of BookQA, and our ability to draw conclusions that will generalize to other question types. Given a *Who* question, our system retrieves a set of relevant passages from the book, which are then used by a memory network to infer the answer in multiple hops. A BERT-based trained retrieval system, together with the usage of artificial question-answer pairs to pretrain the memory network, allowed our system to significantly outperform the lexical frequency-based baselines. The use of BERT-retrieved contexts improved upon a simpler IR-based method although, in both cases, only partial evidence was found in the selected contexts for the majority of questions. Increasing the number of retrieved passages did not result in better performance, highlighting the significant challenge of accurate context selection. Pretraining on artificially generated questions provided promising improvements, but the automatic construction of realistic questions that require multi-hop reasoning remains an open problem. These results confirm the difficulty of the BookQA challenge, and indicate that there is need for novel research in order to achieve high-quality BookQA. Future work on the task must focus on several aspects of the problem, including: (a) improving context selection, by combining IR and neural methods to remove noise in the selected passages, or by jointly optimizing for context selection and answer extraction (Das et al., 2019); (b) using better methods for encoding questions, sentences, and candidate answers, as embedding averaging results in information loss; (c) pretraining tactics that better mimic the real BookQA task; (d) incorporation of commonsense knowledge and structure, which was not addressed in this paper.

Acknowledgments We would like to thank Hugo Zaragoza and Alex Klementiev for their valuable insights, feedback and support on the work presented in this paper.

References

David Bamman, Ted Underwood, and Noah A. Smith. 2014. A bayesian mixed effects model of literary character. In *Proceedings of the 52nd Annual Meeting of the Association for Computational Linguistics (Volume 1: Long Papers)*, pages 370–379. Association for Computational Linguistics.

Lisa Bauer, Yicheng Wang, and Mohit Bansal. 2018. Commonsense for generative multi-hop question answering tasks. In *Proceedings of the 2018 Conference on Empirical Methods in Natural Language Processing*, pages 4220–4230, Brussels, Belgium. Association for Computational Linguistics.

Antoine Bordes, Sumit Chopra, and Jason Weston. 2014. Question answering with subgraph embeddings. In *Proceedings of the 2014 Conference on Empirical Methods in Natural Language Processing (EMNLP)*, pages 615–620. Association for Computational Linguistics.

Rajarshi Das, Shehzaad Dhuliawala, Manzil Zaheer, and Andrew McCallum. 2019. Multi-step retriever-reader interaction for scalable open-domain question answering. In *ICLR 2019*.

Haohui Deng and Yik-Cheung Tam. 2018. Read and comprehend by gated-attention reader with more belief. In *Proceedings of the 2018 Conference of the North American Chapter of the Association for Computational Linguistics: Student Research Workshop*, pages 83–91, New Orleans, Louisiana, USA. Association for Computational Linguistics.

Jacob Devlin, Ming-Wei Chang, Kenton Lee, and Kristina Toutanova. 2019. BERT: Pre-training of deep bidirectional transformers for language understanding. In *Proceedings of the 2019 Conference of the North American Chapter of the Association for Computational Linguistics: Human Language Technologies, Volume 1 (Long and Short Papers)*, pages 4171–4186, Minneapolis, Minnesota. Association for Computational Linguistics.

Lea Frermann and György Szarvas. 2017. Inducing semantic micro-clusters from deep multi-view representations of novels. In *Proceedings of the 2017 Conference on Empirical Methods in Natural Language Processing*, pages 1873–1883. Association for Computational Linguistics.

Sathish Reddy Indurthi, Seunghak Yu, Seohyun Back, and Heriberto Cuayáhuitl. 2018. Cut to the chase: A context zoom-in network for reading comprehension. In *Proceedings of the 2018 Conference on Empirical Methods in Natural Language Processing*, pages 570–575, Brussels, Belgium. Association for Computational Linguistics.

Mohit Iyyer, Anupam Guha, Snigdha Chaturvedi, Jordan Boyd-Graber, and Hal Daumé III. 2016. Feuding families and former friends: Unsupervised learning for dynamic fictional relationships. In *Proceedings of the 2016 Conference of the North American Chapter of the Association for Computational Linguistics: Human Language Technologies*, pages 1534–1544. Association for Computational Linguistics.

Tomas Kocisky, Jonathan Schwarz, Phil Blunsom, Chris Dyer, Karl Moritz Hermann, Gabor Melis, and Edward Grefenstette. 2018. The narrativeqa reading comprehension challenge. *Transactions of the Association for Computational Linguistics*, 6:317–328.

André F. T. Martins and Ramón F. Astudillo. 2016. From softmax to sparsemax: A sparse model of attention and multi-label classification. In *Proceedings of the 33rd International Conference on International Conference on Machine Learning - Volume 48*, ICML'16, pages 1614–1623. JMLR.org.

Tomas Mikolov, Ilya Sutskever, Kai Chen, Greg Corrado, and Jeffrey Dean. 2013. Distributed representations of words and phrases and their compositionality. In *Proceedings of the 26th International Conference on Neural Information Processing Systems - Volume 2*, NIPS'13, pages 3111–3119, USA. Curran Associates Inc.

Alexander Miller, Adam Fisch, Jesse Dodge, Amir-Hossein Karimi, Antoine Bordes, and Jason Weston. 2016. Key-value memory networks for directly reading documents. In *Proceedings of the 2016 Conference on Empirical Methods in Natural Language Processing*, pages 1400–1409. Association for Computational Linguistics.

Sewon Min, Victor Zhong, Richard Socher, and Caiming Xiong. 2018. Efficient and robust question answering from minimal context over documents. In *Proceedings of the 56th Annual Meeting of the Association for Computational Linguistics (Volume 1:*

Long Papers), pages 1725–1735. Association for Computational Linguistics.

Kyosuke Nishida, Itsumi Saito, Kosuke Nishida, Kazutoshi Shinoda, Atsushi Otsuka, Hisako Asano, and Junji Tomita. 2019. Multi-style generative reading comprehension. In *Proceedings of the 57th Annual Meeting of the Association for Computational Linguistics*, pages 2273–2284, Florence, Italy. Association for Computational Linguistics.

Yelong Shen, Po-Sen Huang, Jianfeng Gao, and Weizhu Chen. 2017. Reasonet: Learning to stop reading in machine comprehension. In *Proceedings of the 23rd ACM SIGKDD International Conference on Knowledge Discovery and Data Mining*, KDD '17, pages 1047–1055, New York, NY, USA. ACM.

Yi Tay, Anh Tuan Luu, and Siu Cheung Hui. 2018a. Multi-granular sequence encoding via dilated compositional units for reading comprehension. In *Proceedings of the 2018 Conference on Empirical Methods in Natural Language Processing*, pages 2141–2151, Brussels, Belgium. Association for Computational Linguistics.

Yi Tay, Luu Anh Tuan, Siu Cheung Hui, and Jian Su. 2018b. Densely connected attention propagation for reading comprehension. In *Proceedings of the 32Nd International Conference on Neural Information Processing Systems*, NIPS'18, pages 4911–4922, USA. Curran Associates Inc.

Yi Tay, Shuohang Wang, Anh Tuan Luu, Jie Fu, Minh C. Phan, Xingdi Yuan, Jinfeng Rao, Siu Cheung Hui, and Aston Zhang. 2019. Simple and effective curriculum pointer-generator networks for reading comprehension over long narratives. In *Proceedings of the 57th Annual Meeting of the Association for Computational Linguistics*, pages 4922–4931, Florence, Italy. Association for Computational Linguistics.

Ellen M. Voorhees. 2001. The trec question answering track. *Natural Language Engineering*, 7(4):361–378.

Hugo Zaragoza, Nick Craswell, Michael J Taylor, Suchi Saria, and Stephen E Robertson. 2004. Microsoft cambridge at trec 13: Web and hard tracks. In *TREC*, volume 4, pages 1–1.

FlowDelta: Modeling Flow Information Gain in Reasoning for Conversational Machine Comprehension

Yi-Ting Yeh
National Taiwan University
r07922064@csie.ntu.edu.tw

Yun-Nung Chen
National Taiwan University
y.v.chen@ieee.org

Abstract

Conversational machine comprehension requires deep understanding of the dialogue flow, and the prior work proposed FlowQA to implicitly model the context representations in reasoning for better understanding. This paper proposes to explicitly model the *information gain* through dialogue reasoning in order to allow the model to focus on more informative cues. The proposed model achieves state-of-the-art performance in a conversational QA dataset QuAC and sequential instruction understanding dataset SCONE, which shows the effectiveness of the proposed mechanism and demonstrates its capability of generalization to different QA models and tasks [1]

1 Introduction

Machine reading comprehension has been increasingly studied in the NLP area, which aims to read a given passage and then answer questions correctly. However, human usually seeks answers in a conversational manner by asking follow-up questions given the previous answers. Traditional machine reading comprehension (MC) tasks such as SQuAD (Rajpurkar et al., 2016) focus on a single-turn setting, and there is no connection between different questions and answers to the same passage. To address the multi-turn issue, several datasets about conversational question answering (QA) were introduced, such as CoQA (Reddy et al., 2018) and QuAC (Choi et al., 2018).

Most existing machine comprehension models apply single-turn methods and augment the input with question and answer history, ignoring previous reasoning processes in the models. Recently proposed FlowQA (Huang et al., 2018) attempted at modeling such multi-turn reasoning in dialogues in order to improve performance for

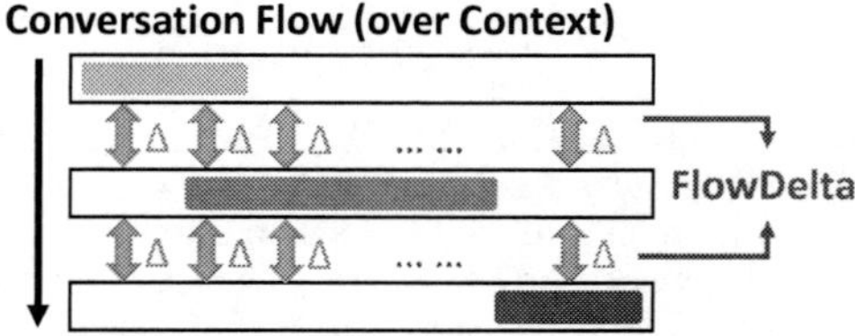

Figure 1: Illustration of the flow information gain modeled by the FlowDelta mechanism.

conversational QA. However, the proposed FLOW operation is expected to incorporate salient information in an *implicit* manner, because the learned representations captured by FLOW would change during multi-turn questions. It is unsure whether such change correlates well with the current answer or not. In order to *explicitly* model the information gain in FLOW and further relate the current answer to the corresponding context, we present a novel mechanism, FlowDelta, which focuses on modeling the difference between the learned context representations in multi-turn dialogues illustrated in Figure 1. The contributions are 3-fold:

- This paper proposes a simple and effective mechanism to explicitly model information gain in flow-based reasoning for multi-turn dialogues, which can be easily incorporated in different MC models.
- FlowDelta consistently improves the performance on various conversational MC datasets, including CoQA and QuAC.
- The proposed method achieves the state-of-the-art results on QuAC and sequential instruction understanding task (SCONE).

2 Background

Given a document (context), previous conversation history (i.e., question/answer pairs) and the current question, the goal of conversational QA is to find the correct answer. We denote the

---

[1]Our code can be found in https://github.com/MiuLab/FlowDelta.

Proceedings of the Second Workshop on Machine Reading for Question Answering, pages 86–90
Hong Kong, China, November 4, 2019. ©2019 Association for Computational Linguistics

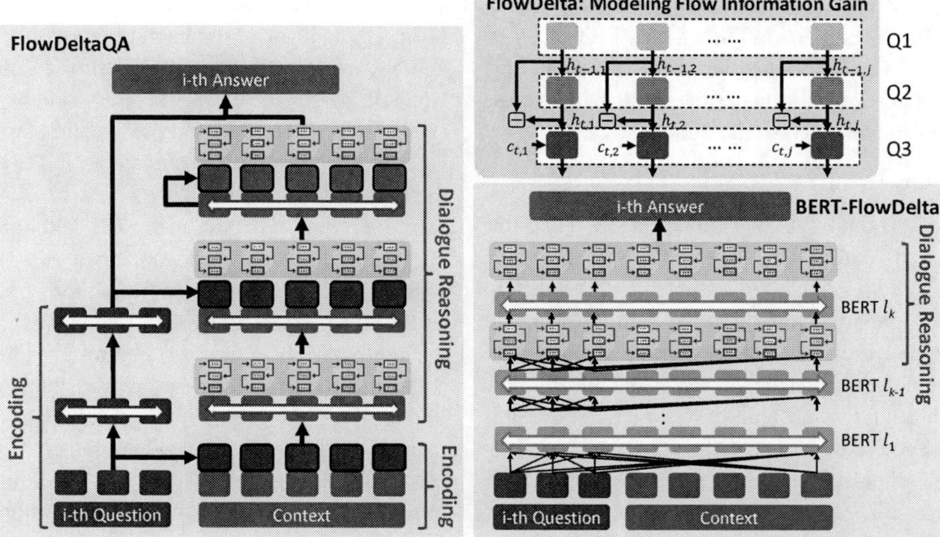

Figure 2: Illustration of the proposed FlowDelta models.

context document as a sequence of m words $C = \{c_1, c_2, \ldots c_m\}$, and the i-th question $Q_i = \{q_1, q_2, \ldots, q_n\}$ as a sequence of n words. In the extractive setting, the i-th answer A_i is guaranteed to be a span in the context. The main challenge in conversational QA is that current question may depend on the conversation history, which differs from the classic machine comprehension. Therefore, how to incorporate previous history into the QA model is especially important for better understanding. Prior work (Huang et al., 2018) proposes an effective way to model the reasoning in multi-turn dialogues summarized below.

FLOW Operation Instead of only using shallow history like previous questions and answers, Huang et al. (2018) proposed the FLOW operation that feeds the model with entire hidden representations generated during the reasoning process when answering previous questions. FLOW is defined as *a sequence of latent representations based on the context tokens* and is demonstrated effective for conversational QA tasks, because it well incorporates multi-turn information in dialogue reasoning.

Let the context representation for i-th question be $C_i = c_{i,1}, \ldots, c_{i,m}$ and the dialogue length is t. When answering questions in the dialogue, there are t context sequences of length m, one for each question. We reshape it to become m sequences of length t, one for each context word, and then pass each sequence into a unidirectional GRU. All context word representation j ($1 \leq j \leq m$) are

processed in parallel in order to model the information via the FLOW direction (vertical direction illustrated in Figure 1).

$$h_{1,j}, \ldots, h_{t,j} = GRU(c_{1,j}, \ldots, c_{t,j}) \quad (1)$$

Then we reshape the outputs from GRU back and form $F_i = \{h_{i,1}, \ldots, h_{i,m}\}$, where F_i is the output of the FLOW layer.

FlowQA The FLOW layer described above is incorporated in FLOWQA for conversational MC, which is built on the single-turn MC model FusionNet (Huang et al., 2017), and the full structure is shown in the left part of Figuire 2. Briefly, FLOWQA first performs word-level attention to fuse the information of i-th question Q_i into context C. Then it uses two LSTM cells combined with FLOW layers to integrate the context representations, followed by the context-question attention computation. Finally, FLOWQA performs self-attention (Yu et al., 2018) on the context and predict the answer span. Modeling FLOW is shown effective to improve the performance for conversational MC.

3 Proposed Approaches

This paper extends the concept of FLOW and proposes a flow-based approach, FLOWDELTA, to *explicitly* model information gain in flow during dialogues illustrated in Figure 2. The proposed mechanism is flexible to integrate with different models, including FlowQA and others. To examine such flexibility and generalization capability, we further apply FLOW and FLOWDELTA to BERT (Devlin et al., 2018), a pretrained language understanding model that shows strong performance in MC tasks, to allow model to grasp dialogue history.

3.1 FlowDeltaQA

In the original FLOW operation in (1), the k-th step computation of GRU is $h_{k,j} = GRU(c_{k,j}, h_{k-1,j})$. We assume that the difference of previous hidden representations $h_{k-1,j}$ and $h_{k-2,j}$ indicates whether the flow change is important, which can be viewed as the information gain through the reasoning process. For example, 3 consecutive questions Q_{k-2}, Q_{k-1}, Q_k. Q_{k-1} and Q_k all discuss the same event described in the span $\{c_j, c_{j+1}, \ldots, c_l\}$ of the context, while Q_{k-2} is about another topic. We expect the hidden state $\{h_{k-1,j}, h_{k-1,j+1} \ldots, h_{k-1,l}\}$ of the span in turn $k-1$ is dissimilar to the hidden state in the turn $k-2$, because their topics are different. By explicitly modeling such difference, our model more easily relates the current reasoning process to the corresponding context.

Following the intuition above, we propose FLOWDELTA by modifying the single step computation of FLOW into:

$$h_{k,j} = GRU([c_{k,j}; h_{k-1,j} - h_{k-2,j}], h_{k-1,j}), \quad (2)$$

where $[x; y]$ is the concatenation of the vectors x and y. We also investigate other variants such as Hadamard product ($h_{k-1,j} * h_{k-2,j}$) detailed in Appendix C.

3.2 BERT-FlowDelta

BERT (Devlin et al., 2018) with fine-tuning recently has reached the state-of-the-art in many single-turn MC tasks, such as SQuAD (Rajpurkar et al., 2016, 2018). However, how to extend BERT to the multi-turn setting remains unsolved. We propose to incorporate the FLOWDELTA mechanism to deal with the multi-turn problem, where the FLOW layer automatically integrates multi-turn information instead of tuning the number of QA pairs for inclusion.

Each layer of BERT is a Transformer block (Vaswani et al., 2017) that consists of multi-head attention (MH) and fully-connected feed forward network (FFN):

$$h_{l+1} = \text{Transfomer}(h_l) = LN(h_l + SA(h_l)),$$
$$SA(h) = FFN(LN(h + MH(h)),$$

where h_l is the hidden representation of the l-th layer, LN is layer normalization (Ba et al., 2016) and SA means self-attention. To utilize L layers from BERT for the extractive question answering task, we feed the hidden representation from last layer h_L to a fully-connected layer (NN) to predict the answer span, written as $P^S, P^E = NN(h_L)$, where P^S and P^E are span start and span end probability for each word respectively.

BERT-FlowDelta incorporates the proposed FLOWDELTA mechanisms for two parts shown in the bottom right corner of Figure 2. First, we add FLOWDELTA layer before the final prediction layer, $P^S, P^E = NN([h_L; \text{FlowDelta}(h_L)])$. Second, we further insert FLOWDELTA into the last BERT layer, considering that modeling dialogue history *within* BERT may be benefitial.

$$h_L = LN(h_{L-1} + SA(h_{L-1}) + \text{FlowDelta}(h_{L-1}))$$

These two modifications are called exFlowDelta and inFlowDelta respectively, and the latter also meets the idea from Stickland and Murray who added additional parameters into BERT layers to improve the performance of multi-task learning. In our experiments, we only modify the last BERT layer to avoid largely increasing model size.

4 Experiments

To evaluate the effectiveness of the proposed FLOWDELTA, various tasks that contains dialogue history for understanding are performed in the following experiments.

4.1 Setup

Our models are tested on two conversational MC datasets, CoQA (Reddy et al., 2018) and QuAC (Choi et al., 2018), and a sequential instruction understanding dataset, SCONE (Long et al., 2016). For QuAC, we also report the Human Equivalence Score (HEQ). HEQ-Q and HEQ-D represent the percentage of exceeding the model performance over the human evaluation for each question and dialogue respectively. While CoQA and QuAC both follow the conversational QA setting, SCONE is the task requiring model to understand a sequence of natural language instructions and modify the word state accordingly. We follow Huang et al. (2018) to reduce instruction understanding to machine comprehension. Appendix A contains the example and reduction detail of SCONE for reference.

Model	CoQA			QuAC			
	Dev	Test		Dev	Test		
	F1	Child/Liter/Mid/News/Wiki/Reddit/Sci	F1	F1	F1	HEQ-Q	HEQ-D
BiDAF++ (N-ctx)	69.2	66.5 65.7 70.2 71.6 72.6 60.8 67.1	67.8	60.6	60.1	54.8	4.0
FlowQA	76.7	73.7 71.6 76.8 79.0 80.2 67.8 76.1	75.0	63.9	64.1	59.6	5.8
SDNet (Zhu et al., 2018)	78.0	75.4 73.9 77.1 80.3 **83.1** 69.8 76.8	76.6	-	-	-	-
ConvBERT (unpublished)	-	-	**86.8**	-	**68.0**	63.5	9.1
FlowDeltaQA	77.6	-	-	64.8	-	-	-
BERT-FlowDelta	**79.4**	**75.9 75.6 80.1 82.1** 82.3 **69.8 78.8**	77.7	**68.6**	67.8	**63.6**	**12.1**
Human	89.8	90.2 88.4 89.8 88.6 89.9 86.7 88.1	88.8	80.8	81.1	100	100

Table 1: Conversational QA results on CoQA and QuAC, where (N-ctx) refers to using previous N QA pairs (%).

Model	CoQA F1	QuAC F1
BERT-FlowDelta	**79.4**	**68.6**
- inFlowDelta	79.0	66.2
- exFlowDelta	78.0	64.5
BERT-Flow	79.2	66.8

Table 2: The ablation study of BERT-FlowDelta (%).

Model	Scene	Tangrams	Alchemy
Long et al. (2016)	14.7	27.6	52.3
Guu et al. (2017)	46.2	37.1	52.9
Suhr and Artzi (2018)	66.4	60.1	62.3
Fried et al. (2017)	72.7	69.6	72.0
FusionNet	58.2	67.9	74.1
FlowQA	74.5	72.3	**76.4**
FlowDeltaQA	**75.1**	**72.5**	76.1

Table 3: Dialogue accuracy for SCONE test (%).

4.2 Results

Table 1 reports model performance on CoQA and QuAC. It can be found that FlowDeltaQA yields substantial improvement over FlowQA on both datasets (+ 0.9 % F1 on both CoQA and QuAC), showing the usefulness of explicitly modeling the information gain in the FLOW layer. Furthermore, BERT-FlowDelta outperforms the published models on CoQA and achieves the state-of-the-art scores on the QuAC leaderboard on Apr 24, 2019. Specifically, BERT-FlowDelta outperforms ConvBERT by a large margin in HEQ-D on QuAC, showing the superiority of our model in modeling whole dialogue. Note that FLOWDELTA actually introduced few additional parameters compared to FLOW, since it only augments the input dimension of GRU. The consistent improvement from both data demonstrates the generalization capability of applying the proposed mechanism to various models.

Table 2 shows the ablation study of BERT-FlowDelta, where two proposed modules are both important for achieving such results. It is interesting that the proposed inFlowDelta and exFlowDelta boost the performance more on QuAC. As Yatskar (2018) mentioned, the topics in a dialogue shift more frequently on QuAC than on CoQA, and we can see vanilla BERT also performs well on CoQA in the ablation of FLOW which provides long term dialog history information. Therefore, we can conclude that while FLOWDELTA improves the ability to grasp information gain in the dialog, it bring less performance improvement in the setting we do not need much contexts to answer the question.

Table 3 shows the performance of our FlowDeltaQA on the SCONE [2]. Our model outperforms FlowQA and achieves the state-of-the-art in SCENE and TANGRAMS domains. The small performance drop in ALCHEMY aligns well with the statement in the ablation study. Because experiments show that removing FLOW affects performance in ALCHEMY less when comparing between FlowQA and FusionNet (Huang et al., 2017) (same models except FLOW), we claim that the previous dialogue history is less important in this domain. Thus replaying FLOW with FlowDelta does not bring any improvement in the ALCHEMY domain. The detailed qualitative study can be found in Appendix D.

5 Conclusion

This paper presents a simple and effective extension of FLOW named FLOWDELTA, which is capable of explicitly modeling the dialogue history in reasoning for better conversational machine comprehension. The proposed FlowDelta is flexible to apply to other machine comprehension models including FlowQA and BERT. The experiments on three datasets show that the proposed mechanism can model the information flow in the multi-turn dialogues more comprehensively, and further boosts the performance consistently. In the future, we will investigate more efficient ways to model the dialogue flow for conversational tasks.

---

[2] The results of BERT-FlowDelta are not shown, since SCONE is a relatively small and synthetic dataset.

References

Jimmy Lei Ba, Jamie Ryan Kiros, and Geoffrey E Hinton. 2016. Layer normalization. *arXiv preprint arXiv:1607.06450*.

Eunsol Choi, He He, Mohit Iyyer, Mark Yatskar, Wentau Yih, Yejin Choi, Percy Liang, and Luke Zettlemoyer. 2018. Quac: Question answering in context. In *Proceedings of the 2018 Conference on Empirical Methods in Natural Language Processing*, pages 2174–2184.

Jacob Devlin, Ming-Wei Chang, Kenton Lee, and Kristina Toutanova. 2018. Bert: Pre-training of deep bidirectional transformers for language understanding. *arXiv preprint arXiv:1810.04805*.

Daniel Fried, Jacob Andreas, and Dan Klein. 2017. Unified pragmatic models for generating and following instructions. *arXiv preprint arXiv:1711.04987*.

Kelvin Guu, Panupong Pasupat, Evan Zheran Liu, and Percy Liang. 2017. From language to programs: Bridging reinforcement learning and maximum marginal likelihood. *arXiv preprint arXiv:1704.07926*.

Hsin-Yuan Huang, Eunsol Choi, and Wen-tau Yih. 2018. Flowqa: Grasping flow in history for conversational machine comprehension. *arXiv preprint arXiv:1810.06683*.

Hsin-Yuan Huang, Chenguang Zhu, Yelong Shen, and Weizhu Chen. 2017. Fusionnet: Fusing via fully-aware attention with application to machine comprehension. *arXiv preprint arXiv:1711.07341*.

Reginald Long, Panupong Pasupat, and Percy Liang. 2016. Simpler context-dependent logical forms via model projections. *arXiv preprint arXiv:1606.05378*.

Pranav Rajpurkar, Robin Jia, and Percy Liang. 2018. Know what you don't know: Unanswerable questions for squad. *arXiv preprint arXiv:1806.03822*.

Pranav Rajpurkar, Jian Zhang, Konstantin Lopyrev, and Percy Liang. 2016. Squad: 100,000+ questions for machine comprehension of text. *arXiv preprint arXiv:1606.05250*.

Siva Reddy, Danqi Chen, and Christopher D Manning. 2018. Coqa: A conversational question answering challenge. *arXiv preprint arXiv:1808.07042*.

Asa Cooper Stickland and Iain Murray. 2019. Bert and pals: Projected attention layers for efficient adaptation in multi-task learning. *arXiv preprint arXiv:1902.02671*.

Alane Suhr and Yoav Artzi. 2018. Situated mapping of sequential instructions to actions with single-step reward observation. *arXiv preprint arXiv:1805.10209*.

Ashish Vaswani, Noam Shazeer, Niki Parmar, Jakob Uszkoreit, Llion Jones, Aidan N Gomez, Łukasz Kaiser, and Illia Polosukhin. 2017. Attention is all you need. In *Advances in Neural Information Processing Systems*, pages 5998–6008.

Mark Yatskar. 2018. A qualitative comparison of coqa, squad 2.0 and quac. *arXiv preprint arXiv:1809.10735*.

Adams Wei Yu, David Dohan, Minh-Thang Luong, Rui Zhao, Kai Chen, Mohammad Norouzi, and Quoc V Le. 2018. Qanet: Combining local convolution with global self-attention for reading comprehension. *arXiv preprint arXiv:1804.09541*.

Chenguang Zhu, Michael Zeng, and Xuedong Huang. 2018. Sdnet: Contextualized attention-based deep network for conversational question answering. *arXiv preprint arXiv:1812.03593*.

Do Multi-hop Readers Dream of Reasoning Chains?

Haoyu Wang *[†]   Mo Yu *[†]   Xiaoxiao Guo *[†]   Rajarshi Das *[‡]
Wenhan Xiong *[§]   Tian Gao *[†]
[†] IBM Research   [‡] Umass Amherst   [§] UC Santa Barbara

Abstract

General Question Answering (QA) systems over texts require the multi-hop reasoning capability, i.e. the ability to reason with information collected from multiple passages to derive the answer. In this paper we conduct a systematic analysis to assess such an ability of various existing models proposed for multi-hop QA tasks. Specifically, our analysis investigates that whether providing the full reasoning chain of multiple passages, instead of just one final passage where the answer appears, could improve the performance of the existing QA models. Surprisingly, when using the additional evidence passages, the improvements of all the existing multi-hop reading approaches are rather limited, with the highest error reduction of 5.8% on F1 (corresponding to 1.3% absolute improvement) from the BERT model.

To better understand whether the reasoning chains could indeed help find correct answers, we further develop a co-matching-based method that leads to 13.1% error reduction with passage chains when applied to two of our base readers (including BERT). Our results demonstrate the existence of the potential improvement using explicit multi-hop reasoning and the necessity to develop models with better reasoning abilities.[1]

1 Introduction

More recent development of QA systems (Song et al., 2018; De Cao et al., 2018; Zhong et al., 2019) has started to focus on multi-hop reasoning on text passages, aiming to propose more sophisticated models beyond the shallow matching between questions and answers. Multi-hop reasoning requires the ability to gather information from multiple different passages to correctly answer the question, and generally the task

would be unsolvable by using only similarities between the question and answer. Recent multi-hop QA datasets, such as WikiHop (Welbl et al., 2018), ComplexWebQuestions (Talmor and Berant, 2018), and HotpotQA (Yang et al., 2018), have accelerated the rapid progress of QA models for multi-hop reasoning problems.

There have been several reading comprehension models proposed to address the problem. Some methods (Yang et al., 2018; Zhong et al., 2019) rely on cross-attention among the question and evidence passages. BERT (Devlin et al., 2018) is one successful model of such an approach. Moreover, a substantial amount of query reformulation approaches (Weston et al., 2014; Wu et al., 2016; Shen et al., 2017; Das et al., 2019) have been proposed. Most of these methods adopt a soft version of reformulation, i.e. modifying the question embeddings based on the attention computed from each reasoning step. Similarly, some hard query reformulation approaches (Buck et al., 2018) propose to rewrite the question in the original language space. These methods provide more transparency to the reasoning processes. However, their performance usually lags behind their soft counterparts when no supervision on re-writing is available.

This paper aims to investigate the following two questions for multi-hop reasoning QA systems:

Do existing models indeed have the multi-hop reasoning ability? To answer this question, we design a dataset with chains of passages ordered by the ground-truth reasoning path. Then we conduct the comparisons between two settings: (1) training and evaluating the models with the correct ordering of the passage chains (**the ordered-oracle setting**); (2) training and evaluating the models with only the single passage that contain the answer (**the single-oracle setting**). We hypothesize that if the dataset indeed requires multi-hop rea-

---

[*]Equal contributions.

[1]Code and data released at `https://github.com/helloeve/bert-co-matching`.

Proceedings of the Second Workshop on Machine Reading for Question Answering, pages 91–97
Hong Kong, China, November 4, 2019. ©2019 Association for Computational Linguistics

soning and if a model could conduct multi-hop reasoning, it should perform significantly better in the first setting. However, we discovered that, for all the existing multi-hop reading comprehension models, the performance improvement with the ordered passages is rather limited, with the highest F1 improvement from BERT as 1.29%.

Is it beneficial to explore the usage of the reasoning chains? To answer this question, we try to find a reader model which could indeed make a better use of the the ordered passage information to improve performance. Inspired by the recent progress on the co-matching approaches for answer option selection (Wang et al., 2018; Zhang et al., 2019), we propose to adopt a similar idea for multi-hop question answering. We extend both the HotpotReader (Yang et al., 2018) and the BERT model (Devlin et al., 2018) with co-matching and observe 3.88% and 2.91% F1 improvement in the ordered-oracle setting over the single-oracle setting. These results confirm that the utilization of passage chains is important for multi-hop question answering, and there is untapped potential of designing new models that could perform "real" multi-hop reasoning.

2 Analysis Methods

The goal of this analysis is to validate each model's multi-hop reasoning ability by a specifically designed dataset with three comprehensive experiment settings.

2.1 Dataset

We conduct the analysis over a recently released multihop QA dataset HotpotQA (Yang et al., 2018). We created a new empirical setting based on the HotpotQA distractor setting: for each question-answer pair, two supporting passage are labeled by human annotators that are sufficient for answering the question. We release the data of our analysis setting, to make our results comparable for future works.[2]

There have been several multi-hop QA datasets released, but none of them has the ground truth reasoning chains annotated. The reason we choose HotpotQA is that the provided supporting passages serve as a good start point for identifying the approximately correct reasoning chain of passages, based on the heuristics described below.[3]

The key idea to recover the reasoning chain is that the chain must end at a passage that contains the answer. Specifically, given a question-answer pair (q, a) and its two supporting passages[4] p_0, p_1. Each passage p_i is an abstract paragraph of a Wikipedia page, thus corresponding to a topic entity e_i that is the title of the page. To determine the reasoning chain of passages, we have the following steps:

• We first check whether the answer a appears in any of the passages. If there is only one passage p_i containing the answer, then we have a reasoning chain with p_i as the final link of the chain, i.e., $p_{1-i} \to p_i$.

• If both passages contain a, then we use the following rule to determine the order: we check whether topic entity e_i appears in p_{1-i}. If true, we have the chain $p_{1-i} \to p_i$. If there are still multiple matches, we simply discard the question.

For a chain $p_i \to p_j$, we denote the first passage as the **context passage** and the second as the **answer passage**.

2.2 Analytical Method for the Ability of Multi-Hop Reasoning

Based on the aforementioned dataset, we propose a systematical approach to assess the multi-hop reasoning ability of different QA models. We design three experiment settings for different passage chain compositions.

• **Single-Oracle**, similar to the conventional QA setting that only the question and answer passage are provided while any context passages are omitted.

• **Ordered-Oracle**, that the question and the extracted ordered context and answer passages are provided.

• **Random**, similar to **Ordered-Oracle** but the passages are randomly ordered.

Based on the three settings,[5] we conduct the fol-

---

[2] https://gofile.io/?c=FDsda1.

[3] The HotpotQA also contains a subset of *comparison* questions, which aims to select between two options by comparing a property of theirs queried by the question, e.g., *Did LostAlone and Guster have the same number of members?*. These questions are not typical multi-hop questions by our community from the view of deduction. Therefore in this analysis we focus on non-comparison questions.

[4] This heuristic only works for chains of length 2. To investigate longer chains, more complex rules are required to deal with noise in distant supervision. Popular datasets generally do not require more than 2 hops to answer questions correctly. For example all the questions in HotpotQA has no more than 2 hops. We thus leave this to future work.

[5] Please note that both the Single-Oracle and the Ordered-Oracle settings are not valid realizations of the full task since they require a-priori knowledge of the answers. The settings

lowing analysis that each answers a research question related the multi-hop ability of the reading comprehension models:

First, we evaluate existing models on these settings, to answer the question *Q1: whether the existing models have the multi-hop reasoning ability*. To answer the question, we mainly look at the gap between *Single-Oracle* and *Ordered-Oracle*. A model with strong multi-hop reasoning capacity should have better performance in the *Ordered-Oracle* setting as the reasoning path is given.

Second, if the existing methods do not show great improvement when the reasoning paths are given, we will hope to confirm *Q2: whether our dataset does not require multi-hop reasoning because of some data biases* (see Section 6 for examples and discussions of the biases). It is difficult to directly answer Q2, therefore in our analysis we try to answer a relevant question *Q2′: whether the existing models can be further improved on the same dataset with better reasoning techniques*. Obviously, if there exists a technique that does better with the oracle-order information. It shows the reasoning paths can indeed introduce additional information in our settings, therefore the answer to *Q2* is likely *yes*. Therefore our dataset and settings can be used as a criterion for evaluating different models' multi-hop reasoning ability, i.e. used for answering *Q1*.

3 Baseline Models

For all methods, there are three inputs for the model: q represents the question, p_1 the context passage, and p_2 the answer passage. Accordingly, the word-level encoded hidden sequences for these three inputs are $H^q \in \mathbb{R}^{l \times Q}$, $H^{p_1} \in \mathbb{R}^{l \times P_1}$, and $H^{p_2} \in \mathbb{R}^{l \times P_2}$ respectively.

3.1 Baseline Models

Bi-Attention Reader (HotpotReader) One common state-of-the-art QA system is the HotpotReader (Yang et al., 2018) which is reported to benefit from the context passages. The system includes self-attention and bi-attention which are the standard practice in many question answering systems. We take this as one baseline as many other methods (Liu et al., 2017; Xiong et al., 2017) generally have similar model architectures.

BERT Reader Another strong baseline is to use the pre-trained BERT model to encode q, p_1,

are used in this paper only for analysis purpose.

and p_2 all together, expecting the inner-attention mechanism to capture the order information.

Given the fact that BERT could only take one input which contains the question and answer separated by "[SEP]", one straightforward approach to encode all three inputs by concatenating the two passages p_1 and p_2 to form the answer text "q [SEP] p_1 p_2". A more explicit way to introduce the separation of the two passages is to include a learnable boundary token by using the reserved token "[unused0]". Therefore we design another input for BERT as "q [SEP] p_1 [unused0] p_2". We adopt both approaches for completeness.

4 Multi-hop Reasoning Approaches

We seek to extend these two baseline models with two commonly used approaches for multi-hop reasoning, i.e. query-reformulation and co-matching.

4.1 Query-Reformulation Approach

Query-reformulation is an idea widely used in many multi-step reasoning QA models (Wu et al., 2016; Shen et al., 2017; Das et al., 2019). The key idea is that after the model reads a paragraph, the question representation should be modified according to the matching results between the question and the paragraph. In this way, when the next paragraph comes, the model could focus on "what is not covered" from the history.

Most of the previous methods represent the question as a single vector so that the reformulation is performed in the embedding space. However, representing a question with a single vector performs badly in our task, which is not surprising since most of the top systems on recent QA leaderboards adopt word-by-word attention mechanisms.

Therefore, to have a fair comparison, we need to extend the existing methods from reformulating single vectors to reformulating the whole hidden state sequences H^q. To compare the first passage H^{p_1} with the question H^q, we applied the $BiAtt$ function and result in the matching states $\tilde{H}^q \in \mathbb{R}^{l \times Q}$, where each $\tilde{H}^q[:, i]$ states how the ith word of the question is matched by the passage p_1. Then we use these matching states to reformulate the H^q as follows:

$$\tilde{H}^q = BiAtt(H^{p_1}, H^q)$$
$$M^q = \gamma H^q + (1 - \gamma)\tanh(W[H^q : \tilde{H}^q : H^q - \tilde{H}^q])$$
$$\tilde{H}^{p_2} = BiAtt(M^q, H^{p_2})$$
$$M = BiLSTM(\tilde{H}^{p_2})$$
$$M' = SelfAtt(M) \tag{1}$$

where $\gamma = \sigma(W_g[\tilde{H}^q : H^q : H^q - \tilde{H}^q])$ is a gate function. For the reformulation equation of M^q, we have also tried some other popular options, including only with $M^q = \tanh(W[H^q : \tilde{H}^q : H^q - \tilde{H}^q])$, $M^q = BiLSTM[\tilde{H}^q : H^q : H^q - \tilde{H}^q]$ and directly set $M^q = \tilde{H}^q$. Among them, our gated function achieves the best performance.

4.2 Co-Matching Approach

The work from (Wang et al., 2018) proposed a co-matching mechanism which is used to jointly encode the question and answer with the context passage. We extend the idea to conduct the multi-hop reasoning in our setup. Specifically, we integrate the co-matching to the baseline readers by firstly applying bi-attention described in Equation 2 on (H^q, H^{p_2}), and (H^{p_1}, H^{p_2}) using the same set of parameters.

$$\bar{H}^q = H^q G^q$$
$$G^q = SoftMax((W^g H^q + b^g \otimes e_{p_2})^T H^{p_2})$$
$$\bar{H}^{p_1} = H^{p_1} G^{p_1}$$
$$G^{p_1} = SoftMax((W^g H^{p_1} + b^g \otimes e_{p_2})^T H^{p_2}) \tag{2}$$

where $W^g \in \mathbb{R}^{l \times l}$ and $b^g \in \mathbb{R}^l$ are learnable parameters and $e_{p_2} \in \mathbb{R}^{P_2}$ denotes a vector of all 1s and it is used to repeat the bias vector into the matrix.

We further concatenate the two output hidden sequences $\bar{H}^q$ and $\bar{H}^{p_1}$, followed by a BiLSTM model to get the final hidden sequence for answer prediction as shown in Equation 3. The start and end of the answer span is predicted based on M.

$$M = BiLSTM([\bar{H}^q : \bar{H}^{p_1}]) \tag{3}$$

Co-Matching in HotpotReader We follow the above co-matching approach on the HotporReader's output directly.

Co-Matching in BERT One straightforward way to achieve co-matching in BERT is to separately encode the question, the first passage and the second one with BERT, and then apply the

above co-matching functions on the output hidden sequence as proposed in (Zhang et al., 2019).

However, as observed in the experiments, we believe the inter-attention mechanism (i.e. cross paragraph attention) could capture the order information in an implicit way. Therefore, we still hope to benefit from the cross passage attention inside BERT, but make it better cooperate with three inputs. After the original encoding from BERT, we apply the co-matching[6] on the output sequence to explicitly encourage the reasoning path. H^q, H^{p_1}, and H^{p_2} could be easily obtained by masking the output sequence according to the original text.

5 Experiments

5.1 Settings

We trained and evaluated each model for comparison for each setting separately. Following previous work (Yang et al., 2018), we report the exact-match and F1 score for the answer prediction task.

5.2 Results

In Table 1, the original HotpotReader method does not show significant performance improvement when comparing the Single-Oracle setting with the Ordered-Oracle setting. BERT was able to get a small improvement from its inner cross passage attention which introduces some weak reasoning. Surprisingly, overall the context passage in the reasoning path does not inherently contribute to the performance of these methods, which indicates that the models are not learning much multi-hop reasoning as previously thought.

Model	Single-Oracle		Ordered-Oracle	
	EM	F1	EM	F1
HotpotReader	55.07	70.00	55.17	70.75
Bert	64.08	77.86	65.03	79.15

Table 1: Baseline results for HotpotReader and BERT

We show our proposed improvements in Table 2 and 3. Compared to the Single-Oracle baseline (HotpotReader), when applying the co-matching mechanism in the Ordered-Oracle setting, there is a significant improvement of 4.38% in exact match and 4.26% in F1. The soft query reformulation also improves the performance but not as significantly. In order to confirm that the improvement

---

[6]To follow the original BERT's setup, we also apply the same attention dropout with a probability of 0.9 on the attention scores.

of co-matching does come from the usage of reasoning paths (instead of the higher model capacity), we make another comparison that runs the co-matching model over the Single-Oracle setting. To achieve this, we duplicate the single oracle passage twice as p_1 and p_2. Our results show that this method does not give any improvement. Therefore the co-matching method indeed contributes to the performance gain of multi-hop reasoning.

Model	Order	Performance	
		EM	F1
HotpotReader	Random	52.23	69.80
	Single-Oracle	55.07	70.00
	Ordered-Oracle	55.17	70.75
w/ Query-Reform	Ordered-Oracle	56.89	71.69
w/ Co-Matching	Single-Oracle	55.00	70.23
	Ordered-Oracle	**59.45**	**74.26**

Table 2: Results for HotpotReader on 3 oracle settings

BERT achieved promising results even in the Single-Oracle setting which proves its original capacity for QA. The original BERT was improved by 1.23% in exact match when both context passage and answer passage are provided and separated by an extra token. Nonetheless, the co-matching mechanism contributes to an additional 1.66% exact match improvement which indicates the success of co-matching for reasoning. Co-matching result also shows that multi-hop over passage chain contains additional information, and thus multi-hop ability is necessary in our analysis setting.

Model	Order	Performance	
		EM	F1
BERT	Random	59.18	75.27
	Single-Oracle	64.08	77.86
	Ordered-Oracle	65.03	79.15
w/ split token	Ordered-Oracle	65.31	79.49
w/ Co-Matching	Ordered-Oracle	**66.97**	**80.77**

Table 3: Results for BERT on 3 oracle settings

Among both approaches, co-matching shows promising performance improvement especially for the well pre-trained BERT model. This proves the co-matching mechanism is able to conduct multi-hop reasoning following the passage chains.

Finally, both models perform worse in the Random setting compared to the Single-Oracle setting, although the Random setting contains sufficient information of the whole reasoning chain.

From the analysis, we find that it is difficult for the models to correctly predict the orders from the randomly-ordered passages. For example, we created a binary classification task to predict which passage is the context passage and which is the answer passage. BERT model gives an accuracy of only 87.43% on this task. This gives further evidence that the existing models do not have appropriate inductive biases for utilizing the reasoning chains.

Answers to our research questions The above results answer our research questions as follows: (1) in our experimental setting, the reasoning paths are indeed useful, thus multi-hop reasoning is necessary, as there exists a method, i.e., co-matching, that has demonstrated significant improvement; (2) existing reader models usually cannot fully make use of the reasoning paths, indicating their limited reasoning abilities. Among the existing methods, BERT can do slightly better on making use of the reasoning paths. Our new proposed co-matching approach improves the reasoning abilities over both the two different base models (HotpotReader and BERT).

6 Discussion

Difference from prior work Our work conducts the first analysis of *models' behaviors*. In comparison, a concurrent analysis work (Min et al., 2019), which is also conducted on HotpotQA, focuses more on the properties of the dataset. For example, (Min et al., 2019) finds that for 80% of the questions in HotpotQA, humans do not need the full paths of paragraphs to correctly answer some of the questions. One of the major reasons is the bias of factoid questions that look for certain types of entities as answers. For example, a question asking *"which sports team"* can be directly answered if there is only one sports team mentioned in the documents.

Our analysis focuses on whether the full reasoning paths can help the *machine learning models* to (1) improve their performance on those 80% of the questions, as well as (2) cover the left 20% of questions that indeed require the multi-hop ability. Moreover, compared to the prior analysis, we are the first to analyze the effects of reasoning paths in an explicit way, and construct a dataset for this purpose.

The effect of data biases on our analysis The aforementioned biases make the full reasoning paths less useful for a large portion of data, therefore making it more challenging for reader models to improve with full reasoning paths.

Because of the data bias, it is critical to verify that the dataset we created can still benefit from the improved reasoning skills. That is why answering *Q2* in Section 2.2 is important for the whole analysis. The results in Section 5.2 show that our co-matching methods can indeed benefit from the reasoning paths, confirming the effectiveness of our proposed dataset and settings for the analysis purpose.

Encouraging model design with better evaluation Finally, continued from the previous paragraph, we hope to highlight the problem that the less biased a dataset is, the more likely a model can easily benefit from the availability of reasoning paths. On many existing benchmark datasets that are biased, it is less likely to achieve improvement with specific designs for achieving multi-hop reasoning ability. This makes multi-hop reasoning a less important factor when people design models for these multi-hop QA datasets, if the goal is simply to improve the answer accuracy.

To encourage model design towards real reasoning instead of fitting the data biases, we believe that an improved evaluation is necessary. To this end, one way is certainly to create datasets with fewer biases. While our analysis also suggests the other way: we can keep the biased training data, but created small evaluation datasets with human-labeled reasoning paths. Then during evaluation, we compute the accuracy of the predicted reasoning paths. This is an extension of the idea of HotpotQA that jointly evaluates the support selection and answer extraction, but with a more explicit focus on the reasoning processes.

7   Conclusion

In this paper, we analyze QA models' capability in multi-hop reasoning by assessing if the reasoning chain could help existing multi-hop readers. We observed the general weakness of stat-or-the-art models in multi-hop reasoning and proposed a co-matching based method to mitigate. Despite the fact that co-matching is designed to encode only three input sequences to achieve limited multi-hop reasoning, we consider this as the most promising one that demonstrates the concrete reasoning capability and has the potential for real multi-hop reasoning.

Acknowledgments

We thank the anonymous reviewers for their very valuable comments and suggestions.

References

Christian Buck, Jannis Bulian, Massimiliano Ciaramita, Wojciech Gajewski, Andrea Gesmundo, Neil Houlsby, and Wei Wang. 2018. Ask the right questions: Active question reformulation with reinforcement learning. In *International Conference on Learning Representations*.

Rajarshi Das, Shehzaad Dhuliawala, Manzil Zaheer, and Andrew McCallum. 2019. Multi-step retriever-reader interaction for scalable open-domain question answering. In *International Conference on Learning Representations*.

Nicola De Cao, Wilker Aziz, and Ivan Titov. 2018. Question answering by reasoning across documents with graph convolutional networks. *arXiv preprint arXiv:1808.09920*.

Jacob Devlin, Ming-Wei Chang, Kenton Lee, and Kristina Toutanova. 2018. Bert: Pre-training of deep bidirectional transformers for language understanding. *arXiv preprint arXiv:1810.04805*.

Xiaodong Liu, Yelong Shen, Kevin Duh, and Jianfeng Gao. 2017. Stochastic answer networks for machine reading comprehension. *arXiv preprint arXiv:1712.03556*.

Sewon Min, Eric Wallace, Sameer Singh, Matt Gardner, Hannaneh Hajishirzi, and Luke Zettlemoyer. 2019. Compositional questions do not necessitate multi-hop reasoning. *arXiv preprint arXiv:1906.02900*.

Yelong Shen, Po-Sen Huang, Jianfeng Gao, and Weizhu Chen. 2017. Reasonet: Learning to stop reading in machine comprehension. In *Proceedings of the 23rd ACM SIGKDD International Conference on Knowledge Discovery and Data Mining*, pages 1047–1055. ACM.

Linfeng Song, Zhiguo Wang, Mo Yu, Yue Zhang, Radu Florian, and Daniel Gildea. 2018. Exploring graph-structured passage representation for multi-hop reading comprehension with graph neural networks. *arXiv preprint arXiv:1809.02040*.

Alon Talmor and Jonathan Berant. 2018. Repartitioning of the complexwebquestions dataset. *arXiv preprint arXiv:1807.09623*.

Shuohang Wang, Mo Yu, Shiyu Chang, and Jing Jiang. 2018. A co-matching model for multi-choice reading comprehension. *arXiv preprint arXiv:1806.04068*.

Johannes Welbl, Pontus Stenetorp, and Sebastian Riedel. 2018. Constructing datasets for multi-hop reading comprehension across documents. *Transactions of the Association of Computational Linguistics*, 6:287–302.

Jason Weston, Sumit Chopra, and Antoine Bordes. 2014. Memory networks. *arXiv preprint arXiv:1410.3916*.

Qi Wu, Peng Wang, Chunhua Shen, Anthony Dick, and Anton van den Hengel. 2016. Ask me anything: Free-form visual question answering based on knowledge from external sources. In *Proceedings of the IEEE Conference on Computer Vision and Pattern Recognition*, pages 4622–4630.

Caiming Xiong, Victor Zhong, and Richard Socher. 2017. Dcn+: Mixed objective and deep residual coattention for question answering. *arXiv preprint arXiv:1711.00106*.

Zhilin Yang, Peng Qi, Saizheng Zhang, Yoshua Bengio, William W Cohen, Ruslan Salakhutdinov, and Christopher D Manning. 2018. Hotpotqa: A dataset for diverse, explainable multi-hop question answering. *arXiv preprint arXiv:1809.09600*.

Shuailiang Zhang, Hai Zhao, Yuwei Wu, Zhuosheng Zhang, Xi Zhou, and Xiang Zhou. 2019. Dual co-matching network for multi-choice reading comprehension. *arXiv preprint arXiv:1901.09381*.

Victor Zhong, Caiming Xiong, Nitish Shirish Keskar, and Richard Socher. 2019. Coarse-grain fine-grain coattention network for multi-evidence question answering. *arXiv preprint arXiv:1901.00603*.

Machine Comprehension Improves
Domain-Specific Japanese Predicate-Argument Structure Analysis

Norio Takahashi **Tomohide Shibata**[*] **Daisuke Kawahara** **Sadao Kurohashi**
Graduate School of Informatics, Kyoto University
Yoshida-honmachi, Sakyo-ku, Kyoto, 606-8501, Japan
{ntakahashi, shibata, dk, kuro}@nlp.ist.i.kyoto-u.ac.jp

Abstract

To improve the accuracy of predicate-argument structure (PAS) analysis, large-scale training data and knowledge for PAS analysis are indispensable. We focus on a specific domain, specifically Japanese blogs on driving, and construct two wide-coverage datasets as a form of QA using crowdsourcing: a PAS-QA dataset and a reading comprehension QA (RC-QA) dataset. We train a machine comprehension (MC) model based on these datasets to perform PAS analysis. Our experiments show that a stepwise training method is the most effective, which pre-trains an MC model based on the RC-QA dataset to acquire domain knowledge and then fine-tunes based on the PAS-QA dataset.

1 Introduction

To understand the meaning of a sentence or a text, it is essential to analyze relations between a predicate and its arguments. Such analysis is called semantic role labeling (SRL) or predicate-argument structure (PAS) analysis. For English, the accuracy of SRL has reached approximately 80%-90% (Ouchi et al., 2018; He et al., 2018; Strubell et al., 2018; Tan et al., 2018). However, there are many omissions of arguments in Japanese, and the accuracy of Japanese PAS analysis on omitted arguments is still around 50%-60% (Shibata et al., 2016; Shibata and Kurohashi, 2018; Kurita et al., 2018; Ouchi et al., 2017). A reason for such low accuracy is the shortage of gold datasets and knowledge about PAS analysis, which require a prohibitive cost of creation (Iida et al., 2007; Kawahara et al., 2002).

From the viewpoint of text understanding, machine comprehension (MC) has been actively studied in recent years. In MC studies, QA datasets consisting of triplets of a document, a question and

its answer are constructed, and an MC model is trained using these datasets (e.g., Rajpurkar et al. (2016) and Trischler et al. (2017)). MC has made remarkable progress in the last couple of years, and MC models have even exceeded human accuracy in some datasets (Devlin et al., 2019). However, MC accuracy is not necessarily high for documents that contain anaphoric phenomena and those that need external knowledge or inference (Mihaylov et al., 2018; Yang et al., 2018).

In this paper, we propose a Japanese PAS analysis method based on the MC framework for a specific domain. In particular, we focus on a challenging task of finding an antecedent of a zero pronoun within PAS analysis. We construct a wide-coverage QA dataset for PAS analysis (PAS-QA) in the domain and feed it to an MC model to perform PAS analysis. We also construct a QA dataset for reading comprehension (RC-QA) in the same domain and jointly use the two datasets in the MC model to improve PAS analysis.

We consider the domain of blogs on driving because of the following two reasons. Firstly, we can construct high-quality QA datasets in a short time using crowdsourcing. Crowdworkers can interpret driving blog articles based on the traffic commonsense shared by the society. Secondly, if computers can understand driving situations correctly by extracting driving behavior from blogs, it is possible to predict danger and warn drivers to achieve safer transportation.

Our contributions are summarized as follows.

- We propose an MC-based PAS analysis model and show its superiority to a state-of-the-art neural model.
- We construct PAS-QA and RC-QA datasets in the driving domain using crowdsourcing.
- We improve Japanese PAS analysis by combining the PAS-QA and RC-QA datasets.

---

[*] The current affiliation is Yahoo Japan Corporation.

Proceedings of the Second Workshop on Machine Reading for Question Answering, pages 98–104
Hong Kong, China, November 4, 2019. ©2019 Association for Computational Linguistics

2 Related Work

2.1 QA Dataset Construction

FitzGerald et al. (2018) and Michael et al. (2018) constructed QA-SRL Bank 2.0 and QAMRs using crowdsourcing, respectively. They asked crowdworkers to generate question-answer pairs that represent a PAS. These datasets are similar to our PAS-QA dataset, but different in that we focus on omitted arguments and automatically generate questions (see Section 3.1).

Many RC-QA datasets have been constructed in recent years. For example, Rajpurkar et al. (2016) constructed SQuAD 1.1, which contains 100K crowdsourced questions and answer spans in a Wikipedia article. Rajpurkar et al. (2018) updated SQuAD 1.1 to 2.0 by adding unanswerable questions. Some RC-QA datasets have been built in a specific domain (Welbl et al., 2017; Suster and Daelemans, 2018; Pampari et al., 2018).

2.2 Machine Comprehension Models

Many MC models based on neural networks have been proposed to solve RC-QA datasets. For example, Devlin et al. (2019) proposed an MC model using a language representation model, BERT, which achieved a high-ranked accuracy on the SQuAD 1.1 leaderboard as of September 30, 2019.

As a previous study of transfer learning of MC models to other tasks, Pan et al. (2018) pre-trained an MC model using an RC-QA dataset and transfered the pre-trained knowledge to sequence-to-sequence models. They used SQuAD 1.1 as the RC-QA dataset and experimented on translation and summarization. While they used different models for pre-training and fine-tuning, we use the same MC model by constructing PAS-QA and RC-QA datasets in the same QA form.

3 QA Dataset Construction

We construct PAS-QA and RC-QA datasets in the driving domain. Both the QA datasets consist of triplets of a document, a question and its answer as in existing RC-QA datasets. We employ crowdsourcing to create large-scale datasets in a short time. Figure 1 and Figure 2 show examples of our PAS-QA and RC-QA datasets.

3.1 PAS-QA Dataset

We construct a PAS-QA dataset in which a question asks an omitted argument for a predicate. We

Figure 1: An example of PAS-QA dataset.

Figure 2: An example of RC-QA dataset.

focus on the *ga* case (nominative), the *wo* case (accusative), and the *ni* case (dative), which are targeted in the Japanese PAS analysis literature (Shibata et al., 2016; Shibata and Kurohashi, 2018; Kurita et al., 2018; Ouchi et al., 2017).

As a source corpus, we use blog articles included in the Driving Experience Corpus (Iwai et al., 2019). We first detect a predicate that has an omitted argument of either of the target three cases by applying the existing PAS analyzer KNP[1] to the corpus. KNP tends to overgenerate such predicates, but most erroneous ones are filtered out by the following crowdsourcing step. We extract the sentence that contains the predicate and preceding three sentences as a document. Then, we automatically generate a question using the following template for nominative.

- ［述語］の主語は何か？ (What is the subject of [predicate]?)

All the question templates of PAS-QA datasets are shown in Table 1. We ask crowdworkers to choose one from answer choices, which consist of nouns extracted from the document and special symbols,

---

[1] http://nlp.ist.i.kyoto-u.ac.jp/EN/index.php?KNP

Case	Question
Nominative	［述語］の主語は何か？ (What is the subject of [predicate]?)
Accusative	○○を［述語］、の○○に入るものは何か？ (What is the accusative of [predicate]?)
Dative	○○に［述語］、の○○に入るものは何か？ (What is the dative of [predicate]?)

Table 1: Question templates of PAS-QA datasets.

"author," "other," and "not sure." The details of this procedure are described in the appendix.

We generated questions from 2,146 blog articles. We asked five crowdworkers per question using Yahoo! crowdsourcing[2]. We adopted triplets with three or more votes if they are not "not sure." For accusative and dative PAS-QA questions, we adopted triplets if they are "other." In this case, there is not any antecedent of a zero pronoun in a document, and the answer is "NULL." For nominative PAS-QA questions, we did not adopt triplets if they are "other" because a nominative always exists as a noun in a document or "author." In addition, because "author" is not explicitly expressed in the document, we add a sentence "著者は以下の文章を書きました。" (The author wrote the following document.) to the beginning of the document to deal with "author" in MC models. We record the answers as spans in a document or NULL.

We randomly extracted 100 questions for each case from the PAS-QA dataset and judged whether we can answer them. As a result, 97% nominative, 87% accusative and 68% dative questions were answerable. For accusative and dative, we checked all the questions and chose answerable ones. Finally, we created 12,468 nominative, 3,151 accusative and 1,069 dative triplets including 476 accusative and 126 dative questions whose answers are NULL. It took approximately 32 hours and approximately 210,000 JPY to create this dataset.

3.2 RC-QA Dataset

We construct a driving-domain RC-QA dataset in the same way as SQuAD 1.1. We extract a document from the Driving Experience Corpus and ask three crowdworkers to write questions and their answers about the document. After that, we ask another five crowdworkers to answer a question to validate its answerability and adopt questions with three or more same answers.

---

[2]https://crowdsourcing.yahoo.co.jp/

	Nominative	Accusative	Dative	Other
# Questions	41	28	8	123
Ratio	20.5%	14.0%	4.0%	61.5%
Ratio (Omission)	(5.0%)	(2.5%)	(0.5%)	−

Table 2: Classification of questions in the RC-QA dataset.

Training method		Dataset
MC-single		PAS-QA
Joint training	MC-merged	PAS-QA + RC-QA
	MC-stepwise	RC-QA → PAS-QA

Table 3: Three training methods for PAS analysis.

As a result, we obtained 20,007 RC-QA triplets from 5,146 blog articles. It took approximately 60 hours and approximately 180,000 JPY to create this dataset.

We randomly extracted 200 questions from the RC-QA dataset and judged the question types. The result is shown in Table 2. A question was classified according to whether it is a question asking for any argument of nominative, accusative or dative, and if applicable, whether it is an omission or not. As shown in Table 2, the RC-QA dataset contains nearly 40% of questions asking arguments of nominative, accusative and dative, and a few questions asking for omitted arguments, which are similar to the PAS-QA dataset. There are various other questions asking for arguments other than nominative, accusative and dative, and questions using why and how.

4 PAS Analysis Based on a Machine Comprehension Model

We analyze PAS based on the MC model on our constructed PAS-QA dataset. Each question in the PAS-QA dataset asks an omitted argument and has an answer that is expressed as a span in the given document or NULL. Because the PAS-QA dataset has the same structure as existing MC datasets including NULL, such as SQuAD 2.0, we can employ an existing state-of-the-art MC model that answers a span in the document or NULL.

We refer to the method of MC training based only on the PAS-QA dataset as **MC-single**. We also propose two joint training methods that use both the PAS-QA and RC-QA datasets: **MC-merged** and **MC-stepwise**, as described in Table 3. The purpose of these joint training methods is to verify whether domain knowledge can be learned from the RC-QA dataset and whether it is

	Train	Development	Test
Nominative	11,359	544	565
Accusative	2,756	199	196
Dative	967	50	52

Table 4: Split of the PAS-QA dataset.

Training method	PAS	RC	NOM	ACC	DAT
NN-PAS	-	-	0.39	0.38	0.29
NN-PAS$'$	✓	-	0.74	0.45	0.32
MC-single	✓	-	**0.76**	0.52	0.37
MC-merged	✓	✓	**0.76**	0.52	0.43
MC-stepwise	✓	✓	**0.76**	**0.53**	**0.51**

Table 5: PAS-QA test results of MC models and NN-PAS models. "PAS" and "RC" denote the use of the PAS-QA and RC-QA datasets, respectively. "NOM", "ACC" and "DAT" denote the EM scores of nominative, accusative and dative, respectively.

effective in improving the accuracy of PAS analysis. In MC-merged, the PAS-QA and RC-QA datasets are just merged and used for training. In MC-stepwise, the RC-QA dataset is used for pre-training, and this pre-trained model is fine-tuned using the PAS-QA dataset.

5 Experiments

We conduct PAS analysis experiments of our MC-single/merged/stepwise methods using the PAS-QA and RC-QA datasets. We also compare our methods with the neural network-based PAS analysis model (Shibata and Kurohashi, 2018) (hereafter, NN-PAS), which achieved the state-of-the-art accuracy on Japanese PAS analysis.

5.1 Experimental Settings

We adopt BERT (Devlin et al., 2019) as an MC model. We split the triplets in the PAS-QA dataset as shown in Table 4. All sentences in these datasets are preprocessed using the Japanese morphological analyzer, JUMAN++[3].

We trained a Japanese pre-trained BERT model using Japanese Wikipedia, which consists of approximately 18 million sentences. The input sentences were segmented into words by JUMAN++, and words were broken into subwords by applying BPE (Sennrich et al., 2016). The parameters of BERT are the same as English BERT$_{\text{BASE}}$. The number of epochs for the pre-training was 30.

The state-of-the-art baseline PAS analyzer, NN-PAS, was trained using the existing PAS dataset, KWDLC[4] (Kyoto University Web Document Leads Corpus), as described in Shibata and Kurohashi (2018). We also trained an NN-PAS model using the PAS-QA dataset in addition to KWDLC (hereafter, NN-PAS$'$). For this training, the PAS-QA dataset was converted to the same format as KWDLC, where questions are deleted, and only answers are used.

The PAS-QA test data is used to compare the baseline methods with the proposed methods. As

an evaluation measure, EM (Exact Match) is used for all the MC models. EM is defined as (the number of questions in which the system answer matches the gold answer in the dataset) / (the number of questions in the entire dataset). For each experimental condition, training and testing were conducted five times, and the average scores were calculated.

5.2 Results and Discussion

Table 5 lists evaluation results of the NN-PAS models and the MC-single/merged/stepwise models. First, NN-PAS$'$ significantly outperformed NN-PAS, and thus the construction of the domain-specific PAS-QA dataset was effective in domain adaptation of the NN-PAS model. Furthermore, our proposed MC-* models outperfomed NN-PAS$'$. For the joint training models, MC-stepwise was better than MC-single for the accusative and dative cases. MC-merged was inferior to MC-stepwise.

We compared the results of MC-single and MC-stepwise. In examples shown in Figures 3 and 4, only the outputs of MC-stepwise were correct. We found some cases that MC-stepwise successfully captured knowledge in the driving domain. In the example shown in Figure 4, the correspondence between "坂を 上がる" (climb up the slope) and "坂を 越える" (going up the slope) can be recognized. MC-merged's answer "坂道" (the hill road), which has a coreference relation with "坂" (the slope), looked correct although "坂" (the slope) was the only answer from crowdsourcing. Supplying multiple answers considering coreference relations is our future work. From these results, we think that it is important to use an RC-QA dataset to acquire domain knowledge, and suggest that it is better to construct both PAS-QA and RC-QA datasets to develop a PAS analyzer for a new

[3] http://nlp.ist.i.kyoto-u.ac.jp/EN/index.php?JUMAN++
[4] http://nlp.ist.i.kyoto-u.ac.jp/EN/index.php?KWDLC

・Document :
　彼、「車を返す時ガソリンを満タンにするのか、だいぶ走ったから少なくなったなぁ」
　(He said, "When we return this car, we have to fill up with gasoline. We ran a lot so we ran out of it.")
　同乗者、「勿体無いから坂道はニュートラルで走ろうぜ」
　(The passenger said, "Because It is a waste to consume gasoline, let's run downhill with the gear in neutral.")
　皆それは良いと、賛同して長い坂をニュートラルで下り始めました、直線の長い坂道でした。
　(Everyone agreed that it was good idea, and started to go down a long downhill, which was straight.)
　・・・と彼は下りにガソリンは要らないと、エンジンを切り鍵を抜いて皆に『見せました』。
　(He said that we did not need gasoline to go down, turned off the engine, unlocked the key and "showed" it to everyone.)

・Question :
　○○を『見せました』、の○○に入るものは何か？
　(What is the accusative of "showed"?)

・Answer :
Correct answer	： 鍵 (the key)
MC-single	： 坂道 (downhill)
MC-merged	： 車 (this car)
MC-stepwise	： 鍵 (the key)

Figure 3: An example that is correctly answered by MC-stepwise.

domain.

6　Conclusion

We constructed driving-domain PAS-QA and RC-QA datasets using crowdsourcing[5]. We also proposed an MC-based PAS analysis method. In particular, the stepwise training method based on BERT was the most effective, which outperformed the previous state-of-the-art NN-PAS model. In the future, we will pre-train an MC model based on datasets other than the RC-QA dataset to acquire domain knowledge.

References

Jacob Devlin, Ming-Wei Chang, Kenton Lee, and Kristina Toutanova. 2019. BERT: pre-training of deep bidirectional transformers for language understanding. In *NAACL-HLT2019*, pages 4171–4186.

Nicholas FitzGerald, Julian Michael, Luheng He, and Luke Zettlemoyer. 2018. Large-scale QA-SRL parsing. In *ACL2018*, pages 2051–2060.

Shexia He, Zuchao Li, Hai Zhao, and Hongxiao Bai. 2018. Syntax for semantic role labeling, to be, or not to be. In *ACL2018*, pages 2061–2071.

Ryu Iida, Mamoru Komachi, Kentaro Inui, and Yuji Matsumoto. 2007. Annotating a Japanese text corpus with predicate-argument and coreference relations. In *ACL2007*, pages 132–139.

Ritsuko Iwai, Daisuke Kawahara, Takatsune Kumada, and Sadao Kurohashi. 2018. Annotating a driving experience corpus with behavior and subjectivity. In *PACLIC 32*, pages 222–231.

Ritsuko Iwai, Takatsune Kumada, Norio Takahashi, Daisuke Kawahara, and Sadao Kurohashi. 2019. Development of driving-related dictionary that includes psychological expressions. In *Proceedings of the 25th Annual Meeting of Natural Language Processing (in Japanese)*, pages 1201–1204.

Daisuke Kawahara, Sadao Kurohashi, and Kôiti Hasida. 2002. Construction of a Japanese relevance-tagged corpus. In *LREC2002*, pages 2008–2013.

Shuhei Kurita, Daisuke Kawahara, and Sadao Kurohashi. 2018. Neural adversarial training for semi-supervised Japanese predicate-argument structure analysis. In *ACL2018*, pages 474–484.

Julian Michael, Gabriel Stanovsky, Luheng He, Ido Dagan, and Luke Zettlemoyer. 2018. Crowdsourcing question-answer meaning representations. In *NAACL2018*, pages 560–568.

Todor Mihaylov, Peter Clark, Tushar Khot, and Ashish Sabharwal. 2018. Can a suit of armor conduct electricity? A new dataset for open book question answering. In *EMNLP2018*, pages 2381–2391.

Hiroki Ouchi, Hiroyuki Shindo, and Yuji Matsumoto. 2017. Neural modeling of multi-predicate interactions for Japanese predicate argument structure analysis. In *ACL2017*, pages 1591–1600.

Hiroki Ouchi, Hiroyuki Shindo, and Yuji Matsumoto. 2018. A span selection model for semantic role labeling. In *EMNLP2018*, pages 1630–1642.

・Document :
　屈伸をしながら気合いを入れ直し坂道に挑む。
　(I motivate myself again while bending and stretching, and challenge the hill road.)
　坂を越えたらバイク屋がある。
　(There is a motorbike shop when going up the slope.)
　少し『上っただけで』さっきまで引いていた汗が今まで以上に噴き出す。
　(Just "climbing up" a bit, sweat that stopped until a while ago gushes out more than before.)

・Question :
　○○を『上っただけで』、の○○に入るものは何か？
　(What is the accusative of "climb up"?)

・Answer :
Correct answer	： 坂 (the slope)
MC-single	： 汗 (sweat)
MC-merged	： 坂道 (the hill road)
MC-stepwise	： 坂 (the slope)

Figure 4: An example that is correctly answered by MC-stepwise.

[5]These datasets are available at
http://nlp.ist.i.kyoto-u.ac.jp/EN/
index.php?Driving%20domain%20QA%20datasets

Anusri Pampari, Preethi Raghavan, Jennifer J. Liang, and Jian Peng. 2018. emrQA: A large corpus for question answering on electronic medical records. In *EMNLP2018*, pages 2357–2368.

Boyuan Pan, Yazheng Yang, Hao Li, Zhou Zhao, Yueting Zhuang, Deng Cai, and Xiaofei He. 2018. MacNet: Transferring knowledge from machine comprehension to Sequence-to-Sequence models. In *NeurIPS2018*, pages 6095–6105.

Pranav Rajpurkar, Robin Jia, and Percy Liang. 2018. Know what you don't know: Unanswerable questions for SQuAD. In *ACL2018*, pages 784–789.

Pranav Rajpurkar, Jian Zhang, Konstantin Lopyrev, and Percy Liang. 2016. SQuAD: 100, 000+ questions for machine comprehension of text. In *EMNLP2016*, pages 2383–2392.

Rico Sennrich, Barry Haddow, and Alexandra Birch. 2016. Neural machine translation of rare words with subword units. In *ACL2016*, pages 1715–1725.

Tomohide Shibata, Daisuke Kawahara, and Sadao Kurohashi. 2016. Neural network-based model for Japanese predicate argument structure analysis. In *ACL2016*, pages 1235–1244.

Tomohide Shibata and Sadao Kurohashi. 2018. Entity-centric joint modeling of Japanese coreference resolution and predicate argument structure analysis. In *ACL2018*, pages 579–589.

Emma Strubell, Patrick Verga, Daniel Andor, David Weiss, and Andrew McCallum. 2018. Linguistically-informed self-attention for semantic role labeling. In *EMNLP2018*, pages 5027–5038.

Simon Suster and Walter Daelemans. 2018. CliCR: a dataset of clinical case reports for machine reading comprehension. In *NAACL2018*, pages 1551–1563.

Zhixing Tan, Mingxuan Wang, Jun Xie, Yidong Chen, and Xiaodong Shi. 2018. Deep semantic role labeling with self-attention. In *AAAI2018*, pages 4929–4936.

Adam Trischler, Tong Wang, Xingdi Yuan, Justin Harris, Alessandro Sordoni, Philip Bachman, and Kaheer Suleman. 2017. NewsQA: A machine comprehension dataset. In *ACL2017*, pages 191–200.

Johannes Welbl, Nelson F. Liu, and Matt Gardner. 2017. Crowdsourcing multiple choice science questions. In *EMNLP2017*, pages 94–106.

Zhilin Yang, Peng Qi, Saizheng Zhang, Yoshua Bengio, William W. Cohen, Ruslan Salakhutdinov, and Christopher D. Manning. 2018. HotpotQA: A dataset for diverse, explainable multi-hop question answering. In *EMNLP2018*, pages 2369–2380.

A Details of PAS-QA Dataset Construction

We construct the PAS-QA dataset asking for omitted nominative arguments using the following procedure:

1. We extract four consecutive sentences that satisfy the following conditions from the Driving Experience Corpus constructed by Iwai et al. (2019).

   - The Driving Experience extracting CRF tool (Iwai et al., 2018) judges that three or more sentences out of four sentences are driving experience.
   - Each sentence contains at least one PAS.
   - The PAS analyzer, KNP, judges that there is a PAS whose nominative argument is omitted in the fourth sentence.
   - Sentences include at least one "Driving Characteristic Word" (Iwai et al., 2019).

2. We automatically make crowdsourcing tasks using an extracted document and a PAS whose nominative argument is omitted (See Figure 5 and Figure 6). Each task consists of a document, a question and answer choices. Answer choices consist of nouns extracted from the document and special symbols, "author," "other," and "not sure." For nominative PAS-QA questions, the special symbol "author" can often be an answer, but it is not explicitly expressed in the document. So we add it to the choices. We add "other" so that it can be selected when there is an appropriate answer besides the choices. We add "not sure" so that workers can select it if they cannot find an answer. We add more explanations to crowdsourcing answer screen (See Figure 5 and Figure 6).

3. Using crowdsourcing, we ask five crowdworkers per question to select one or more appropriate answers from the choices. We asked five crowdworkers per question using Yahoo! crowdsourcing. We adopted triplets with three or more votes if they are not "not sure." If they are "other," we handled them as described in the main paper. We finally record the answers as spans in a document or NULL.

運転エピソードに関する以下の文章を読んで、問題にお答えください。
【文章】
そこから先はどうしたか、見てないから知らないけど・・・
車がかなり壊れたみたい。
なんで無理に前に進むかな？？？
バックすれば、そこまで激しく壊れなかったと『思うけど』、気が動転して…

【問題】
上記文章中、最後の文の『思うけど』の主語は何か、以下の選択肢から適切なもの
を一つ以上選択してください（主語は人や物で、複数でも可）。
「その他」を選択した場合は、自由記述欄に適切な言葉をご記入ください。
答えられない場合は、「分からない」を選択してください。

⦿ 先

⦿ 車

⦿ 気

⦿ 著者

⦿ その他

⦿ 分からない

Figure 5: PAS-QA dataset answer screen.

Please read the following document about driving episodes and respond to
the question.
[Document]
I do not know what happened to the point after that ...
The car seems to have broken considerably.
Why was he going to force forward?
(Φ-NOM) "think" that if he backed his car, he did not break it so hard, but
his mind might be upset ...

[Question]
In the above document, what is the subject of "think" in the last sentence?
Please select one or more appropriate answers from the following choices
(subjects are people, things, more than one).
If you select "other", please fill in the appropriate words in the free
description field.
If you can not answer, please select "not sure".

⦿ the point

⦿ his car

⦿ his mind

⦿ author

⦿ other

⦿ not sure

Figure 6: PAS-QA dataset answer screen (English translation version).

On Making Reading Comprehension More Comprehensive

Matt Gardner,[♠] Jonathan Berant,[♠,♣] Hannaneh Hajishirzi,[♠,◇]
Alon Talmor,[♣] and Sewon Min,[◇]
[♠]Allen Institute for Artificial Intelligence
[♣]Tel Aviv University
[◇]University of Washington
mattg@allenai.org

Abstract

Machine reading comprehension, the task of evaluating a machine's ability to comprehend a passage of text, has seen a surge in popularity in recent years. There are many datasets that are targeted at reading comprehension, and many systems that perform as well as humans on some of these datasets. Despite all of this interest, there is no work that systematically defines what reading comprehension *is*. In this work, we justify a question answering approach to reading comprehension and describe the various kinds of questions one might use to more fully test a system's comprehension of a passage, moving beyond questions that only probe local predicate-argument structures. The main pitfall of this approach is that questions can easily have surface cues or other biases that allow a model to shortcut the intended reasoning process. We discuss ways proposed in current literature to mitigate these shortcuts, and we conclude with recommendations for future dataset collection efforts.

1 Introduction

Getting machines to "understand" natural language text is a vast and long-standing problem, made more challenging by the fact that it is not even clear what it means to understand text, or how to judge whether a machine has achieved success at this task. Much recent research in the natural language processing community has converged on an approach to this problem called *machine reading comprehension*, where a system is given a passage of text and a natural language question that presumably requires some level of "understanding" of the passage in order to answer. While there have been many papers in the last few years studying this basic problem, as far as we are aware, there is no paper formally justifying this approach

to "understanding", or discussing its drawbacks.[1]

In this work we aim to motivate question answering as a good, but potentially fraught, means of measuring a machine's comprehension of natural language text. We argue that current reading comprehension datasets, largely inspired by the Stanford Question Answering Dataset (Rajpurkar et al., 2016, SQuAD),[2] are a good start at measuring reading comprehension, but do not go far enough in probing systems' understanding capabilities. Most of these datasets simply require a basic understanding of local predicate-argument structure and entity typing; there is a lot more to understanding text than that, such as tracking entities through a discourse, understanding the implications of text that is read, and recovering the underlying world model that the author intended to convey.

Question answering is a natural format to use when probing these complex phenomena, but it comes with inherent challenges. In particular, it is very easy to write questions that seem like they require deep understanding of text to answer, but in fact give lexical or other cues to a machine that allow the system to bypass the intended reasoning when answering the question. When constructing reading comprehension datasets, it is essential to deal with this issue up front, designing mechanisms in the data collection process that combat these shortcuts. We give many examples of both the shortcuts themselves and methods people have used to mitigate them, such as having mismatched questions and passages, including "no answer" as a possible answer option, and creating adversarial

---

[1]Richardson et al. (2013) give a good overview of the early history of this approach, but provide only very little justification.

[2]Though SQuAD was not nearly the first reading comprehension dataset, its introduction of the span extraction format was innovative and useful, and most new datasets follow its design.

Proceedings of the Second Workshop on Machine Reading for Question Answering, pages 105–112
Hong Kong, China, November 4, 2019. ©2019 Association for Computational Linguistics

examples, among others.

We conclude with a discussion about gaps we see in the literature that should be addressed by future dataset collection efforts.

2 Defining Reading Comprehension

How does one define "understanding a passage of text"? The process which a human uses to recover some notion of meaning when reading a passage is not well understood computationally (Kendeou and Trevors, 2012), so while this would be an ideal benchmark for machine understanding, it is unavailable to us. The natural language processing community has long drawn on linguistic formalisms to represent pieces of this meaning, from syntax trees and word sense disambiguation to semantic roles and coreference resolution. These formalisms only take us so far, however, as there is no linguistic formalism that satisfactorily captures the full meaning of a paragraph.

Instead we turn to ideas that go back at least to Alan Turing's test for machine intelligence (Turing, 1950; Levesque, 2013)—it is through interacting in natural language that an entity can demonstrate their understanding of language. We begin with a postulate: **an entity (human or machine)** *understands* **a passage of text if it can correctly answer** *arbitrary questions* **about that text**. We claim that this is a *sufficient* condition for understanding, but not a *necessary* one; there are surely other ways of demonstrating understanding.

Following this postulate, we define *machine reading comprehension* to be a task aimed at understanding a single coherent passage of text, where a system is given a single passage and a single question about that passage, and must produce an answer. Our definition of "single coherent passage" is somewhat loose; we consider anything longer than, e.g., a typical Wikipedia page to be too long and not a single coherent passage, while single sentences are generally too short. This means that, while they are certainly relevant, we are not including in this strict definition tasks that involve retrieving paragraphs or answering multiple consecutive questions, as they require additional capabilities. The boundaries around "reading comprehension" and which capabilities are related to "reading" or something else are very fuzzy, however, as we will see throughout the rest of this paper. In order to talk formally about the problem, we must pick a concrete definition, and

so this is the definition we choose, while admitting that it is not perfect.

Using natural language questions to test comprehension of natural language text seems like an obvious choice: the meaning of arbitrary open-domain text goes beyond any possible formalism. There are various attempts, such as open information extraction (Etzioni et al., 2011) and abstract meaning representations (Banarescu et al., 2013), to try to capture broad, open domain semantics and the meaning of entire sentences. However, leaving aside the difficulties in training annotators and collecting annotations for these formalisms, any attempt to normalize meaning across disparate surface forms will necessarily lose information that was present in the natural language. The flexibility inherent in natural language as an *annotation* and *query* format is necessary in order to test deep understanding of arbitrary passages.

However, using questions to judge understanding is itself somewhat problematic, as (1) it is not clear a priori what the scope of these questions should be, and (2) collecting these arbitrary questions is very challenging, as questions that seem to be probing a particular kind of understanding might have shortcuts that allow answering them correctly without actually understanding the text at the level that was intended. Section 3 explores the first of these issues, and Section 4 discusses the second, along with ways to mitigate it.

3 What kinds of questions?

Having claimed that the ability to answer arbitrary questions is a natural way for machines to demonstrate understanding of a passage of text, we turn to the obvious question: what exactly is included in "arbitrary questions"? Some questions one could ask about a passage have little to do with understanding the passage. For example, the question *What is the population of the country Trump visited?*, asked about a passage that mentions the country but not its population, does require understanding the passage, but also requires knowing an additional specific fact. Such a requirement of external background knowledge not relevant to the passage is not desirable in a test of reading comprehension.

In this section we attempt to enumerate the high-level phenomena that characterize the understanding of a passage of text, and which can be asked about in reading comprehension questions. This enumeration is by no means exhaustive, but it should be a decent starting place for researchers attempting to build reading comprehension datasets—very few of these phenomena are explicitly queried in existing reading comprehension datasets, and those that are have relatively little coverage. We implicitly assume that the number of high-level phenomena is small enough such that making headway on, say, a few dozen phenomena will substantially improve the ability of models to read and understand text.

There are fuzzy boundaries between all of these phenomena, and no dataset can possibly focus exclusively on one of them. Every dataset, even those that sample from naturally occurring questions, will have some bias in which phenomena are asked about. We advocate being intentional about this bias and trying to be comprehensive in the collection of datasets that we construct.

Sentence-level linguistic structure Most existing reading comprehension datasets implicitly target local predicate-argument structures. The incentives involved in the creation of SQuAD encouraged workers to create questions that were close paraphrases of some part of a paragraph, replacing a noun phrase with a question word. This, and other cloze-style question construction, encourages very local reasoning that amounts to finding and then understanding the argument structure of a single sentence. This is an important aspect of meaning, but one could construct much harder datasets than this. One direction to push on linguistic structure is to move beyond locating a single sentence. DROP (Dua et al., 2019) largely involves the same level of linguistic structural analysis as SQuAD, but the questions require combining pieces from several parts of the passage, forcing a more comprehensive analysis of the passage contents. A separate direction one could push on sentence-level linguistic structure in reading comprehension is to target other phenomena than predicate argument structure. There are many rich problems in semantic analysis, such as negation scope, distributive vs. non-distributive coordination, factuality, deixis, briding and empty elements, preposition senses, noun compounds, and many more. Many of these phenomena have well-defined formalisms that can be used for annotation and evaluation, but it would also be useful to carefully design reading comprehension datasets that require an implicit understanding of these phenomena.

Paragraph-level structure While the input to a reading comprehension dataset is a paragraph of text, most datasets do not explicitly target questions that require understanding the entire paragraph, or how the sentences fit together into a coherent whole. Some post-hoc analyses attempt to reveal the percentage of questions that require more than one sentence, but it is better to design the datasets from the beginning to obtain questions that look at paragraph- or discourse-level phenomena, such as entity tracking, discourse relations, or pragmatics. For example, Quoref (Dasigi et al., 2019) is a dataset that targets entity tracking and coreference resolution. There are few linguistic formalisms targeting structures larger than a paragraph, but those that do exist, such as rhetorical structure theory (Mann and Thompson, 1988), could form the basis of an interesting and useful reading comprehension dataset.

Grounding and background knowledge A key aspect of reading is understanding the text in terms of what you already know, either commonsense knowledge or more domain-specific factual knowledge. After reading a description of a room, for example, people can make commonsense inferences about the objects described, and a lot of training and background knowledge is required to really understand an abstract on PubMed. People exhibit varying levels of comprehension when reading a particular text, depending largely on their ability to situate that text in the context of the appropriate background knowledge. There is room for interesting datasets along these lines. Cosmos QA (Huang et al., 2019) is an attempt to make such a dataset, though the fact that it is multiple choice puts it outside of our strict definition of "reading comprehension".

Implicative reasoning Understanding text includes understanding the implications (or entailments) of that text on other text that might be seen. For example, understanding the text *Bill loves Mary. Mary was just diagnosed with cancer.* means also understanding that Bill will be sad. In some sense this can be seen as "grounding" the predicates in the text to some prior knowledge that includes the implications of that predicate, but it also includes the more general notion of reconstructing a model of the world being described by the text. There are two datasets that just scratch the surface of this kind of reading: ShARC (Saeidi et al., 2018) requires reading rules and applying them to questions asked by users, though its format is not standard reading comprehension; and ROPES (Lin et al., 2019), which requires reading descriptions of causes and effects and applying them to situated questions.

Communicative aspects There are many communicative aspects of text that a human implicitly understands when reading, and which could be queried in reading comprehension datasets. For instance, is a text intended to be expository, narrative, persuasive, or something else? Did the author succeed in their communicative intent? Was there some deeper metaphorical point in the text? A dataset targeted at these sorts of phenomena could be incredibly interesting, and very challenging.

4 Ways to combat shortcuts

As discussed in the previous section, large-scale reading comprehension datasets where crowdworkers ask questions about the given passage have brought significant progress in the community. However, it is very easy to construct datasets where solving the task contributes little to genuine understanding of the text as intended. Chen et al. (2016) argues that 97% of answerable questions on CNNDAILYMAIL (Hermann et al., 2015) are solvable by superficial clues such as word or semantic overlap.[3] Jia and Liang (2017) find that models trained on SQUAD suffer significantly when adversarial input is injected despite no change in the semantics of the original text. Such findings indicate that there are certain shortcuts in solving reading comprehension tasks that allow a model to find the answer by superficial clues such as lexical overlap and entity types (Clark and Gardner, 2018; Sugawara et al., 2018). Accordingly, more recent reading comprehension datasets are constructed with several different approaches to prevent such shortcuts in order to foster natural language understanding.

4.1 Question / passage mismatch

One way to reduce lexical overlap between the question and passage is to expose the author of the question to a different passage that conveys

a similar meaning. Examples include NARRATIVEQA (Kočiský et al., 2018), where question authors were shown a summary of a movie script that will be used for answering questions, and DUORC (Saha et al., 2018), where questions are authored given a passage that is comparable to the one that will later be employed.

Another approach is to collect questions first, and then pair them with a passage, which was done in QUAC (Choi et al., 2018) or with a distantly collected relevant context, which was the method of choice in TRIVIAQA (Joshi et al., 2017).

Last, lexical overlap can be reduced if one has access to natural questions that have been posed by users who do not know the answers and are seeking information (Lee et al., 2019). NATURAL QUESTIONS (Kwiatkowski et al., 2019) and BOOLQ (Clark et al., 2019) are two examples for such datasets. However, access to such questions is usually limited for most researchers.

4.2 "No answer" option

Most of the reasoning shortcuts in existing datasets arise due to the fact that the system can assume that the answer is guaranteed to exist in the given passage. Removing this assumption and requiring the system to identify whether the question is even answerable from the passage can prevent such shortcuts.

One example of this kind of dataset construction is SQUAD 2.0(Rajpurkar et al., 2018), which asked annotators to read the given passage and write a question which the passage does not contain the answer to but contains a plausible negative answer. A drawback of this approach is that annotators see the passage when asking the question, which can introduce its own biases and shortcuts. An alternative is to combine a "no answer" option with the approach the previous section, where an annotator writes questions without knowing the answer, and another annotator verifies whether they are answerable by the paired passage. Example datasets include NEWSQA (Trischler et al., 2016)[4], QUAC (Choi et al., 2018) and NATURAL QUESTIONS (Kwiatkowski et al., 2019).

4.3 Dialog

Questions that require additional context to be understood, such as conversation state, are another

---

[3]They found 75% of questions are answerable, and among them, 73% are solvable by exact match, paragraph and partial clues (word/concept overlap).

[4]Non-answerable questions are provided as the extra challenge apart from answerable portions.

potential means of avoiding reasoning shortcuts. A person is not able to answer a simple question such as *How many?* without the additional context of a prior question describing what is being counted. Care needs to be taken with this method, however, as some datasets are amenable to input reduction (Feng et al., 2018), where there is only one plausible answer to such a short question. If done well, however, this method provides additional challenges such as clarification, coreference resolution, and aggregation of pieces scattered across conversation history. QUAC (Choi et al., 2018) and CoQA (Reddy et al., 2019) are two datasets that focus on such setting.

4.4 Complex reasoning

Tasks which require more advanced forms of reasoning are proposed to prevent answering the question from superficial clues. Examples include tasks requiring discrete and arithmetic reasoning (Dua et al., 2019), textbook question answering which requires understanding various forms of knowledge (Clark et al., 2018; Kembhavi et al., 2017) and multi-hop question answering which requires reading multiple distinct pieces of evidence (Talmor and Berant, 2018; Yang et al., 2018). Despite these attempts, it was found that shortcuts still exist in complex reasoning tasks such as multi-hop QA (Min et al., 2019; Jiang and Bansal, 2019), so careful construction of the dataset is necessary.

One novel method that may by applied to combat such shortcuts and enforce multi-hop reasoning is to check the semantic relations present in the question. In questions requiring a conjunction to be performed, functional or pseudo functional relations (Lin et al., 2010), such as *father* or *founder*, may facilitate arriving at the correct answer by solving only the functional relation and not the full conjunction. On the other hand such relations are desired when requiring a composition to be solved in a question. For example, in the question *What is the capital of the largest economy in Europe?* we would like *the largest economy in Europe* to be one answer we can use to modify the question to *what is the capital of **Germany***.

4.5 Context construction

Shortcuts in solving a reading comprehension questions may also occur when the context is not diverse with respect to the question. (Min et al., 2019) Functional relations and entity types in the question can give away the location of the correct answer when only one such function relation or entity type exists in the context. For instance when asked *What year... ?* having only one available year in the context enable models to easily locate the correct answer, without requiring the rest of the question. One option to avoid these shortcuts is to carefully select or construct the contexts that are used, and various methods of entity and relation type counting in the context may be employed.

4.6 Adversarial construction

One promising means of removing reasoning shortcuts is to encode those shortcuts into a learned system, and use that system to filter out questions that are too easy during dataset construction. DROP (Dua et al., 2019) and Quoref (Dasigi et al., 2019) used a model trained on SQuAD 1.1 (Rajpurkar et al., 2016) as an "adversarial" baseline when having crowd workers write questions. Because the people could see when the system answered their questions correctly, they learned to ask harder questions.

This kind of adversarial construction can introduce its own biases, however, especially if the questions being filtered are generated by machines instead of humans (Zellers et al., 2018). This also makes a dataset dependent on another dataset and model in complex ways, which has both positive and negative aspects to it. In some sense, it is a good thing to get a diverse set of reading comprehension questions, and encoding one dataset's biases into a model to enforce a different distribution for new datasets helps in collecting diverse datasets. If crowd workers end up simply wordsmithing their questions in order to pass the adversary, however, this seems unsatisfying. Overall, however, we believe this is a good method that could be used more widely when collecting reading comprehension datasets.

4.7 Minimal question pairs

ROPES (Lin et al., 2019) borrowed the idea of "minimal pairs" from linguistic analysis in its construction. In order to avoid subtle biases around which entity appears first in a question or paragraph, or simple lexical association biases between question and passage words, crowd workers were instructed to make minimal changes to the questions they wrote in order to change the answer. For example, a question such as *Which city would have more trees?* might be changed to

Which city would have fewer trees?. This method is not applicable in all reading comprehension scenarios, but where it is it can be an effective means of reducing shortcuts—a single question in isolation might exhibit the characteristics of a shortcut, but presumably the other question in the minimal pair would *also* have the same shortcut, leading to a system that relies on the shortcut getting at least one of them wrong.

4.8 Free-form answers

Shortcuts almost always arise because of a limited output space that can be searched over to find simple biases that lead to the correct answer. The problem is largely, though not entirely, with multiple choice answers. This includes span extraction formats, which is still effectively multiple choice with on the order of 100 choices (or many fewer, if the system can reasonably model likely answer candidates from the passage). Requiring free-form answers, especially where the answer is not found in the paragraph, would dramatically reduce the occurrence of reasoning shortcuts. This introduces a separate problem of evaluating the free-form answers, however, which is a pressing problem in reading comprehension research. If we had a good means of automatically evaluating free-form answers, much of this section on designing datasets to avoid reasoning shortcuts would be unnecessary, and we could build much more interesting and challenging datasets.

4.9 Multi-task evaluation

Given the myriad datasets created for reading comprehension, a natural method to reduce the effects of shortcuts is to evaluate models on multiple datasets. Assuming shortcuts are often dataset-specific means that a model that succeeds on all datasets is likely to have better text understanding.

But evaluation on multiple datasets goes even beyond shortcut mitigation. In Section 3 we proposed to enumerate the phenomena required for reading comprehension and build datasets that highlight each category. A possible shortcoming of this approach is that researchers will develop models for specific datasets that do not generalize to other datasets. This will result in a collection of models, none of which fully understands text. Evaluating models on multiple reading comprehension datasets (Talmor and Berant, 2019) will ensure that progress is made towards comprehensive understanding of text.

4.10 Explainability

A possible way to reduce the effect of shortcuts is to demand some sort of explanation for the final answer provided by a reading comprehension model. In that vein, Yang et al. (2018) evaluate in HOTPOTQA not only QA accuracy but also whether the relevant supporting sentences are identified by a reading comprehension model.

5 Recommendations for future research

As evidenced by this survey, reading comprehension datasets have a long way to go before they approach a comprehensive test of a system's ability to read. Future datasets should try to improve coverage by focusing on phenomena that have been thus far neglected. Section 3 lists many possible phenomena that would make for very interesting reading comprehension datasets.

The challenge of creating a dataset without shortcuts has recently emerged as a fundamental one for progress in natural language understanding. Many datasets that have been created at great expense in an attempt to stress-test the abilities of existing models have been found to be simpler than expected due to the shortcuts that lie within them. Developing scientific methods for dataset collection that circumvent such shortcuts is instrumental for making sure the collective effort of our community actually leads to models that better understand text. For example, one possible method may be dropping out parts of a question as a means of insuring the question is not redundant and the model is not learning spurious shortcuts. Questions may be filtered using this technique, and models for shortcut checking may be trained on part of the questions to check if indeed no significant redundancy exists in them, and the model cannot solve the example with, say, only one word in the question (Feng et al., 2018).

In our opinion, evaluating reading comprehension models on many datasets is a promising direction that will prevent over-fitting to the statistical biases in a single dataset, but preventing bias *a priori*, as well as detecting bias and constructing adversarial examples are also important directions for future research.

References

L. Banarescu, C. B. S. Cai, M. Georgescu, K. Griffitt, U. Hermjakob, K. Knight, P. Koehn, M. Palmer, and

N. Schneider. 2013. Abstract meaning representation for sembanking. In *7th Linguistic Annotation Workshop and Interoperability with Discourse*.

Danqi Chen, Jason Bolton, and Christopher D Manning. 2016. A thorough examination of the cnn/daily mail reading comprehension task. In *ACL*.

Eunsol Choi, He He, Mohit Iyyer, Mark Yatskar, Wen tau Yih, Yejin Choi, Percy Liang, and Luke S. Zettlemoyer. 2018. QuAC: Question answering in context. In *EMNLP*.

Christopher Clark and Matt Gardner. 2018. Simple and effective multi-paragraph reading comprehension. In *ACL*.

Christopher Clark, Kenton Lee, Ming-Wei Chang, Tom Kwiatkowski, Michael Collins, and Kristina Toutanova. 2019. BoolQ: Exploring the surprising difficulty of natural yes/no questions. In *NAACL-HLT*.

Peter Clark, Isaac Cowhey, Oren Etzioni, Tushar Khot, Ashish Sabharwal, Carissa Schoenick, and Oyvind Tafjord. 2018. Think you have solved question answering? try arc, the ai2 reasoning challenge. *arXiv preprint arXiv:1803.05457*.

Pradeep Dasigi, Nelson Liu, Ana Marasovic, Noah Smith, and Matt Gardner. 2019. Quoref: A reading comprehension dataset with questions requiring coreferential reasoning. In *EMNLP*.

Dheeru Dua, Yizhong Wang, Pradeep Dasigi, Gabriel Stanovsky, Sameer Singh, and Matt Gardner. 2019. Drop: A reading comprehension benchmark requiring discrete reasoning over paragraphs. In *NAACL*.

O. Etzioni, A. Fader, J. Christensen, S. Soderland, and Mausam. 2011. Open information extraction: the second generation. In *IJCAI*.

Shi Feng, Eric Wallace, Alvin Grissom II, Mohit Iyyer, Pedro Rodriguez, and Jordan Boyd-Graber. 2018. Pathologies of Neural Models Make Interpretations Difficult. In *EMNLP*.

Karl Moritz Hermann, Tomas Kocisky, Edward Grefenstette, Lasse Espeholt, Will Kay, Mustafa Suleyman, and Phil Blunsom. 2015. Teaching machines to read and comprehend. In *NeurIPS*.

Lifu Huang, Ronan Le Bras, Chandra Bhagavatula, and Yejin Choi. 2019. Cosmos qa: Machine reading comprehension with contextual commonsense reasoning. In *EMNLP*.

Robin Jia and Percy Liang. 2017. Adversarial examples for evaluating reading comprehension systems. In *EMNLP*.

Yichen Jiang and Mohit Bansal. 2019. Avoiding reasoning shortcuts: Adversarial evaluation, training, and model development for multi-hop QA. In *ACL*.

Mandar S. Joshi, Eunsol Choi, Daniel S. Weld, and Luke S. Zettlemoyer. 2017. Triviaqa: A large scale distantly supervised challenge dataset for reading comprehension. In *ACL*.

Aniruddha Kembhavi, Minjoon Seo, Dustin Schwenk, Jonghyun Choi, Ali Farhadi, and Hannaneh Hajishirzi. 2017. Are you smarter than a sixth grader? textbook question answering for multimodal machine comprehension. In *CVPR*.

Panayiota Kendeou and Gregory Trevors. 2012. *Quality learning from texts we read: What does it take?*, pages 251–275. Cambridge University Press.

Tomáš Kočiský, Jonathan Schwarz, Phil Blunsom, Chris Dyer, Karl Moritz Hermann, Gábor Melis, and Edward Grefenstette. 2018. The narrativeqa reading comprehension challenge. *TACL*.

Tom Kwiatkowski, Jennimaria Palomaki, Olivia Redfield, Michael Collins, Ankur Parikh, Chris Alberti, Danielle Epstein, Illia Polosukhin, Jacob Devlin, Kenton Lee, et al. 2019. Natural questions: a benchmark for question answering research. *TACL*.

Kenton Lee, Ming-Wei Chang, and Kristina Toutanova. 2019. Latent retrieval for weakly supervised open domain question answering. In *ACL*.

H. J. Levesque. 2013. On our best behaviour. In *IJCAI*.

Kevin Lin, Oyvind Tafjord, Peter Clark, and Matt Gardner. 2019. Reasoning over paragraph effects in situations. *arXiv preprint arXiv:1908.05852*.

Thomas Lin, Mausam, and Oren Etzioni. 2010. Identifying Functional Relations in Web Text. In *EMNLP*.

William C Mann and Sandra A Thompson. 1988. Rhetorical structure theory: Toward a functional theory of text organization. *Text*, 8(3):243–281.

Sewon Min, Eric Wallace, Sameer Singh, Matt Gardner, Hannaneh Hajishirzi, and Luke Zettlemoyer. 2019. Compositional questions do not necessitate multi-hop reasoning. In *ACL*.

Pranav Rajpurkar, Robin Jia, and Percy Liang. 2018. Know what you don't know: Unanswerable questions for squad. In *ACL*.

Pranav Rajpurkar, Jian Zhang, Konstantin Lopyrev, and Percy Liang. 2016. SQuAD: 100, 000+ questions for machine comprehension of text. In *EMNLP*.

Siva Reddy, Danqi Chen, and Christopher D. Manning. 2019. CoQA: A conversational question answering challenge. *TACL*.

Matthew Richardson, Christopher J.C. Burges, and Erin Renshaw. 2013. MCTest: A challenge dataset for the open-domain machine comprehension of text. In *EMNLP*.

Marzieh Saeidi, Max Bartolo, Patrick Lewis, Sameer Singh, Tim Rocktäschel, Mike Sheldon, Guillaume Bouchard, and Sebastian Riedel. 2018. Interpretation of natural language rules in conversational machine reading. In *Proceedings of the 2018 Conference on Empirical Methods in Natural Language Processing*, pages 2087–2097, Brussels, Belgium. Association for Computational Linguistics.

Amrita Saha, Rahul Aralikatte, Mitesh M. Khapra, and Karthik Sankaranarayanan. 2018. DuoRC: Towards complex language understanding with paraphrased reading comprehension. In *ACL*.

Saku Sugawara, Kentaro Inui, Satoshi Sekine, and Akiko Aizawa. 2018. What makes reading comprehension questions easier? In *Proceedings of the 2018 Conference on Empirical Methods in Natural Language Processing*, pages 4208–4219, Brussels, Belgium. Association for Computational Linguistics.

Alon Talmor and Jonathan Berant. 2018. The web as a knowledge-base for answering complex questions. In *NAACL-HLT*.

Alon Talmor and Jonathan Berant. 2019. MultiQA: An empirical investigation of generalization and transfer in reading comprehension. In *ACL*.

Adam Trischler, Tong Wang, Xingdi Yuan, Justin Harris, Alessandro Sordoni, Philip Bachman, and Kaheer Suleman. 2016. Newsqa: A machine comprehension dataset. *arXiv preprint arXiv:1611.09830*.

A. M. Turing. 1950. Computing machinery and intelligence. *Mind*.

Zhilin Yang, Peng Qi, Saizheng Zhang, Yoshua Bengio, William W. Cohen, Ruslan Salakhutdinov, and Christopher D. Manning. 2018. Hotpotqa: A dataset for diverse, explainable multi-hop question answering. In *EMNLP*.

Rowan Zellers, Yonatan Bisk, Roy Schwartz, and Yejin Choi. 2018. Swag: A large-scale adversarial dataset for grounded commonsense inference. In *EMNLP*.

Multi-step Entity-centric Information Retrieval for Multi-Hop Question Answering

Ameya Godbole[1]*, Dilip Kavarthapu[1]*, Rajarshi Das[1]*,
Zhiyu Gong[1], Abhishek Singhal[1], Hamed Zamani[1],
Mo Yu[2], Tian Gao[2], Xiaoxiao Guo[2], Manzil Zaheer[3] and Andrew McCallum[1]
[1]University of Massachusetts Amherst,
[2]IBM Research, [3]Google Research

Abstract

Multi-hop question answering (QA) requires an information retrieval (IR) system that can find *multiple* supporting evidence needed to answer the question, making the retrieval process very challenging. This paper introduces an IR technique that uses information of entities present in the initially retrieved evidence to learn to 'hop' to other relevant evidence. In a setting, with more than **5 million** Wikipedia paragraphs, our approach leads to significant boost in retrieval performance. The retrieved evidence also increased the performance of an existing QA model (without any training) on the HOTPOTQA benchmark by **10.59** F1.

1 Introduction

Multi-hop QA requires finding multiple supporting evidence, and reasoning over them in order to answer a question (Welbl et al., 2018; Talmor and Berant, 2018; Yang et al., 2018). For example, to answer the question shown in figure 1, the QA system has to retrieve two different paragraphs and reason over them. Moreover, the paragraph containing the answer to the question has very little lexical overlap with the question, making it difficult for search engines to retrieve them from a large corpus. For instance, the accuracy of a BM25 retriever for finding *all* supporting evidence for a question decreases from 53.7% to 25.9% on the 'easy' and 'hard' subsets of the HOTPOTQA training dataset.[1]

We hypothesize that an effective retriever for multi-hop QA should have the *"hopiness"* built into it, by design. That is, after retrieving an initial set of documents, the retriever should be able to "hop" onto other documents, if required. We note that, many supporting evidence often share common

---

* Equal contribution. Correspondence to {agodbole, rajarshi}@cs.umass.edu

[1]According to Yang et al. (2018), the easy (hard) subset primarily requires single (multi) hop reasoning. We only consider queries that have answers as spans in at least one paragraph.

Question : What county is Ron Teachworth from?

Ronald S. Teachworth is an American artist, writer and film director from **Rochester Hills**, Michigan.

Rochester Hills is a city in northeast **Oakland County** of the U.S. state of Michigan, in the northern outskirts of Metropolitan Detroit area. As of the 2010 census, the city had a total population of 70,995.

Figure 1: Multi-hop questions require finding multiple evidence and the target document containing the answer has very little lexical overlap with the question.

(*bridge*) entities between them (e.g. "Rochester Hills" in figure 1). In this work, we introduce a model that uses information about entities present in an initially retrieved paragraph to jointly find a passage of text *describing* the entity (*entity-linking*) and also determining whether that passage would be relevant to answer the multi-hop query.

A major component of our retriever is a re-ranker model that uses contextualized entity representation obtained from a pre-trained BERT (Devlin et al., 2018) language model. Specifically, the entity representation is obtained by feeding the query and a Wikipedia paragraph describing the entity to a BERT model. The re-ranker uses representation of both the initial paragraph and the representation of all the entities within it to determine which evidence to gather next.

Essentially, our method introduces a new way of *multi-step* retrieval that uses information about intermediate entities. A standard way of doing multi-step retrieval is via *pseudo-relevance feedback* (Xu and Croft, 1996; Lavrenko and Croft, 2001) in which relevant terms from initial retrieved documents are used to reformulate the initial question. A few recent works learn to reformulate the query using task specific reward such as document recall or performance on a QA task (Nogueira and Cho, 2017; Buck et al., 2018; Das et al., 2019). However, these methods do not necessarily use the information about entities present in the evidence as they might not be the more frequent/salient terms in it.

Proceedings of the Second Workshop on Machine Reading for Question Answering, pages 113–118
Hong Kong, China, November 4, 2019. ©2019 Association for Computational Linguistics

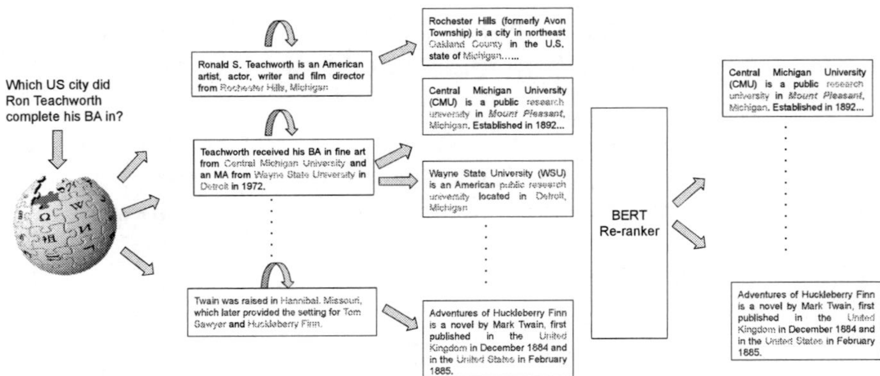

Figure 2: Overview of our approach. We use the entity mentions present in the initially retrieved paragraphs to link to paragraphs describing them. Next, the BERT-based re-ranker scores the chain of initial and the entity-describing paragraph. Note the presence of self-loop from the initial paragraphs to accommodate for questions that do not require 'hopping' to a new paragraph. Finally, the paragraph at the end of every chain is reported in the order in which the chain it belongs to is ranked.

Empirically, our method outperforms all of these methods significantly for multi-hop QA. Our work is most closely related to the recently proposed BERT re-ranker model of Nogueira and Cho (2019). However, unlike us, they do not model the chains of evidence paragraphs required for a multi-hop question. Secondly, they also do not have a entity linking component to identify the relevant paragraphs. Our model out-performs them for multi-hop QA.

To summarize, this paper presents an entity-centric IR approach that jointly performs entity linking and effectively finds relevant evidence required for questions that need multi-hop reasoning from a large corpus containing millions of paragraphs. When the retrieved paragraphs are supplied to the baseline QA model introduced in Yang et al. (2018), it improved the QA performance on the hidden test set by 10.59 F1 points.[2]

2 Methodology

Our approach is summarized in Figure 2. The first component of our model is a standard IR system that takes in a natural language query 'Q' and returns an initial set of evidence. For our experiments, we use the popular BM25 retriever, but this component can be replaced by any IR model. We assume that all spans of entity mentions have been identified in the paragraph text by a one-time pre-processing, with an entity tagger.[3]

---

[2]Code, pre-trained models and retrieved paragraphs are released — https://github.com/ameyagodbole/entity-centric-ir-for-multihop-qa

[3]We plan to explore joint learning of entity tagging with linking and retrieval as future work.

Entity Linking The next component of our model is an entity linker that finds an introductory Wikipedia paragraph describing the entity, corresponding to each entity mention. Several IR approaches (Xiong et al., 2016; Raviv et al., 2016) use an off-the-shelf entity linker. However, most entity linking systems (Ganea and Hofmann, 2017; Raiman and Raiman, 2018) have been trained on Wikipedia data and hence using an off-the-shelf linker would be unfair, since there exists a possibility of test-time leakage. To ensure strictness, we developed our own simple linking strategy. Following the standard approach of using mention text and hyper-link information (Cucerzan, 2007; Ji and Grishman, 2011), we create a mapping (alias table) between them. The alias table stores mappings between a mention string (e.g. "Bill") and various entities it can refer to (e.g. Bill Clinton, Billy Joel, etc). The top-40 documents returned by the BM25 retriever on the dev and test queries are also ignored while building the alias table. At test time, our re-ranker considers all the candidate entity paragraphs that a mention is linked to via the alias table. Although simple, we find this strategy to work well for our task and we plan to use a learned entity linker for future work.

Re-ranker The next component of our model is a BERT-based re-ranker that ranks the chains of paragraphs obtained from the previous two components of the model. Let Q denote the query, D denote a paragraph in the initial set of paragraphs returned by the BM25 retriever. Let e denote an entity mention present in D and E be the linked document returned by the linker for e. If there are multiple linked documents, we consider all of them. Although our retriever is designed for multi-hop questions, in a general setting, most questions are not multi-hop in nature. Therefore to account for questions that do not need hopping to a new paragraph, we also add a 'self-link' (Figure 2) from each of the initial retrieved paragraph, giving the model the ability to stay in the same paragraph.

To train the re-ranker, we form *query-dependent* passage representation for both D and E. The query Q and the paragraph E are concatenated and fed as input to a BERT encoder and the corresponding [CLS] token forms the entity representation **e**. Similarly, the document representation **d** is set to the embedding of the [CLS] token obtained after encoding the concatenation of Q and D. The final score that the entity paragraph E is relevant to Q is computed by concatenating the two query-aware representation **d** and **e** and passing it through a 2-layer feed-forward network as before. It should be noted, the final score is determined by both the evidence paragraphs D and E and as we show empirically, not considering both leads to decrease in performance.

During training, we mark a chain of paragraphs as a positive example, if the last paragraph of the chain is present in the supporting facts, since that is a chain of reasoning that led to a relevant paragraph. All other paragraph chains are treated as negative examples. In our experiments, we consider chains of length 2, although extending to longer chains is straightforward. The training set had on an avg. 6.35 positive chains per example suggesting a multi-instance multi-label learning training setup (Surdeanu et al., 2012). However, for this work, we treat each chain independently. We use a simple binary cross-entropy loss to train the network.

3   Experiments

For all our experiment, unless specified otherwise, we use the open domain corpus[4] released by Yang et al. (2018) which contains over 5.23 million Wikipedia abstracts (introductory paragraphs). To identify spans of entities, we use the implementation of the state-of-the-art entity tagger presented in Peters et al. (2018).[5] For the BERT encoder, we use the BERT-BASE-UNCASED model.[6] We use the implementation of widely-used BM25 retrieval

Model	ACCURACY				
	@2	@5	@10	@20	MAP
BM25	0.093	0.191	0.259	0.324	0.412
PRF-TFIDF	0.088	0.157	0.204	0.258	0.317
PRF-RM	0.083	0.175	0.242	0.296	0.406
PRF-TASK	0.097	0.198	0.267	0.330	0.420
BERT-re-ranker	0.146	0.271	0.347	0.409	0.470
QUERY+E-DOC	0.101	0.223	0.301	0.367	0.568
Our Model	**0.230**	**0.482**	**0.612**	**0.674**	**0.654**

Table 1: Retrieval performance of models on the HOTPOTQA benchmark. A successful retrieval is when *all* the relevant passages for a question are retrieved from more than 5 million paragraphs in the corpus.

available in Lucene.[7]

3.1   IR for MultiHop QA

We introduce a new way of doing multi-step retrieval. A popular way of doing it in traditional IR systems is via pseudo-relevance feedback (PRF). The PRF methods assume that the top retrieved documents in response to a given query are relevant. Based on this assumption, they expand the query in a weighted manner. PRF has been shown to be effective in various retrieval settings (Xu and Croft, 1996). We compare with two widely used PRF models — The Rocchio's algorithm on top of the TF-IDF retrieval model (PRF-TFIDF) (Rocchio, 1971) and the relevance model (RM3) based on the language modeling framework in information retrieval (PRF-RM) (Lavrenko and Croft, 2001). Following prior work (Nogueira and Cho, 2017), we use query likelihood retrieval model with Dirichlet prior smoothing (Zhai and Lafferty, 2001) for first retrieval run.

Nogueira and Cho (2017) proposed a new way of query reformulation — incorporating reward from a document-relevance task (PRF-TASK) and training using reinforcement learning. Recently, Nogueira and Cho (2019) proposed a BERT based passage re-ranker (BERT-re-ranker) that has achieved excellent performance in several IR benchmarks. But, its performance has not been evaluated on multi-hop queries till now. For a fair comparison with our model which looks at paragraphs corresponding to entities, we use top 200 paragraphs retrieved by the initial IR model for BERT-re-ranker instead of 25 for our model.[8]

Table 1 reports the accuracy($@k$) of retrieving

---

[4] https://hotpotqa.github.io/wiki-readme.html
[5] https://allennlp.org/models
[6] https://github.com/google-research/bert

[7] https://lucene.apache.org/
[8] There were 2.725 entities in a paragraph on average. We wanted to make sure to give the BERT-re-ranker baseline atleast 25 × 2.275 paragraphs.

all[9] the relevant paragraphs required for answering a question in HOTPOTQA[10] within the top k paragraphs. We also report the mean average precision score (MAP) which is a strict metric that takes into account the relative position of the relevant document in the ranked list (Kadlec et al., 2017). As we can see, our retrieval technique vastly outperforms other existing retrieval systems with an absolute increase of **26.5%** (accuracy@10) and **18.4%** (MAP), when compared to BERT-re-ranker. The standard PRF techniques do not perform well for this task. This is primarily because the PRF methods rely on statistical features like frequency of terms in the document, and fail to explicitly use information about entities, that may not be frequently occurring the paragraph. In fact, their performance is a little behind the standard retrieval results of BM25, suggesting that this benchmark dataset needs entity-centric information retrieval. The PRF-TASK does slightly better than other PRF models, showing that incorporating task-specific rewards can be beneficial. However, as we find, RL approaches are slow to converge[11] as rewards from a down-stream tasks are sparse and action space in information retrieval is very large.

Ablations. We investigate whether modeling the chain of paragraphs needed to reach the final paragraph is important or not. As an ablation, we ignore the representation of the initial retrieved document D_1 and only consider the final document representing the entity (QUERY+E-DOC). Table 1 shows that, indeed modeling the chain of documents is important. This makes intuitive sense, since to answer questions such as the county where a person is from (figure 1), modeling context about the person, should be helpful. We also evaluate, if our model performs well on single-hop questions as well. This evaluation is a bit tricky to do in HOTPOTQA, since the evaluataion set only contains questions from 'hard' subset (Yang et al., 2018). However, within that hard subset, we find the set of question, that has the answer span present in *all* the supporting passages (SINGLE-HOP (HARD)) and only in *one* of the supporting passages (MULTI-HOP (HARD))[12]. The intuition is that if there are multiple evidence

---

[9]This is different from the usual hits@k metric where at least one relevant evidence is required to be present in the top-k retrieved evidence.

[10]Since, the supporting passage information is only present for train & validation set, we consider the validation set as our hidden test set and consider a subset of train as validation set.

[11]Training took ∼2 weeks for comparable performance.

[12]There were 1184 SINGLE-HOP (HARD) and 4734 MULTI-HOP (HARD) queries.

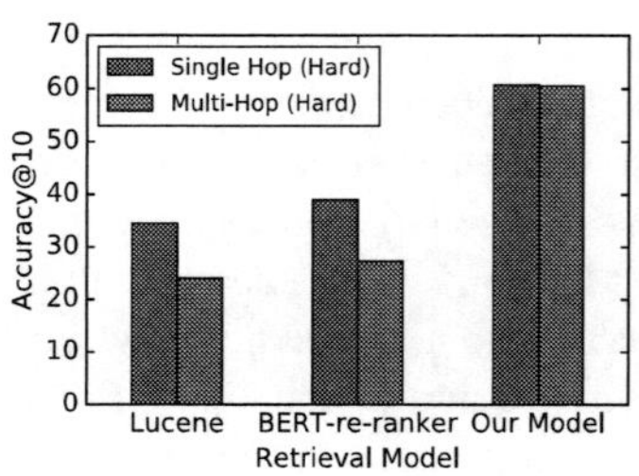

Figure 3: Our retrieval model works equally well for single-hop queries. This can be attributed to the presence of self-loops in the model which can make the model not hop to a different paragraph, if not required.

Model	EM	F1
Baseline Reader (Yang et al., 2018)	23.95	32.89
Our re-implementation	26.06	35.67
+ retrieved result	**35.36**	**46.26**

Table 2: Performance on QA task on hidden test set of HOTPOTQA after adding the retrieved paragraphs

containing the answer spans then it might be a little easier for a downstream QA model to identify the answer span. Figure 3 shows that our model performs equally well on both type of queries and hence can be applied in a practical setting.

3.2 Performance on HOTPOTQA

Table 2 shows the performance on the QA task. We were able to achieve better scores than reported in the baseline reader model of Yang et al. (2018) by using Adam (Kingma and Ba, 2014) instead of standard SGD (our re-implementation). Next, we use the top-10 paragraphs retrieved by our system from the entire corpus and feed it to the reader model. We achieve a **10.59** absolute increase in F1 score than the baseline. It should be noted that we use the simple baseline reader model and we are confident that we can achieve better scores by using more sophisticated reader architectures, e.g. using BERT based architectures. Our results show that retrieval is an important component of an open-domain system and equal importance should be given to both the retriever and reader component.

3.3 Zero-shot experiment on Wikihop

We experiment if our model trained on HOTPOTQA can generalize to another multi-hop dataset – WIKIHOP (Welbl et al., 2018), without any training. In the WIKIHOP dataset, a set of candidate introductory Wikipedia paragraphs are given per question. Hence, we do not need to use our initial BM25 retriever.

We assign the first entity mention occurring in a

Model	acc@2	acc@5
BM25	0.06	0.30
BERT-re-ranker (zs)	0.08	0.27
Our Model (zs)	**0.10**	**0.41**

Table 3: Zero-shot (zs) IR results on WIKIHOP.

paragraph as the textual description of that entity. For instance, if the first entity mention in the paragraph is 'Mumbai', we assign that paragraph as the textual description for the entity 'Mumbai'. This assumption is often true for the introductory paragraphs of a Wikipedia article. Next, we perform entity linking of mentions by just simple string matching (i.e. linking strings such as 'mumbai' to the previous paragraph). After constructing a small subgraph from the candidate paragraphs, we apply our model trained on HOTPOTQA. Since the dataset does not provide explicit supervision for which paragraphs are useful, we mark a paragraph as 'correct' if it contains the answer string. The baseline models we compare to are a BM25 retriever and a BERT-re-ranker model of (Nogueira and Cho, 2019) that ranks all the candidate supporting paragraphs for the question. Table 3 shows our model outperforms both models in zero-shot setting.

4   Related Work

Document retrieval using entities. Analysis of web-search query logs has revealed that there is a large portion of entity seeking queries (Liu and Fang, 2015). There exists substantial work on modeling documents with entities occurring in them. For example, Xiong et al. (2016) represents a document with bag-of-entities and Raviv et al. (2016) use entity-based language modeling for document retrieval. However, they depend on an off-the-shelf entity tagger, where as we jointly perform linking and retrieval. Moreover, we use contextualized entity representations using pre-trained LMs which have been proven to be better than bag-of-words approaches. There has been a lot of work which leverages knowledge graphs (KGs) to learn better entity representations (Xiong and Callan, 2015; Xiong et al., 2017; Liu et al., 2018) and for better query reformulation (Cao et al., 2008; Dalton et al., 2014; Dietz and Verga, 2014). Our work is not tied to any specific KG schema, instead we encode entities using its text description.

Neural ranking models have shown great potential and have been widely adopted in the IR community (Dehghani et al., 2017; Guo et al., 2019; Mitra

et al., 2017; Zamani et al., 2018, inter-alia). Bag-of-words and contextual embedding models, such as word2vec and BERT, have also been explored extensively for various IR tasks, from document to sentence-level retrieval (Padigela et al., 2019; Zamani and Croft, 2016, 2017).

5   Conclusion

We introduce an entity-centric approach to IR that finds relevant evidence required to answer multi-hop questions from a corpus containing millions of paragraphs leading to significant improvement to an existing QA system.

Acknowledgements

This work is funded in part by the Center for Data Science and the Center for Intelligent Information Retrieval, and in part by the National Science Foundation under Grant No. IIS-1514053 and in part by the International Business Machines Corporation Cognitive Horizons Network agreement number W1668553 and in part by the Chan Zuckerberg Initiative under the project Scientific Knowledge Base Construction. Any opinions, findings and conclusions or recommendations expressed in this material are those of the authors and do not necessarily reflect those of the sponsor.

References

Christian Buck, Jannis Bulian, Massimiliano Ciaramita, Wojciech Gajewski, Andrea Gesmundo, Neil Houlsby, and Wei Wang. 2018. Ask the right questions: Active question reformulation with reinforcement learning. In *ICLR*.

Guihong Cao, Jian-Yun Nie, Jianfeng Gao, and Stephen Robertson. 2008. Selecting good expansion terms for pseudo-relevance feedback. In *SIGIR*.

Silviu Cucerzan. 2007. Large-scale named entity disambiguation based on wikipedia data. In *EMNLP-CoNLL*.

Jeffrey Dalton, Laura Dietz, and James Allan. 2014. Entity query feature expansion using knowledge base links. In *SIGIR*.

Rajarshi Das, Shehzaad Dhuliawala, Manzil Zaheer, and Andrew McCallum. 2019. Multi-step retriever-reader interaction for scalable open-domain question answering. In *ICLR*.

Mostafa Dehghani, Hamed Zamani, Aliaksei Severyn, Jaap Kamps, and W. Bruce Croft. 2017. Neural ranking models with weak supervision. In *SIGIR*.

Jacob Devlin, Ming-Wei Chang, Kenton Lee, and Kristina Toutanova. 2018. Bert: Pre-training of deep bidirectional transformers for language understanding. In *NAACL*.

Laura Dietz and Patrick Verga. 2014. Umass at trec web 2014: Entity query feature expansion using knowledge base links. Technical report, MASSACHUSETTS UNIV AMHERST.

Octavian-Eugen Ganea and Thomas Hofmann. 2017. Deep joint entity disambiguation with local neural attention. In *EMNLP*.

Jiafeng Guo, Yixing Fan, Liang Pang, Liu Yang, Qingyao Ai, Hamed Zamani, Chen Wu, W. Bruce Croft, and Xueqi Cheng. 2019. A deep look into neural ranking models for information retrieval. *arXiv preprint arXiv:1903.06902*.

Heng Ji and Ralph Grishman. 2011. Knowledge base population: Successful approaches and challenges. In *ACL*.

Rudolf Kadlec, Ondrej Bajgar, and Jan Kleindienst. 2017. Knowledge base completion: Baselines strike back. *arXiv preprint arXiv:1705.10744*.

Diederik P Kingma and Jimmy Ba. 2014. Adam: A method for stochastic optimization. *arXiv preprint arXiv:1412.6980*.

Victor Lavrenko and W Bruce Croft. 2001. Relevance-based language models. In *SIGIR*.

Xitong Liu and Hui Fang. 2015. Latent entity space: a novel retrieval approach for entity-bearing queries. *Information Retrieval Journal*.

Zhenghao Liu, Chenyan Xiong, Maosong Sun, and Zhiyuan Liu. 2018. Entity-duet neural ranking: Understanding the role of knowledge graph semantics in neural information retrieval. In *ACL*.

Bhaskar Mitra, Fernando Diaz, and Nick Craswell. 2017. Learning to match using local and distributed representations of text for web search. In *WWW*.

Rodrigo Nogueira and Kyunghyun Cho. 2017. Task-oriented query reformulation with reinforcement learning. In *EMNLP*.

Rodrigo Nogueira and Kyunghyun Cho. 2019. Passage re-ranking with bert. *arXiv preprint arXiv:1901.04085*.

Harshith Padigela, Hamed Zamani, and W. Bruce Croft. 2019. Investigating the successes and failures of BERT for passage re-ranking. *arXiv preprint arXiv:1905.01758*.

Matthew E Peters, Mark Neumann, Mohit Iyyer, Matt Gardner, Christopher Clark, Kenton Lee, and Luke Zettlemoyer. 2018. Deep contextualized word representations. In *NAACL*.

Jonathan Raphael Raiman and Olivier Michel Raiman. 2018. Deeptype: multilingual entity linking by neural type system evolution. In *AAAI*.

Hadas Raviv, Oren Kurland, and David Carmel. 2016. Document retrieval using entity-based language models. In *SIGIR*.

J. J. Rocchio. 1971. Relevance feedback in information retrieval. In *The SMART Retrieval System - Experiments in Automatic Document Processing*. Prentice Hall.

Mihai Surdeanu, Julie Tibshirani, Ramesh Nallapati, and Christopher D Manning. 2012. Multi-instance multi-label learning for relation extraction. In *EMNLP*.

Alon Talmor and Jonathan Berant. 2018. The web as a knowledge-base for answering complex questions. In *NAACL*.

Johannes Welbl, Pontus Stenetorp, and Sebastian Riedel. 2018. Constructing datasets for multi-hop reading comprehension across documents. In *TACL*.

Chenyan Xiong and Jamie Callan. 2015. Esdrank: Connecting query and documents through external semi-structured data. In *CIKM*.

Chenyan Xiong, Jamie Callan, and Tie-Yan Liu. 2016. Bag-of-entities representation for ranking. In *ICTIR*.

Chenyan Xiong, Jamie Callan, and Tie-Yan Liu. 2017. Word-entity duet representations for document ranking. In *SIGIR*.

Jinxi Xu and W Bruce Croft. 1996. Quary expansion using local and global document analysis. In *SIGIR*.

Zhilin Yang, Peng Qi, Saizheng Zhang, Yoshua Bengio, William W Cohen, Ruslan Salakhutdinov, and Christopher D Manning. 2018. Hotpotqa: A dataset for diverse, explainable multi-hop question answering. In *EMNLP*.

Hamed Zamani and W. Bruce Croft. 2016. Embedding-based query language models. In *ICTIR*.

Hamed Zamani and W. Bruce Croft. 2017. Relevance-based word embedding. In *SIGIR*.

Hamed Zamani, Mostafa Dehghani, W Bruce Croft, Erik Learned-Miller, and Jaap Kamps. 2018. From neural re-ranking to neural ranking: Learning a sparse representation for inverted indexing. In *CIKM*.

Chengxiang Zhai and John Lafferty. 2001. A study of smoothing methods for language models applied to ad hoc information retrieval. In *SIGIR*.

Evaluating Question Answering Evaluation

Anthony Chen[1], Gabriel Stanovsky[2], Sameer Singh[1], and Matt Gardner[3]

[1]University of California, Irvine, USA
[2]Allen Institute for Artificial Intelligence, Seattle, Washington, USA
[3]Allen Institute for Artificial Intelligence, Irvine, California, USA
anthony.chen@uci.edu

Abstract

As the complexity of question answering (QA) datasets evolve, moving away from restricted formats like span extraction and multiple-choice (MC) to free-form answer generation, it is imperative to understand how well current metrics perform in evaluating QA. This is especially important as existing metrics (BLEU, ROUGE, METEOR, and F1) are computed using n-gram similarity and have a number of well-known drawbacks. In this work, we study the suitability of existing metrics in QA. For generative QA, we show that while current metrics do well on existing datasets, converting multiple-choice datasets into free-response datasets is challenging for current metrics. We also look at span-based QA, where F_1 is a reasonable metric. We show that F_1 may not be suitable for all extractive QA tasks depending on the answer types. Our study suggests that while current metrics may be suitable for existing QA datasets, they limit the complexity of QA datasets that can be created. This is especially true in the context of free-form QA, where we would like our models to be able to generate more complex and abstractive answers, thus necessitating new metrics that go beyond n-gram based matching. As a step towards a better QA metric, we explore using BERTScore, a recently proposed metric for evaluating translation, for QA. We find that although it fails to provide stronger correlation with human judgements, future work focused on tailoring a BERT-based metric to QA evaluation may prove fruitful.

1 Introduction

Question answering (QA) has emerged as a burgeoning research field driven by the availability of large datasets. These datasets are built to test a variety of reading comprehension skills such as multihop (Welbl et al., 2017), numerical (Dua et al.,

Context: ... After Peter returns, they eventually figure out her proper care, right down to diaper changes, baths, and feedings. The next day, **two men** (who are drug dealers) arrive at the apartment to pick up the package...

Question: Who comes to pick up the package the next day?

Gold Answers: drug dealers, the drug dealer
Prediction: two men

Human Judgement: 5 out of 5
ROUGE-L: 0
METEOR: 0

(a) Example from the generative **NarrativeQA** dataset.

Context: ...David got five exercise tips from his personal trainer, **tip A**, tip B ... Tip A involves weight lifting, but tip B does not involve weight lifting ...
Question: In which tip the skeletal muscle would not be bigger, tip A or tip B?

Gold Answers: tip B
Prediction: tip A

Human Judgement: 1 out of 5
F1: 0.66

(b) Example from the span-based **ROPES** dataset.

Figure 1: Examples where existing **n-gram based metrics fail to align with human judgements**. Human judgements are between 1 and 5. (a) illustrates that because existing metrics do not use the context, they fail to capture coreferences. (b) illustrates that changing a single token can make a prediction incorrect while F_1 assigns a non-zero score.

2019), and commonsense (Talmor et al., 2018) reasoning. A key component of a QA dataset is the evaluation metric associated with it, which aims to automatically approximate human accuracy judgments of a predicted answer against a gold answer.

The metrics used to evaluate QA datasets have a number of ramifications. The first is that they drive research focus. Models that rank higher on a leaderboard according to a metric will receive

Proceedings of the Second Workshop on Machine Reading for Question Answering, pages 119–124
Hong Kong, China, November 4, 2019. ©2019 Association for Computational Linguistics

more community attention. The second is that just as good datasets drive model development, good metrics drive dataset development. As QA datasets become more complex and models are expected to produce more free-form and abstract answers, it is crucial that the metrics we use are able to assign scores that accurately reflect human judgements. Despite the value of metrics as drivers of research, a comprehensive study of QA metrics across a number of datasets has yet to be completed. This is important as present metrics are based on n-gram matching, which have a number of shortcomings (Figure 1).

In this work, we survey the landscape of evaluation metrics for QA and study how well current metrics approximate (i.e. correlate with) human judgements. We conduct our study on three datasets: NarrativeQA (Kociský et al., 2017), ROPES (Lin et al., 2019), and SemEval-2018 Task 11 (Ostermann et al., 2018). For the generative NarrativeQA dataset, we find that existing metrics provide reasonable correlation with human accuracy judgements while still leaving considerable room for improvement. We also study the span-based ROPES dataset, finding that it presents an interesting case where F1 struggles due to the high overlap in right and wrong answers. Finally, we convert the multiple-choice SemEval-2018 Task 11 dataset into a generative QA dataset. This produces a more difficult generative QA dataset compared to NarrativeQA as answers in SemEval are often more free-form in nature and have less overlap with the context. Here we find existing n-gram based metrics perform considerably worse in comparison to NarrativeQA.

These results signify that as QA systems are expected to perform more free-form answer generation, new metrics will be required. In exploring other metrics that go beyond n-gram matching, we study the recently proposed BERTScore. BERTScore computes a score by leveraging contextualized word representations, allowing it to go beyond exact match and capture paraphrases better. We find that it falls behind existing metrics on all three datasets. We propose a potential step in constructing a better QA metric by extending BERTScore to incorporate the context and the question when computing the similarity between two answers. We show that extending BERTScore in this way slightly improves results when evaluating generative QA, though not to an extant that is sta-

tistically significant. Overall, our results indicate that studying the evaluation of QA is an under-researched area with substantial room for further experimentation.

2 Metrics

We provide a summary of popular n-gram based metrics, as well as sentence mover's similarity, BERTScore, and an extension of BERTScore which we call conditional BERTScore. In this work, we study all mentioned metrics in the context of question answering.

BLEU is a precision-based metric developed for evaluating machine translation (Papineni et al., 2001). BLEU scores a candidate by computing the number of n-grams in the candidate that also appear in a reference. n is varied from 1 up to a specified N and the scores for varying n are aggregated with a geometric mean. In this work, we look at BLEU-1 and BLEU-4, where $N = 1$ and $N = 4$ respectively.

METEOR is an F-measure metric developed for evaluating machine translation which operates on unigrams (i.e. tokens) (Banerjee and Lavie, 2005). METEOR first creates an alignment by attempting to map each token in a candidate to a token in a reference (and vice versa). A token is aligned to another token if they are the same, are synonyms, or their stems match. The alignment is aggregated into precision and recall values, which are combined into an F-measure score in which more weight is given to recall.

ROUGE is an F-measure metric designed for evaluating translation and summarization (Lin, 2004). There are a number of variants of ROUGE however in this work we focus on ROUGE-L. ROUGE-L is computed based on the longest common subsequence (LCS), which searches for the longest co-occurring set of tokens common to both reference and candidate. An advantage of ROUGE-L is that no predefined n-gram size is required.

F$_1$ While the previously mentioned metrics have been adapted for evaluating generative question answering, F$_1$ has been generally reserved for evaluating span-based question answering (Rajpurkar et al., 2016). It is computed over tokens in the candidate and reference.

Sentence Mover's Similarity (SMS) is a recent metric based on earth mover's distance for evaluated multi-sentence texts such as machine-generated summaries (Clark et al., 2019) .[1] SMS

---

[1]https://github.com/eaclark07/sms

first computes an embedding for each sentence in a document as an average its ELMo word representations (Peters et al., 2018). A linear program is then solved to obtain the distance of "moving" a candidate document's sentences to match a reference document. SMS has shown better results over ROUGE-L in evaluating generated summaries and student essays.

BERTScore is recent metric for evaluating translation (Zhang et al., 2019).[2] BERTScore first obtains BERT representations of each word in the candidate and reference by feeding the candidate and reference through a BERT model separately. An alignment is then computed between candidate and reference words by computing pairwise cosine similarity. This alignment is then aggregated in to precision and recall scores before being aggregated into a (modified) F1 score that is weighted using inverse-document-frequency values. BERTScore has been shown to align better to human judgements in evaluating translation compared to existing metrics. Additionally, because it uses word representations and not exact match, BERTScore has also been shown to capture paraphrases better than existing metrics. We include BERTScore and SMS in this work because they have not yet been studied in the context of QA.

Conditional BERTScore A key difference between machine translation and QA is that determining the correctness of a predicted answer requires using information from the context and question (Figure 1a). While BERTScore can potentially handle phenomena like paraphrases better than existing metrics, it still overlooks the context and question. We propose an extension to BERTScore that incorporates the context and question when calculating the answer word representations. More specifically, we concatenate the context, question, and answer delineated by BERT separator tokens as the input to BERT. We then extract the BERT representations of the answer words and compute BERTScore. In this way, the representation of the answer words are *conditioned* (i.e. contextualized) with the context and question.

3   Datasets

We describe the three QA datasets we use with examples in Table 1.

NarrativeQA is a generative QA dataset on books and movie scripts (Kociský et al., 2017). The contexts are plot summaries taken from Wikipedia and each question has two reference answers. The official evaluation metrics of NarrativeQA are BLEU-1, BLEU-4, METEOR, and ROUGE-L.

SemEval-2018 Task 11 (which we refer to as SemEval for brevity) is a multiple-choice QA dataset which focuses on commonsense reasoning about everyday scenarios (Ostermann et al., 2018). We convert this into a generative QA dataset by using the correct answer choice as a target for a generative QA system. We hypothesize that this results in a more difficult generative QA dataset compared to NarrativeQA as a number of the answers in the SemEval dataset have no overlap with the question or context.

ROPES is a recent span-based QA dataset with questions that focus on cause-and-effect relationships (Lin et al., 2019). Each question is accompanied by a *background* passage with auxiliary information and a *situation* passage. We concatenate the background and situation to use as the context. The official evaluation metric of ROPES is F_1. A unique characteristic of ROPES is that questions generally present two possible answer choices, one of which is incorrect (Table 1). Because incorrect and correct answers often have some n-gram overlap, we believe F_1 will struggle to accurately assign scores (Figure 1b).

4   Models

We describe the models used to generate predictions for our datasets. These models have publicly available code and have reasonable performance compared to the current state-of-the-art models.

Multi-hop Point Generator For NarrativeQA and SemEval, we use a multi-hop pointer generator (MHPG) model (Bauer et al., 2018)[3]. MHPG represents its input using ELMo embeddings. The embeddings are then fed into a sequence of BiDAF (Seo et al., 2017) cells, where the output of one BiDAF cell is fed as the input into another BiDAF cell. This allows multi-hop reasoning over the context. The output layer consists of a generative decoder with a copying mechanism. We evaluate MHPG's predictions using BLEU-1, BLEU-4, ROUGE-L, METEOR, SMS, BERTScore and Conditional BERTScore.

BERT For ROPES, we finetune BERT as a span based QA model following the procedure used for

---

Dataset	# QA Pairs	Context	Question	Gold Answer
NarrativeQA	32,747	… An earthquake triggers the transfer, bringing the ship into the present … After carrying the men through hyperspace, the ship lands on a planet where faltering robots refuel the ship …	How were the men able to find fuel for the spaceship?	The first planet had robots that fueled the ship.
SemEval	9,731	One evening, I noticed my alarm clock had stopped working … I lifted the plastic cover and checked what batteries it required: two AA-sized batteries …	Why did they throw away the old batteries?	They were no longer useful
ROPES	11,202	… A catalyst is a chemical that speeds up chemical reactions … [Mark] conducts two tests, test A and test B, on an organism. In test A he reduces catalysts from the organism, but in test B he induces catalysts in the organism …	Which test would see reactions taking place slower, test A or test B?	test A

Table 1: Examples for the datasets we use in our study. The *# of QA Pairs* column refers to the number of QA pairs in the training sets.

SQuAD (Devlin et al., 2019). We evaluate BERT's predictions using F_1, SMS, BERTScore, and Conditional BERTScore.

5 Evaluating QA Metrics using Human Judgements

5.1 Collecting Human Judgements

After training our models on the three datasets, we extract 500, 500, and 300 data points from the validation sets of NarrativeQA, ROPES, and SemEval, respectively, along with the model predictions. When extracting data points to label, we filter out data points where the predicted answer exactly matches the gold answer. This filtering step is done as we are interested on how well metrics do when it cannot resort to exact string matching.

For the extracted data points, we ask annotators to rate how closely a prediction captures the same information as a gold answer. Annotations are on a scale from 1 to 5. Two of the authors annotated all data points in-house. We find strong agreement between the two annotators across the three datasets (see Table 3). We note that because we have removed exact matches, the distribution of human judgement scores is right-skewed for each dataset. This is most prominent in ROPES, where around 400 predictions are labeled as a 1.

5.2 Correlation with Human Judgements

We first normalize the judgements for each annotator following Blatz et al. (2004) and then average the judgements of the two annotators to obtain a single gold annotation per data point. We then compute the Spearman and Kendall correlation of the gold annotations to the scores assigned by automatic metrics. The correlation results are presented in Table 2.

5.3 Discussion

Of NarrativeQA's four evaluation metrics, ME-TEOR aligns closest with human judgements, while leaving considerable room for improvement. ROPES proves to be a challenging dataset for F1 to evaluate. This highlights the fact that while F1 is a reasonable metric for many span-based QA datasets, the types of questions and answers can influence how well it works in practice and care should be taken when adapting evaluation metrics. For the SemEval dataset, which we converted to a generative QA dataset from a multiple-choice dataset, we find that existing metrics do considerably worse compared to NarrativeQA. This aligns with our hypothesis that more free-form generative QA datasets leads to a degradation in n-gram based metrics' performance. Similar to NarrativeQA, METEOR aligns best with human judgements on SemEval. We make the recommendation based on these results that for evaluating generative QA, METEOR is currently the metric that should be given the most consideration.

Both BERTScore and sentence mover's similarity fall behind the best metric for each dataset. This points to the fact that metrics that perform well for evaluating summarization and translation do not necessarily indicate success in evaluating question answering. Conditional BERTScore slightly

Metrics	NarrativeQA		SemEval		ROPES	
	Spearman	Kendall	Spearman	Kendall	Spearman	Kendall
BLEU-1	0.617	0.483	0.443	0.351	-	-
BLEU-4	0.563	0.433	0.437	0.350	-	-
METEOR	**0.752**	**0.614**	**0.642**	**0.542**	-	-
ROUGE-L	0.707	0.577	0.570	0.489	-	-
Sentence Mover's Similarity	0.474	0.365	0.488	0.384	0.376	0.307
BERTScore	0.733	0.573	0.406	0.323	0.448	0.365
Conditional BERTScore	0.741	0.581	0.415	0.330	0.434	0.353
F1	-	-	-	-	**0.591**	**0.540**

Table 2: **Human Judgments and Metrics:** Correlation between metrics and human judgments using Spearman's rho (ρ) and Kendall's tau (τ) rank correlation coefficients. "-" indicates the metric is not used for the dataset.

Dataset	κ	r	ρ
NarrativeQA	0.747	0.951	0.944
SemEval	0.854	0.970	0.976
ROPES	0.962	0.997	0.992

Table 3: **Inter-annotator agreement** computed using Cohen's kappa (κ), Pearson correlation (r), and Spearman's correlation (ρ).

improves results over BERTScore on our two generative QA tasks, which is a promising sign that incorporating the context and question in a QA metric is a worthwhile pursuit. In the cases where Conditional BertScore improves over BERTScore, the gains are not statistically significant. One thing to note is that the BERT model was never exposed to context/question/answer triples during its pre-training. Finetuning a BERT model on QA datasets can potentially yield a better BERTScore-based metric.

6 Related Work

N-gram based metrics such as BLEU and METEOR were originally developed and tested for evaluation of machine translation. These metrics have grown to become popular choices in evaluating all forms of natural language generation, including image captioning, question answering, and dialog systems. As these metrics continue to be used, there have been a number of papers that try to assess how suitable these metrics are for different domains. Nema and Khapra (2018) show that for question generation, n-gram metrics assign scores that correlate poorly to the notion of answerability

(i.e., is a generated question answerable). Yang et al. (2018) study the effect of using BLEU and ROUGE in evaluating QA, focusing on yes-no and entity questions on the Chinese DuReader dataset (He et al., 2017). For these types of questions, changing a single word from a gold answer can lead to an incorrect answer. In these cases, BLEU and ROUGE assign scores that do not necessarily reflect the correctness of an answer. Our work is continuation of this line of work in assessing the quality of current metrics for use in evaluating question answering across a number of datasets.

Because of the inherent limitations of n-gram metrics, recent work has focused on using metrics that have been learned or are based on word representations. In image captioning, Cui et al. (2018) train a model that takes as input an image, a reference caption, and a candidate caption and learns to predict if the two captions are semantically equivalent. Using this trained model as a metric leads to better scores compared to n-gram based metrics. As mentioned earlier, sentence mover's similarity and BERTScore leverage contextualized word representations for evaluating summarization and translation respectively, also obtaining better results compared to existing metrics. We hope to push the evaluation of question answering in this direction and study SMS and BERTScore in the context of QA as a first step in this direction.

7 Conclusion

In this work, we present a systematic study of existing n-gram based metrics by comparing their correlation to human accuracy judgements on three QA datasets. We find that while existing metrics do fairly well on NarrativeQA, for the more free-form

SemEval dataset, existing metrics fare significantly worse. Our results indicate that as generative QA datasets become more abstractive in nature, better metrics that go beyond n-gram matching will be required. We also find that F_1 struggles in evaluating the ROPES dataset, signaling that a better metric can also help improve span-based QA evaluation. In the search of a better metric, we also study BERTScore along with a conditional BERTScore that incorporates the context and question. Incorporating the context and question into BERTScore slightly improves results, indicating that a BERT-based model that uses the context and question is a promising research direction. Future work also involves the collection of more data. This includes collecting human annotations on more datasets, generating model predictions using more reading comprehension models, and also evaluating metrics on human generated answers.

References

Satanjeev Banerjee and Alon Lavie. 2005. Meteor: An automatic metric for mt evaluation with improved correlation with human judgments. In *IEEvaluation@ACL*.

Lisa Bauer, Yicheng Wang, and Mohit Bansal. 2018. Commonsense for generative multi-hop question answering tasks. In *ACL*.

John Blatz, Erin Fitzgerald, George F. Foster, Simona Gandrabur, Cyril Goutte, Alex Kulesza, Alberto Sanchís, and Nicola Ueffing. 2004. Confidence estimation for machine translation. In *COLING*.

Elizabeth Clark, Asli elikyilmaz, and Noah A. Smith. 2019. Sentence mover's similarity: Automatic evaluation for multi-sentence texts. In *ACL*.

Yin Cui, Guandao Yang, Andreas Veit, Xun Huang, and Serge J. Belongie. 2018. Learning to evaluate image captioning. *2018 IEEE/CVF Conference on Computer Vision and Pattern Recognition*, pages 5804–5812.

Jacob Devlin, Ming-Wei Chang, Kenton Lee, and Kristina Toutanova. 2019. Bert: Pre-training of deep bidirectional transformers for language understanding. *NAACL-HLT*.

Dheeru Dua, Yizhong Wang, Pradeep Dasigi, Gabriel Stanovsky, Sameer Singh, and Matt Gardner. 2019. Drop: A reading comprehension benchmark requiring discrete reasoning over paragraphs. In *NAACL-HLT*.

Wei He, Kai Liu, Jing Liu, Yajuan Lyu, Shiqi Zhao, Xinyan Xiao, Yuan Liu, Yizhong Wang, Hua Wu, Qiaoqiao She, Xuan Liu, Tian Wu, and Haifeng Wang. 2017. Dureader: a chinese machine reading comprehension dataset from real-world applications. In *QA@ACL*.

Tomás Kociský, Jonathan Schwarz, Phil Blunsom, Chris Dyer, Karl Moritz Hermann, Gábor Melis, and Edward Grefenstette. 2017. The narrativeqa reading comprehension challenge. *Transactions of the Association for Computational Linguistics*, 6:317–328.

Chin-Yew Lin. 2004. Rouge: A package for automatic evaluation of summaries. In *ACL*.

Kevin Lin, Oyvind Tafjord, Peter Clark, and Matt Gardner. 2019. Reasoning over paragraph effects in situations. *ArXiv*, abs/1908.05852.

Preksha Nema and Mitesh M. Khapra. 2018. Towards a better metric for evaluating question generation systems. In *EMNLP*.

Simon Ostermann, Michael Roth, Ashutosh Modi, Stefan Thater, and Manfred Pinkal. 2018. Semeval-2018 task 11: Machine comprehension using commonsense knowledge. In *SemEval@NAACL-HLT*.

Kishore Papineni, Salim Roukos, Todd Ward, and Wei-Jing Zhu. 2001. Bleu: a method for automatic evaluation of machine translation. In *ACL*.

Matthew E. Peters, Mark Neumann, Mohit Iyyer, Matt Gardner, Christopher Blake Clark, Kenton Lee, and Luke S. Zettlemoyer. 2018. Deep contextualized word representations. volume abs/1802.05365.

Pranav Rajpurkar, Jian Zhang, Konstantin Lopyrev, and Percy Liang. 2016. Squad: 100, 000+ questions for machine comprehension of text. In *EMNLP*.

Min Joon Seo, Aniruddha Kembhavi, Ali Farhadi, and Hannaneh Hajishirzi. 2017. Bidirectional attention flow for machine comprehension. In *ICLR*.

Alon Talmor, Jonathan Herzig, Nicholas Lourie, and Jonathan Berant. 2018. Commonsenseqa: A question answering challenge targeting commonsense knowledge. In *NAACL-HLT*.

Johannes Welbl, Pontus Stenetorp, and Sebastian Riedel. 2017. Constructing datasets for multi-hop reading comprehension across documents. *Transactions of the Association for Computational Linguistics*, 6:287–302.

An Yang, Kai Liu, Jing Liu, Yajuan Lyu, and Sujian Li. 2018. Adaptations of rouge and bleu to better evaluate machine reading comprehension task. *ArXiv*, abs/1806.03578.

Tianyi Zhang, Varsha Kishore, Felix Wu, Kilian Q. Weinberger, and Yoav Artzi. 2019. Bertscore: Evaluating text generation with bert. *ArXiv*, abs/1904.09675.

Bend but Don't Break? Multi-Challenge Stress Test for QA Models

Hemant Pugaliya*   James Route*   Kaixin Ma*   Yixuan Geng   Eric Nyberg
Language Technologies Institute
Carnigie Mellon University
{hpugaliy, jroute, kaixinm, yixuang, ehn}@cs.cmu.edu

Abstract

The field of question answering (QA) has seen rapid growth in new tasks and modeling approaches in recent years. Large scale datasets and focus on challenging linguistic phenomena have driven development in neural models, some of which have achieved parity with human performance in limited cases. However, an examination of state-of-the-art model output reveals that a gap remains in reasoning ability compared to a human, and performance tends to degrade when models are exposed to less-constrained tasks. We are interested in more clearly defining the strengths and limitations of leading models across diverse QA challenges, intending to help future researchers with identifying pathways to generalizable performance. We conduct extensive qualitative and quantitative analyses on the results of four models across four datasets and relate common errors to model capabilities. We also illustrate limitations in the datasets we examine and discuss a way forward for achieving generalizable models and datasets that broadly test QA capabilities.

1 Introduction

Advancements in question answering, where a system generates a response to a natural language query, have led AI agents to demonstrate competency at increasingly sophisticated linguistic patterns and concepts. Neural models have achieved particularly strong results in machine reading and comprehension (MRC), a related task where a model answers questions from a given text passage. High scores on some MRC datasets, some of which even exceed human performance, seemingly imply that models are attaining a level of linguistic reasoning that approaches a human's. However, we suspect that the raw scores on MRC datasets do not fully convey the strengths and weaknesses of models, and we propose a more in-depth exploration of model results.

We investigate four publicly-available models, each of which take a different approach to QA and have attained high scores on at least one MRC dataset. We also select four MRC datasets that present a different set of challenges for the models. We aim to characterize how models perform on each challenge, going beyond reporting of standard scores like F1 or BLEU. Our goal is to understand how different models generalize to a wider range of challenges than a single dataset can provide, and determine if aspects of model design adapt well to certain conditions. We manually examine error cases and random samples of results from each model-dataset pair and employ a regression framework to model evaluation scores on various dataset characteristics.[1] Our analysis has revealed some key findings, as follows:

- Scores of high performing models are often underestimated because of noise or errors in the dataset (e.g., over 10% of a model's errors are factually correct answers scored as incorrect, as indicated in Sections 6.2-6.4).

- Manual error analysis, often overlooked when reporting new approaches, reveals useful model strengths. One example is the QANet model's apparent strong performance on multi-hop inference questions.

- Regression analysis can pinpoint dataset features that challenge models; for example, indicating that HotpotQA's difficulty stems from distractor sentences and at least partially from multihop inference, rather than simply resulting from long context lengths.

---

* Equal contribution

[1]Annotations are available at https://github.com/jamesrt95/Neural-QA-Eval

Proceedings of the Second Workshop on Machine Reading for Question Answering, pages 125–136
Hong Kong, China, November 4, 2019. ©2019 Association for Computational Linguistics

Based on our findings, we conclude with some guidelines which future researchers can benefit from while building new models and datasets.

2 Related Work

Wadhwa et al. (2018) explored the performance of several MRC models on SQuAD and inferred common areas of difficulty. Kaushik and Lipton (2018) examined model performance across several MRC datasets, including SQuAD. This study questioned the effective difficulty of MRC tasks by varying the amount of input data available to the models. Rondeau and Hazen (2018) presented a systematic approach for identifying the most salient features for a question's difficulty on SQuAD. They define question categories based on the number of models that could get the correct output on the question. Sugawara et al. (2017) analyzed 6 MRC datasets on the metrics of prerequisite skills and readability, which are defined from a human's perspective. Feng et al. (2018) explored model explainability on MRC and other tasks by reducing input spans until a given model failed to generate a correct prediction. Talmor and Berant (2019) investigated generalization and transferability of 10 MRC datasets and analyzed factors that contribute to these characteristics.

Our study casts a broader net by testing four MRC datasets against four models. The study tests a greater range of linguistic phenomena and examines a larger proportion of question-answer pairs. In addition, our quantitative analysis scales to larger data sizes. We focus on characterizing model outputs and errors, and in the process, make inferences about the MRC challenges. We adopt both automatic and manual analysis of QA pairs across all dataset-model pairs. We do not focus on explainability in this study, although we aim to conclude why a model performs in a certain way throughout our analysis.

3 Datasets

We selected four datasets for evaluating model performance, each of which we describe briefly. We chose datasets that are relatively well-known and test a variety of non-overlapping capabilities. Table 1 summarizes key characteristics for the datasets.

SQuAD (Rajpurkar et al., 2016) is one of the first large-scale extractive question answering datasets. We include SQuAD in this study because it is

Dataset	Data	Source	Answer	Size
SQuAD	Wikipedia	Crowd	Span	100K
HotpotQA	Wikipedia	Crowd	Span	113K
SearchQA	Web	Jeopardy	Span	140K
MSMARCO	Web	Bing	Free-form	1.01M

Table 1: Dataset Summary

well-understood, and it tests a model's tolerance for paraphrasing and coreferences between the question and context. Although SQuAD 2.0 (Rajpurkar et al., 2018) is the most recent version of this dataset, we focus on SQuAD 1.1 because our selected models are not designed to handle the unanswerable questions in SQuAD 2.0.

HotpotQA (Yang et al., 2018) is similar to SQuAD but includes additional linguistic phenomena. HotpotQA stresses multihop reasoning, which requires a model to aggregate information from multiple relevant passages to locate the answers. It also contains questions that require a model to compare two entities and select the correct one. We use the distractor version of HotpotQA, where 10 passages are provided per question; two of the passages are relevant and the remaining eight contain keywords that appear in the question. We selected HotpotQA to test how well models handle consistently challenging multihop and comparison questions.

SearchQA (Dunn et al., 2017) is built using a different approach than SQuAD or HotpotQA. All question-answer pairs from the Jeopardy Challenge are collected and then augmented with text snippets from web pages retrieved by a search engine. Each question includes up to 51 snippets, and questions and snippets are cleaned to remove tokens such as stopwords. We selected SearchQA because it requires models to locate an answer within a uniquely large and noisy context, and the cleaning process creates a much more terse and uninterpretable text compared to the other datasets.

MSMARCO (Nguyen et al., 2016) is also a search-based dataset and was created using Bing queries from real users as questions and corresponding documents returned by the search engine as contexts. We include MSMARCO as the only dataset that requires models to freely generate answer sequences instead of selecting a span. Although most of the models we test are span-based, we aim to evaluate how well the models adapt to a different answer type.

4 Models

We also focus on diversity when selecting models. Each of the models described in this section is developed for a different task and they have relatively heterogeneous architecture. We specifically chose models that had strong performance on at least one popular QA dataset, particularly the ones used in this study. Some of the models were not designed to handle the challenges presented by one or more of the datasets; this is an intentional choice to measure how well a model generalizes to an out of domain task. We reduce the size of some models so that all training can be accomplished using equal hardware resources (single GPU)[2]. All changes are described in Section 5.

QANet (Yu et al., 2018) was originally developed for the SQuAD dataset and was state-of-the-art on the leaderboard in earlier 2018. The model consists of several convolutional encoding blocks, self-attention layers (Vaswani et al., 2017) and feed-forward layers. Finally, answer pointer layers (Seo et al., 2016) are used to predict start and end indices of the answer span. We used Google's implementation for our experiments[3]. To train QANet on single GPU, we reduce the number of encoder layers from 7 to 1.

BERT (Devlin et al., 2018) consists of stacked bidirectional transformer encoders and is pretrained on large corpora for masked language modeling task and next sentence prediction. BERT has achieved state-of-the-art performance on several NLP tasks after fine-tuning, and a BERT ensemble occupied the top position on the SQuAD leaderboard. A final layer is added to BERT that predicts the start and end indices of the answer span. We select BERT for this study because we hypothesize that its strong performance across NLP tasks is indicative of generalizability on multiple QA datasets. We use the Pytorch implementation of BERT[4] and use the smaller BERT-base model. BERT-base SQuAD results are consistent with the Pytorch implementation but lower than the official SQuAD leaderboard which uses BERT-large.

Denoising Distantly Supervised(DS)-QA (Lin et al., 2018) is mainly aimed at improving Open-Domain Question Answering. The model employs a paragraph selector to filter out noisy paragraphs and a paragraph reader to extract the correct answer from those denoised paragraphs. The paragraph selector encodes all paragraphs and the question using LSTM layers and self-attention. A paragraph reader then estimates a probability distribution over all possible spans. This architecture is shown to be effective on many open-domain datasets like Quasar-T(Dhingra et al., 2017), SearchQA(Dunn et al., 2017), TriviaQA(Joshi et al., 2017) and CuratedTREC(Baudis and Sedivý, 2015). We use the official implementation of this model.[5]

CommonSenseMultihop(CSM) (Bauer et al., 2018) generates an answer sequence rather than selecting a span. It uses an attention mechanism to reason over context and a pointer-generator decoder (See et al., 2017) to synthesize the answer. The model also applies common sense knowledge from an external knowledge base Concept-Net (Speer et al., 2016). The model encodes the context and question using Bi-LSTM layers, and BiDAF attention (Seo et al., 2016), then applies self-attention (Cheng et al., 2016) to perform multihop reasoning. The context is also attended by an encoded commonsense representation. Finally, the decoder generates the answer sequence and copies key spans from the context. This model has achieved promising performance on the NarrativeQA (Kocisky et al., 2018) and WikiHop (Welbl et al., 2018) datasets. We choose this model to test how it generalizes to extractive datasets and whether common sense knowledge is helpful for other QA tasks. We use the official implementation of this model. [6]

5 Experiments

We train the four selected models on each dataset as outlined in Sections 3 and 4, and where possible replicate the same training procedures used for the original models. Many of the datasets have features that the models were not designed to handle, in these cases, we perform preprocessing to adapt the dataset to the model without conferring an unfair advantage. We use official evaluation scripts to compute scores for the models.[7]

---

[2] Some models accept the number of layers/encoders as hyperparameters

[3] https://github.com/tensorflow/tpu/tree/master/models/experimental/QANet

[4] https://github.com/huggingface/pytorch-pretrained-BERT

[5] https://github.com/thunlp/OpenQA

[6] https://github.com/yicheng-w/CommonSenseMultiHopQA

[7] We used SQuAD's scripts for HotpotQA and SearchQA

Models	SQuAD		HotpotQA		SearchQA		MSMARCO	
	EM	F1	EM	F1	EM	F1	Rouge-L	Bleu1
QANet	71.08	80.33	**49.78**	**63.73**	57.33	64.06	33.23	27.90
BERT	**81.25**	**88.45**	44.22	56.84	**62.36**	**68.18**	**42.99**	33.00
CSM	57.90	69.49	48.09	50.60	54.03	60.03	39.25	**38.57**
DS-QA	60.24	70.95	35.83	45.99	60.31	65.89	23.42	9.00

Table 2: Results from all experiments

We evaluate models on every dataset's dev set, sample 100 question-answer pairs to characterize the linguistic phenomena and inference type needed to answer correctly, and then inspect performance on the sampled pairs. Definitions and examples of each inference type can be found in supplementary. We perform a further manual evaluation on 100 sampled cases where the prediction is completely incorrect for each dataset-model pair. A single annotator evaluated the samples for each dataset, although we performed limited cross-validation to promote consistency. We characterize errors and relative strengths and weaknesses for models in Section 6.

In addition to manual error analysis, we perform regressions to evaluate model performance on an entire dev set. This enables us to evaluate many course-grained hypotheses, such as the assertion that models perform worse on longer contexts. We performed logistic regression for dataset and model pairs on the EM metric (feature templates and regression tables are provided in supplementary). Although OLS regression on a continuous variable may seem like a more intuitive choice, the F1 score distributions are bimodal and heteroskedastic, which violate key OLS assumptions. We perform stepwise regression using AIC to select features and apply a Bonferroni correction to p-values based on the number of features we originally collected. We do not report regression results for MSMARCO because complete separation occurs for two features (discussed further in Section 6).

5.1 Data Preprocessing

Here we describe preprocessing decisions and experimental adaptations for the datasets.

SQuAD's contexts are relatively small, so no substantial preprocessing was done. We disabled the paragraph selector in DS-QA since each context is a single paragraph.

HotpotQA contains questions with *yes* / *no* answers, and we prepend these tokens to the context spans so extractive models can select them. We also exclude supporting evidence annotations because the models do not support these outputs. For QANet and CSM, we concatenate all paragraphs as context. For BERT, we follow Nogueira et al. (2018) and Buck et al. (2017) by concatenating contexts and using a sliding window approach, because of the models' limits on input length. During training we reduce context size to 5 paragraphs by randomly discarding non-relevant segments, so BERT is more likely to see relevant spans in one window.

SearchQA We concatenate the first 10 passages and discard the remainder for the training and dev sets for all models except DS-QA. For BERT, we follow the same sliding window approach as HotpotQA.

MSMARCO is an order of magnitude larger than the other datasets and since our primary interest is in exploring model performance, we randomly sample 20% of the training and dev QA pairs. We also remove all unanswerable questions, resulting in 101K training samples and 11K for dev. The QANet, BERT, and DS-QA model require answers to be extracted spans for training, so for each QA pair, we locate the span in the answer-bearing document with the highest Rouge score compared to the true answer and use the corresponding start and end indices for training. We also append *yes* and *no* tokens to the context so these answers are available to the extractive models. For QANet, BERT and CSM, we concatenate all snippets as context.

6 Results and Error Analysis

The evaluation scores across all models and datasets are shown in Table 2. In the remainder of this section, we examine model performance on a per-dataset basis and explore possible reasons that explain the results. For each dataset, we break down performance by the types of inference required to answer the question. We also introduce categories for common errors observed across all datasets below; Table 3 shows examples for every

Error Type	Question	Answer	Prediction
Random Guess	How high do plague fevers run?	38-41C	near 100%
Same Entity Type	What team lost Super Bowl XXXIII?	Atlanta Falcons	Denver
Sentence Selection	What did Marlee Matlin translate?	the national anthem	American Sign Language
Copying From Question	What was Apple Talk?	proprietary suite of networking protocols	AppleTalk
Factually Correct	How long are car loans typically?	60-month	5 years
Reasonable Answer	What did Edison offer Tesla ...	$10 a week raise	payment
Multihop Inference	How long is the river for which Frenchmans Creek is a Tributary?	2844 km	729 km
Span Selection	Which "Roseanne" star is in Scream 2?	Laurie Metcalf	Rebecca Gayheart
Confused By Question	What type of word play does "What Are Little Girls Made Of?" and "What Are Little Boys Made "Of" have in common?	ryhme	rock
Entity Choice	Which band has released more albums with their original members, Sick Puppies or Third Eye Blind?	Sick Puppies	Third Eye Blind
Yes/No Choice	Are Uber Goober and American Jobs both documentaries about gaming?	No	Yes
Numeric Inference	Which genus is native to more continents, Nothoscordum or Callirhoe ?	Nothoscordum	Callirhoe
Answer Missing	jan 20 , 2009 man lose 400,000 year plus 50 grand expenses federal ...	george w bush	willie pearl russell

Table 3: Examples of frequent error types from all 4 datasets

error type. We refer readers to supplementary for dataset specific examples of these error categories.

Random Guess: The answer appeared randomly selected, with no clear logic behind the choice.

Same Entity Confusion: The model selected the right type of entity (e.g., a person) but chose the wrong span.

Sentence Selection: The model predicted a span from an irrelevant sentence that shared one or more words with the question.

Copying From Question: The model picked a span that appeared in the question.

Factually Correct: The model's answer is correct but does not match a reference answer.

Reasonable Answer: The prediction makes sense semantically to the question but is not exactly correct.

Multihop Inference: In a "bridge" type question, the model's answer was only informed by one of the supporting facts. Typically the selected span answers part of the question but fails to address an additional clue or constraint.

Span Selection: The model located the answer-bearing sentence but chose the wrong span. These errors frequently happen when the correct answer is a date or number and the model chooses a nearby number instead.

Confused by Question: The question is malformed or the true answer is illogical, causing the model to choose a loosely related or random span.

Entity Choice: The question provided a choice of two entities and the model picked the wrong one.

Yes/No Choice: The question required a Yes/No response and the model picked the incorrect one.

Numeric Inference: The question required the model to choose between two numeric quantities, such as which is greater or came first. The models largely appear to guess at these questions, because none of them are designed to perform such evaluations.

Answer Missing: The answer span does not appear in the context, therefore making it impossible for the model to locate the answer.

Overall, we observe that BERT achieves the highest performance on extractive datasets with relatively straightforward questions (SQuAD and SearchQA). BERT's extensive pretraining as a language model and sentence predictor probably confers a strong advantage in these settings. QANet performs best on HotpotQA: it can process longer contexts than BERT, and our error analysis finds that QANet handles questions that require multihop inference better than the other models. BERT achieves the highest Rouge-L score on MSMARCO, but CSM has the highest Bleu1 score. This is somewhat unexpected because MS-MARCO answers are often not contiguous spans, which would seem to favor CSM as the only model that generates answer sequences. We discuss these findings in more detail below.

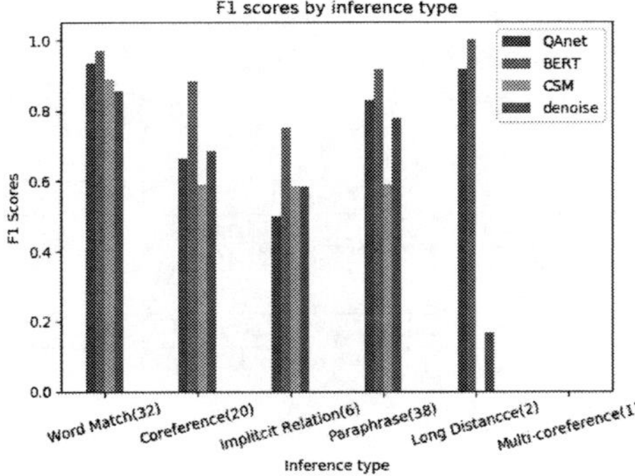

Figure 1: Comparison of Model Performance on SQuAD By Question Inference Types (numbers beside the labels indicate how many samples out of 100 fall into that category)

Error Type	QANet	BERT	CSM	DS-QA
Random Guess	28%	16%	26%	35%
Same Entity Type	30%	34%	24%	39%
Sent. Selection	20%	22%	10%	7%
Copy From Ques.	4%	0%	10%	2%
Factually Correct.	7%	11%	3%	5%
Reasonable Ans.	5%	8%	6%	3%
Regression Feature	**QANet**	**BERT**	**CSM**	**DS-QA**
Q-A Jaccard	22.3	15.0	16.6	23.0
"Who" Q	2.58	2.83	2.49	2.07
"When" Q	3.70	4.05	2.92	2.93
"How Many" Q	3.04	2.78	3.30	2.58

Table 4: Common Types of Errors on SQuAD (top) and Select SQuAD Regression Features and Odds Ratios (bottom)

6.1 SQuAD

Figure 1 compares results by inference type on SQuAD. All models did well on questions that require simple word match and BERT's advantage is less obvious. BERT is less affected by challenging inference types such as coreference and implicit relation, resulting in a large lead over other models.

Table 4 shows the error distribution for all models. The numbers in each column may not sum to 100% because multiple categories may apply to a single QA pair and we do not include error types that rarely occur.

We find that BERT is relatively precise at locating answer spans: it makes the fewest random guesses, and its most common mistake is confusing a similar entity with the answer. QANet is prone to the same error type; however, because this kind of mistake is relatively subtle, it may also be an indicator of stronger performance.

We note that 10% of the CSM model's errors are the result of selecting words that appear in the question, which is much more frequent than other models. We hypothesize that the model's copying mechanism assigns a higher probability to question keywords that appear frequently in the context, making these words more likely to appear during generation. Given that other models do not have the score aggregation step, they are less susceptible to copying words from the question.

Here we describe the features used for regression analysis and some details of how we compute them.

Lengths: The number of tokens in the question and answer respectively.

Word Match: Binary feature indicating if the sentence that has most words overlap with question contains the answer.

Question-Answer: The Jaccard similarity between the question and the answer bearing sentence. All tokens in the question and the context sentence are lemmatized using Spacy[8].

Question-Sentence: The number of overlapping words between question and answer bearing sentence.

Avg Word Match: We first segment the context into sentences and compute the average number of overlapping words between the question and sentences.

Question Types: Dummy variables signifying if a question keyword appears anywhere in the question.

Entity Counts - Question: We use Spacy to annotate entities in the question and count the number of entities.

Pronouns (Passage): We count the number of pronouns in the context from Spacy annotation.

Regression analysis shows that the Jaccard similarity between the question and answer-bearing sentence is highly predictive of EM score for all models: an increase in Jaccard similarity of 0.1 correlates with at least a 30% increase of a model answering correctly (Table 4. Questions asking *who*, *when* and *how many* are easier to answer for all models (the chances of a correct answer increase by 2-4 times). The effects are particularly strong for "when" and "how many," because the answers are numeric and distinctive from other tokens in the context. Complete regression results, including p-values, are given in supplemental (re-

---

[8] https://spacy.io/

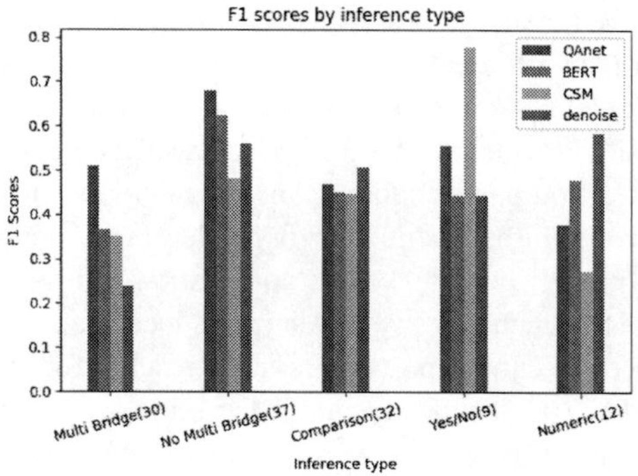

Figure 2: Comparison of Model Performance on Hot-potQA By Question Inference Types

Error Type	QANet	BERT	CSM	DS-QA
Multihop Inference	13%	8%	12%	35%
Sent. Selection	12%	18%	29%	34%
Span Selection	33%	22%	19%	7%
Confused By Ques.	9%	14%	15%	7%
Factually Correct	13%	12%	7%	5%
Entity Choice	10%	16%	11%	9%
Yes/No Choice	10%	9%	5%	4%
Numeric Inference	8%	2%	8%	6%
Regression Feature	**QANet**	**BERT**	**CSM**	**DS-QA**
Ans Len	.956	.954	.962	.966
Fact Dist	.992	.992	.993	-
Context Len	-	-	-	-
Question Type	-	-	-	-

Table 5: Common Types of Errors on HotpotQA (top) and Select HotpotQA Regression Features and Odds Ratios (bottom, - denotes insignificant results)

sults in Table 4 are all significant).

6.2 HotpotQA

QANet unexpectedly recorded a higher score than BERT, a departure from the other extractive datasets. QANet is the only model with CNN layers, which may be suited to identifying related text in long contexts, necessary for multihop inference. As shown in Table 5, the most frequent errors in HotpotQA involve distractor sentences and multihop inference. QANet and BERT clearly make these errors less frequently than the other models. We attribute this to the models' more extensive attention mechanisms that better model interactions and dependencies in the context.

Nearly 25% of QANet and BERT errors are due to problems with the question or answer. This is almost certainly due to the complexity of HotpotQA questions, which increases the chances of crowd-workers erroneously formulating the question and answer. As a result, the true performance for QANet and BERT may be well over 10% higher than the actual evaluation scores; this is an issue we observe in MSMARCO as well.

Many HotpotQA questions do not require multihop inference. The question often contains a keyword or phrase that occurs only near the correct answer, or the question asks for an entity type that appears once in the context. During the manual evaluation, this was the only question type that all four models could frequently answer without error. We *only* assigned the multihop inference label to a QA pair if the correct answer could not be deduced from reading a single passage in the context. Here are some of the regression features we used besides ones that are identical to those in SQuAD.

Dist between Sup. Facts The number of tokens (in hundreds) between the starting point of each paragraph that contains a supporting fact. This is computed after concatenating the paragraphs into a single context.

Question-Answer Overlap: The number of tokens common to the question and the answer-bearing sentence.

Distractor Sentences: The number of sentences with at least the same amount of overlap as the question and answer-bearing sentence.

Yes/No: Dummy variable set to 1 if the question requires a yes or no answer.

Comparison: Dummy variable set to 1 if the answer is a selection between 2 entities.

Numeric: Dummy variable set to 1 if the answer is a number.

Regression analysis indicates that question type (e.g., "who" or "when") has insignificant predictive power, which is unusual. This is probably because knowledge of the answer's entity type does not help narrow candidate spans when questions truly require multihop inference. We also find that context length has no significant predictive power, and we even exclude it from the final regression because it worsens fit. HotpotQA is notable in that its contexts are long compared to other datasets, and this result indicates that HotpotQA's difficulty is not simply the result of long contexts. There is one case where context size matters, which is the distance in tokens between passages with supporting facts. For three of the models, an increase of 100 tokens between supporting facts correlates with approximately a halved probability of a correct answer. There is also a negative correlation for all models with answer span length. We find

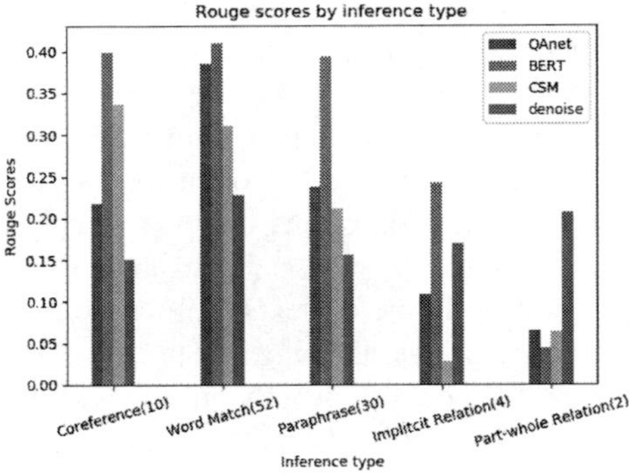

Figure 3: Comparison of Model Performance on MS-MARCO By Question Inference Types

Error Type	QANet	BERT	CSM	DS-QA
Random Guess	42%	14%	26%	48%
Same Entity Type	10%	18%	23%	25%
Sent. Selection	9%	15%	16%	6%
Factually Correct	14%	40%	12%	11%
Reasonable Ans.	17%	11%	11%	4%
Yes/No Choice	8%	11%	4%	0%

Table 6: Common Types of Errors on MSMARCO

that long answers are more likely to be faulty or badly chosen. More than half of the dev set answers that contain least 10 words are improperly chosen or contain spurious information, making it very unlikely for a model to choose the exact span.

6.3 MSMARCO

Figure 3 compares Rouge scores across question inference types for MSMARCO. We primarily focus on the first three inference types since there are relatively more samples. Although QANet's performance is comparable to BERT on word match, BERT is better on questions involving coreference resolution or paraphrasing. We again attribute this to BERT's pre-training, which we suspect makes it more robust to variations in language. The error types we observed in MSMARCO are identical to those in previous sections.

Table 6 shows the distribution of common errors on MSMARCO. Similar to SQuAD, BERT is least likely to guess randomly. To our surprise, 40% of BERT's predictions that are scored as 0 are correct, and another 11% are at least reasonable. This indicates that MSMARCO's annotations are noisy and that model performance may be systematically understated. In practical terms, however, MSMARCO's questions are based on real user queries, many of which are open-ended and

have too many correct answers to exhaustively list. It is worth mentioning that the reason the DS-QA model makes no yes/no choice errors is because it failed to identify the correct answer type and instead outputs random spans. Essentially, higher errors in the yes/no category at least indicate that a model can detect a yes/no question and provide an applicable answer, even if it is incorrect.

We do not report regression results for MS-MARCO. The Rouge and Bleu scores are continuous but cannot be well-modeled by OLS for the same reason as F1 scores on the other datasets (see Section 5). Logistic regression is non-ideal because the scores must be coerced to either 0 or 1, and in any case, complete separation occurs because two variables trivially predict whether a question can be perfectly answered. For the CSM model, any question with an answer longer than approximately 50 words is never perfectly answered. For the remaining models, if no contiguous span from the context matches the true answer, the question is never perfectly answered.

6.4 SearchQA

As SearchQA is built by collecting documents from a search query, and aggressive preprocessing has been performed to remove common words, the inference types used for other datasets do not hold. However, each search query may have one or more clues pointing to the answer. Figure 4 shows model performance by the number of clues in a query. Model performance generally improves with more clues, and we observe that a higher number of clues correlates with more answer mentions in the provided documents.

From Table 7, we see that the Same Entity Type is the major error across all models. All the models have a similar number of Same Entity Type errors. For the Random Guess error, we see that QANet, BERT and DS-QA have similar error distributions; however, CSM has a high random error rate. This could be attributed to the decoding layer copying something useless from the context when it is unsure. Similarly, a high number of word match distractions were expected for DS-QA as its initial paragraph selector has a simple architecture and is expected to be distracted by lexical matches. Another thing to notice is that the last three error types (Factually Correct, Reasonable Answer and Answer Missing) make up between 14-24% of the errors across the models. This suggests that the

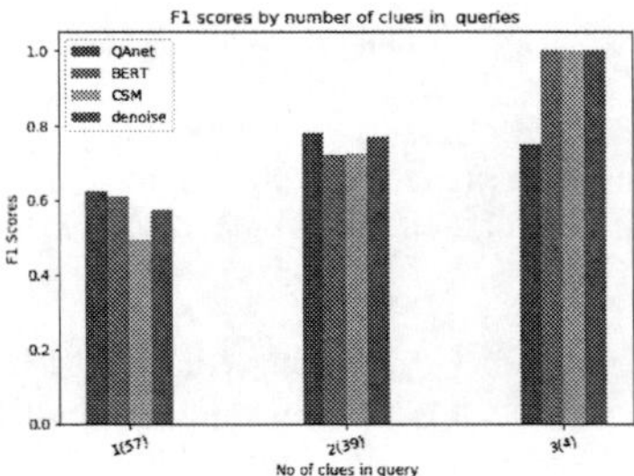

Figure 4: Comparison of Performance on SearchQA By Number of clues in Question

Error Type	QANet	BERT	CSM	DS-QA
Random Guess	19%	16%	28%	18%
Same Entity Type	30%	29%	32%	37%
Sent. Selection	20%	22%	19%	24%
Factually Correct	8%	10%	7%	6%
Reasonable Ans.	6%	7%	6%	4%
Answer Missing	5%	7%	5%	4%
Regression Feature	**QANet**	**BERT**	**CSM**	**DS-QA**
Ans Len	1.34	1.27	1.16	-
Q Len	1.03	1.03	1.02	1.03
Context Len	1.02	1.03	1.02	1.03
Any Entity Type	$\geq$1.29	$\geq$1.30	$\geq$1.45	$\geq$1.50

Table 7: Common Types of Errors on SearchQA (top) and Select SearchQA Regression Features and Odds Ratios (bottom, - denotes insignificant results)

actual model performance is better than what is portrayed in Table 2. Regarding regression analysis, we describe only features that are new for SearchQA:

Passage (Avg): Average number of tokens in all passages in the context.

Answer-Bearing Passages: The number of passages in the context that contain the correct answer.

Answer Mentions: The number of times the correct answer appears in the context.

Answer Entity Type: Dummy variable signifying the entity type of the correct answer.

Based on the regressions done on model scores (Table 7), an interesting common trend is suggested across all models. Whenever the answer is an entity[9], the odds that the models get the answer right increases significantly, frequently by a factor of 2 or 3. Although somewhat counterintuitive, the lengths of the question, answer, and context all correlate positively with the odds of selecting the right answer. We attribute this to the terse language of SearchQA, as longer questions and answers often include useful clues to narrow the list of possible answers. We further speculate that large contexts may have lengthy sections of irrelevant text that are easier to exclude during answer selection.

7 Conclusion

We conclude our discussion by presenting suggestions for good future practices when building and presenting new models and datasets. We constructively offer these points and have no intent to criticize authors whose prior work we reference.

Diverse Selection of Datasets. QA models are frequently evaluated on a single dataset, and even when multiple datasets are used, they tend to be similar. We encourage future authors to evaluate performance against a dataset with substantial differences from the one used for initial evaluation. For datasets like SQuAD, where the leaderboard is crowded with high-performing models, results on an additional challenge may provide better information on an approach's strengths and limits.

Limited Dataset Annotation. To assist in characterizing model performance, future datasets could include a small set of QA pairs that have been manually annotated with data on inference types or linguistic phenomena being tested. This information would provide a much more detailed view of model performance than a raw score, and could be incorporated into the evaluation script for an automatic presentation.

Question-Answer Quality Control. Model performance is consistently underestimated because correct answers are scored as wrong, and some questions are unanswerable because of human error. Crowdsourced datasets could include an additional task where a separate pool of workers checks QA pairs for mistakes or adds additional accepted answers to the QA pair. Standardization of answers, such as whether to include "the" before an entity, would also make scoring more precise.

---

[9]Detected using Google Natural language API

References

Petr Baudis and Jan Sedivý. 2015. Modeling of the question answering task in the yodaqa system. In *CLEF*.

Lisa Bauer, Yicheng Wang, and Mohit Bansal. 2018. Commonsense for generative multi-hop question answering tasks. In *Proceedings of the 2018 Conference on Empirical Methods in Natural Language Processing*, pages 4220–4230, Brussels, Belgium. Association for Computational Linguistics.

Christian Buck, Jannis Bulian, Massimiliano Ciaramita, Andrea Gesmundo, Neil Houlsby, Wojciech Gajewski, and Wei Wang. 2017. Ask the right questions: Active question reformulation with reinforcement learning. *CoRR*, abs/1705.07830.

Jianpeng Cheng, Li Dong, and Mirella Lapata. 2016. Long short-term memory-networks for machine reading. In *Proceedings of the 2016 Conference on Empirical Methods in Natural Language Processing*, pages 551–561, Austin, Texas. Association for Computational Linguistics.

Jacob Devlin, Ming-Wei Chang, Kenton Lee, and Kristina Toutanova. 2018. BERT: pre-training of deep bidirectional transformers for language understanding. *CoRR*, abs/1810.04805.

Bhuwan Dhingra, Kathryn Mazaitis, and William W Cohen. 2017. Quasar: Datasets for question answering by search and reading. *arXiv preprint arXiv:1707.03904*.

Matthew Dunn, Levent Sagun, Mike Higgins, V. Ugur Güney, Volkan Cirik, and Kyunghyun Cho. 2017. Searchqa: A new q&a dataset augmented with context from a search engine. *CoRR*, abs/1704.05179.

Shi Feng, Eric Wallace, Alvin Grissom II, Mohit Iyyer, Pedro Rodriguez, and Jordan Boyd-Graber. 2018. Pathologies of neural models make interpretations difficult. In *Proceedings of the 2018 Conference on Empirical Methods in Natural Language Processing*, pages 3719–3728, Brussels, Belgium. Association for Computational Linguistics.

Mandar Joshi, Eunsol Choi, Daniel S. Weld, and Luke Zettlemoyer. 2017. Triviaqa: A large scale distantly supervised challenge dataset for reading comprehension. In *Proceedings of the 55th Annual Meeting of the Association for Computational Linguistics*, Vancouver, Canada. Association for Computational Linguistics.

Divyansh Kaushik and Zachary C. Lipton. 2018. How much reading does reading comprehension require? a critical investigation of popular benchmarks. In *Proceedings of the 2018 Conference on Empirical Methods in Natural Language Processing*, pages 5010–5015, Brussels, Belgium. Association for Computational Linguistics.

Tomas Kocisky, Jonathan Schwarz, Phil Blunsom, Chris Dyer, Karl Moritz Hermann, Gábor Melis, and Edward Grefenstette. 2018. The NarrativeQA reading comprehension challenge. *Transactions of the Association for Computational Linguistics*, TBD:TBD.

Yankai Lin, Haozhe Ji, Zhiyuan Liu, and Maosong Sun. 2018. Denoising distantly supervised open-domain question answering. In *Proceedings of the 56th Annual Meeting of the Association for Computational Linguistics (Volume 1: Long Papers)*, pages 1736–1745, Melbourne, Australia. Association for Computational Linguistics.

Tri Nguyen, Mir Rosenberg, Xia Song, Jianfeng Gao, Saurabh Tiwary, Rangan Majumder, and Li Deng. 2016. Ms marco: A human generated machine reading comprehension dataset.

Rodrigo Nogueira, Jannis Bulian, and Massimiliano Ciaramita. 2018. Learning to coordinate multiple reinforcement learning agents for diverse query reformulation. *CoRR*, abs/1809.10658.

Pranav Rajpurkar, Robin Jia, and Percy Liang. 2018. Know what you don't know: Unanswerable questions for SQuAD. In *Proceedings of the 56th Annual Meeting of the Association for Computational Linguistics (Volume 2: Short Papers)*, pages 784–789, Melbourne, Australia. Association for Computational Linguistics.

Pranav Rajpurkar, Jian Zhang, Konstantin Lopyrev, and Percy Liang. 2016. SQuAD: 100,000+ questions for machine comprehension of text. In *Proceedings of the 2016 Conference on Empirical Methods in Natural Language Processing*, pages 2383–2392, Austin, Texas. Association for Computational Linguistics.

Marc-Antoine Rondeau and T. J. Hazen. 2018. Systematic error analysis of the Stanford question answering dataset. In *Proceedings of the Workshop on Machine Reading for Question Answering*, pages 12–20, Melbourne, Australia. Association for Computational Linguistics.

Abigail See, Peter J. Liu, and Christopher D. Manning. 2017. Get to the point: Summarization with pointer-generator networks. In *Proceedings of the 55th Annual Meeting of the Association for Computational Linguistics (Volume 1: Long Papers)*, pages 1073–1083, Vancouver, Canada. Association for Computational Linguistics.

Min Joon Seo, Aniruddha Kembhavi, Ali Farhadi, and Hannaneh Hajishirzi. 2016. Bidirectional attention flow for machine comprehension. *CoRR*, abs/1611.01603.

Robert Speer, Joshua Chin, and Catherine Havasi. 2016. Conceptnet 5.5: An open multilingual graph of general knowledge. In *AAAI Conference on Artificial Intelligence*.

Saku Sugawara, Yusuke Kido, Hikaru Yokono, and Akiko Aizawa. 2017. Evaluation metrics for machine reading comprehension: Prerequisite skills and readability. In *Proceedings of the 55th Annual Meeting of the Association for Computational Linguistics (Volume 1: Long Papers)*, pages 806–817, Vancouver, Canada. Association for Computational Linguistics.

Alon Talmor and Jonathan Berant. 2019. MultiQA: An empirical investigation of generalization and transfer in reading comprehension. In *Proceedings of the 57th Annual Meeting of the Association for Computational Linguistics*, pages 4911–4921, Florence, Italy. Association for Computational Linguistics.

Ashish Vaswani, Noam Shazeer, Niki Parmar, Jakob Uszkoreit, Llion Jones, Aidan N Gomez, Ł ukasz Kaiser, and Illia Polosukhin. 2017. Attention is all you need. In I. Guyon, U. V. Luxburg, S. Bengio, H. Wallach, R. Fergus, S. Vishwanathan, and R. Garnett, editors, *Advances in Neural Information Processing Systems 30*, pages 5998–6008. Curran Associates, Inc.

Soumya Wadhwa, Khyathi Chandu, and Eric Nyberg. 2018. Comparative analysis of neural QA models on SQuAD. In *Proceedings of the Workshop on Machine Reading for Question Answering*, pages 89–97, Melbourne, Australia. Association for Computational Linguistics.

Johannes Welbl, Pontus Stenetorp, and Sebastian Riedel. 2018. Constructing datasets for multi-hop reading comprehension across documents. *Transactions of the Association for Computational Linguistics*, 6:287–302.

Zhilin Yang, Peng Qi, Saizheng Zhang, Yoshua Bengio, William Cohen, Ruslan Salakhutdinov, and Christopher D. Manning. 2018. HotpotQA: A dataset for diverse, explainable multi-hop question answering. In *Proceedings of the 2018 Conference on Empirical Methods in Natural Language Processing*, pages 2369–2380, Brussels, Belgium. Association for Computational Linguistics.

Adams Wei Yu, David Dohan, Thang Luong, Rui Zhao, Kai Chen, and Quoc Le. 2018. Qanet: Combining local convolution with global self-attention for reading comprehension.

A Inference Types

A.1 SQuAD

Word Match: The model can simply match keys words in the question to find the answer bearing sentence and select the correct span.

Coreference: The model need to resolve a pronoun in the answer bearing sentence to find the answer.

Implicit Relation: Key entities in the context share a relationship that is not explicitly stated in the question. The model must infer the relationship to select the answer.

Paraphrase: The question paraphrases the answer bearing sentence.

Long Distance: Evidence for the answer is separated by a long sequence of irrelevant words.

Multi-coreference: The model needs to infer that one pronoun is referring to multiple entities.

Table 8 shows an example for each inference type.

A.2 HotpotQA

Multi Bridge: The model must perform multihop inference by finding and evaluating both supporting facts in the context. Each supporting fact is linked by a common "bridge" entity.

No Multi Bridge: Context clues alone can identify the answer. No multihop inference required.

Comparison: The question compares two entities, and the model must select the correct one.

Yes/No: The model must choose between a yes or no answer.

Numeric: The model must compare numeric quantities to choose the answer.

A.3 MSMARCO

There is only one new category in MSMARCO:

Part-whole Relation The model would need to infer that one entity is an example or a subset of another entity and leverage inherited properties to answer the question. An example would be:

Question: *cannot uninstall windirstat*

Gold Context: *Windows Add/ Remove Programs offers users a way to uninstall the program ... Click Start menu and run Control Panel ...*

Answer: *Click Start menu and run Control Panel...*

The model would have to understand that windirstat is a program to make correct prediction.

ReQA: An Evaluation for End-to-End Answer Retrieval Models

Amin Ahmad, Noah Constant, Yinfei Yang, Daniel Cer
Google Research, Mountain View, USA
{aahmad, nconstant, yinfeiy, cer}@google.com

Abstract

Popular QA benchmarks like SQuAD have driven progress on the task of identifying answer spans within a specific passage, with models now surpassing human performance. However, retrieving relevant answers from a huge corpus of documents is still a challenging problem, and places different requirements on the model architecture. There is growing interest in developing scalable answer retrieval models trained end-to-end, bypassing the typical document retrieval step. In this paper, we introduce Retrieval Question-Answering (ReQA), a benchmark for evaluating large-scale sentence-level answer retrieval models. We establish baselines using both neural encoding models as well as classical information retrieval techniques. We release our evaluation code to encourage further work on this challenging task.

1 Introduction

Popular QA benchmarks like SQuAD (Rajpurkar et al., 2016) have driven impressive progress on the task of identifying spans of text within a specific passage that answer a posed question. Recent models using BERT pretraining (Devlin et al., 2019) have already surpassed human performance on SQuAD 1.1 and 2.0.

While impressive, these systems are not yet sufficient for the end task of answering user questions at scale, since in general, we don't know which documents are likely to contain an answer. On the one hand, typical document retrieval solutions fall short here, since they aren't trained to directly model the connection between questions and answers in context. For example, in Figure 1, a relevant answer appears on the Wikipedia page for New York, but this document is unlikely to be retrieved, as the larger document is not highly relevant to the question. On the other hand,

> **Question**: Which US county has the densest population?
>
> **Wikipedia Page**: New York City
>
> **Answer**: Geographically co-extensive with New York County, the borough of Manhattan's 2017 population density of 72,918 inhabitants per square mile ($28,154/km^2$) makes it the highest of any county in the United States and higher than the density of any individual American city.

Figure 1: A hypothetical example of end-to-end answer retrieval, where the document containing the answer is not "on topic" for the question.

QA models with strong performance on reading comprehension can't be used directly for large-scale retrieval. This is because competitive QA models use interactions between the question and candidate answer in the early stage of modeling (e.g. through cross-attention) making it infeasible to score a large set of candidates at inference time.

There is growing interest in training end-to-end retrieval systems that can efficiently surface relevant results without an intermediate document retrieval phase (Gillick et al., 2018; Cakaloglu et al., 2018; Seo et al., 2019; Henderson et al., 2019). We are excited by this direction, and hope to promote further research by offering the Retrieval Question-Answering (ReQA) benchmark, which tests a model's ability to retrieve relevant answers efficiently from a large set of documents. Our code is available at https://github.com/google/retrieval-qa-eval.

The remainder of the paper is organized as follows. In Section 2, we define our goals in developing large-scale answer retrieval models. Section 3 describes our method for transforming within-document reading comprehension tasks into Retrieval Question-Answering (ReQA) tasks, and de-

Proceedings of the Second Workshop on Machine Reading for Question Answering, pages 137–146
Hong Kong, China, November 4, 2019. ©2019 Association for Computational Linguistics

tails our evaluation procedure and metrics. Section 4 describes various neural and non-neural baseline models, and characterizes their performance on several ReQA tasks. Finally, Section 5 discusses related work.

2 Objectives

What properties would we like a large-scale answer retrieval model to have? We discuss five characteristics below that motivate the design of our evaluation.

First, we would like an **end-to-end** solution. As illustrated in Figure 1, some answers are found in surprising places. Pipelined systems that first retrieve topically relevant documents and then search for answer spans within only those documents risk missing good answers from documents that appear to have less overall relevance to the question.

Second, we need **efficient** retrieval, with the ability to scale to billions of answers. Here we impose a specific condition that guarantees scalability. We require the model to encode questions and answers *independently* as high-dimensional (e.g. 512d) vectors, such that the relevance of a QA pair can be computed by taking their dot-product, as in Henderson et al. (2017).[1] This technique enables retrieval of relevant answers using approximate nearest neighbor search, which is sub-linear in the number of documents, and in practice close to log(N). This condition rules out the powerful models like BERT that perform best on reading comprehension metrics. Note, these approaches could be used to rerank a small set of retrieved candidate answers, but the evaluation of such multi-stage systems is out of the scope of this work.

Third, we focus on **sentence-level** retrieval. In practice, sentences are a good size to present a user with a "detailed" answer, making it unnecessary to highlight specific spans for many use cases.[2] While the experiments in this paper primarily target sentence-level retrieval, we recognize that some domains may be best served by retrieval at a different granularity, such as phrase or passage. The evaluation techniques described in Section 3 can be easily extended to cover these different granularities.

Fourth, a retrieval model should be **context aware**, in the sense that the context surrounding a sentence should affect its appropriateness as an answer. For example, an ideal QA system should be able to tell that the bolded sentence in Figure 2 is a good answer to the question, since the context makes it clear that "The official language" refers to the official language of Nigeria.

Question: What is Nigeria's official language?

Answer in Context: [...] Nigeria has one of the largest populations of youth in the world. The country is viewed as a multinational state, as it is inhabited by over 500 ethnic groups, of which the three largest are the Hausa, Igbo and Yoruba; these ethnic groups speak over 500 different languages, and are identified with wide variety of cultures. **The official language is English.** [...]

Figure 2: An example from SQuAD 1.1 where looking at the surrounding context is necessary to determine the relevance of the answer sentence.

Finally, we believe a strong model should be **general purpose**, with the ability to generalize to new domains and datasets gracefully. For this reason, *we advocate using a retrieval evaluation drawn from a specific task/domain that is never used for model training*. In the case of our tasks built on SQuAD and Natural Questions (NQ), we evaluate on retrieval over the entire training sets, with the understanding that all data from these sets is off-limits for model training. Additionally, we recommend not training on any Wikipedia data, as this is the source of the SQuAD and NQ document text. However, should this latter recommendation prove impractical, then, at the very least, the use of Wikipedia during training should be noted when reporting results on ReQA, being as specific as possible as to which subset was used and in what manner. This increases our confidence that a model that evaluates well on our retrieval metrics can be applied to a wide range of open-domain QA tasks.[3]

---

[1]Other distance metrics are possible. Another popular option for nearest neighbor search is cosine distance. Note, models using cosine distance can still compute relevance through a dot-product, provided the final encoding vectors are L2-normalized.

[2]In cases where highlighting the relevant span within a sentence is important, a separate highlighting module could be learned that takes a retrieved sentence as input.

[3]We strongly assert that when NLP models are used in applied systems, it is generally preferable to evaluate alternative models using data that is as distinct as reasonably possible from model training data. While this is common practice in some sub-fields of NLP such as machine translation, it is still unfortunately very common to assess other NLP

3 ReQA Evaluation

In this section, we describe our method for constructing *Retrieval Question-Answering* (ReQA) evaluation tasks from existing machine reading based QA challenges. To perform this evaluation over existing QA datasets, we first extract a large pool of candidate answers from the dataset. Models are then evaluated on their ability to correctly retrieve and rank answers to individual questions using two metrics, *mean reciprocal rank* (MRR) and *recall at N* (R@N). In Eq (1), Q is the set of questions, and $rank_i$ is the rank of the first correct answer for the ith question. In Eq (2), A_i^* is the set of correct answers for the ith question, and A_i is a scored list of answers provided by the model, from which the top N are extracted.

$$\text{MRR} = \frac{1}{|Q|} \sum_{i=1}^{|Q|} \frac{1}{rank_i} \tag{1}$$

$$\text{R@N} = \frac{1}{|Q|} \sum_{i=1}^{|Q|} \frac{|\max_N(A_i) \cap A_i^*|}{|A_i^*|} \tag{2}$$

We explore using the ReQA evaluation on both SQuAD 1.1 and Natural Questions. However, the technique is general and can be applied to other datasets as well.

3.1 ReQA SQuAD

SQuAD 1.1 is a reading comprehension challenge that consists of over 100,000 questions composed to be answerable by text from Wikipedia articles. The data is organized into paragraphs, where each paragraph has multiple associated questions. Each question can have one or more answers in its paragraph.[4]

We choose SQuAD 1.1 for our initial ReQA evaluation because it is a widely studied dataset, and covers many question types.[5] To turn SQuAD into a retrieval task, we first split each paragraph into sentences using a custom sentence-breaking tool included in our public release. For the SQuAD 1.1 train set, splitting 18,896 paragraphs produces 91,707 sentences. Next, we construct an "answer index" containing each sentence as a candidate answer. The model being evaluated computes an answer embedding for each answer (using any encoding strategy), given only the sentence and its surrounding paragraph as input. Crucially, this computation must be done independently of any specific question. The answer index construction process is described more formally in Algorithm 1.

Algorithm 1 Constructing the answer index

Input: c is a representation of a dataset in SQuAD format[6]; S is a function that accepts a string of text, s, and returns a sequence of sentences, $[s_0, s_1, \cdots, s_n]$; E_a is the embedding function, which takes answer text, a, into points in $\mathbb{R}^n$.

Output: A list of $\langle$sentence, encoding$\rangle$ tuples.

1: **function** ENCODEINDEX(c, S, E_a)
2:     I $\leftarrow$ new list
3:     **for** x in c.data **do**   ▷ for every passage
4:         **for** p in x.paragraphs **do**
5:             **for** s in $S(p$.context$)$ **do**
6:                 $s_e \leftarrow E_a(s, p$.context$)$
7:                 append $\langle s, s_e \rangle$ to I
8:     **return** I

Similarly, we embed each question using the model's question encoder, with the restriction that only the question text be used. For the SQuAD 1.1 train set, this gives around 88,000 questions.

After all questions and answers are encoded, we compute a "relevance score" for each question-answer pair by taking the dot-product of the question and answer embeddings, as shown in Al-

---

models on dev and test data that is very similar to its training data (e.g., harvested from the same source using a common pipeline and a common pool of annotators). This makes it more difficult to interpret claims of models approaching "human-level" performance.

[4]Typically, multiple answers come from the same sentence. For example, the question "Where did Super Bowl 50 take place?" is associated with three answers found within the sentence "The game was played on February 7, 2016, at Levi's Stadium in the San Francisco Bay Area at Santa Clara, California." The answer spans are: [Santa Clara, California], [Levi's Stadium] and [Levi's Stadium in the San Francisco Bay Area at Santa Clara, California.].

[5]SQuAD 2.0 adds questions that have no answer in the paragraph. While these questions are useful for testing machine reading over fixed passages, their value in a large-scale retrieval evaluation is less clear. Specifically, we can't be sure that such questions aren't answered by another sentence in the larger corpus.

[6]The SQuAD JSON format consists of a top-level list of *data* elements that represent Wikipedia articles, each containing a list of *paragraphs*. Every paragraph defines a *context*, which is its text, and a corresponding list of questions and answers. For clarity, the algorithm definition uses the same names (lines 3-6).

gorithm 2. These scores can be used to rank all (around 92,000) candidate answers for each question, and compute standard ranking metrics such as mean reciprocal rank (MRR) and recall (R@k).[7]

Algorithm 2 Scoring questions and answers

Input: $Q_{[q \times n]}$ is a matrix of question embeddings in $\mathbb{R}^n$, arranged so that the i-th row, $Q[i]$, corresponds to the embedding of q_i; $A_{[a \times n]}$ is a matrix of answer embeddings, also in $\mathbb{R}^n$, derived from the answer index, I, and arranged so that the i-th row, $A[i]$, corresponds to the embedding of a_i.

Output: $R_{[q \times a]}$ a matrix of ranking data that can be used to compute metrics such as MRR and R@k. It is arranged so that i-th row is a vector of dot-product scores for q_i, that is, $[q_i \cdot a_0, q_i \cdot a_1, \cdots, q_i \cdot a_a]$

1: **function** SCORE(Q, A)
2:     $S_{[q \times a]} \leftarrow QA^T$ ▷ compute dot-products
3:     $R_{[q \times a]} \leftarrow$ new matrix
4:     **for** $i \leftarrow 1$ to q **do**
5:         $R[i] \leftarrow$ rankdata[8]($S[i]$)
6:     **return** R

3.2 ReQA NQ

Natural Questions (NQ) consists of over 320,000 examples, where each example contains a question and an entire Wikipedia article. The questions are real questions issued by multiple users to the Google search engine, for which a Wikipedia page appeared in the top five search results. The examples are annotated by humans as to whether the returned article contains an answer to the question, and if so where. For roughly 36% of examples, the article is found to contain a "short answer": a span of text (or rarely multiple spans) that directly answers the question.

Our procedure for converting NQ into a ReQA task is similar to that described for SQuAD above. We restrict to questions with a single-span short

answer, contained within an HTML <P> (paragraph) block, as opposed to answers within a list or table. When applied to the NQ training set, this filtering produces around 74,000 questions. As with SQuAD, we consider the enclosing paragraph as context (available for the model in building an answer embedding), and split the paragraph into sentences. The target answer is the sentence containing the short answer span. Each sentence in the paragraph is added to the answer index as a separate answer candidate, resulting in around 240,000 candidates overall.[9]

As with ReQA SQuAD, *we advocate excluding all of Wikipedia from model training materials*. Models satisfying this restriction give us more confidence that they can be extended to perform answer retrieval in new domains.

3.3 Dataset Statistics

The number of questions and candidate answers in the ReQA SQuAD and ReQA NQ datasets is shown in Table 1. While the number of questions is similar, ReQA SQuAD has around 2.6x fewer candidate answer sentences, making it an easier task overall. This difference is due to the fact that SQuAD itself was constructed to have many different questions answered by the same Wikipedia paragraphs.

	SQuAD	NQ
Questions	87,599	74,097
Candidate Sentences	91,707	239,013
Candidate Paragraphs	18,896	58,699

Table 1: The number of questions and candidates in the constructed datasets ReQA SQuAD and ReQA NQ.

Table 2 lists the average number of tokens in question and sentence-level answer text, as well as the "query coverage", which is the percentage of tokens in the question that also appear in the answer. The token coverage for ReQA SQuAD is much larger than for ReQA NQ, indicating more lexical overlap between the question and answer. This is likely due to the original SQuAD construction process whereby writers "back-wrote" questions to be answerable by the given documents.

---

[7]Rarely, the same question is asked in different contexts. For example, the question "How tall is Mount Olympus?" appears twice in SQuAD, with answers on the pages for both Greece and Cyprus. In this case, we consider both answers correct for the purposes of our evaluation metrics.

[8]This function assigns ranks to data, in this case assigning 1 to the largest dot-product, 2 to the second-largest dot-product, and so forth. For more details, see scipy.stats.rankdata.

[9]Since NQ includes the entire Wikipedia article, we could consider adding all sentences from *all* paragraphs as candidate answers. However even restricting to sentences from paragraphs containing short answers already produced a large index and challenged existing models, so we opted not to increase the search space further.

By comparison, NQ questions are naturally occurring anonymized, aggregated search queries, where users had no access to the answering document ahead of time.

Table 3 shows the distribution of question types for each dataset. Nearly half (47.7%) of ReQA SQuAD questions are *what* questions, with the next most frequent being *who* (9.6%) and *how* (9.3%). ReQA NQ is more balanced across question types, with the leading types being *who* (32.6%), *when* (20.3%) and *what* (15.3%).

We note that neither dataset contains many *why* questions. Performing well on this type of question may require additional reasoning ability, so it would be interesting to explore *why* questions further through more targeted ReQA datasets.

	SQuAD	NQ
Average Length (tokens)		
Question	10.1	9.1
Answer	24.0	22.9
Query Coverage (%)		
Mean	31.7	24.3
Standard Deviation	18.9	16.9

Table 2: Token-level statistics of the constructed datasets. **Average Length** is the average number of tokens in the question and sentence-level answer text. **Query Coverage** is the percentage of tokens in the question that also appear in the sentence-level answer.

Question Type	SQuAD	NQ
what	47.7	15.3
who	9.6	32.6
how	9.3	5.0
when	6.2	20.3
which	5.5	2.0
where	3.8	13.1
why	1.4	0.6
other	16.5	11.1

Table 3: The distribution of question types in ReQA SQuAD and ReQA NQ. A question is assigned to a question type if it starts with the question type word. Note, types *what* and *which* include questions where a preposition (e.g. *at, by, in, on, with*) appears before the *wh-* word.

3.4 Discussion

A defining feature of the SQuAD dataset is that the questions are "back-written", with advance knowledge of the target answer and its surrounding context. One concern when adapting this data for a ReQA task is that questions may become ambiguous or underspecified when removed from the context of a specific document and paragraph. For example, SQuAD 1.1 contains the question "What instrument did he mostly compose for?". This question makes sense in the original context of the Wikipedia article on Frédéric Chopin, but is underspecified when asked in isolation, and could reasonably have other answers. One possible resolution would be to include the context title as part of the question context. However this is unrealistic from the point of view of end systems where the user doesn't have a specific document in mind.

This concern can be avoided by switching from "back-written" datasets to "web-search based" datasets. These include MS MARCO (Nguyen et al., 2016), TriviaQA (Joshi et al., 2017) and Natural Questions (Kwiatkowski et al., 2019). For these sets, questions are taken from natural sources, and a search engine is used in the process of constructing QA pairs.

However, there is an important caveat to mention when using web-search data to build ReQA tasks. In these datasets, the answers are derived from web documents retrieved by a search engine, where the question is used as the search query. This introduces a bias toward answers that are already retrievable through traditional search methods. By comparison, answers in SQuAD 1.1 may be found in "off-topic" documents, and it is valuable for an evaluation to measure the ability to retrieve such answers. Since both types of datasets (back-written and web-search based) have their advantages, we believe there is value in evaluating on ReQA tasks of both types.

4 Models and Results

In this section we evaluate neural models and classic information retrieval techniques on the ReQA SQuAD and ReQA NQ benchmark tasks.

4.1 Neural Baselines

Dual encoder models are learned functions that collocate queries and results in a shared embedding space. This architecture has shown strong performance on sentence-level retrieval tasks, including conversational response retrieval (Henderson et al., 2017; Yang et al., 2018), translation pair retrieval (Guo et al., 2018; Yang et al., 2019b) and similar text retrieval (Gillick et al., 2018). A dual encoder for use with ReQA has the schematic shape illustrated in Figure 3.

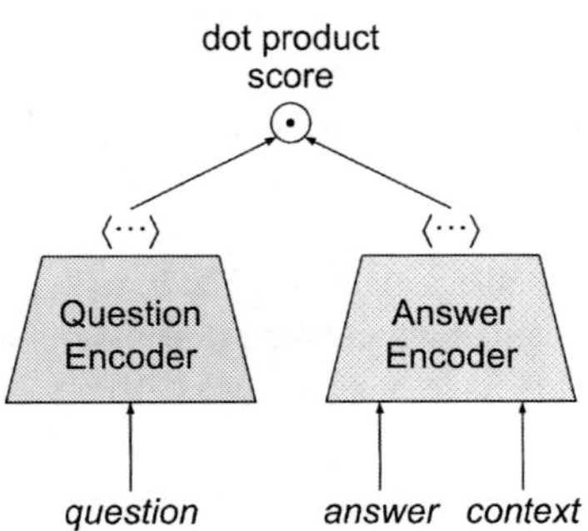

Figure 3: A schematic dual encoder for question-answer retrieval.

As our primary neural baseline, we take the recently released universal sentence encoder QA (USE-QA) model from Yang et al. (2019c)[10]. This is a multilingual QA retrieval model that co-trains a question-answer dual encoder along with secondary tasks of translation ranking and natural language inference. The model uses sub-word tokenization, with a 128k "sentencepiece" vocabulary (Kudo and Richardson, 2018). Question and answer text are encoded independently using a 6-layer transformer encoder (Vaswani et al., 2017), and then reduced to a fixed-length vector through average pooling. The final encoding dimensionality is 512. The training corpus contains over a billion question-answer pairs from popular online forums and QA websites like Reddit and Stack-Overflow.

As a second neural baseline, we include an internal QA model (QA_{Lite}) designed for use on mobile devices. Like USE-QA, this model is trained over online forum data, and uses a transformer-based text encoder. The core differences are reduction in width and depth of model layers, reduction of sub-word vocabulary size, and a decrease in the output embedding size from 512 dimensions to only 100.

Finally, we include the text embedding system InferSent, which, although not explicitly designed for question answering tasks, nevertheless produces strong results on a wide range of semantic tasks without requiring additional fine-tuning (Conneau et al., 2017). Note, however, that at 4096 dimensions, its embeddings are significantly larger than the other baselines presented. Other systems in this class include Skip-thought (Kiros et al., 2015), ELMo (Peters et al., 2018), and the Universal Sentence Encoder[11].

Table 4 presents the ReQA results for our baseline models. As expected, the larger USE-QA model outperforms the smaller QA_{Lite} model. The recall@1 score of 0.439 on ReQA SQuAD indicates that USE-QA is able to retrieve the correct answer from a pool of 91,707 candidates roughly 44% of the time. The ReQA NQ scores are lower, likely due to both the larger pool of candidate answers, as well as the lower degree of lexical overlap between questions and answers.

Table 5 illustrates the tradeoff between model accuracy and resource usage.

Model	MRR	R@1	R@5	R@10
ReQA SQuAD				
USE-QA	0.539	0.439	0.656	0.727
QA_{Lite}	0.412	0.325	0.507	0.576
InferSent	0.317	0.240	0.402	0.468
ReQA NQ				
USE-QA	0.234	0.147	0.317	0.391
QA_{Lite}	0.172	0.103	0.233	0.297
InferSent	0.080	0.043	0.109	0.145

Table 4: Mean reciprocal rank (MRR) and recall@K performance of neural baselines on ReQA SQuAD and ReQA NQ.

Model	Size (MB)	Latency[12] (ms)	Memory (MB)
USE-QA	392.9	17.3	71.8
QA_{Lite}	2.6	10.2	3.6

Table 5: Time and space tradeoffs of different models. Latency was measured on an Intel Xeon CPU E5-1650 v3 @ 3.50GHz, which has 6 cores and 12 threads.

---

[10]https://tfhub.dev/google/universal-sentence-encoder-multilingual-qa/1

[11]The non-QA versions of the Universal Sentence Encoder produce general semantic embeddings of text.

[12]This is the latency for encoding a single piece of text. However, by batching the encoding requests, it's possible to significantly reduce the amortized encoding time. In practice, batch sizes of 200 provide an amortized speedup of up to 5x.

4.2 BM25 Baseline

While neural retrieval systems are gaining popularity, TF-IDF based methods remain the dominant method for document retrieval, with the BM25 family of ranking functions providing a strong baseline (Robertson and Zaragoza, 2009). Unlike the neural models described above that can directly retrieve content at the sentence level, such methods generally consist of two stages: document retrieval, followed by sentence highlighting (Mitra and Craswell, 2018). Previous work in open domain question answering has shown that BM25 is a difficult baseline to beat when questions were written with advance knowledge of the answer (Lee et al., 2019).

To obtain our baseline using traditional IR methods, we constructed a paragraph-level retrieval task which allows a direct comparison between the neural systems in Table 4 and BM25.[13] We evaluate BM25 by measuring its ability to recall the paragraph containing the answer to the question.[14] To get a paragraph retrieval score for our neural baselines, we run sentence retrieval as before, and use the retrieved sentence to select the enclosing paragraph. As shown in Table 6, the USE-QA neural baseline outperforms BM25 on paragraph retrieval.

Model	MRR	R@1	R@5	R@10
ReQA SQuAD				
USE-QA	**0.634**	**0.533**	**0.756**	**0.823**
QA$_{Lite}$	0.503	0.407	0.613	0.689
InferSent	0.369	0.279	0.469	0.548
BM25[15]	0.602	0.517	0.702	0.755
ReQA NQ				
USE-QA	**0.366**	**0.247**	**0.486**	**0.578**
QA$_{Lite}$	0.274	0.177	0.366	0.450
InferSent	0.145	0.082	0.199	0.258
BM25	0.103	0.066	0.140	0.175

Table 6: Performance of various models on paragraph-level retrieval.

---

[13]We opted not to evaluate BM25 on sentence-level retrieval as earlier work has shown that traditional term-based document retrieval technologies are unsuccessful when applied to sentence-level retrieval (Allan et al., 2003).

[14]Our experiments make use of the implementation at `https://github.com/nhirakawa/BM25` with default hyperparameter settings.

[15]BM25 statistics were computed over the first 10,000 questions of each dataset, due to slow scoring speed.

5 Related Work

Open domain question answering is the problem of answering a question from a large collection of documents (Voorhees and Tice, 2000). Successful systems usually follow a two-step approach to answer a given question: first retrieve relevant articles or blocks, and then scan the returned text to identify the answer using a reading comprehension model (Jurafsky and Martin, 2018; Kratzwald and Feuerriegel, 2018; Yang et al., 2019a; Lee et al., 2019). While the reading comprehension step has been widely studied with many existing datasets (Rajpurkar et al., 2016; Nguyen et al., 2016; Dunn et al., 2017; Kwiatkowski et al., 2019), machine reading at scale is still a challenging task for the community.

Chen et al. (2017) recently proposed DrQA, treating Wikipedia as a knowledge base over which to answer factoid questions from SQuAD (Rajpurkar et al., 2016), CuratedTREC (Baudiš and Šedivý, 2015) and other sources. The task measures how well a system can successfully extract the answer span given a question, but it still relies on a document retrieval step. The ReQA eval differs from DrQA task by skipping the intermediate step and retrieving the answer sentence directly.

There is also a growing interest in answer selection at scale. Surdeanu et al. (2008) constructs a dataset with 142,627 question-answer pairs from Yahoo! Answers, with the goal of retrieving the right answer from all answers given a question. However, the dataset is limited to "how to" questions, which simplifies the problem by restricting it to a specific domain. Additionally the underlying data is not as broadly accessible as SQuAD and other more recent QA datasets, due to more restrictive terms of use.

WikiQA (Yang et al., 2015) is another task involving large-scale sentence-level answer selection. The candidate sentences are, however, limited to a small set of documents returned by Bing search, and is smaller than the scale of our ReQA tasks. WikiQA consists of 3,047 questions and 29,258 candidate answers, while ReQA SQuAD and ReQA NQ each contain over 20x that number of questions and over 3x that number of candidates (see Table 1). Moreover, as discussed in Section 3.4, restricting the domain of answers to top search engine results limits the evaluation's applicability for testing end-to-end retrieval.

Cakaloglu et al. (2018) made use of SQuAD for a retrieval task at the paragraph level. We extend this work by investigating sentence level retrieval and by providing strong sentence-level and paragraph-level baselines over a replicable construction of a retrieval evaluation set from the SQuAD data. Further, while Cakaloglu et al. (2018) trained their model on data drawn from SQuAD, we would like to highlight that our own strong baselines do not make use of any training data from SQuAD. We advocate for future work to attempt a similar approach of using sources of model training and evaluation data that are distinct as possible in order to provide a better picture of how well models generally perform a task.

Finally, Seo et al. (2018) construct a phrase-indexed question answering challenge that is similar to ReQA in requiring the question and the answer be encoded separately of one another. However, while ReQA focuses on sentence-based retrieval, their benchmark retrieves phrases, allowing for a direct F_1 and exact-match evaluation on SQuAD. Seo et al. (2019) demonstrate an implementation of a phrase-indexed question answering system using a combination of dense (neural) and sparse (term-frequency based) indices.

We believe that ReQA can help guide development of such systems by providing a point of evaluation between SQuAD, whose passages are too small to test retrieval performance, and SQuAD-Open (Chen et al., 2017), which operates at a realistic scale but is expensive and slow to evaluate. In practice, our evaluation runs completely in memory and finishes within two hours on a developer workstation, making it easy to integrate directly into the training process, where it can, for instance, trigger early stopping.

6   Conclusion

In this paper, we introduce Retrieval Question-Answering (ReQA) as a new benchmark for evaluating end-to-end answer retrieval models. The task assesses how well models are able to retrieve relevant sentence-level answers to queries from a large corpus. We describe a general method for converting reading comprehension QA tasks into cross-document answer retrieval tasks. Using SQuAD and Natural Questions as examples, we construct the ReQA SQuAD and ReQA NQ tasks, and evaluate several models on sentence- and paragraph-level answer retrieval. We find that a freely available neural baseline, USE-QA, outperforms a strong information retrieval baseline, BM25, on paragraph retrieval, suggesting that end-to-end answer retrieval can offer improvements over pipelined systems that first retrieve documents and then select answers within. We release our code for both evaluation and conversion of the datasets into ReQA tasks.

Acknowledgments

We thank our teammates from Descartes and other Google groups for their feedback and suggestions. We would like to recognize Javier Snaider, Igor Krivokon and Ray Kurzweil. Special thanks goes to Jonni Kanerva for developing the tailored sentence-breaking algorithm.

References

James Allan, Courtney Wade, and Alvaro Bolivar. 2003. Retrieval and novelty detection at the sentence level. In *Proceedings of the 26th Annual International ACM SIGIR Conference on Research and Development in Informaion Retrieval*, SIGIR '03, pages 314–321, New York, NY, USA. ACM.

Petr Baudiš and Jan Šedivý. 2015. Modeling of the question answering task in the yodaqa system. In *Proceedings of the 6th International Conference on Experimental IR Meets Multilinguality, Multimodality, and Interaction - Volume 9283*, CLEF'15, pages 222–228, Berlin, Heidelberg. Springer-Verlag.

Tolgahan Cakaloglu, Christian Szegedy, and Xiaowei Xu. 2018. Text embeddings for retrieval from a large knowledge base. *CoRR*, abs/1810.10176.

Danqi Chen, Adam Fisch, Jason Weston, and Antoine Bordes. 2017. Reading Wikipedia to answer open-domain questions. In *Proceedings of the 55th Annual Meeting of the Association for Computational Linguistics (Volume 1: Long Papers)*, pages 1870–1879, Vancouver, Canada. Association for Computational Linguistics.

Alexis Conneau, Douwe Kiela, Holger Schwenk, Loïc Barrault, and Antoine Bordes. 2017. Supervised learning of universal sentence representations from natural language inference data. In *Proceedings of the 2017 Conference on Empirical Methods in Natural Language Processing*, pages 670–680, Copenhagen, Denmark. Association for Computational Linguistics.

Jacob Devlin, Ming-Wei Chang, Kenton Lee, and Kristina Toutanova. 2019. BERT: Pre-training of deep bidirectional transformers for language understanding. In *Proceedings of the 2019 Conference of the North American Chapter of the Association for Computational Linguistics: Human Language*

Technologies, Volume 1 (Long and Short Papers), pages 4171–4186, Minneapolis, Minnesota. Association for Computational Linguistics.

Matthew Dunn, Levent Sagun, Mike Higgins, V. Ugur Güney, Volkan Cirik, and Kyunghyun Cho. 2017. Searchqa: A new q&a dataset augmented with context from a search engine. *CoRR*, abs/1704.05179.

Daniel Gillick, Alessandro Presta, and Gaurav Singh Tomar. 2018. End-to-end retrieval in continuous space. *CoRR*, abs/1811.08008.

Mandy Guo, Qinlan Shen, Yinfei Yang, Heming Ge, Daniel Cer, Gustavo Hernandez Abrego, Keith Stevens, Noah Constant, Yun-Hsuan Sung, Brian Strope, and Ray Kurzweil. 2018. Effective parallel corpus mining using bilingual sentence embeddings. In *Proceedings of the Third Conference on Machine Translation: Research Papers*, pages 165–176, Belgium, Brussels. Association for Computational Linguistics.

Matthew Henderson, Rami Al-Rfou, Brian Strope, Yun-Hsuan Sung, László Lukács, Ruiqi Guo, Sanjiv Kumar, Balint Miklos, and Ray Kurzweil. 2017. Efficient natural language response suggestion for smart reply. *CoRR*, abs/1705.00652.

Matthew Henderson, Ivan Vulić, Daniela Gerz, Iñigo Casanueva, Paweł Budzianowski, Sam Coope, Georgios Spithourakis, Tsung-Hsien Wen, Nikola Mrkšić, and Pei-Hao Su. 2019. Training neural response selection for task-oriented dialogue systems. *arXiv preprint arXiv:1906.01543*.

Mandar Joshi, Eunsol Choi, Daniel S. Weld, and Luke Zettlemoyer. 2017. TriviaQA: A large scale distantly supervised challenge dataset for reading comprehension. In *Proceedings of the 55th Annual Meeting of the Association for Computational Linguistics*, Vancouver, Canada. Association for Computational Linguistics.

Daniel Jurafsky and James H. Martin. 2018. *Speech and Language Processing (3rd Edition, in draft)*. Prentice-Hall, Inc., Upper Saddle River, NJ, USA.

Ryan Kiros, Yukun Zhu, Ruslan Salakhutdinov, Richard S. Zemel, Antonio Torralba, Raquel Urtasun, and Sanja Fidler. 2015. Skip-thought vectors. In *Proceedings of the 28th International Conference on Neural Information Processing Systems - Volume 2*, NIPS'15, pages 3294–3302, Cambridge, MA, USA. MIT Press.

Bernhard Kratzwald and Stefan Feuerriegel. 2018. Adaptive document retrieval for deep question answering. In *Proceedings of the 2018 Conference on Empirical Methods in Natural Language Processing*, pages 576–581, Brussels, Belgium. Association for Computational Linguistics.

Taku Kudo and John Richardson. 2018. SentencePiece: A simple and language independent subword tokenizer and detokenizer for neural text processing.

In *Proceedings of the 2018 Conference on Empirical Methods in Natural Language Processing: System Demonstrations*, pages 66–71, Brussels, Belgium. Association for Computational Linguistics.

Tom Kwiatkowski, Jennimaria Palomaki, Olivia Redfield, Michael Collins, Ankur Parikh, Chris Alberti, Danielle Epstein, Illia Polosukhin, Matthew Kelcey, Jacob Devlin, Kenton Lee, Kristina N. Toutanova, Llion Jones, Ming-Wei Chang, Andrew Dai, Jakob Uszkoreit, Quoc Le, and Slav Petrov. 2019. Natural questions: a benchmark for question answering research. *Transactions of the Association of Computational Linguistics*.

Kenton Lee, Ming-Wei Chang, and Kristina Toutanova. 2019. Latent retrieval for weakly supervised open domain question answering. *arXiv preprint arXiv:1906.00300*.

Bhaskar Mitra and Nick Craswell. 2018. An introduction to neural information retrieval. *Foundations and Trends in Information Retrieval*, 13(1):1–126.

Tri Nguyen, Mir Rosenberg, Xia Song, Jianfeng Gao, Saurabh Tiwary, Rangan Majumder, and Li Deng. 2016. MS MARCO: A human generated machine reading comprehension dataset. *CoRR*, abs/1611.09268.

Matthew E. Peters, Mark Neumann, Mohit Iyyer, Matt Gardner, Christopher Clark, Kenton Lee, and Luke Zettlemoyer. 2018. Deep contextualized word representations. In *Proc. of NAACL*.

Pranav Rajpurkar, Jian Zhang, Konstantin Lopyrev, and Percy Liang. 2016. SQuAD: 100,000+ questions for machine comprehension of text. In *Proceedings of the 2016 Conference on Empirical Methods in Natural Language Processing*, pages 2383–2392, Austin, Texas. Association for Computational Linguistics.

Stephen Robertson and Hugo Zaragoza. 2009. The probabilistic relevance framework: Bm25 and beyond. *Found. Trends Inf. Retr.*, 3(4):333–389.

Minjoon Seo, Tom Kwiatkowski, Ankur Parikh, Ali Farhadi, and Hannaneh Hajishirzi. 2018. Phrase-indexed question answering: A new challenge for scalable document comprehension. In *Proceedings of the 2018 Conference on Empirical Methods in Natural Language Processing*, pages 559–564, Brussels, Belgium. Association for Computational Linguistics.

Minjoon Seo, Jinhyuk Lee, Tom Kwiatkowski, Ankur Parikh, Ali Farhadi, and Hannaneh Hajishirzi. 2019. Real-time open-domain question answering with dense-sparse phrase index. In *Proceedings of the 57th Annual Meeting of the Association for Computational Linguistics*, pages 4430–4441, Florence, Italy. Association for Computational Linguistics.

Mihai Surdeanu, Massimiliano Ciaramita, and Hugo Zaragoza. 2008. Learning to rank answers on large online QA collections. In *Proceedings of ACL-08:*

HLT, pages 719–727, Columbus, Ohio. Association for Computational Linguistics.

Ashish Vaswani, Noam Shazeer, Niki Parmar, Jakob Uszkoreit, Llion Jones, Aidan N Gomez, Łukasz Kaiser, and Illia Polosukhin. 2017. Attention is all you need. In *Proceedings of NIPS*. Curran Associates, Inc.

Ellen M. Voorhees and Dawn M. Tice. 2000. Building a question answering test collection. In *Proceedings of the 23rd Annual International ACM SIGIR Conference on Research and Development in Information Retrieval*, SIGIR '00, pages 200–207, New York, NY, USA. ACM.

Wei Yang, Yuqing Xie, Aileen Lin, Xingyu Li, Luchen Tan, Kun Xiong, Ming Li, and Jimmy Lin. 2019a. End-to-end open-domain question answering with BERTserini. In *Proceedings of the 2019 Conference of the North American Chapter of the Association for Computational Linguistics (Demonstrations)*, pages 72–77, Minneapolis, Minnesota. Association for Computational Linguistics.

Yi Yang, Wen-tau Yih, and Christopher Meek. 2015. WikiQA: A challenge dataset for open-domain question answering. In *Proceedings of the 2015 Conference on Empirical Methods in Natural Language Processing*, pages 2013–2018, Lisbon, Portugal. Association for Computational Linguistics.

Yinfei Yang, Gustavo Hernández Ábrego, Steve Yuan, Mandy Guo, Qinlan Shen, Daniel Cer, Yun-Hsuan Sung, Brian Strope, and Ray Kurzweil. 2019b. Improving multilingual sentence embedding using bi-directional dual encoder with additive margin softmax. *CoRR*, abs/1902.08564.

Yinfei Yang, Daniel Cer, Amin Ahmad, Mandy Guo, Jax Law, Noah Constant, Gustavo Hernandez Abrego, Steve Yuan, Chris Tar, Yun-Hsuan Sung, Brian Strope, and Ray Kurzweil. 2019c. Multilingual universal sentence encoder for semantic retrieval. *arXiv preprint arXiv:1907.04307*.

Yinfei Yang, Steve Yuan, Daniel Cer, Sheng-yi Kong, Noah Constant, Petr Pilar, Heming Ge, Yun-Hsuan Sung, Brian Strope, and Ray Kurzweil. 2018. Learning semantic textual similarity from conversations. In *Proceedings of The Third Workshop on Representation Learning for NLP*, pages 164–174, Melbourne, Australia. Association for Computational Linguistics.

ORB: An Open Reading Benchmark
for Comprehensive Evaluation of Machine Reading Comprehension

Dheeru Dua[♣], Ananth Gottumukkala[♣], Alon Talmor[♡],
Sameer Singh[♣], and Matt Gardner[♠]
[♣]University of California, Irvine, USA
[♡]Allen Institute for Artificial Intelligence, Seattle, Washington, USA
[♠]Allen Institute for Artificial Intelligence, Irvine, California, USA
ddua@uci.edu

Abstract

Reading comprehension is one of the crucial tasks for furthering research in natural language understanding. A lot of diverse reading comprehension datasets have recently been introduced to study various phenomena in natural language, ranging from simple paraphrase matching and entity typing to entity tracking and understanding the implications of the context. Given the availability of many such datasets, comprehensive and reliable evaluation is tedious and time-consuming for researchers working on this problem. We present an evaluation server, **ORB**, that reports performance on seven diverse reading comprehension datasets, encouraging and facilitating testing a single model's capability in understanding a wide variety of reading phenomena. The evaluation server places no restrictions on how models are trained, so it is a suitable test bed for exploring training paradigms and representation learning for general reading facility. As more suitable datasets are released, they will be added to the evaluation server. We also collect and include synthetic augmentations for these datasets, testing how well models can handle out-of-domain questions.

1 Introduction

Research in reading comprehension, the task of answering questions about a given passage of text, has seen a huge surge of interest in recent years, with many large datasets introduced targeting various aspects of reading (Rajpurkar et al., 2016; Dua et al., 2019; Dasigi et al., 2019; Lin et al., 2019). However, as the number of datasets increases, evaluation on all of them becomes challenging, encouraging researchers to overfit to the biases of a single dataset. Recent research, including MultiQA (Talmor and Berant, 2019) and the MRQA workshop shared task, aim to facilitate training and evaluating on several reading comprehension datasets at the same time. To further aid in this direction, we present an evaluation server that can test a single model across many different datasets, including on their hidden test sets in some cases. We focus on datasets where the core problem is natural language understanding, not information retrieval; models are given a single passage of text and a single question and are required to produce an answer.

As our goal is to provide a broad suite of questions that test a single model's reading ability, we additionally provide synthetic augmentations to some of the datasets in our evaluation server. Several recent papers have proposed question transformations that result in out-of-distribution test examples, helping to judge the generalization capability of reading models (Ribeiro et al., 2018, 2019; Zhu et al., 2019). We collect the best of these, add some of our own, and keep those that generate reasonable and challenging questions. We believe this strategy of evaluating on many datasets, including distribution-shifted synthetic examples, will lead the field towards more robust and comprehensive reading comprehension models.

Code for the evaluation server, including a script to run it on the dev sets of these datasets and a leaderboard showing results on their hidden tests, can be found at https://leaderboard.allenai.org/orb

2 Datasets

We selected seven existing datasets that target various complex linguistic phenomena such as coreference resolution, entity and event detection, etc., capabilities which are desirable when testing a model for reading comprehension. We chose datasets that adhere to two main properties: First, we exclude from consideration any multiple choice dataset, as these typically require very different model architectures, and they often have biases in how the dis-

Proceedings of the Second Workshop on Machine Reading for Question Answering, pages 147–153
Hong Kong, China, November 4, 2019. ©2019 Association for Computational Linguistics

tractor choices are generated. Second, we require that the dataset be originally designed for answering isolated questions over a single, given passage of text. We are focused on evaluating *reading* performance, not *retrieval*; reading a single passage of text is far from solved, so we do not complicate things by adding in retrieval, conversation state, or other similar complexities.

It is our intent to add to the evaluation server any high-quality reading comprehension dataset that is released in the future that matches these restrictions.

We now briefly describe the datasets that we include in the initial release of ORB. Table 1 gives summary statistics of these datasets. Except where noted, we include both the development and test sets (including hidden test sets) in our evaluation server for all datasets.

SQuAD (Rajpurkar et al., 2016) requires a model to perform lexical matching between the context and the question to predict the answer. This dataset provides avenues to learn predicate-argument structure and multi-sentence reasoning to some extent. It was collected by asking crowd-workers to create question-answer pairs from Wikipedia articles such that the answer is a single-span in the context. The dataset was later updated to include unanswerable questions (Rajpurkar et al., 2018), giving a harder question set without as many reasoning shortcuts. We include only the development sets of SQuAD 1.1 and SQuAD 2.0 in our evaluation server.

DuoRC (Saha et al., 2018) tests if the model can generalize to answering semantically similar but syntactically different paraphrased questions. The questions are created on movie summaries obtained from two sources, Wikipedia and IMDB. The crowd-workers formalized questions based on Wikipedia contexts and in turn answered them based on the IMDB context. This ensured that the model will not rely solely on lexical matching, but rather utilize semantic understanding. The answer can be either a single-span from context or free form text written by the annotator.

Quoref (Dasigi et al., 2019) focuses on understanding coreference resolution, a challenging aspect of natural language understanding. It helps gauge how a model can handle ambiguous entity and event resolution to answer a question correctly. This dataset was created by asking crowd workers to write questions and multi-span answers from Wikipedia articles that centered around pronouns in the context.

DROP (Dua et al., 2019) attempts to force models to have a more comprehensive understanding of a paragraph, by constructing questions that query many parts of the paragraph at the same time. These questions involve reasoning operations that are mainly rudimentary mathematical skills such as addition, subtraction, maximum, minimum, etc. To perform well on this dataset a model needs to locate multiple spans associated with questions in the context and perform a set of operations in a hierarchical or sequential manner to obtain the answer. The answer can be either a set of spans from the context, a number or a date.

ROPES (Lin et al., 2019) centers around understanding the implications of a passage of text, particularly dealing with the language of causes and effects. A system is given a background passage, perhaps describing the effects of deforestation on local climate and ecosystems, and a grounded situation involving the knowledge in the background passage, such as, *City A has more trees than City B*. The questions then require grounding the effects described in the background, perhaps querying which city would more likely have greater ecological diversity. This dataset can be helpful in understanding how to apply the knowledge contained in a passage of text to a new situation.

NewsQA (Trischler et al., 2017) dataset focuses on paraphrased questions with predicate-argument structure understanding. To some extent it is similar to DuoRC, however the examples are collected from news articles and offers diverse linguistic structures. This crowd-sourced dataset was created by asking annotators to write questions from CNN/DailyMail articles as context.

NarrativeQA (Kočiský et al., 2018) focuses on understanding temporal reasoning among various events that happen in a given movie plot. It also tests the models ability to "hop" between various parts of the context and not rely solely on sequential reasoning. The dataset was constructed by aligning books from Gutenberg [1] with the summaries of their movie adaptations from various web resources. The crowd workers were asked to create complex questions about characters, narratives, events etc. from summaries and typically can be answered

---

[1] http://www.gutenberg.org/

Dataset	Dev Size	Test Size	Context Length (Avg)	Answer Length (Avg)
SQuAD1.1	10,570	-	123.7	4.0
SQuAD2.0	10,570	-	127.5	4.2
DuoRC	12,233	13,449	1113.6	2.8
Quoref	2,418	2,537	348.2	2.7
DROP	9,536	9,622	195.1	1.5
ROPES	1,204	1,015	177.1	1.2
NewsQA	5,166	5,126	711.3	5.1
NarrativeQA	3,443	10,557	567.9	4.7

Table 1: Dataset Statistics

Dataset	IC	MWC	Imp	No-Ans	SEARs
NewsQA	0	0	501	347	16009
QuoRef	0	0	79	385	11759
DROP	1377	457	113	284	16382
SQuAD	16	0	875	594	28188
ROPES	637	119	0	201	2909
DuoRC	22	0	2706	-	45020

Table 2: Yields of augmented datasets

from summaries. In addition, crowd workers were required to provide answers that do not have high overlap with the context. In accordance with our format, we only use the version with the summaries as context in our evaluation server.

3 Synthetic Augmentations

Prior works (Jia and Liang, 2017) have shown that RC models are brittle to minor perturbations in original dataset. Hence, to test the model's ability to generalize to out-of-domain syntactic structures and be logically consistent in its answers, we automatically generate questions based on various heuristics. These heuristics fall in two broad categories.

1. The question is paraphrased to a minimal extent to create new syntactic structures, keeping the semantics of the question largely intact and without making any changes to the original context and answer.

2. The predicate-argument structures of a given question-answer pair are leveraged to create new WH-questions based on the object in the question instead of the subject. This rule-based method, adopted from (Ribeiro et al., 2019), changes the question and answer keeping the context fixed.

We use five augmentation techniques, where the first four techniques fall into the first category and the last technique falls into the second category.

Invert Choice transforms a binary choice question by changing the order in which the choices are presented, keeping the answer the same.

More Wrong Choice transforms a binary choice question by substituting the wrong choice in the question with another wrong choice from the passage.

No Answer substitutes a name in the question for a different name from the passage to create with high probability a new question with no answer.

SEARs creates minimal changes in word selection or grammar while maintaining the original meaning of the question according to the rules described by Ribeiro et al. (2018).

Implication creates a new question-answer pair, where the object of the original question is replaced with the answer directly resulting in creation of a new WH-question where the answer is now the object of the original question. These transformations are performed based on rules described by Ribeiro et al. (2019).

We attempted all the above augmentation techniques on all the datasets (except NarrativeQA where entity and event tracking is complex and these simple transformations can lead to a high number of false positives). Table 2 shows the number of augmentations generated by each augmentation technique-dataset pair. A few sample augmentations are shown in Table 3.

After generating all the augmented datasets, we manually identified the augmentation technique-dataset pairs which led to high-quality augmentations. We sample 50 questions from each augmented dataset and record whether they satisfy the three criteria given below.

1. Is the question understandable, with little to no grammatical errors?
2. Is the question semantically correct?
3. Is the new answer the correct answer for the new question?

Table 4 shows the number of high-quality questions generated for each dataset. We keep the augmentation technique-dataset pairs where at least 90% of the question-answer pairs satisfy the above three criteria. We further test the performance of these augmentations (Section 4) on a BERT (Devlin et al., 2019b) based model to establish if the dataset has a sufficiently different question distribu-

Template Type	Context (truncated)	Original QA Pair	Generated QA Pair
Invert Choice	... before halftime thanks to a David Akers 32-yard field goal, giving Detroit a 17-14 edge ... in the third, Washington was able to equalize with John Potter making his first career field goal from 43 yards out ... in the fourth, Detroit took the lead again, this time by way of Akers hitting a 28-yard field goal, giving Detroit a 20-17 lead...	**Q:** Which player scored more field goals, David Akers or John Potter? **A:** David Akers	**Q:** Which player scored more field goals, John Potter or David Akers? **A:** David Akers
More Wrong Choice	The first issue in 1942 consisted of denominations of 1, 5, 10 and 50 centavos and 1, 5, and 10 Pesos. ... 1944 ushered in a 100 Peso note and soon after an inflationary 500 Pesos note. In 1945, the Japanese issued a 1,000 Pesos note...	**Q:** Which year ushered in the largest Peso note, 1944 or 1945? **A:** 1945	**Q:** Which year ushered in the largest Peso note, 1942 or 1945? **A:** 1945
Implication	... In 1562, naval officer Jean Ribault led an expedition that explored Florida and the present-day Southeastern U.S., and founded the outpost of Charlesfort on Parris Island, South Carolina...	**Q:** When did Ribault first establish a settlement in South Carolina? **A:** 1562	**Q:** Who established a settlement in South Carolina in 1562? **A:** Ribault
No Answer	From 1975, Flavin installed permanent works in Europe and the United States, including ... the Union Bank of Switzerland, Bern (1996). ... The 1930s church was designed by Giovanni Muzio...	**Q:** Which permanent works did Flavin install in 1996? **A:** Union Bank of Switzerland, Bern	**Q:** Which permanent works did Giovanni Muzio install in 1996? **A:** No Answer
SEARs	... Dhul-Nun al-Misri and Ibn Wahshiyya were the first historians to study hieroglyphs, by comparing them to the contemporary Coptic language used by Coptic priests in their time...	**Q:** What did historians compare to the Coptic language? **A:** hieroglyphs	**Q:** What'd historians compare to the Coptic language? **A:** hieroglyphs

Table 3: Examples of generated augmentations with various templates.

Dataset	IC	MWC	Imp	No-Ans	SEARs
NewsQA	-	-	47	47	50
QuoRef	-	-	45	48	50
DROP	46	42	36	48	50
SQuAD	15/16	-	47	48	50
ROPES	48	36	-	11	50
DuoRC	18/22	-	47	-	50

Table 4: Quality of augmented datasets (# of good questions out of 50 sampled)

tion from the original and has enough independent value to be incorporated into the evaluation server.

4 Experiments

4.1 Model

We train a numerically-aware BERT-based model[2] (NABERT) on all the seven datasets and test its performance on existing datasets and synthetic augmentations. NABERT is a BERT based model with the ability to perform discrete operations like counting, addition, subtraction etc. We added support for "impossible" answers in the existing NABERT architecture by extending the answer type predictor which classifies the type of reasoning involved given a question into one of the following five categories: *number, span, date, count, impossible*. All the hyper-parameter settings were kept the same.

[2]https://github.com/raylin1000/drop-bert

We noticed *catastrophic forgetting* on randomly sampling a minibatch for training, from all the datasets pooled together. To alleviate this problem, we sampled uniformly from each dataset in the beginning and then switched to sampling in proportion to the size of each dataset towards the end of the epoch (Stickland and Murray, 2019). This helped improve the performance on several dataset by 3-4% in EM, however, there is still a lot of room for improvement on this front. We also tried a simple BERT model (Devlin et al., 2019a) and MultiQA (Talmor and Berant, 2019) but NABERT gave the best results on the seven development sets.

In case of DuoRC and NarrativeQA, some answers are free-form human generated and do not have an exact overlap with the context. However, the NABERT model is trained to predict a span's start and end indices in the context. So for answers, which are not exact spans from the context we pick a span which has the highest ROUGE-L with the gold answer to serve as labels for training. However, for evaluation we use the original gold answer and not the extracted passage span for evaluating the model's performance.

4.2 Existing Dataset Performance

Table 5 shows the result of evaluating on all of the development and test sets using our evalua-

Dataset	Dev		Test	
	EM	F_1	EM	F_1
NewsQA	29.34	45.40	29.69	46.19
Quoref	34.49	42.65	30.13	38.39
DROP	19.09	23.16	17.69	21.87
SQuAD 1.1	68.03	78.55	-	-
SQuAD 2.0	33.70	39.17	-	-
ROPES	40.03	49.07	47.96	56.06
DuoRC	25.65	34.28	23.44	31.73

Narrative QA	BLEU-1	BLEU-4	METEOR	ROUGE-L (F1)
Dev Set	0.17	0.021	0.33	0.52
Test Set	0.16	0.019	0.33	0.53

Table 5: Performance on baseline BERT model on different datasets

tion server. We chose the official metrics adopted by the individual datasets to evaluate the performance of our baseline model. As can be seen in the table, the results are quite poor, significantly below single-dataset state-of-the-art on all datasets. The training of our initial baseline appears to be dominated by SQuAD 1.1, or perhaps SQuAD 1.1 mainly tests reasoning that is common to all of the other datasets. Significant research is required to build reading systems and develop training regimes that are general enough to handle multiple reading comprehension datasets at the same time, even when all of the datasets are seen at training time.

4.3 Synthetic Augmentations

Table 6 shows the performance of the baseline model on various development sets and heuristically generated questions. The **More Wrong Choice** augmentation is omitted since a high enough quality and/or yield of questions could not be ensured for any of the datasets. When evaluated on out-of-domain linguistic structures, performance drops significantly for some augmentation-dataset pairs but only marginally for others. For questions generated by the **Invert Choice** augmentation, the model struggles to grasp the correct reasoning behind two answer options like *Art Euphoric or Trescott Street* and changes the prediction when the choices are flipped. However, relative to the dev set performances on the original datasets, the performance drop is almost nonexistent. For the **SEARs** based augmentation the generated linguistic variations are close to in-domain syntactic structure so we do not see much performance drop in most of the datasets except for ROPES and

NewsQA. The **Implication** style questions create a large performance drop for NewsQA and SQuAD while having a performance boost for DuoRC. Finally, the **No-Ans** type questions have the worst performance across board for all datasets.

5 Related Work

Generalization and multi-dataset evaluation Recently there has been some work aimed at exploring the relation and differences between multiple reading comprehension datasets.

MULTIQA (Talmor and Berant, 2019) investigates over ten RC datasets, training on one or more source RC datasets, and evaluating generalization, as well as transfer to a target RC dataset. This work analyzes the factors that contribute to generalization, and shows that training on a source RC dataset and transferring to a target dataset substantially improves performance. MultiQA also provides a single format including a model and infrastructure for training and comparing question answering datasets. We provide no training mechanism, instead focusing on very simple evaluation that is compatible with any training regime, including evaluating on hidden test sets.

MRQA19, the Machine Reading for Question Answering workshop, introduced a shared task, which tests whether existing machine reading comprehension systems can generalize beyond the datasets on which they were trained. The task provides six large-scale datasets for training, and evaluates generalization to ten different hidden test datasets. However these datasets were modified from there original version, and context was limited to 800 tokens. In addition this shared task only tests for generalization with no intra-domain evaluation. In contrast, our evaluation server simply provides a single-model evaluation on many different datasets, with no prescriptions about training regimes.

NLP evaluation benchmarks The General Language Understanding Evaluation benchmark or GLUE (Wang et al., 2018) is a tool for evaluating and analyzing the performance of models across a diverse range of existing NLU tasks. A newer version, Super-GLUE (Wang et al., 2019) is styled after GLUE with a new set of more difficult language understanding tasks. In this line of work another standard toolkit for evaluating the quality of universal sentence representations is SENTE-VAL (Conneau and Kiela, 2018). Similar to GLUE,

	Dev		IC		Imp		No-Ans		SEARs	
	EM	F_1	EM	F_1	EM	F_1	EM	F_1	EM	F_1
NewsQA	29.34	45.40	-	-	23.35	34.36	0.02	0.02	21.34	33.33
QuoRef	34.49	42.65	-	-	32.91	44.84	0.0	0.0	34.84	42.11
DROP	19.09	23.16	40.23	48.03	-	-	0.0	0.0	16.97	21.65
SQuAD	68.03	78.55	56.25	64.58	46.74	57.97	0.0	0.0	56.53	71.25
ROPES	40.03	49.07	24.08	31.74	-	-	-	-	14.05	19.12
DuoRC	25.65	34.28	27.27	34.19	30.30	35.23	-	-	21.51	28.85

Template Type	Answered Incorrectly	Answered Correctly
Invert Choice	Original: Which art gallery was founded first, Art Euphoric or Trescott Street? Generated: Which art gallery was founded first, Trescott Street or Art Euphoric?	Original: Who scored more field goals, Nate Kaeding or Dan Carpenter? Generated: Who scored more field goals, Dan Carpenter or Nate Kaeding?
Implication	Original: When did the Huguenots secure the right to own land in the Baronies? Generated: Who secured the right to own land in baronies in 1697?	Original: When did Henry issue the Edict of Nantes? Generated: What did Henry issue in 1598?
SEARs	Original: What was the theme of Super Bowl 50? Generated: So what was the theme of Super Bowl 50?	Original: Who won Super Bowl 50? Generated: So who won Super Bowl 50?

Table 6: Quantitative and qualitative analysis of generated augmentations. We only show performance for high yield and high-quality augmentations.

SENTEVAL also encompasses a variety of tasks, including binary and multi-class classification, natural language inference and sentence similarity. We differ from GLUE and SENTEVAL by focusing on reading comprehension tasks, and only evaluating a single model on all datasets, instead of allowing the model to be tuned to each dataset separately.

Evaluation Platforms and Competitions in NLP
The use of online evaluation platform with private test labels has been exercised by various leaderboards on Kaggle and CodaLab, as well as shared tasks at the SemEval and CoNLL conferences.

Additional benchmarks such as PARLAI (Miller et al., 2017) and BABI (Weston et al., 2016) proposed a hierarchy of tasks towards building question answering and reasoning models and language understanding. However these frameworks do not include a standardized evaluation suite for system performance nor do they offer a wide set of reading comprehension tasks.

6 Conclusion

We have presented ORB, an open reading benchmark designed to be a comprehensive test of reading comprehension systems, in terms of their generalizability, understanding of various natural language phenomenon, capability to make consistent predictions, and ability to handle out-of-domain questions. This benchmark will grow over time as more interesting and useful reading comprehension datasets are released. We hope that this benchmark will help drive research on general reading systems.

References

A. Conneau and D. Kiela. 2018. Senteval: An evaluation toolkit for universal sentence representations. *Association for Computational Linguistics (ACL)*.

Pradeep Dasigi, Nelson Liu, Ana Marasovic, Noah Smith, and Matt Gardner. 2019. Quoref: A reading comprehension dataset with questions requiring coreferential reasoning. In *EMNLP*.

J. Devlin, M. Chang, K. Lee, and K. Toutanova. 2019a. Bert: Pre-training of deep bidirectional transformers for language understanding. In *North American Association for Computational Linguistics (NAACL)*.

Jacob Devlin, Ming-Wei Chang, Kenton Lee, and Kristina Toutanova. 2019b. Bert: Pre-training of deep bidirectional transformers for language understanding. *North American Association for Computational Linguistics (NAACL)*.

D. Dua, Y. Wang, P. Dasigi, G. Stanovsky, S. Singh, and M. Gardner. 2019. Drop: A reading comprehension benchmark requiring discrete reasoning over paragraphs. In *North American Association for Computational Linguistics (NAACL)*.

R. Jia and P. Liang. 2017. Adversarial examples for evaluating reading comprehension systems. In *Empirical Methods in Natural Language Processing (EMNLP)*.

T. Kočiský, J. Schwarz, P. Blunsom, C. Dyer, K. Hermann, G. Melis, and E. Grefenstette. 2018. The narrativeqa reading comprehension challenge. *Transactions of the Association for Computational Linguistics (TACL)*, 6:317–328.

Kevin Lin, Oyvind Tafjord, Peter Clark, and Matt Gardner. 2019. Reasoning over paragraph effects in situations. *arXiv preprint arXiv:1908.05852*.

A. H. Miller, W. Feng, A. Fisch, J. Lu, D. Batra, A. Bordes, D. Parikh, and J. Weston. 2017. Parlai: A dialog research software platform. In *Empirical Methods in Natural Language Processing (EMNLP)*, pages 79–84.

P. Rajpurkar, R. Jia, and P. Liang. 2018. Know what you don't know: Unanswerable questions for SQuAD. In *Association for Computational Linguistics (ACL)*.

P. Rajpurkar, J. Zhang, K. Lopyrev, and P. Liang. 2016. SQuAD: 100,000+ questions for machine comprehension of text. In *Empirical Methods in Natural Language Processing (EMNLP)*.

Marco Tulio Ribeiro, Carlos Guestrin, and Sameer Singh. 2019. Are red roses red? evaluating consistency of question-answering models. In *Proceedings of the 57th Conference of the Association for Computational Linguistics*, pages 6174–6184.

Marco Tulio Ribeiro, Sameer Singh, and Carlos Guestrin. 2018. Semantically equivalent adversarial rules for debugging nlp models. In *Proceedings of the 56th Annual Meeting of the Association for Computational Linguistics (Volume 1: Long Papers)*, pages 856–865.

A. Saha, R. Aralikatte, M. Khapra, and K. Sankaranarayanan. 2018. Duorc: Towards complex language understanding with paraphrased reading comprehension. In *Association for Computational Linguistics (ACL)*.

Asa Cooper Stickland and Iain Murray. 2019. BERT and PALs: Projected attention layers for efficient adaptation in multi-task learning. In *Proceedings of the 36th International Conference on Machine Learning*, volume 97 of *Proceedings of Machine Learning Research*, pages 5986–5995, Long Beach, California, USA. PMLR.

Alon Talmor and Jonathan Berant. 2019. Multiqa: An empirical investigation of generalization and transfer in reading comprehension. *57th Annual Conference of the Association for Computational Linguistics (ACL)*, abs/1905.13453.

A. Trischler, T. Wang, X. Yuan, J. Harris, A. Sordoni, P. Bachman, and K. Suleman. 2017. NewsQA: A machine comprehension dataset. In *Workshop on Representation Learning for NLP*.

A. Wang, Y. Pruksachatkun, N. Nangia, A. Singh, J. Michael, F. Hill, O. Levy, and S. Bowman. 2019. Superglue: A stickier benchmark for general-purpose language understanding systems. In *Advances in Neural Information Processing Systems (NeurIPS)*.

Alex Wang, Amanpreet Singh, Julian Michael, Felix Hill, Omer Levy, and Samuel Bowman. 2018. GLUE: A multi-task benchmark and analysis platform for natural language understanding. In *Proceedings of the 2018 EMNLP Workshop BlackboxNLP: Analyzing and Interpreting Neural Networks for NLP*, pages 353–355, Brussels, Belgium. Association for Computational Linguistics.

J. Weston, A. Bordes, S. Chopra, and T. Mikolov. 2016. Towards AI-complete question answering: A set of prerequisite toy tasks. *ICLR*.

Haichao Zhu, Li Dong, Furu Wei, Wenhui Wang, Bing Qin, and Ting Liu. 2019. Learning to ask unanswerable questions for machine reading comprehension. In *Proceedings of the 57th Annual Meeting of the Association for Computational Linguistics*, pages 4238–4248, Florence, Italy. Association for Computational Linguistics.

A Recurrent BERT-based Model for Question Generation

Ying-Hong Chan
Department of Computer Science
National Chung Hsing University
Taichung, Taiwan
harry831120@gmail.com

Yao-Chung Fan
Department of Computer Science
National Chung Hsing University
Taichung, Taiwan
yfan@nchu.edu.tw

Abstract

In this study, we investigate the employment of the pre-trained BERT language model to tackle question generation tasks. We introduce three neural architectures built on top of BERT for question generation tasks. The first one is a straightforward BERT employment, which reveals the defects of directly using BERT for text generation. Accordingly, we propose another two models by restructuring our BERT employment into a sequential manner for taking information from previous decoded results. Our models are trained and evaluated on the recent question-answering dataset SQuAD. Experiment results show that our best model yields state-of-the-art performance which advances the BLEU 4 score of the existing best models from 16.85 to 22.17.

1 Introduction

Question generation (QG) problem, which takes a context text and an answer phase as input and generates a question corresponding to the given answer phase, has received tremendous interests in recent years from both industrial and academic natural language processing communities (Zhao et al., 2018; Zhou et al., 2017; Du et al., 2017). The state-of-the-art model mainly adopts neural QG approaches: training a neural network based on sequence-to-sequence framework. So far, the best performing result is reported in (Zhao et al., 2018), which advances the state-of-the-art results from 13.9 to 16.85 (BLEU 4).

The existing QG models mainly rely on recurrent neural networks (RNN), e.g. long short-term memory LSTM network (Hochreiter and Schmidhuber, 1997) or gated recurrent unit (Chung et al., 2014), augmented by attention mechanisms (Luong et al., 2015). However, the inherent sequential nature of the RNN models suffers from the problem of handling long sequences. Therefore, the existing QG models (Du et al., 2017; Zhou et al.,

2017) mainly use only sentence-level information as a context text for question generation. When applied to a paragraph-level context, the existing models show significant performance degradation. However, as indicated by (Du et al., 2017), providing paragraph-level information can improve QG performance. For handling long context, the work (Zhao et al., 2018) introduces a maxout pointer mechanism with a gated self-attention encoder for processing paragraph-level input. The work reports state-of-the-art performance.

Recently, the NLP community has seen the excitement around neural learning models that make use of pre-trained language models (Devlin et al., 2018; Radford et al., 2018). The latest development is BERT, which has shown significant performance improvement over various natural language understanding tasks, such as document summarization, document classification, etc.

Given the success of the BERT model, a natural question follows: can we leverage the BERT models to further advance the state-of-the-art for QG tasks? By our study, the answer is yes. Intuitively, the BERT employment brings two advantages for tackling the QG problem. First, as reported by studies (Devlin et al., 2018; Radford et al., 2018), employing pre-training language models has shown to be effective for improving NLP tasks. Second, the BERT model is a stack of multi-layer Transformer block (Vaswani et al., 2017), which eschews recurrence structure and relies entirely on self-attention mechanism to draw global dependencies between input sequences. With the Transformer blocks, processing paragraph-level contexts for QG are therefore to be possible.

In this study, we investigate the employment of the pre-trained BERT language model to tackle question generation tasks. We introduce three neural architectures built on top of BERT for question generation tasks. The first one is a straightforward

Proceedings of the Second Workshop on Machine Reading for Question Answering, pages 154–162
Hong Kong, China, November 4, 2019. ©2019 Association for Computational Linguistics

BERT employment, which reveals the defects of directly using BERT for text generation. As will be shown in the experiment, the naive BERT employment (called BERT-QG, BERT Question Generation) offers poor performance, as by construction, BERT produces all tokens at a time without considering decoding results in previous steps. We find that the question generated by the naive employment is not even a readable sentence. As a result, we propose a sequential question generation model based on BERT as our second model called BERT-SQG (BERT-Sequential Question Generation) for taking information from previous decoded results. As will shown in the performance evaluation, the BERT-SQG model outperforms the exiting best model (Zhao et al., 2018) by advancing the state-of-the-art results from 16.85 to 21.04 (BLEU 4).

Furthermore, we propose an augmented model called BERT-HLSQG (Highlight Sequential Question Generation) for further enhancing the performance of the BERT-SQG. Our BERT-HLSQG model works by marking the answer with [HL] tokens to avoid possible ambiguity in specifying answers for question generation. Such design further improves the BLEU 4 score from 21.04 to 22.17.

The contribution of this paper is summarized as follows.

- In this paper, we investigate the employment of using the BERT model for QG tasks. We show that the sequential structure is important for the decoding of text generation. Aiming at this point, we propose two sequential question generation models based on BERT in this paper.

- Furthermore, we propose a simple but effective input encoding scheme, which inserts special highlighting tokens [HL] before and after the given answer span, to address the ambiguity issue when an answer phase appears multiple times in the question.

- Extensive experiments are conducted using benchmark datasets, and the experiment results show the effectiveness of our question generation model. Our model outperforms the existing best models (Zhao et al., 2018) and pushes the state-of-the-art result from 16.85 to 22.17 (BLEU 4).

The rest of this paper is organized as follows. In Section 2, we discuss the related work for QG generation. In Section 3, we review the BERT model (the basic building block for our model). In Section 4, we introduce our models for question generation, and Section 5 provides the experiment results. In Section 6, we conclude the paper and discuss future work.

2 Related Work

The question generation has been mainly tackled with two types of approaches. One is built on top of heuristic rules that creates questions with manually constructed template and ranks the generated results (Heilman and Smith, 2010; Mazidi and Nielsen, 2014; Labutov et al., 2015). In (Labutov et al., 2015), the authors propose to use a crowdsourcing policy to generate question templates from a large amount of text to generate question. The research in (Heilman and Smith, 2010) proposes to use manually written rules to perform a sequence of general-purpose syntactic transformations to turn declarative sentences into questions. The generated questions are then ranked by a logistic regression model to select the qualified questions for later use. And, the research in (Yao et al., 2012) proposes to convert the sentence into a Minimal Recursion Semantics (MRS) representation through linguistic parsing, and then construct semantic structures and grammar rules from the representation to generate questions through the manually designed rules. Those approaches heavily depend on human effort, which makes them hard to scale up and being generalized in various domains.

The other one, which is becoming increasingly popular, is to train an end-to-end neural network from scratch by using sequence to sequence or encoder-decoder framework, e.g. (Du et al., 2017; Yuan et al., 2017; Song et al., 2017; Zhou et al., 2017; Zhao et al., 2018).

(Du et al., 2017) pioneered the work of automatic QG tasks using an end-to-end trainable seq2seq neural model. Automatic and human evaluation results showed that the proposed model outperformed the previous rule-based systems (Heilman and Smith, 2010; Rus et al., 2010). However, in their study, there was no control about which part of the context text the generated question was asking about.

On the other hands, the work (Zhou et al., 2017;

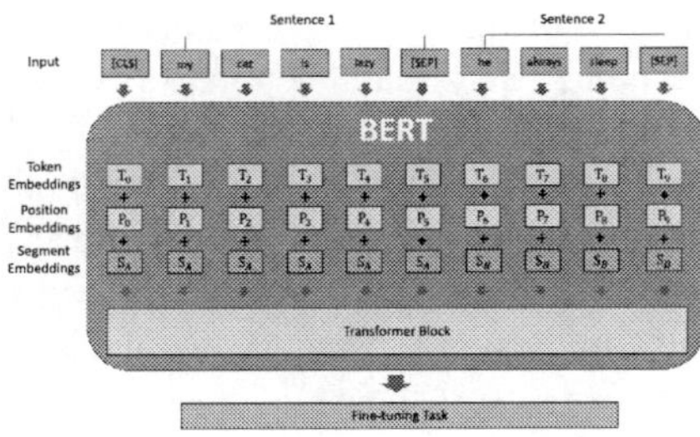

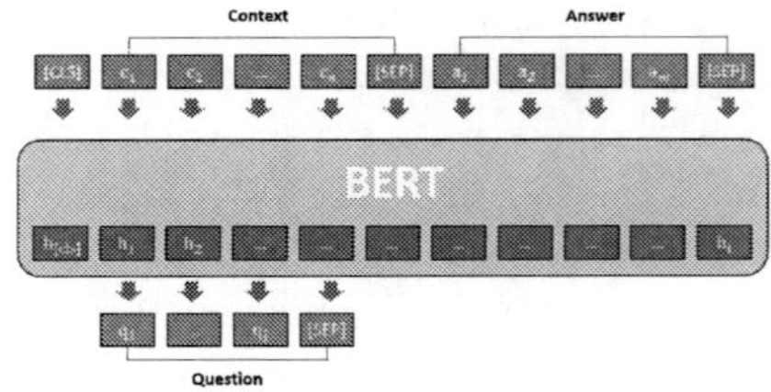

Figure 2: The BERT-QG architecture

Figure 1: BERT input architecture. Input Transformer block embedding is the sum of the three embeddings, and then use the hidden vector to fine tune each task.

Subramanian et al., 2017; Yuan et al., 2017) propose to encode answer location information using an annotation vector corresponding to the answer word positions. (Zhou et al., 2017) utilized rich features of the passage including answer positions. (Subramanian et al., 2017) deployed a two-stage neural model that detects important phrases and accordingly generates questions conditioned on the important phases. (Yuan et al., 2017) combined supervised and reinforcement learning in the training of their model using policy gradient techniques to maximize several rewards that measure question quality. Instead of using an annotation vector to tag the answer locations, the (Song et al., 2017) propose to employ a unified framework for QG and question answering by encoding both the answer and the passage with a multi-perspective matching mechanism. Further, (Tang et al., 2017; Wang et al., 2017) proposed joint models to address QG and question answering as a multi-task learning setting. (Duan et al., 2017) conducted QG for improving question answering. Due to the mixed objectives including question answering, the performance reported by their work was lower than the state-of-the-art results. In (Zhao et al., 2018), authors propose a maxout pointer mechanism with a gated self-attention encoder to solve the problem of processing long context for question generation.

All above-mentioned models are RNN base models, which suffers from the issue of processing long context/sequences. Compared with the RNN based model, our models based on BERT composed by transformer models (Vaswani et al., 2017). As shown in the later section, the question generated by our model is more semantically coherent and fluent.

3   BERT Overview

The BERT model is built by a stack of multi-layer bidirectional Transformer encoder (Vaswani et al., 2017). The BERT model has three architecture parameter settings: the number of layers (i.e., transformer blocks), the hidden size, and the number of self-attention heads in a transformer block.

For using BERT model, the input is required to be aligned as the BERT's specific input sequence. In general, a special token [CLS] is inserted as the first token for BERT's input sequence. The final hidden state of the [CLS] token is designed to be used as a final sequence representation for classification tasks. The input token sequence can be a pack of multiple sentences. To distinguish the information from different sentences, a special token [SEP] is added between the tokens of two consecutive sentences. In addition, a learned embedding is added to every token to denote whether it belongs to which sentence. For example, given a sentence pair (s_i, s_j) where s_i contains $|s_i|$ tokens and s_j contains $|s_j|$ tokens, the BERT input sequence is formulated as a sequence in the following form:

$$X = (\text{[CLS]}, t_{i,1}, ..., t_{i,|s_i|}, \text{[SEP]}, t_{j,1}..., t_{j,|s_j|})$$

As shown in Figure 1, the input representation of a given token is the sum of three embeddings: the token embeddings, the segmentation embeddings, and the position embeddings. Then the input representation is fed forward into extra layers to perform a fine-tuning procedure. The BERT model can be employed in three language modeling tasks: sequence-level classification, span-level prediction, and token-level prediction tasks. The fine-tuning procedure is performed in a task-specific manner. The details of our fine-tuning procedure are introduced in the later subsections.

4 BERT for Question Generation

In the following subsections, we introduce our models for QG. In Subsection 4.1, we introduce the naive BERT employment (BERT-QG), which serves as a first cut for using BERT for QG. BERT-QG offer poor performance but draws some insights for using BERT in QG tasks. Further, in Subsection 4.2, we introduce BERT-SQG by considering sequential information when generating questions. Last, in Subsection 4.3, we introduce BERT-HLSQG which shows the SOTA results for QG based on BERT.

4.1 BERT-QG

As an initial attempt, we first adapt the BERT model for QG as follows. First, for a given context paragraph $C = [c_1, ..., c_{|C|}]$ and an answer phase $A = [a_1, ..., a_{|A|}]$, the input sequence X is aligned as

$$X = (\text{[CLS]}, C, \text{[SEP]}, A, \text{[SEP]})$$

Let BERT() be the BERT model. We first obtain the hidden representation $\mathbf{H} \in \mathbb{R}^{|X| \times h}$ by $\mathbf{H} = \text{BERT}(X)$, where $|X|$ is the length of the input sequence and h is the size of the hidden dimension. Then, $\mathbf{H}$ is passed to a dense layer $\mathbf{W} \in \mathbb{R}^{h \times |V|}$ followed by a softmax function as follows.

$$Pr(w|x_i) = softmax(\mathbf{H} \cdot \mathbf{W} + \mathbf{b}), \forall x_i \in X$$

$$\hat{q}_i = \text{argmax}_w Pr(w|x_i)$$

The softmax is applied along the dimension of the sequence. All of the parameters of BERT and $\mathbf{W}$ are fine-tuned jointly to maximize the log-probability of the correct token q_i. The model architecture is shown in Figure 2. As such, a sequence of tokens $[w_1, ..., w_{|x|}]$ is generated and we use the first generated [SEP] symbol as the end of the generated question sentence.

4.2 BERT-SQG

In text generation tasks, as proposed by (Sutskever et al., 2014), considering the previous decoded results has significant impacts on the quality of the generated text. However, in BERT-QG, the token generation is performed without previous decoded result information. Due to this consideration, we propose a sequential question generation model based on BERT (called BERT-SQG).

In BERT-SQG, we take into consideration the previous decoded results for decoding a token. We adapt the BERT model for question generation as follows. First, for a given context paragraph $C = [c_1, ..., c_{|C|}]$ and an answer phase $A = [a_1, ..., a_{|A|}]$, and $\hat{Q} = [\hat{q}_1, ..., \hat{q}_i]$ the input sequence X_i is formulated as

$$X_i = (\text{[CLS]}, C, \text{[SEP]}, A, \text{[SEP]}, \hat{q}_1,$$
$$..., \hat{q}_i, \text{[MASK]})$$

Then, the input sequence X_i is represented by the BERT embedding layers and then travel forward into the BERT model. After that, we take the final hidden state (i.e., the output of the Transformer blocks) for the last token [MASK] in the input sequence. We denote the final hidden vector of [MASK] as $\mathbf{h}_{\text{[MASK]}} \in \mathbb{R}^h$. We adapt BERT model by adding an affine layer $\mathbf{W}_{\text{SQG}} \in \mathbb{R}^{h \times |V|}$ to the output of the [MASK] token. We compute the label probabilities $Pr(w|X_i) \in R^{|V|}$ by a softmax function as follows.

$$Pr(w|X_i) = softmax(\mathbf{h}_{\text{[MASK]}} \cdot \mathbf{W}_{\text{SQG}} + \mathbf{b}_{\text{SQG}})$$

$$\hat{q}_i = \text{argmax}_w Pr(w|X_i)$$

Subsequently, the newly generated token $\hat{q}_i$ is appended into X and the question generation process is repeated (as illustrated in Figure 3) with the new X until [SEP] is predicted. We report the generated tokens as the predicted question. In Table 1, we give an example of the actual running of the model.

4.3 BERT-HLSQG

In BERT-SQG, we find there are two shortcomings for producing quality results. First, when processing lengthy context, we find that the generated question is often with lower quality. Second, when an answer phase appears multiple times in the context, there is ambiguity for select which one to generate questions. As a result, poor results are reported when we use the BLEU score for performance evaluation. To address these shortcomings, we propose to further restructure BERT-SQG as follows. First, for a given context paragraph $C = [c_1, ..., c_{|C|}]$ and an answer phase $A = [a_1, ..., a_{|A|}]$, we integrate C and A into a new C' in the following form.

$$C' = [c_1, c_2, ..., \text{[HL]}, a_1, ..., a_{|A|}, \text{[HL]}, ..., c_{|C|}]$$

	X	x_i
iter0	[CLS] The Super Bowl 50 was played at Santa Clara, California. [SEP] Santa Clara, California. [SEP] [MASK]	Where
iter1	[CLS] The Super Bowl 50 was played at Santa Clara, California. [SEP] Santa Clara, California. [SEP] Where [MASK]	did
iter2	[CLS] The Super Bowl 50 was played at Santa Clara, California. [SEP] Santa Clara, California. [SEP] Where did [MASK]	Super
iter3	[CLS] The Super Bowl 50 was played at Santa Clara, California. [SEP] Santa Clara, California. [SEP] Where did Super [MASK]	Bowl
iter4	[CLS] The Super Bowl 50 was played at Santa Clara, California. [SEP] Santa Clara, California. [SEP] Where did Super Bowl [MASK]	50
iter5	[CLS] The Super Bowl 50 was played at Santa Clara, California. [SEP] Santa Clara, California. [SEP] Where did Super Bowl 50 [MASK]	take
iter6	[CLS] The Super Bowl 50 was played at Santa Clara, California. [SEP] Santa Clara, California. [SEP] Where did Super Bowl 50 take [MASK]	place?
iter7	[CLS] The Super Bowl 50 was played at Santa Clara, California. [SEP] Santa Clara, California. [SEP] Where did Super Bowl 50 take place [MASK]	[SEP]
iter8	[CLS] The Super Bowl 50 was played at Santa Clara, California. [SEP] Santa Clara, California. [SEP] Where did Super Bowl 50 take place [SEP] [MASK]	

Table 1: BERT-SQG Running Example

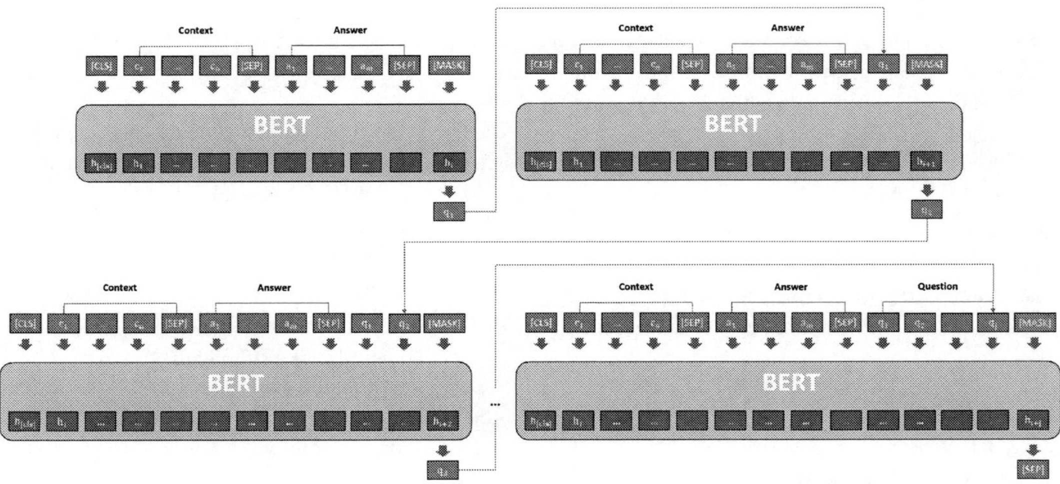

Figure 3: The BERT-SQG architecture

In C', we design and insert a new token (i.e., [HL]) to indicate the answer phase in the context. The observation for doing so is that we observe that for a long context, the answer phase often appears multiple times in the context, which causes ambiguity for the model for knowing which one as a target to generate question sentence. Thus, we design [HL] token to avoid possible ambiguity. With C', the input sequence X can be formulated as

$$X_i = ([\text{CLS}], C', [\text{SEP}], \hat{q}_1, ..., \hat{q}_i, [\text{MASK}])$$

Figure 4 shows the BERT-HLSQG model architecture. At each iteration, for generating q_i, we take the final hidden state vector $\mathbf{h}_{[\text{MASK}]} \in \mathbb{R}^h$ of the last token [MASK] in the input sequence. and connect it to an affine layer $\mathbf{W}_{\text{HLSQG}} \in \mathbb{R}^{h \times |V|}$. We compute the label probabilities $Pr(w|X_i) \in R^{|V|}$ by a softmax function as follows.

$$Pr(w|X_i) = softmax(\mathbf{h}_{[\text{MASK}]} \cdot \mathbf{W}_{\text{HLSQG}} + \mathbf{b}_{\text{HLSQG}})$$

$$\hat{q}_i = \operatorname{argmax}_w Pr(w|X_i)$$

We show a running example of BERT-HLSQG in Table 2.

5 Performance Evaluation

In this section, we present the performance evaluation results on the QG task on SQuAD (Rajpurkar et al., 2016) dataset.

5.1 Datasets

The SQuAD dataset contains 536 Wikipedia articles and 100K reading comprehension questions (and the corresponding answers) posed about the articles. Answers of the questions are text spans in the articles.

We use the same data split settings as the previous work on the QG tasks (Du et al., 2017; Zhao et al., 2018) to directly compare the state-of-the-art results on QG tasks. Table 3 summarizes statistics for the compared datasets.

- **SQuAD 73K** In this set, we follow the same setting as (Du et al., 2017); the accessible parts of the SQuAD training data are randomly divided into a training set (80%), a development set (10%), and a test set (10%). We report results on the 10% test set.

	X	x_i
iter0	[CLS] The Super Bowl 50 was played at [HL] Santa Clara, California [HL] . [SEP][MASK]	Where
iter1	[CLS] The Super Bowl 50 was played at [HL] Santa Clara, California [HL] . [SEP] Where [MASK]	did
iter2	[CLS] The Super Bowl 50 was played at [HL] Santa Clara, California [HL] . [SEP] Where did [MASK]	Super
iter3	[CLS] The Super Bowl 50 was played at [HL] Santa Clara, California [HL] . [SEP] Where did Super [MASK]	Bowl
iter4	[CLS] The Super Bowl 50 was played at [HL] Santa Clara, California [HL] . [SEP] Where did Super Bowl [MASK]	50
iter5	[CLS] The Super Bowl 50 was played at [HL] Santa Clara, California [HL] . [SEP] Where did Super Bowl 50 [MASK]	take
iter6	[CLS] The Super Bowl 50 was played at [HL] Santa Clara, California [HL] . [SEP] Where did Super Bowl 50 take [MASK]	place?
iter7	[CLS] The Super Bowl 50 was played at [HL] Santa Clara, California [HL] . [SEP] Where did Super Bowl 50 take place [MASK]	[SEP]
iter8	[CLS] The Super Bowl 50 was played at [HL] Santa Clara, California [HL] . [SEP] Where did Super Bowl 50 take place [SEP] [MASK]	

Table 2: BERT-HLSQG Running Example

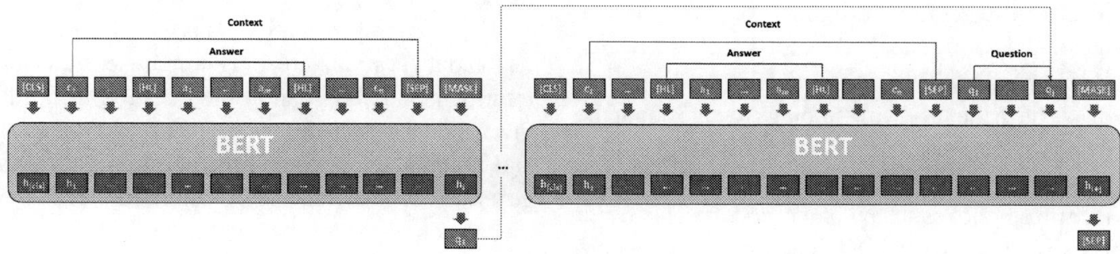

Figure 4: The BERT-HLSQG architecture

	Train	Test	Dev
SQuAD 73K	73240	11877	10570
SQuAD 81K	81577	8964	8964

Table 3: Dataset statistics: SQuAD 73K is the setting of (Du et al., 2017), and SQuAD 81K is the setting of (Zhao et al., 2018).

- **SQuAD 81K** In this set, we follow the same setting as (Zhao et al., 2018); the accessible SQuAD development data set is divided into a development set (50%), and a test set (50%). We report results on the 50% test set.

5.2 Performance Metrics

We use the evaluation package released by (Sharma et al., 2017). The package includes BLEU 1, BLEU 2, BLEU 3, BLEU 4 (Papineni et al., 2002), METEOR (Denkowski and Lavie, 2014) and ROUGE (Lin, 2004) evaluation scripts. BLEU measures the average n-gram precision on a set of reference sentences, with a penalty for overly short sentences. BLEU-n is a BLEU score variant that uses up to n-grams for counting co-occurrences. METEOR is a recall-oriented metric, which computes the similarity between the generated sentences and ground truth sentences by considering synonyms, stemming and paraphrases. ROUGE is commonly employed to evaluate n-grams recall of the summaries with gold standard sentences as references. ROUGE-L (measured based on the longest common subsequence) results are reported.

5.3 Implementation Details

We use the PyTorch version of BERT [1] to train our BERT-QG, BERT-SQG and BERT-HLSQG models. The pre-trained model uses the officially provided **BERT**$_{\text{base}}$ model (12 layers, 768 hidden dimensions, and 12 attention heads.) with a vocab of 30522 words. Dropout probability is set to 0.1 between transformer layers. The Adamax optimizer is applied during the training process, with an initial learning rate of 5e-5. The batch size for the update is set at 28. All our models use two TITAN RTX GPUs for 5 epochs training. We use Dev. data for epoch model to make predictions and select the highest accuracy rate as our score evaluation model. Also, in our BERT-SQG and BERT-HLSQG model, we use the Beam Search strategy for sequence decoding. The beam size is set to 3.

5.4 Model Comparison

In this paper, we compare our models with the best performing models (Du et al., 2017; Zhao et al., 2018) in the literature. The compared models in the experiment are:

- **NQG-RC** (Du et al., 2017): A seq2seq question generation model based on bidirectional LSTMs.

- **PLQG** (Zhao et al., 2018): A seq2seq network which contains a gated self-attention encoder and a maxout pointer decoder to en-

---

[1] https://github.com/huggingface/pytorch-pretrained-BERT

able the capability of handling long text input. The PLQG model is the state-of-the-art models for QG tasks.

5.5 Quantitative Results

Table 5 shows the comparison results using sentence-level context texts and Table 6 shows the results on paragraph-level context. We compare the models using standard metric BLEU, ROUGE-L, and METEOR.

We have the following findings to note about the results. First, as can be observed, BERT-QG offers poor performance. The performance of BERT-QG is far from the results by other models. This result is expected as BERT-QG generates the sentences without considering the previous decoded results. However, when taking into account the previous decoded results (BERT-SQG), we effectively utilize the power of BERT and yield the state-of-the-art result compared with the existing RNN variants for QG. Also, we see that BERT-HLSQG successfully address the limitation of BERT-SQG. As shown in Table 5, BERT-HLSQG outperforms the existing best performing model by 4-5% on both benchmark datasets.

Second, the results in Table 6 further show that BERT-SQG successfully processes the paragraph-level contexts and further push the state-of-the-art from 16.85 to 21.04 in terms of BLEU 4 score. Note that NQG-RC and PLQG both use the RNN architecture, and the RNN-based models all suffer from the issue of consuming long text input. We see that the BERT model based on Transformer blocks effectively addresses the issue of processing long text. In addition, the improvement of BERT-HLSQG is more obvious under paragraph-level, which advances the score from 21.04 to 22.17 in terms of BLEU 4 score. Again, this result validates that our BERT-HLSQG model does improve the shortcomings of BERT-SQG and achieves the best score at the paragraph-level context.

5.6 Evaluation Result on Reading Comprehension Task

One issue we find in our performance evaluation is that we observe questions generated by our models are good but with a very low BLEU score. The problem for this result comes from that BLEU score is token-basis; the generated question is compared with a golden standard based on the token similarity. A question might be expressed in different ways (but semantically the same); there are many different ways of describing the same thing/question. We think the score computed based on tokens can not truly reflect the performance of our model.

In order to demonstrate the effectiveness of our model, we further evaluate our model through reading comprehension (RC) tasks. Given a context and a question, a reading comprehension task returns the answer span to the question from the given context. In this experiment, we compare and examine the impact of the question sentences generated by the BERT-SQG and BERT-HLSQG models on the RC task to further validate our model.

5.6.1 Implementation Details

In this set of experiments, our goal is to examine the difference between using human-generated questions and questions generated by our QG models to train a reading comprehension model. Specifically, we use the training data set provided by the SQuAD and divided the training data set into QG set (50%) and RC set (50%). Then, we train BERT-SQG and BERT-HLSQG models using QG sets. The model is then used to generate questions to generate the RC-SQG and RC-HLSQG sets. Finally, we use RC, RC-SQG and RC-HLSQG sets for reading comprehension task training, and compare Exact Match and F1 score with the RC model (the one trained by RC set).

Our RC model is also implemented based on the PyTorch version BERT model and fine-tuned on the officially $BERT_{base}$ pre-training model. The dropout rate is set to 0.1 for all Transformer layers. The optimizer is performed using AdamW, with an initial learning rate of 3e-5. The batch size for the update is set at 8. All RC models use two TITAN RTX GPUs for 2 epochs training.

5.6.2 Results and Analysis

Table 4 shows the human question and generated question experiment comparison results. We observe that the RC-SQG and RC-HLSQG data sets generated using the model for question generation differed only 4-5% from the results of the human question data set on the Exact Match and the F1 Score is only 3-4%. The average token on the question is also close to the human question. These results demonstrate that the quality of the problems generated by our model is close to hu-

	Exact Match	F1 score	Question avg. tokens
RC	79.09	86.82	12.29
RC-SQG	74.07	82.91	12.09
RC-HLSQG	74.36	83.07	12.06

Table 4: Reading comprehension evaluation results

	Model	BLEU 1	BLEU 2	BLEU 3	BLEU 4	METEOR	ROUGE-L
	NQG-RC	43.09	25.96	17.50	12.28	16.62	39.75
	PLQG	43.47	28.23	20.40	15.32	19.29	43.91
SQuAD 73K	BERT-QG	34.17	15.52	8.36	4.47	14.78	37.60
	BERT-SQG	48.38	**33.15**	24.75	19.08	22.43	46.94
	BERT-HLSQG	**48.29**	33.12	**24.78**	**19.14**	**22.89**	**47.07**
	PLQG	44.51	29.07	21.06	15.82	19.67	44.24
SQuAD 81K	BERT-QG	34.18	15.51	8.57	4.97	14.57	37.65
	BERT-SQG	50.18	35.03	26.60	20.88	23.84	48.37
	BERT-HLSQG	**50.71**	**35.44**	**26.95**	**21.20**	**24.02**	**48.68**

Table 5: Comparison between our model and the published methods using sentence level context

	Model	BLEU 1	BLEU 2	BLEU 3	BLEU 4	METEOR	ROUGE-L
	NQG-RC	42.54	25.33	16.98	11.86	16.28	39.37
	PLQG	45.07	29.58	21.60	16.38	20.25	44.48
SQuAD 73K	BERT-QG	37.49	18.32	10.47	6.10	16.80	41.01
	BERT-SQG	**50.00**	34.54	25.98	20.11	23.88	48.12
	BERT-HLSQG	49.73	**34.60**	**26.13**	**20.33**	23.88	**48.23**
	PLQG	45.69	30.25	22.16	16.85	20.62	44.99
SQuAD 81K	BERT-QG	32.61	14.50	7.70	4.08	14.18	37.94
	BERT-SQG	50.89	35.49	26.87	21.04	24.25	48.66
	BERT-HLSQG	**51.54**	**36.45**	**27.96**	**22.17**	**24.80**	**49.68**

Table 6: Comparison between our model and the published methods using paragraph level context

mans, and the use of reading comprehension tasks also has effective.

6 Conclusion

In this paper, we propose models that generate a question from the input context (sentence or paragraph) and the target answer based on BERT models. Our models are transformer models which can handle long-term dependencies well. To make the generation process sequential, we propose to restructure our model to generate one word at a time, using the encoded task inputs and the previously generated words as inputs to the transformer. The best model outperforms previous RNN-based state-of-the-arts in terms of standard NLG metrics (BLEU, ROUGE, METEOR) and of whether a standard QA model can correctly answer the generated questions. While our model is simple, our model achieves state-of-the-art performance at both sentence-level and paragraph-level input and provides strong baselines for future research.

Acknowledgments

This work is supported in part by the Ministry of Science and Technology, Taiwan, under grant No: 107-2221-E-005-064-MY2.

References

Junyoung Chung, Caglar Gulcehre, KyungHyun Cho, and Yoshua Bengio. 2014. Empirical evaluation of gated recurrent neural networks on sequence modeling. *arXiv preprint arXiv:1412.3555*.

Michael Denkowski and Alon Lavie. 2014. Meteor universal: Language specific translation evaluation for any target language. In *Proceedings of the ninth workshop on statistical machine translation*, pages 376–380.

Jacob Devlin, Ming-Wei Chang, Kenton Lee, and Kristina Toutanova. 2018. Bert: Pre-training of deep bidirectional transformers for language understanding. *arXiv preprint arXiv:1810.04805*.

Xinya Du, Junru Shao, and Claire Cardie. 2017. Learning to ask: Neural question generation for reading comprehension. *arXiv preprint arXiv:1705.00106*.

Nan Duan, Duyu Tang, Peng Chen, and Ming Zhou. 2017. Question generation for question answering. In *Proceedings of the 2017 Conference on Empirical Methods in Natural Language Processing*, pages 866–874.

Michael Heilman and Noah A Smith. 2010. Good question! statistical ranking for question generation. In *Human Language Technologies: The 2010 Annual Conference of the North American Chapter of the Association for Computational Linguistics*, pages 609–617. Association for Computational Linguistics.

Sepp Hochreiter and Jürgen Schmidhuber. 1997. Long short-term memory. *Neural computation*, 9(8):1735–1780.

Igor Labutov, Sumit Basu, and Lucy Vanderwende. 2015. Deep questions without deep understanding. In *Proceedings of the 53rd Annual Meeting of the Association for Computational Linguistics and the 7th International Joint Conference on Natural Language Processing (Volume 1: Long Papers)*, volume 1, pages 889–898.

Chin-Yew Lin. 2004. Rouge: A package for automatic evaluation of summaries. *Text Summarization Branches Out*.

Minh-Thang Luong, Hieu Pham, and Christopher D Manning. 2015. Effective approaches to attention-based neural machine translation. *arXiv preprint arXiv:1508.04025*.

Karen Mazidi and Rodney D Nielsen. 2014. Linguistic considerations in automatic question generation. In *Proceedings of the 52nd Annual Meeting of the Association for Computational Linguistics (Volume 2: Short Papers)*, volume 2, pages 321–326.

Kishore Papineni, Salim Roukos, Todd Ward, and Wei-Jing Zhu. 2002. Bleu: a method for automatic evaluation of machine translation. In *Proceedings of the 40th annual meeting on association for computational linguistics*, pages 311–318. Association for Computational Linguistics.

Alec Radford, Karthik Narasimhan, Tim Salimans, and Ilya Sutskever. 2018. Improving language understanding by generative pre-training. *URL https://s3-us-west-2. amazonaws. com/openai-assets/research-covers/languageunsupervised/language understanding paper. pdf*.

Pranav Rajpurkar, Jian Zhang, Konstantin Lopyrev, and Percy Liang. 2016. Squad: 100,000+ questions for machine comprehension of text. *arXiv preprint arXiv:1606.05250*.

Vasile Rus, Brendan Wyse, Paul Piwek, Mihai Lintean, Svetlana Stoyanchev, and Cristian Moldovan. 2010. The first question generation shared task evaluation challenge.

Shikhar Sharma, Layla El Asri, Hannes Schulz, and Jeremie Zumer. 2017. Relevance of unsupervised metrics in task-oriented dialogue for evaluating natural language generation. *arXiv preprint arXiv:1706.09799*.

Linfeng Song, Zhiguo Wang, and Wael Hamza. 2017. A unified query-based generative model for question generation and question answering. *arXiv preprint arXiv:1709.01058*.

Sandeep Subramanian, Tong Wang, Xingdi Yuan, Saizheng Zhang, Yoshua Bengio, and Adam Trischler. 2017. Neural models for key phrase detection and question generation. *arXiv preprint arXiv:1706.04560*.

Ilya Sutskever, Oriol Vinyals, and Quoc V Le. 2014. Sequence to sequence learning with neural networks. In *Advances in neural information processing systems*, pages 3104–3112.

Duyu Tang, Nan Duan, Tao Qin, Zhao Yan, and Ming Zhou. 2017. Question answering and question generation as dual tasks. *arXiv preprint arXiv:1706.02027*.

Ashish Vaswani, Noam Shazeer, Niki Parmar, Jakob Uszkoreit, Llion Jones, Aidan N Gomez, Łukasz Kaiser, and Illia Polosukhin. 2017. Attention is all you need. In *Advances in neural information processing systems*, pages 5998–6008.

Tong Wang, Xingdi Yuan, and Adam Trischler. 2017. A joint model for question answering and question generation. *arXiv preprint arXiv:1706.01450*.

Xuchen Yao, Gosse Bouma, and Yi Zhang. 2012. Semantics-based question generation and implementation. *Dialogue & Discourse*, 3(2):11–42.

Xingdi Yuan, Tong Wang, Caglar Gulcehre, Alessandro Sordoni, Philip Bachman, Sandeep Subramanian, Saizheng Zhang, and Adam Trischler. 2017. Machine comprehension by text-to-text neural question generation. *arXiv preprint arXiv:1705.02012*.

Yao Zhao, Xiaochuan Ni, Yuanyuan Ding, and Qifa Ke. 2018. Paragraph-level neural question generation with maxout pointer and gated self-attention networks. In *Proceedings of the 2018 Conference on Empirical Methods in Natural Language Processing*, pages 3901–3910.

Qingyu Zhou, Nan Yang, Furu Wei, Chuanqi Tan, Hangbo Bao, and Ming Zhou. 2017. Neural question generation from text: A preliminary study. In *National CCF Conference on Natural Language Processing and Chinese Computing*, pages 662–671. Springer.

Let Me Know What to Ask: Interrogative-Word-Aware Question Generation

Junmo Kang[*]   **Haritz Puerto San Roman**[*]   **Sung-Hyon Myaeng**

School of Computing, KAIST

Daejeon, Republic of Korea

{junmo.kang, haritzpuerto94, myaeng}@kaist.ac.kr

Abstract

Question Generation (QG) is a Natural Language Processing (NLP) task that aids advances in Question Answering (QA) and conversational assistants. Existing models focus on generating a question based on a text and possibly the answer to the generated question. They need to determine the type of interrogative word to be generated while having to pay attention to the grammar and vocabulary of the question. In this work, we propose Interrogative-Word-Aware Question Generation (IWAQG), a pipelined system composed of two modules: an interrogative word classifier and a QG model. The first module predicts the interrogative word that is provided to the second module to create the question. Owing to an increased recall of deciding the interrogative words to be used for the generated questions, the proposed model achieves new state-of-the-art results on the task of QG in SQuAD, improving from 46.58 to 47.69 in BLEU-1, 17.55 to 18.53 in BLEU-4, 21.24 to 22.33 in METEOR, and from 44.53 to 46.94 in ROUGE-L.

1 Introduction

Question Generation (QG) is the task of creating questions about a text in natural language. This is an important task for Question Answering (QA) since it can help create QA datasets. It is also useful for conversational systems like Amazon Alexa. Due to the surge of interests in these systems, QG is also drawing the attention of the research community. One of the reasons for the fast advances in QA capabilities is the creation of large datasets like SQuAD (Rajpurkar et al., 2016) and TriviaQA (Joshi et al., 2017). Since the creation of such datasets is either costly if done manually or prone to error if done automatically, reliable and mean-

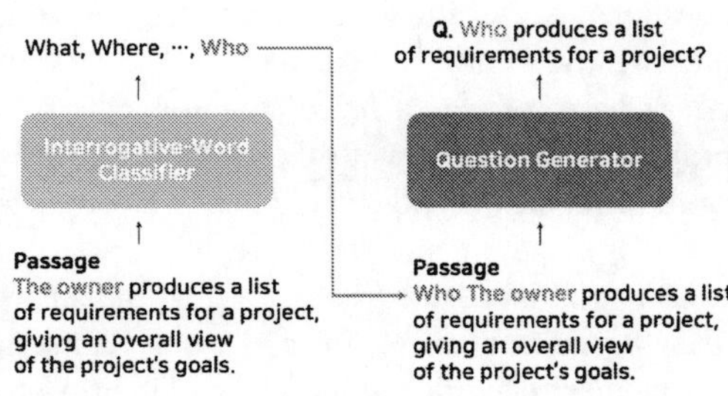

Figure 1: High-level overview of the proposed model.

ingful QG can play a key role in the advances of QA (Lewis et al., 2019).

QG is a difficult task due to the need for understanding of the text to ask about and generating a question that is grammatically correct and semantically adequate according to the given text. This task is considered to have two parts: *what to ask* and *how to ask*. The first one refers to the identification of relevant portions of the text to ask about. This requires machine reading comprehension since the system has to understand the text. The latter refers to the creation of a natural language question that is grammatically correct and semantically precise. Most of the current approaches utilize sequence-to-sequence models, composed of an encoder model that first transforms a passage into a vector and a decoder model that given this vector, generates a question about the passage (Liu et al., 2019; Sun et al., 2018; Zhao et al., 2018; Pan et al., 2019).

There are different settings for QG. Some authors like (Subramanian et al., 2018) assumes that only a passage is given, attempts to find candidate key phrases that represent the core of the questions to be created. Others follow an answer-aware setting, where the input is a passage and the answer to the question to create (Zhao et al., 2018). We assume this setting and consider that the answer is a span of the passage, as in SQuAD. Follow-

---

[*]Equal contribution.

Proceedings of the Second Workshop on Machine Reading for Question Answering, pages 163–171

Hong Kong, China, November 4, 2019. ©2019 Association for Computational Linguistics

ing this approach, the decoder of the sequence-to-sequence model has to learn to generate both the interrogative word (i.e., wh-word) and the rest of the question simultaneously.

The main claim of our work is that separating the two tasks (i.e., interrogative-word classification and question generation) can lead to a better performance. We posit that the interrogative word must be predicted by a well-trained classifier. We consider that selecting the right interrogative word is the key to generate high-quality questions. For example, a question with a wrong interrogative word for the answer "the owner" is: "what produces a list of requirements for a project?". However, with the right interrogative word, *who*, the question would be: "who produces a list of requirements for a project?", which is clear that is more adequate regarding the answer than the first one. According to our claim, the independent classification model can improve the recall of interrogative words of a QG model because 1) the interrogative word classification task is easier to solve than generating the interrogative word along with the full question in the QG model and 2) the QG model would be able to generate the interrogative word easily by using the copy mechanism, which can copy parts of the input of the encoder. With these hypotheses, we propose Interrogative-Word-Aware Question Generation (IWAQG), a pipelined system composed of two modules: an interrogative-word classifier that predicts the interrogative word and a QG model that generates a question conditioned on the predicted interrogative word. Figure 1 shows a high-level overview of our approach.

The proposed model achieves new state-of-the-art results on the task of QG in SQuAD, improving from 46.58 to 47.69 in BLEU-1, 17.55 to 18.53 in BLEU-4, 21.24 to 22.33 in METEOR, and from 44.53 to 46.94 in ROUGE-L.

2 Related Work

Question Generation (QG) problem has been approached in two ways. One is based on heuristics, templates and syntactic rules (Heilman and Smith, 2010; Mazidi and Nielsen, 2014; Labutov et al., 2015). This type of approach requires a heavy human effort, so they do not scale well. The other approach is based on neural networks and it is becoming popular due to the recent progress of deep learning in NLP (Pan et al., 2019). Du et al. (2017)

is the first one to propose an sequence-to-sequence model to tackle the QG problem and outperformed the previous state-of-the-art model using human and automatic evaluations.

Sun et al. (2018) proposed a similar approach to us, an answer-aware sequence-to-sequence model with a special decoding mode in charge of only the interrogative word. However, we propose to predict the interrogative word before the encoding stage, so that the decoder can focus more on the rest of the question rather than on the interrogative word. Besides, they cannot train the interrogative-word classifier using golden labels because it is learned implicitly inside the decoder. Duan et al. (2017) proposed, in a similar way to us, a pipeline approach. First, the authors create a long list of question templates like "who is author of", and "who is wife of". Then, when generating the question, they select first the question template and next, they fill it in. To select the question template, they proposed two approaches. One is a retrieval-based question pattern prediction, and the second one is a generation-based question pattern prediction. The first one has the problem that is computationally expensive when the question pattern size is large, and the second one, although it yields to better results, it is a generative approach and we argue that just modeling the interrogative word prediction as a classification task is easier and can lead to better results. As far as we know, we are the first one to propose an explicit interrogative-word classifier that provides the interrogative word to the question generator.

3 Interrogative-Word-Aware Question Generation

3.1 Problem Statement

Given a passage P, and an answer A, we want to find a question Q, whose answer is A. More formally:

$$\overline{Q} = \arg\max_{Q} Prob(Q|P, A)$$

We assume that P is a paragraph composed of a list of words: $P = \{x_t\}_{t=1}^{M}$, and the answer is a subspan of P.

We model this problem with a pipelined approach. First, given P and A, we predict the interrogative word I_w, and then, we input into QG module P, A, and I_w. The overall architecture of our model is shown in 2.

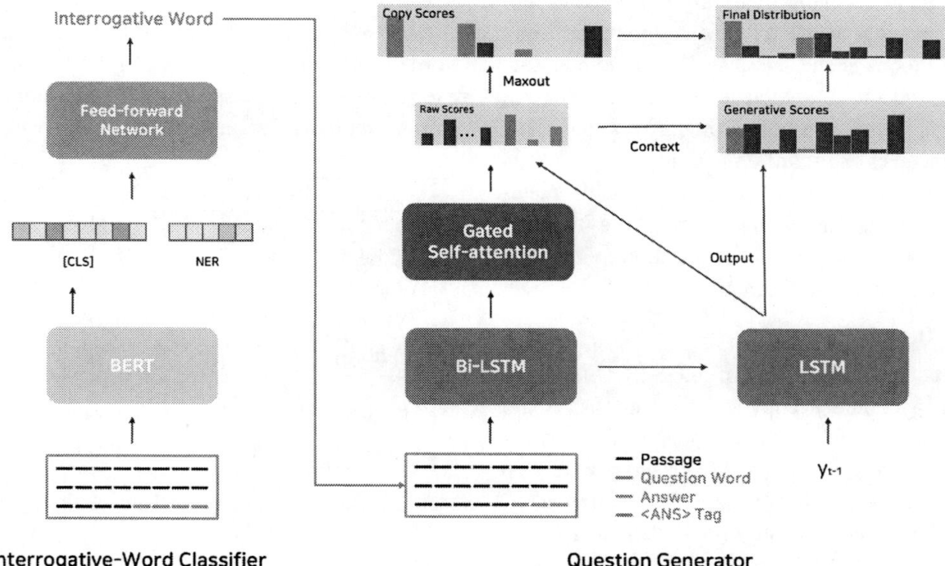

Figure 2: Overall architecture of IWAQG.

3.2 Interrogative-Word Classifier

As discussed in section 5.2, any model can be used to predict interrogative words if its accuracy is high enough. Our interrogative-word classifier is based on BERT, a state-of-the-art model in many NLP tasks that can successfully utilize the context to grasp the semantics of the words inside a sentence (Devlin et al., 2018). We input a passage that contains the answer of the question we want to build and add the special token [ANS] to let BERT knows that the answer span has a special meaning and must be used differently to the rest of the passage. As required by BERT, the first token of the input is the special token [CLS], and the last is [SEP]. This [CLS] token embedding originally was designed for classification tasks. In our case, to classify interrogative words, it learns how to represent the context and the answer information.

On top of BERT, we build a feed-forward network that receives as input the [CLS] token embedding concatenated with a learnable embedding of the entity type of the answer, as shown on the left side of Figure 2. We propose to utilize the entity type of the answer because there is a clear correlation between the answer type of the question and the entity type of the answer. For example, if the interrogative word is *who*, the answer is very likely to have an entity type *person*. Since we are using [CLS] token embedding as a representation of the context and the answer, we consider that using an explicit entity type embedding of the answer could help the system.

3.3 Question Generator

For the QG module, we employ one of the current state-of-the-art QG models (Zhao et al., 2018). This model is a sequence-to-sequence neural network that uses a gated self-attention in the encoder and an attention mechanism with maxout pointer in the decoder.

One way to connect the interrogative-word classifier to the QG model is to use the predicted interrogative word as the first output token of the decoder by default. However, we cannot expect a perfect interrogative-word classifier and also, the first word of the questions is not necessarily an interrogative word. Therefore, in this work, we add the predicted interrogative word to the input of the QG model to let the model decide whether to use it or not. In this way, we can condition the generated question on the predicted interrogative word effectively.

3.3.1 Encoder

The encoder is composed of a Recurrent Neural Network (RNN), a self-attention network, and a feature fusion gate (Gong and Bowman, 2018). The goal of this fusion gate is to combine two intermediate learnable features into the final encoded passage-answer representation. The input of this model is the passage P. It includes the answer and the predicted interrogative word I_w, which is located just before the answer span. The RNN receives the word embedding of the tokens of this text concatenated with a learnable meta-embedding that tags if the token is the interrogative word, the answer of the question to generate or the context of the answer.

3.3.2 Decoder

The decoder is composed of an RNN with an attention layer and a copy mechanism (Gu et al., 2016). The RNN of the decoder at time step t receives its hidden state at the previous time step $t - 1$ and the previously generated output y_{t-1}. At $t = 0$, it receives the last hidden state of the encoder. This model combines the probability of generating a word and the probability of copying that word from the input as shown on the right side of Figure 2. To compute the generative scores, it uses the outputs of the decoder, and the context of the encoder, which is based on the raw attention scores. To compute the copy scores, it uses the outputs of the RNN and the raw attention scores of the encoder. Zhao et al. (2018) observed that the repetition of words in the input sequence tends to create repetitions in the output sequence too. Thus, they proposed a maxout pointer mechanism instead of the regular pointer mechanism (Vinyals et al., 2015). This new pointer mechanism limits the magnitude of the scores of the repeated words to their maximum value. To do that, first, the attention scores are computed over the input sequence and then, the score of a word at time step t is calculated as the maximum of all scores pointing to the same word in the input sequence. The final probability distribution is calculated by applying the softmax function on the concatenation of copy scores and generative scores and summing up the probabilities pointing to the same words.

4 Experiments

In our experiments, we study our proposed system on SQuAD dataset v1.1. (Rajpurkar et al., 2016), prove the validity of our hypothesis and compare it with the current state of the art.

4.1 Dataset

In order to train our interrogative-word classifier, we use the training set of SQuAD v1.1 (Rajpurkar

et al., 2016). This dataset is composed of 87599 instances, however, the number of interrogative words is not balanced as seen in 1. To train the interrogative-word classifier, we downsample the training set to have a balanced dataset.

Class	Original	After Downsampling
What	50385	4000
Which	6111	4000
Where	3731	3731
When	5437	4000
Who	9162	4000
Why	1224	1224
How	9408	4000
Others	9408	4000

Table 1: SQuAD training set statistics. Full training set and downsampled training set.

For a fair comparison with previous models, we train the QG model on the training set of SQuAD and split by half the dev set into dev and test randomly as Zhou et al. (2017).

4.2 Implementation

The interrogative-word classifier is made using the PyTorch implementation of BERT-base-uncased made by HuggingFace[1]. It was trained for three epochs using cross entropy loss as the objective function. The entity types are obtained using spaCy[2]. If spaCy cannot return an entity for a given answer, we label it as None. The dimension of the entity type embedding is 5. The input dimension of the classifier is 773 (768 from BERT base hidden size and 5 from the entity type embedding size) and the output dimension is 8 since we predict the interrogative words: *what, which, where, when, who, why, how,* and *others*. The feed-forward network consists of a single layer. For optimization, we used Adam optimizer with weight decay and learning rate of 5e-5. The QG model is based on the model proposed by (Zhao et al., 2018) with small modifications using PyTorch. The encoder uses a BiLSTM and the decoder uses an LSTM. During training, the QG model uses the golden interrogative words to enforce the decoder to always copy the interrogative word. On the other hand, during inference, it uses

____

[1] https://github.com/huggingface/pytorch-transformers
[2] https://spacy.io/

the interrogative word predictions from the classifier.

4.3 Evaluation

We perform an automatic evaluation using the metrics: BLUE-1, BLUE-2, BLUE-3, BLUE-4 (Papineni et al., 2002), METEOR (Lavie and Denkowski, 2009) and ROUGE-L (Lin, 2004). In addition, we perform a qualitative analysis where we compare the generated questions of the baseline (Zhao et al., 2018), our proposed model, the upper bound performance of our model, and the golden question.

5 Results

5.1 Comparison with Previous Models

Our interrogative-word classifier achieves an accuracy of 73.8% on the test set of SQuAD. Using this model for the pipelined system, we compare the performance of the QG model with respect to the previous state-of-the-art models. Table 2 shows the evaluation results of our model and the current state-of-the-art models, which are briefly described below.

- Zhou et al. (2017) is one of the first authors who proposed a sequence-to-sequence model with attention and copy mechanism. They also proposed the use of POS and NER tags as lexical features for the encoder.

- Zhao et al. (2018) proposed the model in which we based our QG module.

- Kim et al. (2019) proposed QG architecture that treats the passage and the target answer separately.

- Liu et al. (2019) proposed a sequence-to-sequence model with a clue word predictor using a Graph Convolutional Networks to identify if each word in the input passage is a potential clue that should be copied into the generated question.

Our model outperforms all other models in all the metrics. This improvement is consistent, around 2%. This is due to the improvement in the recall of the interrogative words. All these measures are based on the overlap between the golden question and the generated question, so using the right interrogative word, we can improve these scores. In addition, generating the right interrogative word also helps to create better questions since the output of the RNN of the decoder at time step t also depends on the previously generated word.

5.2 Upper Bound Performance of IWAQG

We analyze the upper bound improvement that our QG model can have according to different levels of accuracy of the interrogative-word classifier. In order to do that, instead of using our interrogative-word classifier, we use the golden labels of the test set and generated noise to simulate a classifier with different accuracy levels. Table 3 and Figure 3 show a linear relationship between the accuracy of the classifier and the IWAQG. This demonstrates the effectiveness of our pipelined approach regardless of the interrogative-word classifier model.

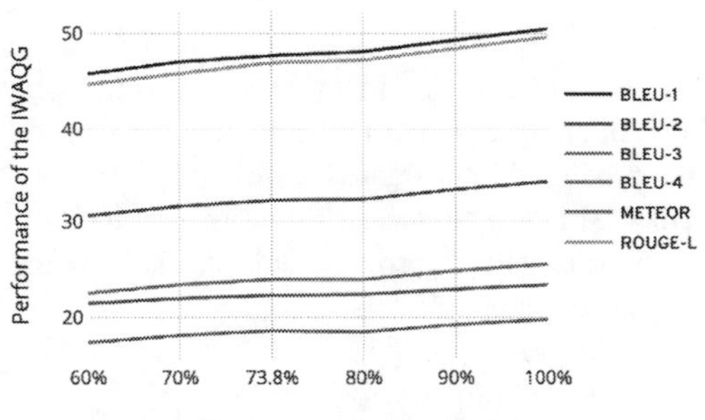

Figure 3: Performance of the QG model with respect to the accuracy of the interrogative-word classifier.

In addition, we analyze the recall of the interrogative words generated by our pipelined system. As shown in the Table 4, the total recall of using only the QG module is 68.29%, while the recall of our proposed system, IWAQG, is 74.10%, an improvement of almost 6%. Furthermore, if we assume a perfect interrogative-word classifier, the recall would be 99.72%, a dramatic improvement which proves the validity of our hypothesis.

5.3 Effectiveness of the input of interrogative words into the QG model

In this section, we show the effectiveness of inserting explicitly the predicted interrogative word into the passage. We argue that this simple way of connecting the two models exploits the characteristics of the copy mechanism successfully. As we can

Model	BLEU-1	BLEU-2	BLEU-3	BLEU-4	METEOR	ROUGE-L
Zhou et al. (2017)	-	-	-	13.29	-	-
Zhao et al. (2018)*	45.69	29.58	22.16	16.85	20.62	44.99
Kim et al. (2019)	-	-	-	16.17	-	-
Liu et al. (2019)	46.58	30.90	22.82	17.55	21.24	44.53
IWAQG	**47.69**	**32.24**	**24.01**	**18.53**	**22.33**	**46.94**

Table 2: Comparison of our model with the baselines. "*" is our QG module.

Accuracy	BLEU-1	BLEU-2	BLEU-3	BLEU-4	METEOR	ROUGE-L
Only QG*	**45.63**	**30.43**	**22.51**	**17.30**	**21.06**	**45.42**
60%	45.80	30.61	22.57	17.30	21.47	44.70
70%	47.05	31.62	23.46	18.05	22.00	45.88
IWAQG (73.8%)	**47.69**	**32.24**	**24.01**	**18.53**	**22.33**	**46.94**
80%	48.11	32.36	24.00	18.42	22.43	47.22
90%	49.33	33.43	24.91	19.20	22.98	48.41
Upper Bound (100%)	**50.51**	**34.28**	**25.60**	**19.75**	**23.45**	**49.65**

Table 3: Performance of the QG model with respect to the accuracy of the interrogative-word classifier. "*" is our implementation of the QG module without our interrogative-word classifier (Zhao et al., 2018).

see in Figure 4, the attention score of the generated interrogative word, *who*, is relatively high for the predicted interrogative word and lower for the other words. This means that it is very likely that the interrogative word inserted into the passage is copied as intended.

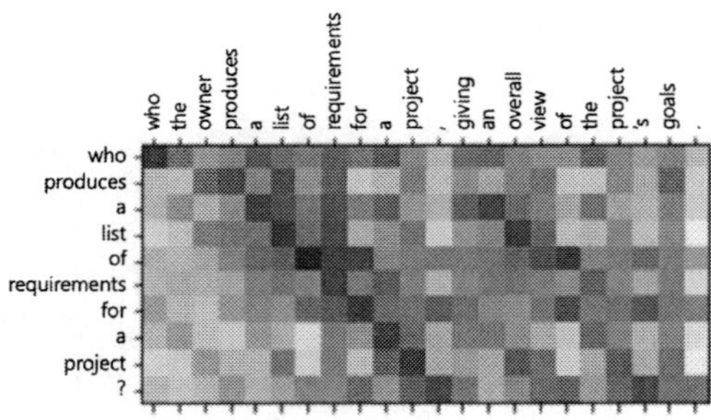

Figure 4: Attention matrix between the generated question (Y-axis) and the given passage (X-axis).

5.4 Qualitative Analysis

In this section, we present a sample of the generated questions of our model, the upper bound model (interrogative-word classifier accuracy is 100%), the baseline (Zhao et al., 2018), and the golden questions to show how our model improves the recall of the interrogative words with respect to the baseline. In general, our model has a better recall of interrogative words than the baseline which leads us to a better quality of questions. However,

since we are still far from a perfect interrogative-word classifier, we also show that questions that our current model cannot generate correctly could be generated well if we had a better classifier.

As we can see in Table 5, in the first three examples the interrogative words generated by the baseline are wrong, while our model is right. In addition, due to the wrong selection of interrogative words, in the second example, the topic of the question generated by the baseline is also wrong. On the other hand, since our model selects the right interrogative word, it can create the right question. Each generated word depends on the previously generated word because of the generative LSTM model, so it is very important to select correctly the first word, i.e. the interrogative word. However, the performance of our proposed interrogative-word classifier is not perfect, if it had a 100% accuracy, then, we could improve the quality of the generated questions like in the last two examples.

5.5 Ablation Study

We tried to combine different features shown in Table 6 for the interrogative-word classifier. In this section, we analyze their impact on the performance of the model.

The first model is only using the [CLS] BERT token embedding (Devlin et al., 2018) that represents the input passage. In this model, the input

Model	What	Which	Where	When	Who	Why	How	Others	Total
Only QG*	82.24%	0.29%	51.90%	60.82%	68.34%	12.66%	60.62%	2.13%	68.29%
IWAQG	87.66%	1.46%	66.24%	49.41%	76.41%	50.63%	70.26%	14.89%	74.10%
Upper Bound	99.87%	99.71%	100.00%	99.71%	99.84%	98.73%	99.67%	89.36%	99.72%

Table 4: Recall of interrogative words of the QG model. "*" is our implementation of the QG module without our interrogative-word classifier (Zhao et al., 2018).

is the passage where the answer appears but, the model does not know where the answer is. The second model is the previous one with the entity type of the answer as an additional feature. The performance of this model is a bit better than the first one but it is not enough to be utilized effectively for our pipeline. In the third model, the input is the passage. This model uses the average of the answer token embeddings generated by BERT along with the [CLS] token embedding. As we can see, the performance noticeably increased, which indicates that answer information is the key to predict the interrogative word needed. In the fourth model, we added the special token [ANS] at the beginning and at the end of the answer span to let BERT knows where the answer is in the passage. So the input to the feed-forward network is only the [CLS] token embedding. This model clearly outperforms the previous one, which shows that BERT can exploit the answer information better if it is tagged with the [ANS] token. The fifth model is the same as the previous one but with the addition of the entity-type embedding of the answer. The combination of the three features (answer, answer entity type, and passage) yields to the best performance.

Classifier	Accuracy
CLS	56.0%
CLS + NER	56.6%
CLS + AE	70.3%
CLS + AT	73.3%
CLS + AT + NER	**73.8%**

Table 6: Ablation Study of our interrogative-word classifier.

In addition, we provide the recall and precision per class for our final interrogative-word classifier (CLS + AT in Table 7). As we can see, the overall recall is high, and it is also higher than just using the QG module (Table 4), which proves our hypothesis that modeling the interrogative-word prediction task as an independent classification problem yields to a higher recall than generating them

with the full question. However, the recall of *which* is very low. This is due to the intrinsic difficulty of predicting this interrogative words. Questions like "what country" and "which country" can be correct depending on the context, but the meaning is very similar. Our model has also problem with *why* due to the lack of training instances for this class. Lastly, the recall of 'when is also low because many questions of this type can be formulated with other interrogative words, e.g.: instead of "When did WWII start?", we can ask "In which year did WWII start?".

Class	Recall	Precision
What	87.7%	76.0%
Which	1.4%	38.0%
Where	65.9%	55.8%
When	49.2%	69.8%
Who	76.9%	66.7%
Why	50.1%	74.1%
How	70.5%	79.0%
Others	10.5%	57.0%

Table 7: Recall and precision of interrogative words of our interrogative-word classifier.

6   Conclusion and Future Work

In this work, we proposed an Interrogative-Word-Aware Question Generation (IWAQG), a pipelined model composed of an interrogative-word classifier and a question generator to tackle the question generation task. First, we predict the interrogative word. Then, the Question Generation (QG) model generates the question using the predicted interrogative word. Thanks to this independent interrogative-word classifier and the copy mechanism of the question generation model, we are able to improve the recall of the interrogative words in the generated questions. This improvement also leads to a better quality of the generated questions. We prove our hypotheses through quantitative and qualitative experiments, showing that our pipelined system outperforms the previous state-of-the-art models. Lastly, we also prove that

id	Only QG*	IWAQG	Upper Bound	Golden	Answer
1	what produces a list of requirements for a project?	who produces a list of requirements for a project?	who produces a list of requirements for a project?	who produces a list of requirements for a project, giving an overall view of the project's goals?	The owner
2	how many tunnels were constructed through newcastle city centre?	what type of tunnels constructed through newcastle city centre?	what type of tunnels constructed through newcastle city centre ?	what type of tunnels are constructed through newcastle 's city center?	deep-level tunnels
3	who received a battering during the siege of newcastle?	what received a battering during the siege of newcastle ?	what received a battering during the siege of newcastle ?	what received a battering during the siege of newcastle?	The church tower
4	what system is newcastle international airport connected to?	what system is newcastle international airport connected to?	how is newcastle international airport connected to ?	how is newport 's airport connected to the city?	via the Metro Light Rail system
5	who was the country most dependent on arab oil?	what country was the most dependent on arab oil?	which country was the most dependent on arab oil?	which country is the most dependent on arab oil?	Japan

Table 5: Qualitative Analysis. Comparison between the baseline, our proposed model, the upper bound of our model, the golden question and the answer of the question. "*" is our implementation of the QG module without our interrogative-word classifier (Zhao et al., 2018).

our methodology is remarkably effective, showing a theoretical upper bound of the potential improvement using a more accurate interrogative-word classifier.

In the future, we would like to improve the interrogative-word classifier, since it would clearly improve the performance of the whole system as we showed. We also expect that the use of the Transformer architecture(Vaswani et al., 2017) could improve the QG model. In addition, we plan to test our approach on other datasets to prove its generalization capability. Finally, an interesting application of this work could be to utilize QG to improve Question Answering systems.

Acknowledgements

This research was supported by Next-Generation Information Computing Development Program through the National Research Foundation of Korea (NRF) funded by the Ministry of Science and ICT (2017M3C4A7065962).

References

Jacob Devlin, Ming-Wei Chang, Kenton Lee, and Kristina Toutanova. 2018. Bert: Pre-training of deep bidirectional transformers for language understanding. *arXiv preprint arXiv:1810.04805*.

Xinya Du, Junru Shao, and Claire Cardie. 2017. Learning to ask: Neural question generation for reading comprehension. In *Association for Computational Linguistics (ACL)*.

Nan Duan, Duyu Tang, Peng Chen, and Ming Zhou. 2017. Question generation for question answering. In *EMNLP*.

Yichen Gong and Samuel Bowman. 2018. Ruminating reader: Reasoning with gated multi-hop attention. In *Proceedings of the Workshop on Machine*

Reading for Question Answering, pages 1–11, Melbourne, Australia. Association for Computational Linguistics.

Jiatao Gu, Zhengdong Lu, Hang Li, and Victor O.K. Li. 2016. Incorporating copying mechanism in sequence-to-sequence learning. *Proceedings of the 54th Annual Meeting of the Association for Computational Linguistics (Volume 1: Long Papers)*.

Michael Heilman and Noah A. Smith. 2010. Good question! statistical ranking for question generation. In *Human Language Technologies: The 2010 Annual Conference of the North American Chapter of the Association for Computational Linguistics*, pages 609–617, Los Angeles, California. Association for Computational Linguistics.

Mandar Joshi, Eunsol Choi, Daniel Weld, and Luke Zettlemoyer. 2017. Triviaqa: A large scale distantly supervised challenge dataset for reading comprehension. *Proceedings of the 55th Annual Meeting of the Association for Computational Linguistics (Volume 1: Long Papers)*.

Yanghoon Kim, Hwanhee Lee, Joongbo Shin, and Kyomin Jung. 2019. Improving neural question generation using answer separation. In *Proceedings of the AAAI Conference on Artificial Intelligence*, volume 33, pages 6602–6609.

Igor Labutov, Sumit Basu, and Lucy Vanderwende. 2015. Deep questions without deep understanding. In *Proceedings of the 53rd Annual Meeting of the Association for Computational Linguistics and the 7th International Joint Conference on Natural Language Processing*, pages 889–898.

Alon Lavie and Michael J. Denkowski. 2009. The meteor metric for automatic evaluation of machine translation. *Machine Translation*, 23(2-3):105–115.

Patrick Lewis, Ludovic Denoyer, and Sebastian Riedel. 2019. Unsupervised question answering by cloze translation. In *Proceedings of the 57th Annual Meeting of the Association for Computational Linguistics (Volume 1: Long Papers)*.

Chin-Yew Lin. 2004. ROUGE: A package for automatic evaluation of summaries. In *Text Summarization Branches Out*, pages 74–81, Barcelona, Spain. Association for Computational Linguistics.

Bang Liu, Mingjun Zhao, Di Niu, Kunfeng Lai, Yancheng He, Haojie Wei, and Yu Xu. 2019. Learning to generate questions by learningwhat not to generate. In *The World Wide Web Conference*, WWW '19, pages 1106–1118, New York, NY, USA. ACM.

Karen Mazidi and Rodney Nielsen. 2014. Linguistic considerations in automatic question generation. In *52nd Annual Meeting of the Association for Computational Linguistics, ACL 2014 - Proceedings of the Conference*, volume 2.

Liangming Pan, Wenqiang Lei, Tat-Seng Chua, and Min-Yen Kan. 2019. Recent advances in neural question generation. *arXiv preprint arXiv:1905.08949*.

Kishore Papineni, Salim Roukos, Todd Ward, and Wei-Jing Zhu. 2002. Bleu: A method for automatic evaluation of machine translation. In *Proceedings of the 40th Annual Meeting on Association for Computational Linguistics*, ACL '02, pages 311–318, Stroudsburg, PA, USA. Association for Computational Linguistics.

Pranav Rajpurkar, Jian Zhang, Konstantin Lopyrev, and Percy Liang. 2016. Squad: 100,000+ questions for machine comprehension of text. *Proceedings of the 2016 Conference on Empirical Methods in Natural Language Processing*.

Sandeep Subramanian, Tong Wang, Xingdi Yuan, Saizheng Zhang, Adam Trischler, and Yoshua Bengio. 2018. Neural models for key phrase extraction and question generation. In *Proceedings of the Workshop on Machine Reading for Question Answering*, pages 78–88.

Xingwu Sun, Jing Liu, Yajuan Lyu, Wei He, Yanjun Ma, and Shi Wang. 2018. Answer-focused and position-aware neural question generation. In *Proceedings of the 2018 Conference on Empirical Methods in Natural Language Processing*, pages 3930–3939, Brussels, Belgium. Association for Computational Linguistics.

Ashish Vaswani, Noam Shazeer, Niki Parmar, Jakob Uszkoreit, Llion Jones, Aidan N Gomez, Łukasz Kaiser, and Illia Polosukhin. 2017. Attention is all you need. In *Advances in neural information processing systems*, pages 5998–6008.

Oriol Vinyals, Meire Fortunato, and Navdeep Jaitly. 2015. Pointer networks. In *Advances in Neural Information Processing Systems*, pages 2692–2700.

Yao Zhao, Xiaochuan Ni, Yuanyuan Ding, and Qifa Ke. 2018. Paragraph-level neural question generation with maxout pointer and gated self-attention networks. In *Proceedings of the 2018 Conference on Empirical Methods in Natural Language Processing*, pages 3901–3910.

Qingyu Zhou, Nan Yang, Furu Wei, Chuanqi Tan, Hangbo Bao, and Ming Zhou. 2017. Neural question generation from text: A preliminary study. In *NLPCC*.

Extractive NarrativeQA with Heuristic Pre-Training

Lea Frermann[*]
School of Computing and Information Systems
The University of Melbourne, Australia
lea.frermann@unimelb.edu.au

Abstract

Although advances in neural architectures for NLP problems and unsupervised pre-training led to impressive improvements on question answering and natural language inference, reasoning over long texts still poses a great challenge. Here, we consider the task of question answering from full narratives (e.g., books or movie scripts), or their summaries, tackling the NarrativeQA challenge (NQA; Kocisky et al. (2018)). We introduce a heuristic *extractive* version of the data set, which allows us to approach the more feasible problem of answer extraction (rather than generation). We develop models for passage retrieval and answer span prediction using this data set. We use pre-trained BERT embeddings for injecting prior knowledge into our system. We show that our setup leads to state of the art performance on *summary-level* QA. On *narrative-level* QA, our model performs competitively on the METEOR metric. We analyze the relative contributions of BERT embeddings and the extractive model setup, and provide a detailed error analysis.

1 Introduction

With recent advances in machine learning techniques, the availability of sizable data sets as well as compute power, natural language processing has made impressive advances across a variety of NLP tasks. A striking gap between machine and human performance, however, remains the ability to *comprehend* text and make *inferences* over multiple pieces of information.

Automatic question answering (QA) from text has received much recent attention as a task designed towards bridging this gap. A variety of question answering tasks and data sets with different levels of difficulty have been proposed recently, ranging from questions paired with short,

relevant documents containing immediately inferable answers (SQUAD; Rajpurkar et al. (2016)), over questions to be answered from sets of documents and requiring to connect facts through multi-step inferences (WikiHop; Welbl et al. (2018)) to naturally occurring questions as Google search queries, paired with sets of Wikipedia pages (Natural Questions; Kwiatkowski et al. (2019)).

Common characteristics of those data sets are (1) sets of (question, document, answer)-tuples in the order of tens- to hundreds of thousands training and test examples; (2) *extractive* answers which can be pin-pointed in the reference documents; (3) the reference documents from which answers are derived are of comparatively short length (e.g., an average of 100 tokens per reference for WikiHop, vs 60K tokens in NQA). All recently proposed successful QA systems were trained in a supervised way, heavily relying on the availability of answer-annotated data sets as described above.

In this work we consider the highly challenging task of narrative question answering (NQA), as introduced by Kocisky et al. (2018). In NQA, a system is presented with a question on the plot of a narrative (a book or a movie) and produces a free-text answer given the raw book or movie script text.[1] The data set was created by pairing each original narrative with a human-created summary, and crowd sourcing a large set of of question-answer pairs based on the summary. Questions are derived from the summaries to deliberately avoid answers to be straightforwardly extractable from the full narrative texts.

Several interesting challenges arise in NQA: (1) although answers are typically localized in the summary, the corresponding answer in the book

---

[*]Work done while the author was employed at Amazon.

[1]Although the NQA data set includes both books and movie scripts, and we will refer collectively to *books* for simplicity.

Proceedings of the Second Workshop on Machine Reading for Question Answering, pages 172–182
Hong Kong, China, November 4, 2019. ©2019 Association for Computational Linguistics

often requires reasoning across paragraphs or even chapters; (2) answers are *abstractive* and as such not necessarily verbatim in the reference documents; (3) the size of the data set, shown in Table 2, is comparatively small making supervised training challenging.

This paper explores the utility of heuristic, but inexpensive training data sets for NQA. We formulate NQA as an extractive question answering task, leveraging the fact that by construction of the data set, answers tend to be extractable locally from the summary text (cf., Table 1 for examples). While ultimately an abstractive system, which synthesizes an answer based on information in the text, is desirable, a conceptually simpler extractive approach can serve as a first and more feasible step towards the goal of answer generation. Our evaluation shows that our extractive system performs competitively on summary- and book-level NQA.

We construct a heuristic extractive NQA data set by leveraging characteristics of the generating process of the original data. Specifically, since question-answer pairs were synthesized based on the summaries, we hypothesize that the answer to a question can typically be found in a single summary sentence (or subspan thereof). We develop heuristics to retrieve those spans.

Based on our heuristic extractive data set we train models for two tasks: (1) Question-based sentence retrieval, which, given a question, selects relevant passages for a question (which may serve as input to a sophisticated QA model); and (2) SQUAD-style answer extraction, where the system learns to point to the beginning and end of the answer in the reference text. We train systems for sentence-retrieval and answer extraction on top of pre-trained BERT embeddings (Devlin et al., 2018), which serve as a source of prior knowledge.

We train question answering systems on summary-question-answer tuples, and evaluate the systems on (1) *summary references* and (2) on the *full book text*. Although summaries are required for training, our model can answer questions on unseen test books with no need for a summary.

While a variety of systems has been proposed for summary-level based NQA, the full NQA challenge of answering questions based on the full, raw narrative text has received less attention. Conceptually similar to our approach of deriving heuristics from question-answer-summary tuples, very recent work proposes heuristic generative

pre-training directly on book passages (Tay et al., 2019). They use pointer-generator networks (See et al., 2017) which allow to produce an answer by sampling from the vocabulary (*generate*) even when the answer cannot be *pointed* to directly in the context passage.

Our system achieves state-of-the-art results on summary-level answer extraction, and performs competitively on the book-level specifically on METEOR, a semantically informed evaluation metric which scores semantic relevance beyond word overlap.

In summary, our contributions are:

1. Augmentation of existing (sparse) data sets with heuristic, inexpensive and supervised training data, with an application to extractive question answering for NQA

2. State-of-the-art results on the summary level NQA benchmark; and competitive results on the book-level NQA task under the METEOR metric, which takes into account synonymy in addition to word overlap

3. An analysis of common errors shedding light on shortcomings in model performance as well as evaluation

2 Task Description

The NarrativeQA data set (Kocisky et al., 2018) provides a testbed for question answering on raw narrative text. It consists of over 1,567 publicly available full-length narrative documents (books or movie scripts), each paired with a human-created plot summary. For each document a set of question-answer pairs was collected by presenting human annotators with the summary. The annotators generated a set of questions (30 per summary) together with free-text answers (two answers per question, from distinct annotators), for a total of 46,765 question-answer pairs. Considering the variety in question types, narrative styles (books and movie scripts of different genres), sheer length of the documents, and the fact that answers need to be synthesized, this data set is too small to train models in a purely in-domain supervised way.

We address the above challenges in two ways. First, we incorporate prior knowledge in the form of pre-trained word embeddings (Devlin et al., 2018). Second, we recognize that by construction of the data set, answers to questions can generally be localized in the summaries, even though

| **Q:** Why does Nora track Mark down? | **G1:** Malcom's suicide |
| | **G2:** to confront him after Malcolm commits suicide |

E: Nobody knows the true identity of Hard Harry [...] until Nora Diniro (Mathis), a fellow student, tracks him down and confronts him the day after a student named **Malcolm commits suicide** after Harry attempts to reason with him.

| **Q:** Why did the couple visit medium Shaun San Dena in Pasadena in 1969? | **G1:** their son has been hearing voices from evil spirits |
| | **G2:** because their son was hearing evil spirits voices |

E: In 1969 Pasadena, California, a couple seeks the aid of the medium Shaun San Dena (Flor de Maria Chahua) saying their **son (Shiloh Selassie) has been hearing evil spirits' voices** after stealing a silver necklace [...]

| **Q:** How was Hadley's Hope Colony destroyed? | **G1:** the nuclear blast from the damaged power plant |
| | **G2:** an explosion |

E: All four escape moments before the station explodes with the colony consumed by the **nuclear blast**.

Table 1: Example questions (Q) from the NarrativeQA data set, with gold free-text answers (G), the most relevant sentence as automatically extracted from the summary (E) and the most relevant sub-sentence level span (boldface).

the free-text answers are typically not found verbatim in the summary. We leverage this property to construct *extractive* data sets for sentence-level and sub-sentence level answer extraction.

3 Data Sets for Extractive NarrativeQA

We derive data sets for supervised query-based sentence retrieval (Section 3.1), and answer span extraction (Section 3.2).

3.1 Sentence Retrieval Data Set

For each question, and its corresponding summary, we proceed as follows. We first obtain a relevance score of each summary sentence s to the input question q: we concatenate the question[2] q with both human-created free text answers $a1, a2$,

$$z = [q; a1; a2], \quad (1)$$

and obtain a relevance score of each summary sentence s w.r.t. z by passing both through the Universal Sentence Encoder (USE)[3] (Cer et al., 2018) and computing the cosine similarity between the encodings,

$$rel_z(s) = cos(\text{USE}(z), \text{USE}(s)). \quad (2)$$

We can thus rank summary sentences by their relevance to input qa-pair z. Our method can serve as

---

[2] We remove the question mark and the first word if it indicates a wh-question.

[3] In preliminary experiments we tested ROUGE-L as an alternative to USD, but found a bias towards mapping to short sentences.

a sentence or passage retrieval system, providing pre-selected input to a more sophisticated question answering model. Assuming the top-ranked sentence to be the true relevant sentence (and all other sentences to be irrelevant), we train supervised retrieval models given a question as input. We further use sentence relevance scores as a basis for heuristic answer-span annotation as described in the following section. Example questions, together with the most relevant retrieved sentence, are shown in Table 1.

3.2 Answer Span Prediction Data Set

Although sentence retrieval is an important step towards question answering from narratives, ultimately a more flexible answer granularity is desirable. Building on sentence-level relevance scores, given a question-answer pair, we extract the most relevant contiguous word sequence to a question q in the summary. We employ the following back-off strategy:

1. if available, return an exact match of one of the reference answers (if both answer candidates match, choose one at random)

2. if unsuccessful: considering the three most question-relevant sentences as determined by the USE (Section 3.1) find the longest substring bounded by content words in the answers

3. if unsuccessful: considering any sentence in the summary, return the longest substring

	train	valid	test
# QA-pairs	32,170	3,461	10,557
# documents	1,102	115	355

Table 2: Statistics of the NarrativeQA data set (Kocisky et al., 2018). We obtain a heuristic answer match for each original question, and maintain the original train/valid/test splits.

bounded by content words in the answers

Our resulting dataset of questions paired with answer-annotated summaries containing the answers, allows us to train SQUAD-style answer prediction systems (cf., Section 5; Rajpurkar et al. (2016); Devlin et al. (2018)). Figure 1 shows examples of automatically annotated answer spans in NarrativeQA summaries (boldfaced).

4 Experiment Setup

We train systems for sentence retrieval and answer span prediction on questions paired with answer-annotated summaries, obtained as described in Sections 3.1 and 3.2. We evaluate sentence retrieval and answer span prediction performance on both summary level data, and full narrative texts. We evaluate our extractive model predictions against the original, *abstractive* NarrativeQA gold answers using the evaluation setup proposed in the original paper to ensure comparability.

Our experiments investigate (a) the effectiveness of a heuristic training data set on sentence retrieval and answer span prediction in the context of NQA; (b) the extent of generalization of systems trained on summary data to book full texts; and (c) the utility of prior knowledge in the form of pre-trained word embeddings. We train sentence retrieval and span prediction models on top of pre-trained BERT embeddings (Devlin et al., 2018).

4.1 BERT

BERT embeddings (Devlin et al., 2018) are contextualized word representations, pre-trained on enormous training corpora on unsupervised word- and sentence prediction tasks using bi-directional transformers. They have been shown to encode substantial semantic and syntactic information, and have been efficiently fine-tuned towards a variety of NLP tasks leading to new state-of-the-art results (Devlin et al., 2018). Here, we fine-tune

	accuracy	precision	recall	f1
$p_{rel} > 0.5$	0.87	0.88	0.83	0.86

Table 3: Results on summary-level sentence-relevance classification on the NQA test set of 25K question-answer pairs. We set the relevance threshold to $p > 0.5$.

BERT embeddings for NQA sentence retrieval and answer span selection, as described below.

5 Sentence Retrieval

Given a question and a reference text, our models retrieve the most relevant sentences from the reference to the query by computing a relevance score for each sentence in the reference.

Approach Given a large set of sentence-question pairs, we train a relevance prediction model on top of BERT embeddings. Following closely the architecture for BERT-based sentence classification, our system takes as input the BERT-embedded query q concatenated with a single BERT-embedded summary sentence s. The two sequences are separated with a special separation token ($[SEP]$) and pre-pended with another special token $[CLS]$ which will be trained to capture the aggregate sentence pair representation,

$$z = [CLS]enc(q)[SEP]enc(s). \qquad (3)$$

The final sentence pair representation $[CLS]$ is passed through a single linear layer followed by a softmax layer to produce an output class (*relevant* vs *irrelevant* in our case). We use queries paired with top-ranked summary sentences (Section 3.1) as positive examples, and queries paired with random sentences from the same summary as negative examples, and minimize cross-entropy classification loss.

For each sentence-query pair we obtain a relevance score $\in [0, 1]$, from which we can derive a summary sentence ranking by query relevance. We retrieve the top n most relevant sentences from this ranking for further predictions.

We use the default parameters from the original BERT implementation.[4]

Summary-level results We apply our model to the book summaries from test data set of NarrativeQA. We evaluate the extent to which truly

<hr>

[4] `https://github.com/google-research/bert`

	p@1	p@5	MRR
BM25f	10.53	51.42	0.276
BERT	13.80	53.02	0.305

Table 4: Fraction of correct answers contained in the top {1 / 5} answer candidates, and MRR of the correct answer in passages retrieved by the BERT-based retrieval method (BERT) or an IR method (BM25f).

relevant sentences (as extracted by our heuristic method) were assigned a relevance probability $p > 0.5$. Results are shown in Table 3, and show that the model detects the most relevant summary sentence for a question accurately across a variety of metrics.

Book-level results We apply our model to the considerably harder task of NQA on full documents, computing a question-specific relevance score for each sentence in the document. Note that we cannot evaluate retrieval scores directly, because we do not have access to a gold standard of relevant book sentences for a given question. Instead, we treat our system as a passage retrieval model given an input question. As an approximation to the quality of the retrieved passages we compute the extent to which the correct answer is found in the N most frequent answer candidates.[5]

We compare our BERT-retrieval with an IR-style retrieval system (BM25f; Zaragoza et al. (2004)) which retrieves text passages of five consecutive sentences based on word token and character mention overlap with the question. From both systems, we retrieve the 20 most relevant predicted sentences, each in a context of ± 2 sentences.

The results are shown in Table 4. We can observe that BERT-based retrieval outperforms the IR retrieval-based model. We will also incorporate this model as a passage-preselection module for book-level answer span prediction in Section 6.

Qualitatively, we observed that most book sentences receive a very low relevance probability in our BERT-based retrieval system, which makes the model amenable for the task of narrowing down the context to few relevant passages. For example, on average across all books, only 1.4% of

[5]We evaluate our system only in the context of *who?* questions with an entity as answer and consider all book entities as candidate answers. We extract character mentions using the BookNLP pipeline (Bamman et al., 2014).

all sentences are predicted as relevant with $p >= 0.8$ and 4.3% with $p >= 0.01\%$.

6 Answer Span Prediction

Given a question and a reference text (summary or full narrative), the task is to predict a contiguous sub-span of arbitrary length in the reference text as the answer to the question.

Approach We fine-tune BERT embeddings for answer extraction, similar to the approach for BERT-based SQUAD question answering in Devlin et al. (2018). Given a query q and a text passage c, we map both to BERT embeddings, and concatenate the embedded representations,

$$z = [CLS]enc(q)[SEP]enc(c). \qquad (4)$$

BERT fine-tuning for answer-span prediction involves training a start-vector representation S and an end-vector representation E. The probability of a word $i \in enc(c)$ being the start of the answer is the dot-product between $enc(c)_i$ and S, softmax-normalized over all words in $enc(c)$; and the probability distribution over end tokens is computed analogously. The probability of a span from word i to word j, s.th. $i < j$, is the sum of its start and end position

$$S \times enc(c)_i + E \times enc(c)_j. \qquad (5)$$

Pointing to the $[CLS]$ token, the model also has the capacity to predict no answer at all. We use the start and end positions of our heuristic answer spans (Section 3.2) as gold training examples, and maximize the sum of log likelihoods of the start and end position as our training objective.

While we use the whole summaries as contexts for summary-based QA, considering full narrative texts is prohibitive. To this end, we leverage the sentence retrieval model from Section 5 to obtain a subset of relevant sentences. In our experiment we retrieve the 100 most likely sentences given a question, each in a context of ± 2 sentences, resulting in contexts of (up to) 500 sentences per question.

Even after this pre-selection, memory constraints prohibit processing of the full contexts, or summary texts. Following Kocisky et al. (2018), we limit context length to a maximum of 384 words, split the original reference documents into multiple such segments, and pass each segment individually as context, and return the most likely

model	BLEU-1	BLEU-4	METEOR	Rouge-L
BiDAF Span Prediction (Kocisky et al., 2018)	33.45	15.69	15.68	36.74
DecaProp (Tay et al., 2018)	42.00	23.42	21.80	44.69
ConZNet (Indurthi et al., 2018)	42.76	22.49	19.24	46.67
BERT SQUAD train	36.22	17.14	23.61	48.58
BERT SQUAD train 31K	40.71	20.60	19.78	45.06
BERT heur	**50.36**	**24.24**	**27.09**	**58.50**

Table 5: Summary-level answer extraction results by previous models and our systems trained on out-of-domain SQUAD data (BERT SQUAD *), and our heuristic data set (BERT heur). All results reported on the NarrativeQA test split.

model	BLEU-1	BLEU-4	METEOR	Rouge-L
BiDAF Span Prediction (Kocisky et al., 2018)	5.68	0.25	3.72	6.22
AS Reader 10 chunks (Kocisky et al., 2018)	**19.09**	1.81	4.29	14.03
AS Reader 20 chunks (Kocisky et al., 2018)	19.06	**2.11**	4.37	14.02
IAL-CL (Tay et al., 2019)[★]	**22.92**	**2.47**	**5.59**	**17.67**
BERT SQUAD train	9.06	1.03	4.29	10.58
BERT SQUAD train 31K	9.23	1.47	3.55	10.29
BERT heur	12.26	2.06	**5.28**	**15.15**

Table 6: Book-level answer extraction results by previous models and our systems trained on out-of-domain SQUAD data (BERT SQUAD *), and our heuristic data set (BERT heur). All results reported on the NarrativeQA test split. [★]: Work developed concurrently with ours; added post acceptance.

span across all passages as an answer. For each test input, we return the most likely non-empty answer candidate returned by the model.

In order to disentangle the contribution of powerful BERT embeddings from the utility of our heuristic training corpus, we also trained an answer extraction model using SQUAD-V2.0 training data (Rajpurkar et al. (2018); BERT SQUAD). We train the models using either the full SQUAD data set, or a random subset of 31,000 training items, comparable in size to our heuristic training data set. On the one hand, this data set is a gold-standard of perfect context-span to answer correspondences. On the other hand, the data stems from a different domain, and thus potentially less informative for the NarrativeQA task.

We evaluate the predicted answers against the human-provided free-text answers using BLEU (Papineni et al., 2002) and METEOR (Banerjee and Lavie, 2005) scores. We report results given (1) summaries as contexts, and (2) the full narrative texts, and compare against previously reported results on the respective tasks.

Summary-level Results Table 5 displays summary-level answer span extraction results for previous models (top), the BERT-based span prediction model trained on SQUAD data (center), and the same model trained on our heuristic extractive NQA corpus (bottom).

BiDAF is a span prediction model, conceptually similar to our own and was used as a baseline method in Kocisky et al. (2018). DecaProp (Tay et al., 2018) is a neural network which, through dense connections between neighboring layers, is designed to distill information from hierarchical passage representations (over words, sentences, and paragraphs). CoZNet (Indurthi et al., 2018) is a neural network architecture designed to 'zoom into' relevant passages of contiguous, long text passages, using co-attention on query and passage and reinforcement learning with answer generation as target. The latter models *generate*, rather than extract, an answer. All models were evaluated against the human free-text answers.

Our model trained on the heuristic data set outperforms all prior work. The model trained on SQUAD data compares poorly against all other models, demonstrating that the prior information from BERT embeddings by themselves do not automatically lead to improvements on NQA. Interestingly, the SQUAD-data trained model perform better with fewer data (31K) compared with the full training data set, suggesting that fitting the model to SQUAD-data prediction decreases its generalization ability to out-of-domain NQA test data. The strong performance with our heuristic training corpus suggests that a heuristic and potentially noisy in-domain data set is of great utility for summary-level answer span extraction.

Note that our model scores higher than the human results reported in (Kocisky et al., 2018), where the automatic evaluation metrics were computed by evaluating one human annotation against the other. By extracting the answer string from the summary, our system is frequently in agreement with at least one human annotator; however, as humans were allowed to provide free-text answers, the two annotations often do not match exactly, resulting in overly pessimistic automatic scores. We discuss shortcomings of automatic evaluation metrics like BLEU in the context of NarrativeQA in more detail in Section 7.

Q1 Who is Mark Hunter?
G   he is a high school student in Phoenix
E   high school student (✓)

Q2 Why do more students tune into Mark's show?
G   Mark talks about what goes on at school and in the community
E   speaks his mind (✓)

Q3 Why do Faulkland and Julia always fight?
G   he thinks she's unfaithful
E   jealous suspicion. He is constantly fretting himself about her fidelity (✓)

Q4 Who was Murphy's ghost?
G   Cooper from the future
E   a poltergeist (✗)

Figure 1: Example questions (Q) with gold (G) and top-ranking model-extracted answer (E) from the book summaries. ✓: correct; ✗: incorrect.

Book-level Results Although a range of prior models have been proposed for summary-level QA, the only prior work that tackles the full NarrativeQA task has been developed concurrently with our work (IAL-CL; Tay et al. (2019)). IAL-CL is a pipelined approach of tfidf/cosine similarity-based passage retrieval pointer-generator networks for question answering model, together with sophisticated block-based alignment (IAL) strategy, trained with curriculum learning (CL). We also compare against the most competitive systems described in the original paper (Kocisky et al., 2018).

All results are shown in Table 6. We compare our own model trained on the heuristic training corpus (bottom), against another span prediction model, Bi-Directional Attention Flow (BiDAF; Seo et al. (2016)), as reported in Kocisky et al. (2018), as well as their most competitive model, an adaptation of the Attention Sum Reader (Kadlec et al., 2016) (AS Reader). AS Reader follows an encoder-decoder architecture with attention, where the decoder is an LSTM sequence decoder which can synthesize an answer (rather than extract). Both prior models are combined with a passage pre-selection method (similar to our own), which is based on tf-idf based cosine similarity of answers (for training sets) and questions for (test sets). Like for the summary-level task, we compare our architecture fine-tuned on quality out-of-domain training data (SQUAD).

Tay et al. (2019) achieve the most competitive results across the board. Our model outperforms the conceptually similar span extraction model (BiDAF). The AS Reader performs similarly to our model, with the ranking depending on the metric used. Our model outperforms previous systems in terms of METEOR score. METEOR includes synonym matching and as such recognizes semantically similar predictions to the gold standard. The error analysis (Section 7), provides a variety of examples which demonstrate that model predictions are indeed often correct, despite having little word overlap with the gold standard. Like in the summary-level evaluation, models trained on our own corpus outperform the SQUAD-based models, suggesting again the utility of training on easily obtainable, inexpensive but heuristic in-domain data.

7 Error Analysis

We inspect a variety of examples on both summary- and narrative level QA to shed light on shortcomings of the model and evaluation. We show qualitative support for our model's discrepancy in METEOR and BLEU performance (Ta-

Q5 What is Tom trying to desperately get working?

G his latest invention

E a photo telephone (✓)

C I 'm trying to make **a photo telephone**. I have the telephone part down Pat, but I can't see anything of the photo image.

Q6 What is Dubuches passion besides painting?

G music

E music (✓)

C his landscapes were at least conscientiously painted, excellent in intention; **but his real passion was music**, a madness for music, a cerebral bonfire which set him on a level with the wildest of the band.

Q7 How does Claude die?

G he hangs himself

E knocked down by a little hand-truck (✗)

C **Claude**, stepping back, **narrowly escaped being knocked down by a little hand-truck** which two big full-bearded fellows brought up

---

Q8 How does Mr. Peters feel about Tom not allowing him access to the patents?

G he gets angry

E embarrassed (✗)

C "Who are these men?" **Tom felt a little embarrassed** over what he had said. "Couldn't he make him pay?" asked Tom.

Q9 What were Owen and George found doing the morning after Brenda died?

G they were laughing and singing

E singing snatches of songs (?)

C George and Owen were **singing snatches of songs** and gibbering like two great apes.

Q10 How long does Jimmy Gator have to live?

G just a few months

E two months (✓)

C [[Jimmy Gator]]: I have about **two months**, I have no time.

Q11 What happened to the doctor who was called to the house after Mortimer's brothers went insane?

G he collapsed at the sight of Brenda's body

E fell into a chair (✓)

C you will recollect that Mortimer Tregennis, in describing the episode of his last visit to his brother's house, remarked that **the doctor on entering the room fell into a chair?**

Q12 How does Linda try to commit suicide?

G by overdosing on Earls prescription medication

E swallows a whole bottle of pills (✓)

C **Linda** takes some pills. Then she takes some more... Then she takes some more... Then **she swallows a whole bottle of pills**... She drinks from a small bottle of vodka

---

Q13 What is ironic about Donnie's teeth being knocked out when he falls from the pole?

G he no longer has to worry about getting braces on his teeth

E Donnie's mouth is full of blood and his teeth (✗)

C he.he . **Donnie's mouth is full of blood and his teeth are broken** ... [[Donnie]]: My teeff ... My teeef .... [[Jim Kurring]]: You 're ok

---

Figure 2: Example questions (Q), gold (G) and extracted (E) answers, and local extraction contexts (C) for NQA on full narrative texts. Correct (✓), incorrect (✗) or undecidable (?) answers.

ble 6), with model predictions frequently *para-phrasing* gold answers. Furthermore, incorrect answer predictions are often still topically relevant to the question, which highlights a need for models that go beyond word co-occurrence based prior knowledge (as obtained through pre-trained embeddings like BERT).

Figure 1 displays example questions with gold and model predicted answers from the summaries as reference documents. Example Q1 shows a case where the correct answer is conceptually simple and easily extractable. In examples Q2 and Q3, answers are complex concepts as indicated by the more verbose human and model-produced answers. Still, the model predictions are correct in both cases. For Example Q4 the model prediction is incorrect, even though the predicted span is clearly semantically related to the question.

We show questions with gold and model answers based on passages from the full narrative in Figure 2. We also include the local context from which the model answer was extracted (the full context is up to 500 sentences long). Examples Q5, Q6, Q10, Q11 and Q12 are predicted correctly. Note that some predicted answers have very little lexical overlap with the gold answer, although the prediction is correct as supported by the context. Example Q7 illustrates a case where the model-predicted answer is wrong, however, the proposed passage refers to a situation which is similar to the correct answer (nearly escaping a potentially deadly situation, rather than real death of the same person). Example Q8 is a wrong prediction, a result of confusing semantic roles of the participants. Example Q9 seems to be correct, however, from the context it is not clear whether the extracted passage indeed refers to *the morning after brenda died*. Example Q13 shows another wrong prediction, however, the extracted context is arguably semantically relevant to the query.

Overall, the error analysis suggests that purely data-driven models tend to overly rely on surface semantic similarity and local contexts. We also find that automatic evaluation scores like BLEU and METEOR, which rely on word overlap, are overly conservative regarding the output of our model. A series of recent papers discussed problems of comparing models on abstractive NLI tasks using automatic metrics as the ones listed above (Novikova et al., 2017; Chaganty et al., 2018). While there is decent agreement between human and automatic judgments on bad model outputs, disagreements tend to be substantial on good outputs. Our analysis provides further support for these observations.

8 Conclusion

Answering questions on the basis of long and comples texts is a major challenge even for the most advanced NLP methods. While the NarrativeQA data set provides an excellent benchmark for this task, it is comparatively small, and not designed for developing *extractive* question answering models, an arguably more straightforward task compared to extractive Q&A. We heuristically constructed an extractive summary-level Q&A data set and showed that it can be used to train accurate sentence- and span-level answer extraction systems from summary text. We also applied our models to full book text and showed that it outperforms IR-based retrieval systems when incorporated in a entity classification network.

On book-level QA, our model achieves competitive METEOR results. Our results and error analysis suggest that pure word overlap-based evaluation methods can lead to misleading results. The model produced answers were often correct despite lacking lexical overlap with the gold answers. Word overlap-based methods like BLEU or METEOR are agnostic of such hits. METEOR, in contrast takes synonymy into account, and our methods outperformed previous systems in this metric. Our observation follows recent published work on evaluating abstractive NLI systems (Chaganty et al., 2018). Concurrently with improving NLI methodology, it is worth investing in the development of evaluation methods that reflect progress faithfully.

We believe that general, prior knowledge is necessary for successful narrative understanding. We incorporated prior knowledge through pre-trained BERT embeddings, and used heuristic but inexpensive data for supervised training. We hope that our approach opens up avenues for more sophisticated data creation methods for future work, including background knowledge and better models of the full stories.

Acknowledgments

Many thanks to Alex Klementiev, Stefanos Angelidis, Roi Blanco, Lluiz Marquez, Diego Marcheggiani and Hugo Zaragoza for helpful feedback.

References

David Bamman, Ted Underwood, and Noah A. Smith. 2014. A Bayesian mixed effects model of literary character. In *Proceedings of the 52nd Annual Meeting of the Association for Computational Linguistics (Volume 1: Long Papers)*, pages 370–379, Baltimore, Maryland. Association for Computational Linguistics.

Satanjeev Banerjee and Alon Lavie. 2005. METEOR: An automatic metric for MT evaluation with improved correlation with human judgments. In *Proceedings of the ACL Workshop on Intrinsic and Extrinsic Evaluation Measures for Machine Translation and/or Summarization*, pages 65–72, Ann Arbor, Michigan. Association for Computational Linguistics.

Daniel Cer, Yinfei Yang, Sheng-yi Kong, Nan Hua, Nicole Limtiaco, Rhomni St John, Noah Constant, Mario Guajardo-Cespedes, Steve Yuan, Chris Tar, et al. 2018. Universal sentence encoder. *arXiv preprint arXiv:1803.11175*.

Arun Chaganty, Stephen Mussmann, and Percy Liang. 2018. The price of debiasing automatic metrics in natural language evalaution. In *Proceedings of the 56th Annual Meeting of the Association for Computational Linguistics (Volume 1: Long Papers)*, pages 643–653, Melbourne, Australia. Association for Computational Linguistics.

Jacob Devlin, Ming-Wei Chang, Kenton Lee, and Kristina Toutanova. 2018. Bert: Pre-training of deep bidirectional transformers for language understanding. *arXiv preprint arXiv:1810.04805*.

Sathish Reddy Indurthi, Seunghak Yu, Seohyun Back, and Heriberto Cuayahuitl. 2018. Cut to the chase: A context zoom-in network for reading comprehension. In *Proceedings of the 2018 Conference on Empirical Methods in Natural Language Processing*, pages 570–575, Brussels, Belgium. Association for Computational Linguistics.

Rudolf Kadlec, Martin Schmid, Ondřej Bajgar, and Jan Kleindienst. 2016. Text understanding with the attention sum reader network. In *Proceedings of the 54th Annual Meeting of the Association for Computational Linguistics (Volume 1: Long Papers)*, pages 908–918, Berlin, Germany. Association for Computational Linguistics.

Tomas Kocisky, Jonathan Schwarz, Phil Blunsom, Chris Dyer, Karl Moritz Hermann, Gabor Melis, and Edward Grefenstette. 2018. The narrativeqa reading comprehension challenge. *Transactions of the Association for Computational Linguistics*, 6:317–328.

Tom Kwiatkowski, Jennimaria Palomaki, Olivia Redfield, Michael Collins, Ankur Parikh, Chris Alberti, Danielle Epstein, Illia Polosukhin, Matthew Kelcey, Jacob Devlin, Kenton Lee, Kristina N. Toutanova, Llion Jones, Ming-Wei Chang, Andrew Dai, Jakob Uszkoreit, Quoc Le, and Slav Petrov. 2019. Natural questions: a benchmark for question answering research. *Transactions of the Association of Computational Linguistics*.

Jekaterina Novikova, Ondřej Dušek, Amanda Cercas Curry, and Verena Rieser. 2017. Why we need new evaluation metrics for NLG. In *Proceedings of the 2017 Conference on Empirical Methods in Natural Language Processing*, pages 2241–2252, Copenhagen, Denmark. Association for Computational Linguistics.

Kishore Papineni, Salim Roukos, Todd Ward, and Wei-Jing Zhu. 2002. Bleu: a method for automatic evaluation of machine translation. In *Proceedings of the 40th Annual Meeting of the Association for Computational Linguistics*, pages 311–318, Philadelphia, Pennsylvania, USA. Association for Computational Linguistics.

Pranav Rajpurkar, Robin Jia, and Percy Liang. 2018. Know what you don't know: Unanswerable questions for SQuAD. In *Proceedings of the 56th Annual Meeting of the Association for Computational Linguistics (Volume 2: Short Papers)*, pages 784–789, Melbourne, Australia. Association for Computational Linguistics.

Pranav Rajpurkar, Jian Zhang, Konstantin Lopyrev, and Percy Liang. 2016. Squad: 100,000+ questions for machine comprehension of text. In *Proceedings of the 2016 Conference on Empirical Methods in Natural Language Processing*, pages 2383–2392, Austin, Texas. Association for Computational Linguistics.

Abigail See, Peter J. Liu, and Christopher D. Manning. 2017. Get to the point: Summarization with pointer-generator networks. In *Proceedings of the 55th Annual Meeting of the Association for Computational Linguistics (Volume 1: Long Papers)*, pages 1073–1083, Vancouver, Canada. Association for Computational Linguistics.

Minjoon Seo, Aniruddha Kembhavi, Ali Farhadi, and Hannaneh Hajishirzi. 2016. Bidirectional attention flow for machine comprehension. *arXiv preprint arXiv:1611.01603*.

Yi Tay, Anh Tuan Luu, Siu Cheung Hui, and Jian Su. 2018. Densely connected attention propagation for reading comprehension. In S. Bengio, H. Wallach, H. Larochelle, K. Grauman, N. Cesa-Bianchi, and R. Garnett, editors, *Advances in Neural Information Processing Systems 31*, pages 4906–4917. Curran Associates, Inc.

Yi Tay, Shuohang Wang, Anh Tuan Luu, Jie Fu, Minh C. Phan, Xingdi Yuan, Jinfeng Rao, Siu Cheung Hui, and Aston Zhang. 2019. Simple and effective curriculum pointer-generator networks for reading comprehension over long narratives. In *Proceedings of the 57th Annual Meeting of the Association for Computational Linguistics*, pages 4922–4931, Florence, Italy. Association for Computational Linguistics.

Johannes Welbl, Pontus Stenetorp, and Sebastian
Riedel. 2018. Constructing datasets for multi-hop
reading comprehension across documents. *Transactions of the Association for Computational Linguistics*, 6:287–302.

Hugo Zaragoza, Nick Craswell, Michael J Taylor,
Suchi Saria, and Stephen E Robertson. 2004. Mi-
crosoft cambridge at trec 13: Web and hard tracks.
In *TREC*, volume 4, pages 1–1.

CLER: Cross-task Learning with Expert Representation to Generalize Reading and Understanding

Takumi Takahashi *

takahashi.takumi@fujixerox.co.jp

Motoki Taniguchi *

motoki.taniguchi@fujixerox.co.jp

Tomoki Taniguchi

Taniguchi.Tomoki@fujixerox.co.jp

Tomoko Ohkuma

Ohkuma.Tomoko@fujixerox.co.jp

Fuji Xerox Co., Ltd.

Abstract

This paper describes our model for the reading comprehension task of the MRQA shared task. We propose CLER, which stands for **C**ross-task **L**earning with **E**xpert **R**epresentation for the generalization of reading and understanding. To generalize its capabilities, the proposed model is composed of three key ideas: multi-task learning, mixture of experts, and ensemble. In-domain datasets are used to train and validate our model, and other out-of-domain datasets are used to validate the generalization of our model's performances. In a submission run result, the proposed model achieved an average F1 score of 66.1 % in the out-of-domain setting, which is a 4.3 percentage point improvement over the official BERT baseline model.

1 Introduction

Reading comprehension (RC) tasks are important to measure machines' capabilities of reading and understanding. Given a question and context, a typical extractive RC task aims to automatically extract an appropriate answer from the given context.

A large number of datasets for RC tasks, which contains various types of context, such as Wikipedia article (Rajpurkar et al., 2016; Yang et al., 2018; Kwiatkowski et al., 2019), newswire (Trischler et al., 2017), and web snipets (Dunn et al., 2017; Joshi et al., 2017), have recently been published. Similarly, many types of RC task, such as multiple passage (Dunn et al., 2017; Joshi et al., 2017), multi-hop reasoning (Yang et al., 2018; Welbl et al., 2018), dialog (Choi et al., 2018; Reddy et al., 2019) and commonsense reasoning (Ostermann et al., 2018; Talmor et al., 2019), are contained in recently published datasets.

Dataset	Size	Context	Question
SQuAD	96K	wikipedia	crowd
NewsQA	78K	newswire	crowd
TriviaQA	69K	snippets	quiz
SearchQA	133K	snippets	quiz
HotpotQA	78K	wikipedia	crowd
NaturalQuestions	116K	wikipedia	crowd
DROP	1,503	wikipedia	crowd
RACE	674	exam	handcraft
BioASQ	1,504	biomedical	handcraft
TextbookQA	1,503	textbook	handcraft
RelationExtraction	2,948	wikipedia	KB
DuoRC	1,501	plot	crowd

Table 1: Characteristics of released datasets for the MRQA shared task. The top part of the table indicates in-domain datasets to train and validate the model, and the bottom part of the table indicates unveiled out-of-domain datasets to validate the generalization of the trained model.

To assess the performance of an RC model on such datasets, basically, we have to train the model on the target domain. This solution requires the same domain dataset as the target domain to appropriately train the model. However, it is difficult to collect the same domain dataset whenever we train a model for an RC task.

To overcome this problem, transfer learning can be applied to create a general model, but there have been few works on this (Chung et al., 2018; Talmor and Berant, 2019; Sun et al., 2019). During training on the source dataset, the model should be generalized to prevent overfitting to the particular domain. In other words, the model should be able to deal with examples on the target domain (i.e., out-of-domain) well.

The MRQA shared task aims to measure generalization capability for RC tasks. The shared task released six-domain datasets (Rajpurkar et al., 2016; Trischler et al., 2017; Joshi et al., 2017; Dunn et al., 2017; Yang et al., 2018; Kwiatkowski et al., 2019) to train and vali-

---

*Authors contributed equally

Proceedings of the Second Workshop on Machine Reading for Question Answering, pages 183–190
Hong Kong, China, November 4, 2019. ©2019 Association for Computational Linguistics

date the model as in-domain settings, and unveiled six out of the twelve test datasets [1] (Dua et al., 2019; Lai et al., 2017; Kembhavi et al., 2017; Levy et al., 2017; Saha et al., 2018) to validate the trained model as out-of-domain settings. The characteristics of released datasets are shown in Table 1. The goal of this competition is to demonstrate high performances on out-of-domain datasets (the bottom part of Table 1 and additionally unseen test datasets) by the trained model which only utilizes in-domain datasets (the top part of Table 1).

In this paper, we propose **CLER**, which stands for **C**ross-task **L**earning with **E**xpert **R**epresentation. CLER is based on BERT (Devlin et al., 2019), which has recently shown great success as a large-scale language model. The proposed model is composed of three concepts; multi-task learning, mixture of experts (MoE), and ensemble.

Our first motivation to employ multi-task learning is inspired by MT-DNN (Liu et al., 2019a). MT-DNN is based on BERT as a shared layer and is trained on four tasks: single-sentence classification, pairwise text similarity, pairwise text classification, and pairwise ranking. In particular, natural language inference (NLI) as a pairwise sentence classification task is related to RC tasks, even in four tasks. Therefore, we train the proposed model for RC and NLI tasks in a multi-task setting.

Our second motivation to employ MoE is inspired by Guo et al. (2018). They demonstrated the effectiveness of the MoE architecture for transfer learning in sentiment analysis and part-of-speech tagging tasks. MoE basically has different neural networks called "experts" and divides a single task into several subtasks so that each subtask is assigned to one expert. Here, we assume that each subtask corresponds to each domain in in-domain settings. Moreover, in MoE, unseen domains (i.e., out-of-domain) are represented as a combination of several domains, such as SQuAD, TriviaQA, and HotpotQA. Therefore, we expect that MoE can deal with examples in any domain well.

Finally, we employ an ensemble to enhance the performance of the proposed model. Because ensemble models have shown superior performances over than single ones (Seo et al., 2016; Devlin et al., 2019), we introduce an ensemble

---

mechanism to improve performance.

The contributions of this paper are as follows:

- We propose a BERT-based model with multi-task learning and mixture of experts called **CLER**.

- We demonstrate that our model has better performances than the official BERT baseline model in both in-domain and out-of-domain settings.

2   Related works

RC models: The state-of-the-art in RC tasks has been rapidly advanced by neural models (Seo et al., 2016; Yu et al., 2018; Devlin et al., 2019). In particular, BERT (Devlin et al., 2019) significantly improves the performance of a wide range of natural language understanding tasks, including RC tasks. BERT is designed to pre-train contextual representations from unlabeled text and fine-tune for downstream tasks. By leveraging large amounts of unlabeled data, BERT can obtain rich contextual representations.

Multi-task learning: Multi-task learning (Caruana, 1997) is a widely used technique in which a model is trained on data from multiple tasks. Multi-task learning provides the model a regularization effect to alleviate overfitting to a specific task, thus enabling universal representations to be learned across tasks. Liu et al. (2019a) proposed the multi-task deep neural network (MT-DNN) based on the BERT model. Similar to the original BERT model, MT-DNN is pre-trained as a language model for learning contextual representations. In the fine-tuning phase, MT-DNN uses multi-task learning instead of training on only a specific task.

Mixture-of-Experts : Guo et al. (2018) introduced the mixture-of-experts (MoE) (Jacobs et al., 1991) approach for unsupervised domain adaptation from multiple sources. MoE is composed of different neural networks, i.e., experts. In the original MoE, a single task is divided into subtasks, and each expert learns to handle a certain subtask. Guo et al. (2018) assumes that different source domains are aligned to different sub-spaces of the target domain.

3   Model

For generalization to RC tasks, we propose CLER, which is based on BERT (Devlin et al., 2019) and

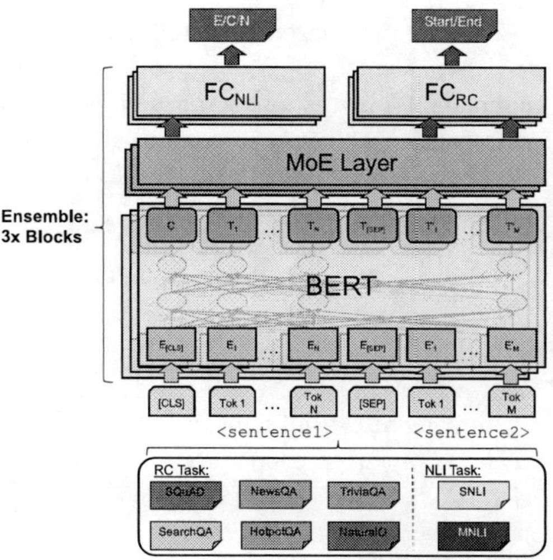

Figure 1: Overview of the proposed model called **CLER**. Each block in the single model consists of BERT, MoE, and FC layers. All three blocks are aggregated into an ensemble CLER. Each block is trained with a different seed.

several other techniques. An overview of the proposed model is illustrated in Figure 1. The core concepts behind our model are multi-task learning, mixture of experts (MoE), and the ensemble mechanism. During training, MoE learns the relationship between domains regardless of the type of task, while the model is trained on RC and NLI tasks simultaneously. We refer to this series of training procedures that trains the model with different experts on two types of task as **cross-task learning**.

3.1 BERT-based model

We utilize BERT$_{\text{LARGE}}$ to encode a pair of sentences composed as `[CLS] <sentence1> [SEP] <sentence2>`. BERT$_{\text{LARGE}}$, which consists of 24 transformer blocks, has already been pre-trained using BooksCorpus (Zhu et al., 2015) and English Wikipedia. For an RC task, the given question and context are set to `<sentence1>` and `<sentence2>`, respectively. Similarly, for an NLI task, the given premise and hypothesis are set to `<sentence1>` and `<sentence2>`, respectively. `[CLS]` and `[SEP]` are special tokens prepared by the default function of BERT. The given pair of sentences is tokenized as a wordpiece token with a sequence length of up to $\tilde{L} = 512$. Finally, all tokens are fed into the MoE layer.

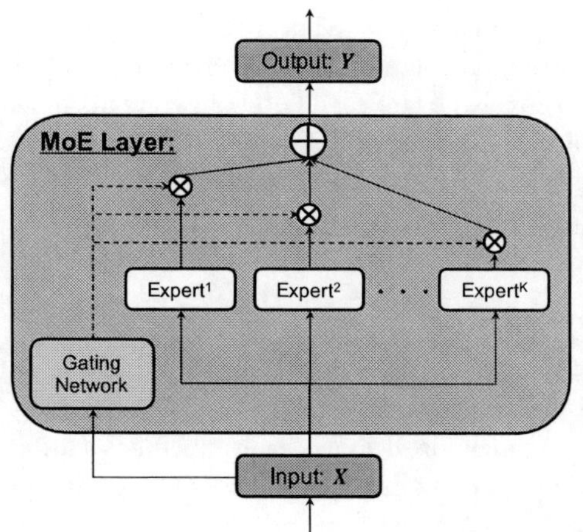

Figure 2: Architecture of the MoE layer. $\otimes$ represents the multiplication operator, and $\oplus$ represents the summation operator.

3.2 Mixture of Experts

To explicitly capture the representation between domains, we introduce a mixture of experts (MoE) (Jacobs et al., 1991) layer after encoding the representation over BERT. As illustrated in Figure 2, MoE is composed of K parts in the expert layer to encode the input representation and a gating network to classify the input representation into the local experts. Intuitively, we expect that each expert is able to interpret domain-wise representations.

Formally, given the representation $\boldsymbol{X} \in \mathbb{R}^{d \times L}$, where d is the number of dimensions of the output of BERT and L indicates the number of input tokens, the equation for output $\boldsymbol{Y} \in \mathbb{R}^{d \times L}$ can be written as follows:

$$\boldsymbol{Y} = \sum_{i=1}^{K} G(\boldsymbol{X})_i E_i(\boldsymbol{X}) \tag{1}$$

where $G(\boldsymbol{x})_i$ indicates the output probability of the i-th expert via the gating network, $E_i(\boldsymbol{x})$ indicates the output representation via the i-th expert layer, and K is the total number of experts.

Here, we give the equations of the gating network $G(\cdot)$ as follows:

$$G(\boldsymbol{X}) = softmax(\boldsymbol{W}_g \boldsymbol{h} + \boldsymbol{b}_g), \tag{2}$$

$$\boldsymbol{h} = [\overrightarrow{h_L}; \overleftarrow{h_1}], \tag{3}$$

$$\overrightarrow{h_L} = \overrightarrow{\text{GRU}}(\boldsymbol{X}), \overleftarrow{h_1} = \overleftarrow{\text{GRU}}(\boldsymbol{X}), \tag{4}$$

where $\overrightarrow{\text{GRU}}$ and $\overleftarrow{\text{GRU}}$ correspond to a forward GRU and backward GRU, respectively, $\boldsymbol{W}_g$ is a weight matrix, $\boldsymbol{b}_g$ is a bias vector, ; indicates a concatenation operator, and L is the number of given tokens. Note that each GRU only outputs the final hidden state vector in Equation 4.

Then, we give the equation of the i-th expert layer $E(\cdot)$ as follows:

$$E_i(\boldsymbol{X}) = \boldsymbol{W}_i \boldsymbol{X} + \boldsymbol{b}_i \tag{5}$$

where $\boldsymbol{W}_i$ is the i-th weight matrix, and $\boldsymbol{b}_i$ is the i-th bias vector.

As mentioned above, each expert has a different weight matrix and bias vector, and the gating network classifies an input example into local experts. Therefore, all experts are able to interpret the input representation with respect to any domain, even if it is unseen in the source domain.

3.3 Multi-task Learning

According to Liu et al. (2019a), multi-task learning is effective for improving models on several NLP tasks. In particular, NLI tasks are related to RC tasks and even several NLP tasks. Therefore, we employ the multi-task learning approach on RC and NLI tasks to enhance the generalization of our model.

BERT-encoder and MoE layer correspond to a shared layer, and both FC_{RC} and FC_{NLI}, which indicate fully connected layers, are task-specific layers in our multi-task setting. For FC_{RC} at prediction time, given the representation of all tokens via the MoE layer, FC_{RC} outputs the span with the maximum logits across all tokens. Specifically, two types of FC_{RC} layer, which are span predictors for the start and end position, estimate the span with the start and end position, individually. For FC_{NLI} at prediction time, given the representation of the first token via the MoE layer corresponding to the [CLS] token, FC_{NLI} outputs a predicted class out of *entailment*, *neutral*, and *contradiction*.

Loss Function

Finally, we minimize the loss function with the multi-task setting as follows:

$$\mathcal{L} = \lambda \mathcal{L}_{RC} + (1 - \lambda)\mathcal{L}_{NLI} + \mathcal{L}_{importance} \tag{6}$$

where $\mathcal{L}_{RC}$ is a negative log likelihood loss for RC tasks, $\mathcal{L}_{NLI}$ is a cross entropy loss for NLI tasks, $\mathcal{L}_{importance}$ is an importance loss, and λ is a weight hyperparameter.

According to Shazeer et al. (2017), we employ an importance loss $\mathcal{L}_{importance}$ to avoid the local minimum. This loss function penalizes some experts that frequently take a large probability via the gating network in any domain. Let us denote the importance loss as follows:

$$\mathcal{L}_{importance} = w_{importance} CV(I(Z))^2 \tag{7}$$

$$I(Z) = \sum_{z \in Z} G(z) \tag{8}$$

where Z represents all samples in the given mini-batch, $CV(\cdot)$ is a coefficient of variation, and $w_{importance}$ is a weight hyperparameter.

3.4 Ensemble

To further enhance the generalization of our model, we employ an ensemble mechanism. The ensemble is only applied at test time.

At test time, we feed examples of RC tasks into our models, which are trained with different seeds, independently. We integrate the logits via FC_{RC} into a merged logit as follows:

$$\boldsymbol{m}_s = \sum_{j=1}^{J} \boldsymbol{o}_s^j, \qquad \boldsymbol{m}_e = \sum_{j=1}^{J} \boldsymbol{o}_e^j, \tag{9}$$

where $\boldsymbol{o}_s^j \in \mathbb{R}^L$ and $\boldsymbol{o}_e^j \in \mathbb{R}^L$ correspond to the logits of our j-th model for the start span and end span, respectively, and J is the total number of models in the ensemble. Finally, we take the span with the maximum logits over $\boldsymbol{m}_s$ and $\boldsymbol{m}_e$.

4 Experiments

4.1 Datasets

Datasets for RC Tasks

MRQA shared task organizers released six types of train and development dataset to train and validate the model for generalization. Additionally, six out of the twelve types of out-of-domain dataset were unveiled to only validate the trained model.

We randomly sampled examples to make the **Test** set from the official train dataset. Note that **Train**, which was created from the official train dataset but is not the same as the official one, does not contain the same examples as in **Test**. The development dataset **Dev.** was used as the same for the official development set. The statistics of the datasets are listed in Table 2.

Dataset	Train	Dev.	Test
SQuAD	76,079	10,507	10,509
NewsQA	69,947	4,212	4,213
TriviaQA	53,902	7,785	7,786
SearchQA	100,403	16,980	16,981
HotpotQA	67,010	5,904	5,902
NaturalQuestions	91,234	12,836	12,837
DROP	-	1,503	-
RACE	-	674	-
BioASQ	-	1,504	-
TextbookQA	-	1,503	-
RelationExtraction	-	2,948	-
DuoRC	-	1,501	-

Table 2: Statistics of datasets for RC tasks. The top part of the table indicates in-domain datasets to train and validate the model, and the bottom part of the table indicates unveiled out-of-domain datasets to only validate the trained model.

Dataset	Train	Dev.
SNLI	550,152	10,000
FICTION	77,348	2,000
GOVERNMENT	77,350	2,000
SLATE	77,306	2,000
TELEPHONE	83,348	2,000
TRAVEL	77,350	2,000

Table 3: Statistics of datasets for NLI tasks. The bottom part of the table indicates genres in the MNLI dataset.

At training time, we took only 75 K examples from each dataset if the total number of examples in the dataset was larger than 75 K. Otherwise, we took all examples in the dataset.

Datasets for NLI Tasks

We introduce two types of NLI datasets to train our model with multi-task learning: SNLI (Bowman et al., 2015) and MultiNLI (Williams et al., 2018). The statistics of these datasets are listed in Table 3.

At training time, the number of examples in each dataset corresponded to the number of examples in the RC task dataset. Specifically, the numbers of examples on SNLI, FICTION, GOVERNMENT, SLATE, TELEPHONE, and TRAVEL were the same as those of SQuAD, NewsQA, TriviaQA, SearchQA, HotpotQA, and NaturalQuestions, respectively.

4.2 Experimental Setup

All of our implementations followed the settings described in this section.

We used the $BERT_{LARGE}$ model for all of our implementations. For the MoE layer, the number of experts was set to 12. We set the hidden unit sizes of the GRU layer and the hidden unit sizes of each expert to 512 and 1024, respectively. For the ensemble model, we trained three models independently with different seeds. The best model of the three evaluated on the out-of-domain development set was chosen as a single model.

We used Adam with a learning rate of 3e-5 to optimize the model. We fine-tuned the model for 2 epochs with a batch size of 24. During training, λ and $w_{importance}$ were set to 0.5 and 0.1, respectively.

Two types of metrics, exact match (EM) and partial match (F1), were employed in the MRQA shared task. EM was 1 if the predicted answer was perfectly the same as the gold answer, but otherwise it was 0. For F1, we calculated the overlap rate between the predicted answer and the gold answer, so the maximum F1 score is 1.

4.3 Comparison Models

As baseline models, we referred to the official evaluation results based on $BERT_{BASE}$ and $BERT_{LARGE}$. To fairly compare the baseline and our models, we prepared $BERT_{STL}$, which is composed of only the BERT-encoder and FC_{RC} with the same settings of our models. $BERT_{STL}$ is different from $BERT_{LARGE}$ with respect to the hyperparameter of scheduling (t_total in Pytorch implementation). Note that $BERT_{STL}$ does not employ both multi-task learning and ensemble.

We also prepared $BERT_{MTL}$ excluding the MoE layer from CLER, as illustrated in Figure 1, to assess the effectiveness of multi-task learning.

4.4 Results

In-domain Evaluation

We evaluated all models on the in-domain development set. Table 4 summarizes the results on the in-domain development set.

CLER with the ensemble setting consistently demonstrated superior performances on all datasets. Also, the multi-task learning ($BERT_{MTL}$) effectively improved overall performances. However, MoE could not improve the performances compared with $BERT_{MTL}$ on in-domain datasets.

Out-of-domain Evaluation

We also evaluated all models on the out-of-domain development set. Table 5 summarizes the evaluation results for out-of-domain.

Model	SQuAD (EM/F1)	NewsQA (EM/F1)	TriviaQA (EM/F1)	SearchQA (EM/F1)	HotpotQA (EM/F1)	NaturalQuestions (EM/F1)	Average (EM/F1)
BERT$_{BASE}$	78.5/86.7	50.8/66.8	65.6/71.6	69.5/76.7	59.8/76.6	65.4/77.4	64.9/76.0
BERT$_{LARGE}$	80.3/88.4	49.6/66.3	68.2/74.7	71.8/79.0	62.4/79.0	67.9/<u>79.8</u>	66.7/77.9
BERT$_{STL}$	83.3/90.5	51.5/67.4	68.5/74.3	72.2/79.3	<u>63.9</u>/<u>80.1</u>	67.7/79.7	67.9/78.5
BERT$_{MTL}$	84.6/91.4	54.1/<u>69.4</u>	<u>70.5</u>/<u>76.0</u>	<u>72.6</u>/<u>79.5</u>	<u>63.9</u>/80.0	67.9/79.5	<u>68.9</u>/<u>79.3</u>
CLER (Single)	<u>84.9</u>/<u>91.6</u>	<u>54.3</u>/<u>69.4</u>	69.9/75.6	72.2/79.0	63.5/79.8	<u>68.1</u>/<u>79.8</u>	68.8/79.2
CLER (Ensemble)	**85.5/91.9**	**55.7/70.5**	**71.8/77.4**	**73.7/80.5**	**64.9/80.9**	**68.5/80.1**	**70.0/80.2**

Table 4: Results on the in-domain development set. Bold values indicate the best scores overall, and the underlined values indicate the best scores for each single model. BERT$_{STL}$ is a single-task learning model composed of only a BERT-encoder and FC$_{RC}$ based on our reimplementation. BERT$_{MTL}$ is a multi-task learning model excluding the MoE layer from CLER.

Model	DROP (EM/F1)	RACE (EM/F1)	BioASQ (EM/F1)	TextbookQA (EM/F1)	RelationExtraction (EM/F1)	DuoRC (EM/F1)	Average (EM/F1)
BERT$_{BASE}$	25.7/34.5	30.4/41.4	47.1/62.7	44.9/53.9	72.6/83.8	44.8/54.6	44.3/55.2
BERT$_{LARGE}$	34.6/43.8	31.3/42.5	51.9/66.8	47.4/55.7	72.7/85.2	46.8/58.0	47.5/58.7
BERT$_{STL}$	38.5/47.3	<u>33.7</u>/45.7	<u>53.9</u>/<u>69.6</u>	48.0/56.6	76.4/86.7	46.9/57.2	49.6/60.5
BERT$_{MTL}$	37.9/46.8	30.4/44.4	53.5/69.0	49.8/58.9	<u>76.9</u>/<u>87.0</u>	51.4/60.8	50.0/61.2
CLER (Single)	<u>39.3</u>/<u>47.8</u>	32.3/**46.6**	52.8/67.4	<u>51.4</u>/<u>61.0</u>	76.3/<u>87.0</u>	<u>51.8</u>/<u>61.8</u>	<u>50.7</u>/<u>62.0</u>
CLER (Ensemble)	**40.2/49.4**	32.2/46.2	52.1/68.4	**52.6/62.3**	**77.3/87.7**	**52.2/61.9**	**51.1/62.7**

Table 5: Results on the out-of-domain development set. Bold values indicate the best scores overall, and the underlined values indicate the best scores for each single model. BERT$_{STL}$ and BERT$_{MTL}$ are the same as in Table 4.

Model	Dev. (EM/F1)	Test (EM/F1)	Average (EM/F1)
BERT$_{BASE}$	43.9/54.6	47.2/62.4	45.5/58.5
BERT$_{LARGE}$	45.7/57.4	50.7/66.1	48.2/61.8
CLER (Ensemble)	**51.1/62.5**	**53.8/69.7**	**52.4/66.1**

Table 6: Results of submission run. BERT$_{BASE}$ and BERT$_{LARGE}$ are the MRQA official baseline models. Bold values indicate the best scores overall.

Overall, the performances of our model were improved compared to the official baseline models. It was observed that CLER drastically improved the EM and F1 scores compared with baseline models on TextbookQA and DuoRC. Moreover, the multi-task learning improved the average F1 score (+0.7 pt) compared with BERT$_{STL}$, and the MoE layer further improved the average F1 score (+0.8 pt) compared with BERT$_{MTL}$. This suggests that both the multi-task learning and MoE are effective for improving generalization for RC tasks.

4.5 Submission Run

For the submission run, 6-domain datasets for the development set and additional 6-domain datasets for the test set were used to evaluate the submitted models. All datasets for the submission run were consistently out-of-domain settings.

Table 6 summarizes the submission run results. CLER drastically improved the performances compared with the official baseline models. We finally ranked 6th of all participants.

5 Conclusion

In this paper, we proposed a BERT-based model with multi-task learning and mixture of experts (MoE) called CLER. To enhance generalization for RC tasks, we introduced an MoE layer and the multi-task learning approach. We also applied an ensemble mechanism to CLER to further improve its performances. Experimental results showed that CLER drastically improved EM and F1 scores compared with the official BERT baseline models.

In future work, we will replace the BERT-encoder with a more powerful model, such as XL-Net (Yang et al., 2019) or RoBERTa (Liu et al., 2019b), which have recently achieved state-of-the-art performances on natural language understanding benchmarks. We will also attempt other training strategies, such as question generation, to automatically augment the training dataset.

Acknowledgement

Computational resource of AI Bridging Cloud Infrastructure (ABCI) provided by National Institute of Advanced Industrial Science and Technology (AIST) was used.

References

Samuel R. Bowman, Gabor Angeli, Christopher Potts, and Christopher D. Manning. 2015. A large annotated corpus for learning natural language inference. In *Proceedings of the 2015 Conference on Empirical Methods in Natural Language Processing*, pages 632–642.

Rich Caruana. 1997. Multitask learning. *Machine Learning*, 28(1):41–75.

Eunsol Choi, He He, Mohit Iyyer, Mark Yatskar, Wentau Yih, Yejin Choi, Percy Liang, and Luke Zettlemoyer. 2018. QuAC: Question answering in context. In *Proceedings of the 2018 Conference on Empirical Methods in Natural Language Processing*, pages 2174–2184.

Yu-An Chung, Hung-Yi Lee, and James Glass. 2018. Supervised and unsupervised transfer learning for question answering. In *Proceedings of the 2018 Conference of the North American Chapter of the Association for Computational Linguistics: Human Language Technologies, Volume 1 (Long Papers)*, pages 1585–1594.

Jacob Devlin, Ming-Wei Chang, Kenton Lee, and Kristina Toutanova. 2019. BERT: Pre-training of deep bidirectional transformers for language understanding. In *Proceedings of the 2019 Conference of the North American Chapter of the Association for Computational Linguistics: Human Language Technologies, Volume 1 (Long and Short Papers)*, pages 4171–4186.

Dheeru Dua, Yizhong Wang, Pradeep Dasigi, Gabriel Stanovsky, Sameer Singh, and Matt Gardner. 2019. DROP: A reading comprehension benchmark requiring discrete reasoning over paragraphs. In *Proceedings of the 2019 Conference of the North American Chapter of the Association for Computational Linguistics: Human Language Technologies, Volume 1 (Long and Short Papers)*, pages 2368–2378.

Matthew Dunn, Levent Sagun, Mike Higgins, V Ugur Guney, Volkan Cirik, and Kyunghyun Cho. 2017. Searchqa: A new q&a dataset augmented with context from a search engine. *arXiv preprint arXiv:1704.05179*.

Jiang Guo, Darsh Shah, and Regina Barzilay. 2018. Multi-source domain adaptation with mixture of experts. In *Proceedings of the 2018 Conference on Empirical Methods in Natural Language Processing*, pages 4694–4703.

Robert A Jacobs, Michael I Jordan, Steven J Nowlan, Geoffrey E Hinton, et al. 1991. Adaptive mixtures of local experts. *Neural computation*, 3(1):79–87.

Mandar Joshi, Eunsol Choi, Daniel Weld, and Luke Zettlemoyer. 2017. TriviaQA: A large scale distantly supervised challenge dataset for reading comprehension. In *Proceedings of the 55th Annual Meeting of the Association for Computational Linguistics*, pages 1601–1611.

Aniruddha Kembhavi, Minjoon Seo, Dustin Schwenk, Jonghyun Choi, Ali Farhadi, and Hannaneh Hajishirzi. 2017. Are you smarter than a sixth grader? textbook question answering for multimodal machine comprehension. In *Proceedings of the IEEE Conference on Computer Vision and Pattern Recognition*, pages 4999–5007.

Tom Kwiatkowski, Jennimaria Palomaki, Olivia Redfield, Michael Collins, Ankur Parikh, Chris Alberti, Danielle Epstein, Illia Polosukhin, Matthew Kelcey, Jacob Devlin, Kenton Lee, Kristina N. Toutanova, Llion Jones, Ming-Wei Chang, Andrew Dai, Jakob Uszkoreit, Quoc Le, and Slav Petrov. 2019. Natural questions: a benchmark for question answering research. *Transactions of the Association of Computational Linguistics*.

Guokun Lai, Qizhe Xie, Hanxiao Liu, Yiming Yang, and Eduard Hovy. 2017. RACE: Large-scale ReAding comprehension dataset from examinations. In *Proceedings of the 2017 Conference on Empirical Methods in Natural Language Processing*, pages 785–794.

Omer Levy, Minjoon Seo, Eunsol Choi, and Luke Zettlemoyer. 2017. Zero-shot relation extraction via reading comprehension. In *Proceedings of the 21st Conference on Computational Natural Language Learning (CoNLL 2017)*, pages 333–342.

Xiaodong Liu, Pengcheng He, Weizhu Chen, and Jianfeng Gao. 2019a. Multi-task deep neural networks for natural language understanding. In *Proceedings of the 57th Annual Meeting of the Association for Computational Linguistics*, pages 4487–4496.

Yinhan Liu, Myle Ott, Naman Goyal, Jingfei Du, Mandar Joshi, Danqi Chen, Omer Levy, Mike Lewis, Luke Zettlemoyer, and Veselin Stoyanov. 2019b. Roberta: A robustly optimized bert pretraining approach. *arXiv preprint arXiv:1907.11692*.

Simon Ostermann, Ashutosh Modi, Michael Roth, Stefan Thater, and Manfred Pinkal. 2018. MCScript: A novel dataset for assessing machine comprehension using script knowledge. In *Proceedings of the Eleventh International Conference on Language Resources and Evaluation (LREC-2018)*.

Pranav Rajpurkar, Jian Zhang, Konstantin Lopyrev, and Percy Liang. 2016. SQuAD: 100,000+ questions for machine comprehension of text. In *Proceedings of the 2016 Conference on Empirical Methods in Natural Language Processing*, pages 2383–2392.

Siva Reddy, Danqi Chen, and Christopher D Manning. 2019. Coqa: A conversational question answering challenge. *Transactions of the Association for Computational Linguistics*, 7:249–266.

Amrita Saha, Rahul Aralikatte, Mitesh M. Khapra, and Karthik Sankaranarayanan. 2018. DuoRC: Towards complex language understanding with paraphrased reading comprehension. In *Proceedings of the 56th Annual Meeting of the Association for Computational Linguistics (Volume 1: Long Papers)*, pages 1683–1693.

Minjoon Seo, Aniruddha Kembhavi, Ali Farhadi, and Hannaneh Hajishirzi. 2016. Bidirectional attention flow for machine comprehension. *arXiv preprint arXiv:1611.01603*.

Noam Shazeer, Azalia Mirhoseini, Krzysztof Maziarz, Andy Davis, Quoc Le, Geoffrey Hinton, and Jeff Dean. 2017. Outrageously large neural networks: The sparsely-gated mixture-of-experts layer. *arXiv preprint arXiv:1701.06538*.

Kai Sun, Dian Yu, Dong Yu, and Claire Cardie. 2019. Improving machine reading comprehension with general reading strategies. In *Proceedings of the 2019 Conference of the North American Chapter of the Association for Computational Linguistics: Human Language Technologies, Volume 1 (Long and Short Papers)*, pages 2633–2643.

Alon Talmor and Jonathan Berant. 2019. MultiQA: An empirical investigation of generalization and transfer in reading comprehension. In *Proceedings of the 57th Annual Meeting of the Association for Computational Linguistics*, pages 4911–4921.

Alon Talmor, Jonathan Herzig, Nicholas Lourie, and Jonathan Berant. 2019. CommonsenseQA: A question answering challenge targeting commonsense knowledge. In *Proceedings of the 2019 Conference of the North American Chapter of the Association for Computational Linguistics: Human Language Technologies, Volume 1 (Long and Short Papers)*, pages 4149–4158.

Adam Trischler, Tong Wang, Xingdi Yuan, Justin Harris, Alessandro Sordoni, Philip Bachman, and Kaheer Suleman. 2017. NewsQA: A machine comprehension dataset. In *Proceedings of the 2nd Workshop on Representation Learning for NLP*, pages 191–200.

Johannes Welbl, Pontus Stenetorp, and Sebastian Riedel. 2018. Constructing datasets for multi-hop reading comprehension across documents. *Transactions of the Association for Computational Linguistics*, 6:287–302.

Adina Williams, Nikita Nangia, and Samuel Bowman. 2018. A broad-coverage challenge corpus for sentence understanding through inference. In *Proceedings of the 2018 Conference of the North American Chapter of the Association for Computational Linguistics: Human Language Technologies, Volume 1 (Long Papers)*, pages 1112–1122.

Zhilin Yang, Zihang Dai, Yiming Yang, Jaime Carbonell, Ruslan Salakhutdinov, and Quoc V Le. 2019. Xlnet: Generalized autoregressive pretraining for language understanding. *arXiv preprint arXiv:1906.08237*.

Zhilin Yang, Peng Qi, Saizheng Zhang, Yoshua Bengio, William Cohen, Ruslan Salakhutdinov, and Christopher D. Manning. 2018. HotpotQA: A dataset for diverse, explainable multi-hop question answering. In *Proceedings of the 2018 Conference on Empirical Methods in Natural Language Processing*, pages 2369–2380.

Adams Wei Yu, David Dohan, Minh-Thang Luong, Rui Zhao, Kai Chen, Mohammad Norouzi, and Quoc V Le. 2018. Qanet: Combining local convolution with global self-attention for reading comprehension. *arXiv preprint arXiv:1804.09541*.

Yukun Zhu, Ryan Kiros, Rich Zemel, Ruslan Salakhutdinov, Raquel Urtasun, Antonio Torralba, and Sanja Fidler. 2015. Aligning books and movies: Towards story-like visual explanations by watching movies and reading books. In *Proceedings of the 2015 IEEE International Conference on Computer Vision (ICCV)*, pages 19–27.

Question Answering Using Hierarchical Attention on Top of BERT Features

Reham Osama, Nagwa El-Makky and Marwan Torki
Computer and Systems Engineering Department
Alexandria University
Alexandria, Egypt
{eng-reham.osama, nagwamakky, mtorki}@alexu.edu.org

Abstract

Machine Comprehension (MC) tests the ability of the machine to answer a question about a given passage. It requires modeling complex interactions between the passage and the question. Recently, attention mechanisms have been successfully extended to machine comprehension. In this work, the question and passage are encoded using BERT language embeddings to better capture the respective representations at a semantic level. Then, attention and fusion are conducted horizontally and vertically across layers at different levels of granularity between question and paragraph. Our experiments were performed on the datasets provided in MRQA shared task 2019 [1]

1 Introduction

The tasks of question answering (QA), especially machine comprehension have gained significant popularity over the past few years within the natural language processing and computer vision communities. Systems trained end-to-end now achieve promising results on a variety of tasks in the text and image domains. The task of machine comprehension is challenging as it requires a comprehensive understanding of natural languages and the ability to do further inference and reasoning. Restricted by the limited volume of the annotated datasets, early studies mainly relied on a pipeline of NLP models to complete this task, such as semantic parsing and linguistic annotation. Benefiting from the availability of large datasets, e.g., SQuAD (Rajpurkar et al., 2016), rapid progress has been made recently.

There have been advancements in multiple variations of the problem including visual question answering and video question answering due to this fast improvement in QA models. Attention mechanisms have a very significant role in increasing

the performance of the models as they focus on the targeted area in the passage. In this paper we use BERT (Devlin et al., 2018) to obtain the representation of both the passage and question, then an encoder layer, which consists of recurrent neural networks, is used to build representations for questions and passages, then a co-attention layer and fusion followed by a self-attention layer are used. Finally, an output layer is added to get the index of both the start and end of the answer.

The rapid progress that has been made recently was mainly due to the availability of SQuAD dataset benchmark. The work in (Wang and Jiang, 2016) was one of the first to investigate the dataset. The authors proposed an end-to-end architecture based on match-LSTM and pointer networks. (Seo et al., 2016) introduced the bi-directional attention flow network which captures the question-document context at different levels of granularity. (Chen et al., 2017) introduced a bilinear match function and a few manual features. (Wang et al., 2017) proposed a gated attention-based recurrent network where self-match attention mechanism is first incorporated. In (Liu et al., 2017) and (Shen et al., 2017) the multi-turn memory networks are designed to simulate multi-step reasoning in machine reading comprehension.

(Devlin et al., 2018) introduced a new language representation model called BERT which is designed to pre-train deep bidirectional representations from unlabeled text by jointly conditioning on both left and right context in all layers. As a result, the pre-trained BERT model can be fine-tuned with just one additional output layer to create state-of-the-art models for a wide range of tasks including question answering. BERT makes use of Transformer (Vaswani et al., 2017) which is an attention mechanism that learns contextual relations between words (or sub-words) in a text. BERT uses the encoder mechanism from the trans-

---

[1] https://mrqa.github.io/shared

Proceedings of the Second Workshop on Machine Reading for Question Answering, pages 191–195
Hong Kong, China, November 4, 2019. ©2019 Association for Computational Linguistics

former as the goal is to generate a language model.

BERT is considered a masked language model as the input to the BERT model is masked before entering the model. 15% of the words in each sequence are replaced with a [MASK] token. The model then attempts to predict the original value of the masked words, based on the context provided by the other, non-masked, words in the sequence.

Due to the great effectiveness of the attention mechanism in the performance of the machine comprehension systems, we used two attention mechanisms in this work similar to (Wang et al., 2018), where in addition to the co-attention mechanism proposed in (Seo et al., 2016) we use a self attention for each of the paragraph and question. So, the output layer can use both of them while predicting the start and end index of the answer.

2 Architecture

The model used in this work was inspired by some of the components of (Devlin et al., 2018) and (Wang et al., 2018).

We chose the components from these 2 models due to their effectiveness in solving the task of machine comprehension. So, we expected that merging the strong components from both models will achieve better results than each one of them individually.

The proposed architecture is explained in this section and is shown in Figure 1.

2.1 Embedding Layer

For the input embeddings we used BERT pre-trained models (Devlin et al., 2018) which is based on word piece level tokenization. BERT has two models that have the same architecture with different sizes

1. BERT base: which consists of 12 transformer blocks, 12 attention heads, and 110 million parameters.

2. BERT large: which consists of 24 transformer blocks, 16 attention heads and, 340 million parameters.

BERT can be used in two ways. The first way is to use it as a model and add a task-specific layer on top of it to produce the required output and train the model with the added layer. The second way is to use it as a pre-trained language model while either keeping the pre-trained weights as they are or training them with your model.

In this work we used a pre-trained BERT base model and we used the second way which is using the pre-trained model with training its weights along with the model. Using BERT large model is expected to yield better results when used. We didn't use it in this work due to the limited resources we had, as the machine we had access to couldn't run BERT large model in its memory.

2.2 Encoder layer

The goal of this layer of the model is to transform the discrete word tokens of question and passage to a sequence of continuous vector representations.

In this layer a Bi-LSTM network is used on top of the embeddings provided by the previous layer to model the temporal interactions between words.

2.3 Co-Attention Layer

This layer is similar to the co-attention layer used in (Seo et al., 2016). Given the question and passage representation from the previous layer, a soft-alignment matrix is built to calculate the shallow semantic similarity between question and passage. We use this similarity matrix to compute the attention between question and passage, which is further used to obtain the attended vectors in passage to question and question to passage direction, respectively.

The output here is a passage-aware question representation and a question-aware passage representation. The question-aware passage representation is calculated using the Passage to Question (P2Q) Attention which signifies the question words that are most relevant to each passage word. The passage-aware question representation is calculated using Question to Passage (Q2P) Attention which signifies the passage words that have the closest similarity to one of the question words and are hence critical for answering the question.

After calculating the aligned passage and question representation, a fusion unit is used to combine the original contextual representations and the corresponding attention vectors for question and passage.

There are several ways to perform the fusion according to (Wang et al., 2018) but one of the simplest ways, which we used here, is a concatenation of the two representations. This fusion is performed due to the importance of the original contextual representations in reflecting the semantics at a more global level.

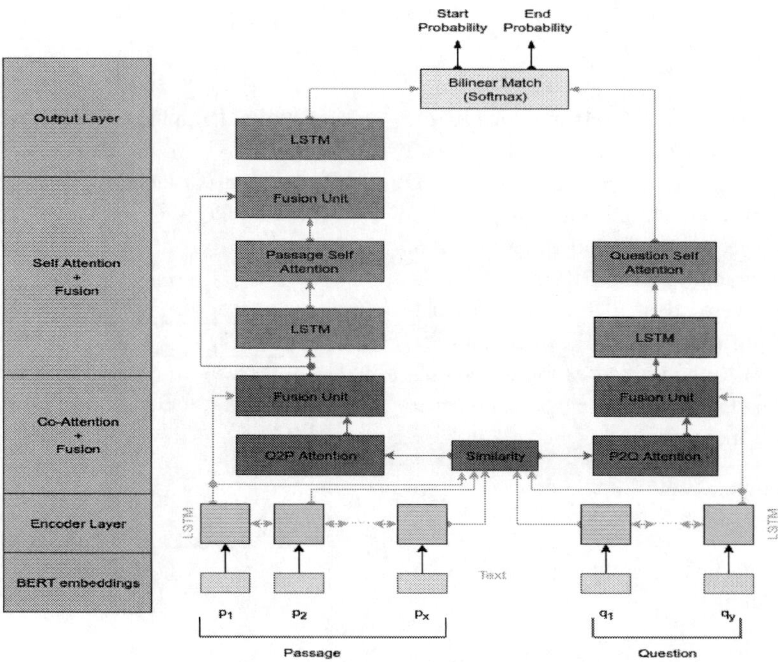

Figure 1: Model Architecture

2.4 Self attention Layer

In this layer, we separately consider the representations of question and passage, and further refine the obtained information from the co-attention layer. Since fusing information among context words allows contextual information to flow close to the correct answer, the self-attention layer is used to further align the question and passage representation against itself, so as to keep the global sequence information in memory.

The idea of benefiting from the advantage of self-alignment attention in addressing the long-distance dependence was taken from (Wang et al., 2017). To allow for more freedom of the aligning process, we used a bilinear self-alignment attention function on the passage representation, introduced in (Wang et al., 2018). We then follow this layer with another fusion unit that combines the question-aware passage representation with the passage self-aware representation. Then, a bidirectional LSTM is used to get the final contextual passage representation.

As for question side we follow the question encoding method used in (Chen et al., 2017) followed by linear transformation to encode the question representation to a single vector. First, another contextual bidirectional LSTM network is applied on top of the fused question representation Then we aggregate the resulting hidden units into one single question vector, with a linear self-alignment.

2.5 Output layer

Instead of predicting the start and end positions based only on the passage representation, a top-level bilinear match function is used to capture the semantic relation between question and passage representation from the previous layer in a matching style.

The top model layer uses a bilinear matching function to capture the interaction between outputs from previous layers and locate the right answer span.

The output layer is application-specific, in Machine comprehension task, we use pointer networks to predict the start and end position of the answer, since it requires the model to find a continuous span of the passage to answer the question.

3 Experiments

In this section, we first present the datasets used for evaluation. Then, we explain the evaluation metrics used, and finally we report the results after training the previously explained model on the given datasets.

3.1 Datasets

In this work we used the datasets provided by the MRQA 2019 shared task. The training datasets included some benchmark datasets such as SQUAD and NewsQA. In-domain and out-of-domain development datasets are also included. Examples of the out-of-domain datasets are DROP and RACE.

The datasets were adapted from several existing datasets from their original formats and settings to conform to the unified extractive setting. The changes made to the datasets to conform to the new settings included:

1. Only a single, length-limited context is provided.

2. There are no unanswerable or non-span answer questions.

3. All questions have at least one accepted answer that is found exactly in the context.

3.2 Evaluation metrics

Performance is measured via two metrics: Exact Match (EM) score and F1 score.

- **Exact Match:** is a binary measure (i.e. true/false) of whether the system output matches the ground truth answer exactly. This is a considered a strict metric.

- **F1:** is a less strict metric. It is the harmonic mean of precision and recall.

A span is judged to be an exact match if it matches the answer string after performing normalization consistent with the SQuAD dataset. Specifically:

1. The text is uncased.

2. All punctuation is stripped.

3. All articles, e.g., a, an ,the, etc. are removed.

4. All consecutive whitespace markers are compressed to just a single normal space ' '.

3.3 Training details

We use the BertAdam optimizer, with a batch size of 6 and initial learning rate of 0.0003. A dropout rate of 0.2 is used for all LSTM layers. We take F1 score as reward with Cross Entropy Loss. We consider the BERT parameters trainable during the training process.

Dataset	EM	F1
BioASQ	43.02	59.09
DROP	24.38	34.78
DuoRC.ParaphraseRC	38.46	49.64
RACE	24.57	37.38
RelationExtraction	67.87	81.30
TextbookQA	32.10	40.49

Table 1: Development Datasets Results.

Dataset	EM	F1
BioProcess	44.29	60.83
ComplexWebQuestions	41.87	51.21
MCTest	54.23	67.88
QAMR	47.97	66.01
QAST	50.91	75.51
TREC	27.72	48.71

Table 2: Test Datasets Results.

The training process takes roughly 48 hours on a single Nvidia Tesla K80 GPU when training the whole provided training and validation datasets, and it takes roughly 12 hours when training a sample size of 20000 instances from each of the training datasets and a sample size of 2000 from each of the development datasets.

3.4 Results

The results of our model on all the development datasets are summarized in Table 1 and the results on all the test datasets are summarized in Table 2. The proposed model achieved an average EM of 41.45 and an average F1 of 56.07 on all datasets (development and test sets combined).

The average F1 obtained for the development datasets is 50.45 and the average F1 obtained for the test datasets is 61.69

3.5 Other Experiments

Other experiments were performed either by changing the model parameters or by trying to add new componenets. But they didn't achieve any increase in the performance of the model.

The following is a brief description of each of the tried experiments

1. Making BERT parameters not trainable.
   In this experiment we tried to use the BERT parameters as they are without retraining, but this caused the performance to decrease significantly.

2. Adding CNN character level embeddings with different number of filters(64, 100).

    In this experiment, the input to the model was the concatenation of BERT embeddings and the character level embeddings. At first we used the settings in (Seo et al., 2016) but we couldn't train the model due to the memory limitations.

    When setting the BERT parameters to be trainable, we cannot add the character level embeddings. However, when we set the parameters to be untrainable ,which causes a big decrease in the performance, the maximum number of filters we could use was 100.

3. Adding L2 regularization.

    We expected that adding the L2 regularizer will make the model achieve better results on the validation and not seen datasets but this didn't happen.

4. Using Adamax optimizer instead of BertAdam.

    In this experiment, we used Adamax optimizer instead of the BertAdam optimizer but we didn't achieve better performance.

4 Conclusion

In this work, we described our machine comprehension system which was designed for the MRQA 2019 Shared Task. When supplied a question and a passage it makes use of the BERT embedding along with the hierarchical attention model which consists of 2 parts, the co-attention and the self-attention, to locate a continuous span of the passage that is the answer to the question.

The proposed model achieved an average EM of 41.45 and an average F1 of 56.07. After analyzing our results, we have identified many ways for improving the system in the future. For instance, other features can be added to the passage and question representations such as adding character embeddings with BERT embeddings. Part-Of-Speech (POS) and Named Entity Recognition (NER) features can also be added in the self-attention layer to better capture the information in the passage.

Another way that will probably increase the performance is using the proposed model with the BERT large model to produce the embeddings instead of BERT base in case there are more resources available.

References

Danqi Chen, Adam Fisch, Jason Weston, and Antoine Bordes. 2017. Reading wikipedia to answer open-domain questions. *arXiv preprint arXiv:1704.00051.*

Jacob Devlin, Ming-Wei Chang, Kenton Lee, and Kristina Toutanova. 2018. Bert: Pre-training of deep bidirectional transformers for language understanding. *arXiv preprint arXiv:1810.04805.*

Rui Liu, Wei Wei, Weiguang Mao, and Maria Chikina. 2017. Phase conductor on multi-layered attentions for machine comprehension. *arXiv preprint arXiv:1710.10504.*

Pranav Rajpurkar, Jian Zhang, Konstantin Lopyrev, and Percy Liang. 2016. Squad: 100,000+ questions for machine comprehension of text. *arXiv preprint arXiv:1606.05250.*

Minjoon Seo, Aniruddha Kembhavi, Ali Farhadi, and Hannaneh Hajishirzi. 2016. Bidirectional attention flow for machine comprehension. *arXiv preprint arXiv:1611.01603.*

Yelong Shen, Po-Sen Huang, Jianfeng Gao, and Weizhu Chen. 2017. Reasonet: Learning to stop reading in machine comprehension. In *Proceedings of the 23rd ACM SIGKDD International Conference on Knowledge Discovery and Data Mining*, pages 1047–1055. ACM.

Ashish Vaswani, Noam Shazeer, Niki Parmar, Jakob Uszkoreit, Llion Jones, Aidan N Gomez, Łukasz Kaiser, and Illia Polosukhin. 2017. Attention is all you need. In *Advances in neural information processing systems*, pages 5998–6008.

Shuohang Wang and Jing Jiang. 2016. Machine comprehension using match-lstm and answer pointer. *arXiv preprint arXiv:1608.07905.*

Wei Wang, Ming Yan, and Chen Wu. 2018. Multi-granularity hierarchical attention fusion networks for reading comprehension and question answering. *arXiv preprint arXiv:1811.11934.*

Wenhui Wang, Nan Yang, Furu Wei, Baobao Chang, and Ming Zhou. 2017. Gated self-matching networks for reading comprehension and question answering. In *Proceedings of the 55th Annual Meeting of the Association for Computational Linguistics (Volume 1: Long Papers)*, pages 189–198.

Domain-agnostic Question-Answering with Adversarial Training

Seanie Lee[*1], **Donggyu Kim**[*1], **Jangwon Park**[*2]

[1]42Maru, Seoul, Korea
[2]Samsung Research, Seoul, Korea
{lsnfamily02,donggyukimc}@42maru.ai, jang1.park@samsung.com

Abstract

Adapting models to new domain without fine-tuning is a challenging problem in deep learning. In this paper, we utilize an adversarial training framework for domain generalization in Question Answering (QA) task. Our model consists of a conventional QA model and a discriminator. The training is performed in the adversarial manner, where the two models constantly compete, so that QA model can learn domain-invariant features. We apply this approach in MRQA Shared Task 2019 and show better performance compared to the baseline model.

1 Introduction

Followed by the success of deep learning in various tasks, it becomes important to build a single model covering various domains without further fine-tuning to out-of-domain distribution. Because for real world application, a model is required to generalize to unseen sources of data.

In case of Question Answering (QA) task which is one of the promising areas in NLP, however, models outperforming human on SQuAD (Rajpurkar et al., 2016) cannot generalize well to other datasets. Models rather overfit to a specific dataset and require additional training on other dataset to adapt to new domain (Yogatama et al., 2019).

Thus, in order to build a domain-agnostic QA model which is capable of handling out-of-domain data, it is necessary for model to learn domain-invariant features rather than specific ones. In this paper, we apply adversarial training framework to train a QA model with domain-agnostic representation. As shown in Figure 1, the model is divided into two components, which are the QA model and the domain discriminator. The discrim-

inator predicts domain label of hidden representation from QA model. During the training, the QA model tries to fool the discriminator so that the hidden representation becomes indistinguishable to the discriminator. Meanwhile the discriminator is trained to identify the domain label correctly. As a result, QA model can learn domain-invariant features. Our framework can be applied to any existing QA model because the architecture of QA model stays unchanged.

We train and validate our method on 12 datasets (6 datasets for training and 6 datasets for validation) which are provided by MRQA Shared Task. Each training dataset is considered different domain for adversarial learning in which QA model learns domain-invariant feature representation by competing with discriminator. Our experimental result shows that the proposed method improves performance compared to baseline.

2 Related Works

Pre-trained Language Model Recently, there have been several applications for using pre-trained language models, such as ELMo (Peters et al., 2018), GPT (Radford et al., 2018), or BERT (Devlin et al., 2018) to transfer the knowledge from pre-training to various downstream NLP tasks.

BERT is pretrained with bidirectional encoder (Vaswani et al., 2017) on large corpora. Unlike other auto-regressive language models (unidirectional or concatenation of forward and backward language model), BERT randomly masks some input tokens and predicts the masked tokens based on its context. The masked language model enables bidirectional representation, which leads to significant improvements on a number of NLP tasks, such as sentence classification, POS tagging or question answering.

---

[*]Equal contribution

Proceedings of the Second Workshop on Machine Reading for Question Answering, pages 196–202
Hong Kong, China, November 4, 2019. ©2019 Association for Computational Linguistics

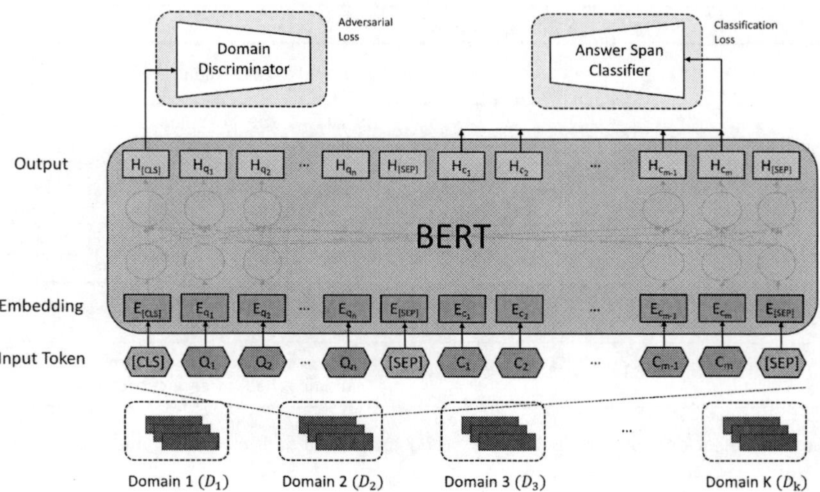

Figure 1: Overall training procedure for learning domain-invariant feature representation. Model learns to predict start and end position in the passage and fool discriminator for domain-invariant representation.

Domain Generalization Even though many deep learning models surpass human-level performance on various task, they perform poorly on out-of-domain dataset. To address this problem, domain adaptation and domain generalization are proposed, making models more robust to out-of-domain data. The difference between domain adaptation and domain generalization is that for domain generalization, data from the target domain is not available during training.

Several methods for domain generalization exist. One of them is to train a model for each in-domain dataset. When testing on out-of-domain, select the most correlated in-domain dataset and use that model for inference (Xu et al., 2014). Other works such as (Ghifary et al., 2015; Muandet et al., 2013), model is trained to learn a domain-invariant feature by using multi-view autoencoders and mean map embedding-based techniques.

Other approaches (Khosla et al., 2012; Li et al., 2017) break down parameters of a model into domain-specific and domain-agnostic components during training with in-domain dataset, and use the domain invariant parameters for predicting data from unseen target domain.

Recently, meta-learning has been proposed for domain generalization. Some methods (Li et al., 2018a; Balaji et al., 2018; Li et al., 2019) leverage meta-learning framework for domain generalization.

Adversarial Training The idea of adversarial training is originally proposed in the field of image generation (Goodfellow et al., 2014), known as Generative Adversarial Network (GAN). GAN is also adopted in text generation (Yu et al., 2017) with policy gradient for bypassing non-differentiable operation. The concept of adversarial training is not limited to the task of generation. It can be extended to text classification (Chen et al., 2016; Liu et al., 2017; Chen and Cardie, 2018), and relation extraction (Wu et al., 2017). Likewise, attempts are made to get language-invariant features with adversarial training (Chen et al., 2016; Zhang et al., 2017).

Adversarial training has been used for domain adaptation or domain generalization as well. In Domain-Adversarial Neural Network (DANN) (Ganin et al., 2016), it has two classifiers: one classifies task-specific class labels, and the other classifies whether the data belong to source or target domain. Recently, One approach (Li et al., 2018b) extends adversarial autoencoder by minimizing maximum mean discrepancy among different domains for domain-invariant feature representation.

3 Proposed Methodology

We assume that there exists domain invariant feature representation such that QA model generalize well to predict answer on unseen out-of-domain. In order to adapt to out-of-domain, adversarial learning procedure is leveraged for learning

Datasets	Samples	Avg.Q.len	Avg.P.len	Source
BioASQ (BA)	1,504	16.4	353.9	Bio-medical literature
DROP (DP)	1,503	12.0	268.4	Wiki + National Football League (NFL) game summaries and history articles
DuoRC (DR)	1,501	9.8	798.9	Wiki + IMDb
RACE (RA)	674	12.4	381.0	English exams for Chinese middle and high school
RelationExtraction (RE)	2,948	11.6	38.0	Wiki (WikiReading dataset)
TextbookQA (TQ)	1,503	12.1	751.0	1k lessons and 26k multi-modal questions, from middle school science curriculum

Table 1: Statistics of out-of-domain validation dataset. $\mathbf{Q}$ and $\mathbf{P}$ stands for question and passage, respectively. Length is calculated based on word-level token.

domain-invariant representation. We present our proposed method in detail in the following sections.

3.1 Problem Definition

We formulate the task as follows: given the K in-domain datasets $\mathcal{D}_i$, consisting of triplets of passage $\mathbf{c}$, question $\mathbf{q}$, and answer $\mathbf{y}$, where $\mathcal{D}_i = \{\mathbf{c}_i^{(k)}, \mathbf{q}_i^{(k)}, \mathbf{y}_i^{(k)}\}_{i=1}^{N_k}$. The model learned from $\{\mathcal{D}_i\}_{i=1}^{K}$ predicts answer $\mathbf{y}_j^l$ from $\mathbf{c}_j^l, \mathbf{q}_j^l$ for each L out-of-domain datasets $\{\mathcal{D}_j\}_{j=1}^{L}$.

3.2 Prediction Model

Our method can be applied to any QA models which learn representation in the joint embedding space of passage and question. In this paper, we use BERT for QA because it is pre-trained on a large corpus and known to be generalized on several different tasks. As for standard QA task, the model is trained to minimize negative log-likelihood of answer $\mathbf{y}$ for all the given in-domain datasets, where $N, \mathbf{y}_{i,s}$, and $\mathbf{y}_{i,e}$ are respectively the total number of in-domain data, the start position and the end position of answer in the passage.

$$\mathcal{L}_{QA} = -\frac{1}{N} \sum_{k=1}^{K} \sum_{i=1}^{N_k} \big[\log P_\theta(\mathbf{y}_{i,s}^{(k)}|\mathbf{x}_i^{(k)}, \mathbf{q}_i^{(k)}) + \log P_\theta(\mathbf{y}_{i,e}^{(k)}|\mathbf{x}_i^{(k)}, \mathbf{q}_i^{(k)}) \big] \quad (1)$$

3.3 Adversarial Training

Minimizing the cross-entropy as in equation (1) does not ensure that the model will generalize on unseen domain. Rather it tends to overfit to certain datasets. Inspired by GAN (Goodfellow et al., 2014), we propose a simple yet effective method to regularize the model such that it learns domain-invariant features.

In the adversarial training procedure, QA model learns to make the discriminator to be uncertain about its prediction. On the other hand, the discriminator is trained to classify the joint embedding of question and passage from QA model into the given K domains. If the QA model can project question and passage into an embedding space where the discriminator cannot tell the difference between embeddings from different K domains, we assume the QA model learns domain-invariant feature representation.

We formulate the adversarial training as follows. A discriminator D is trained to minimize the cross-entropy loss as of equation (2), where l is domain category and $\mathbf{h} \in \mathbb{R}^d$ is the hidden representation of both question and passage. In our experiment, we use [CLS] token representation from BERT for $\mathbf{h}$.

$$\mathcal{L}_D = -\frac{1}{N} \sum_{k=1}^{K} \sum_{i=1}^{N_k} \log P_\phi(l_i^{(k)}|\mathbf{h}_i^{(k)}) \quad (2)$$

For the QA model, it tries to maximize the entropy of $P_\phi(l_i^{(k)}|h_i^{(k)})$. In other words, it minimizes Kullback-Leibler (KL) divergence between uniform distribution over K classes denoted as $\mathcal{U}(l)$ and the discriminator's prediction as in equation (3). Then the final loss for QA model is $\mathcal{L}_{QA} + \lambda \mathcal{L}_{adv}$ where λ is a hyper-parameter for controlling the importance of the adversarial loss. In our experiments, we alternate between optimiz-

Model	BA		DP		DR		RA		RE		TQ		Avg	
	EM	F1	EM	F1	EM	F1	EM	F1	EM	F1	EM	F1	EM	F1
Bert-base	**46.44**	**60.81**	28.31	37.88	42.78	53.32	**28.23**	39.51	**73.33**	**83.89**	44.30	52.03	43.90	54.57
Bert-base-adv	43.35	60.04	**30.51**	**40.01**	**45.97**	**57.89**	26.50	**39.73**	72.67	83.53	**45.62**	**55.67**	**44.10**	**56.15**

Model	BP		CQ		MC		MR		ST		TR		Avg	
	EM	F1	EM	F1	EM	F1	EM	F1	EM	F1	EM	F1	EM	F1
Bert-base	38.36	57.38	47.40	55.29	54.16	66.12	47.83	64.81	**58.64**	**77.02**	36.73	53.96	47.19	62.43
Bert-base-adv	**42.92**	**61.09**	**48.13**	**56.50**	**55.83**	**69.30**	**52.82**	**68.78**	52.73	75.63	**39.08**	**56.79**	**48.59**	**64.68**

Table 2: Model performance on validation and test set. Above is the validation set and below is the test set.

ing QA model and discriminator.

$$\mathcal{L}_{adv} = \frac{1}{N} \sum_{k=1}^{K} \sum_{i=1}^{N_k} KL(\mathcal{U}(l) \parallel P_\phi(l_i^{(k)} | \mathbf{h}_i^{(k)})) \quad (3)$$

4 Experiments and Result

4.1 Dataset

We validate our adversarial model for MRQA Shared Task with 6 different out-of-domain datasets, which are BioASQ (BA) (Tsatsaronis et al., 2012), DROP (DP) (Dua et al., 2019), DuoRC (DR) (Saha et al., 2018), RACE (RA) (Lai et al., 2017), RelationExtraction (RE) (Levy et al., 2017), and TextbookQA (TQ) (Kembhavi et al., 2017). Table 1 shows the statistics and description of these datasets. Each dataset has about 1k samples. However, the number of samples from each dataset varies. Thus, we use stratified sampling in order to make class-balanced stochastic mini-batch having certain amount of samples from all domains. We use maximum sequence length of 64 and 384 for question and passage respectively. But some examples are longer than 384. Therefore each passage is split into several chunks with a window size of 128. We discard samples without answers because all questions are considered to be answerable from given context in MRQA shared task.

Note that the final evaluation shown in the Table 2 is conducted by MRQA organizers with additional 6 out-of-domain undisclosed private test datasets, which are BioProcess (BP) (Scaria et al., 2013), ComplexWebQuestion (CQ) (Talmor and Berant, 2018), MCTest (MC) (Richardson et al., 2013), QAMR (MR) (Michael et al., 2017), QAST (ST) (Jitkrittum et al., 2009) and TREC (TR) (Voorhees, 2001).

4.2 Implementation Details

We implement our model based on the Hugging-Face's open-source BERT implementation[1] in Pytorch (Paszke et al., 2017). The performance of the baseline in our experiment differs from the official baseline of MRQA, which is based on AllenNLP (Gardner et al., 2018). We follow the hyperparameters as BERT for our model. In detail, we use "bert-base-uncased" with a learning rate 3e-5 and a batch size of 64. Additionally, our model requires one more hyperparameter λ, which indicates the importance of adversarial loss as described in the equation (3). We find out that the value of 1e-2 for λ gives the best result in our experiments. The baseline and adversarial model are trained on V100 GPU for about 5 GPU hours. For training, we use 6 in-domain datasets, which are SQuAD, TriviaQA (Joshi et al., 2017), Natural Questions (Kwiatkowski et al., 2019), HotpotQA (Yang et al., 2018), SearchQA (Dunn et al., 2017), and NewsQA (Trischler et al., 2016) provided by MRQA. We select the best performing model on validation set, where models are trained for 1 or 2 epochs. The codes for our model are available at `https://github.com/seanie12/mrqa`.

4.3 Performance Comparison

Table 2 shows the performance evaluation results of models on out-of-domain datasets. In the table, the model trained with our adversarial learning is named with '-adv'. The top of the table is the result of validation datasets while the bottom is the result of test datasets. As shown in the table, overall, the model with adversarial learning has better performance compared to the baseline in terms of both EM and F1 measures.

For validation datasets, the average F1 score of our model is about 1.5 point higher than the baseline. In detail, our model outperforms the baseline

---

[1] https://github.com/huggingface/transformers

in DP, DR, RC, and RA dataset by large margin. But the adversarial learning degrades performance in BA and RE. We can see the same aspect in terms of EM score. Similar to the result of validation datasets, our model shows better performance in terms of EM (Exact Match) and F1 on the most of test datasets except for ST. Overall, our model has superior performance with considerable margin of over 2 point in F1.

5   Discussion

In this section, we discuss some trials that have failed to improve the performance but might be helpful for future works.

5.1   Span Refinement

QA sample consists of a question, a passage, and an answer span. There could exist multiple answer spans because more than one phrase in the passage can be matched with the answer text. For simplicity, only the first occurrence of answer text is used for training in most of the baseline codes. However, considering context and semantic of the given question and answer, a certain phrase in the passage is more likely to be plausible answer span relevant to the question. In order to find the most plausible answer span, a question and sentences in the passage are encoded into fixed-size vectors with universal sentence encoder (Cer et al., 2018). We choose the span in a sentence, which is the most similar to the question in terms of cosine similarity, as golden span. In our experiment, this approach boosts up the performance of some datasets but degrades the performance a lot in the other datasets.

5.2   Meta Learning

We apply meta learning to domain generalization (Li et al., 2018a, 2019; Balaji et al., 2018) to simulate train/test domain shift. For every epoch, one dataset is randomly selected as virtual test domain. As described in (Finn et al., 2017), QA model is trained to maximize meta objective, which leads to improve the performance in train domain, but also in test domain. But this requires to compute Hessian-vector products, which slows down the training. This is even worse for BERT because there are 110M parameters to fine-tune. Moreover, contrary to the previous works, the meta learning for domain generalization does not help improve the performance.

6   Conclusion

We leverage adversarial learning to learn domain-invariant features. In our experiments, the proposed method consistently improves the performance of baseline and it is applicable to any QA model. In future work, we will try adversarial learning for pre-training model with diverse set of domains.

Acknowledgments

We would like to thank Seonghan Ryu, Donghyeon Lee and Nicolas Remond for their valuable feedback, as well as the anonymous reviewers for their insightful comments.

References

Yogesh Balaji, Swami Sankaranarayanan, and Rama Chellappa. 2018. Metareg: Towards domain generalization using meta-regularization. In *Advances in Neural Information Processing Systems*, pages 998–1008.

Daniel Cer, Yinfei Yang, Sheng-yi Kong, Nan Hua, Nicole Limtiaco, Rhomni St John, Noah Constant, Mario Guajardo-Cespedes, Steve Yuan, Chris Tar, et al. 2018. Universal sentence encoder. *arXiv preprint arXiv:1803.11175*.

Xilun Chen, Ben Athiwaratkun, Yu Sun, Kilian Q. Weinberger, and Claire Cardie. 2016. Adversarial deep averaging networks for cross-lingual sentiment classification. *CoRR*, abs/1606.01614.

Xilun Chen and Claire Cardie. 2018. Multinomial adversarial networks for multi-domain text classification. In *Proceedings of the 2018 Conference of the North American Chapter of the Association for Computational Linguistics: Human Language Technologies, Volume 1 (Long Papers)*, pages 1226–1240, New Orleans, Louisiana. Association for Computational Linguistics.

Jacob Devlin, Ming-Wei Chang, Kenton Lee, and Kristina Toutanova. 2018. Bert: Pre-training of deep bidirectional transformers for language understanding. *arXiv preprint arXiv:1810.04805*.

Dheeru Dua, Yizhong Wang, Pradeep Dasigi, Gabriel Stanovsky, Sameer Singh, and Matt Gardner. 2019. Drop: A reading comprehension benchmark requiring discrete reasoning over paragraphs. *arXiv preprint arXiv:1903.00161*.

Matthew Dunn, Levent Sagun, Mike Higgins, V Ugur Guney, Volkan Cirik, and Kyunghyun Cho. 2017. Searchqa: A new q&a dataset augmented with context from a search engine. *arXiv preprint arXiv:1704.05179*.

Chelsea Finn, Pieter Abbeel, and Sergey Levine. 2017. Model-agnostic meta-learning for fast adaptation of deep networks. In *Proceedings of the 34th International Conference on Machine Learning-Volume 70*, pages 1126–1135. JMLR. org.

Yaroslav Ganin, Evgeniya Ustinova, Hana Ajakan, Pascal Germain, Hugo Larochelle, François Laviolette, Mario Marchand, and Victor Lempitsky. 2016. Domain-adversarial training of neural networks. *J. Mach. Learn. Res.*, 17(1):2096–2030.

Matt Gardner, Joel Grus, Mark Neumann, Oyvind Tafjord, Pradeep Dasigi, Nelson F. Liu, Matthew E. Peters, Michael Schmitz, and Luke Zettlemoyer. 2018. Allennlp: A deep semantic natural language processing platform. *arXiv preprint arXiv:1803.07640*.

Muhammad Ghifary, W Bastiaan Kleijn, Mengjie Zhang, and David Balduzzi. 2015. Domain generalization for object recognition with multi-task autoencoders. In *Proceedings of the IEEE international conference on computer vision*, pages 2551–2559.

Ian Goodfellow, Jean Pouget-Abadie, Mehdi Mirza, Bing Xu, David Warde-Farley, Sherjil Ozair, Aaron Courville, and Yoshua Bengio. 2014. Generative adversarial nets. In *Advances in neural information processing systems*, pages 2672–2680.

Wittawat Jitkrittum, Choochart Haruechaiyasak, and Thanaruk Theeramunkong. 2009. QAST: Question answering system for ThaiWikipedia. In *Proceedings of the 2009 Workshop on Knowledge and Reasoning for Answering Questions (KRAQ 2009)*, pages 11–14, Suntec, Singapore. Association for Computational Linguistics.

Mandar Joshi, Eunsol Choi, Daniel S Weld, and Luke Zettlemoyer. 2017. Triviaqa: A large scale distantly supervised challenge dataset for reading comprehension. *arXiv preprint arXiv:1705.03551*.

Aniruddha Kembhavi, Minjoon Seo, Dustin Schwenk, Jonghyun Choi, Ali Farhadi, and Hannaneh Hajishirzi. 2017. Are you smarter than a sixth grader? textbook question answering for multimodal machine comprehension. In *Proceedings of the IEEE Conference on Computer Vision and Pattern Recognition*, pages 4999–5007.

Aditya Khosla, Tinghui Zhou, Tomasz Malisiewicz, Alexei A Efros, and Antonio Torralba. 2012. Undoing the damage of dataset bias. In *European Conference on Computer Vision*, pages 158–171. Springer.

Tom Kwiatkowski, Jennimaria Palomaki, Olivia Redfield, Michael Collins, Ankur Parikh, Chris Alberti, Danielle Epstein, Illia Polosukhin, Jacob Devlin, Kenton Lee, et al. 2019. Natural questions: a benchmark for question answering research. *Transactions of the Association for Computational Linguistics*, 7:453–466.

Guokun Lai, Qizhe Xie, Hanxiao Liu, Yiming Yang, and Eduard Hovy. 2017. Race: Large-scale reading comprehension dataset from examinations. *arXiv preprint arXiv:1704.04683*.

Omer Levy, Minjoon Seo, Eunsol Choi, and Luke Zettlemoyer. 2017. Zero-shot relation extraction via reading comprehension. *arXiv preprint arXiv:1706.04115*.

Da Li, Yongxin Yang, Yi-Zhe Song, and Timothy M Hospedales. 2017. Deeper, broader and artier domain generalization. In *Proceedings of the IEEE International Conference on Computer Vision*, pages 5542–5550.

Da Li, Yongxin Yang, Yi-Zhe Song, and Timothy M Hospedales. 2018a. Learning to generalize: Metalearning for domain generalization. In *Thirty-Second AAAI Conference on Artificial Intelligence*.

Haoliang Li, Sinno Jialin Pan, Shiqi Wang, and Alex C. Kot. 2018b. Domain generalization with adversarial feature learning. In *The IEEE Conference on Computer Vision and Pattern Recognition (CVPR)*.

Yiying Li, Yongxin Yang, Wei Zhou, and Timothy M Hospedales. 2019. Feature-critic networks for heterogeneous domain generalization. *arXiv preprint arXiv:1901.11448*.

Pengfei Liu, Xipeng Qiu, and Xuanjing Huang. 2017. Adversarial multi-task learning for text classification. *CoRR*, abs/1704.05742.

Julian Michael, Gabriel Stanovsky, Luheng He, Ido Dagan, and Luke Zettlemoyer. 2017. Crowdsourcing question-answer meaning representations. *arXiv preprint arXiv:1711.05885*.

Krikamol Muandet, David Balduzzi, and Bernhard Schölkopf. 2013. Domain generalization via invariant feature representation. In *International Conference on Machine Learning*, pages 10–18.

Adam Paszke, Sam Gross, Soumith Chintala, Gregory Chanan, Edward Yang, Zachary DeVito, Zeming Lin, Alban Desmaison, Luca Antiga, and Adam Lerer. 2017. Automatic differentiation in pytorch.

Matthew E Peters, Mark Neumann, Mohit Iyyer, Matt Gardner, Christopher Clark, Kenton Lee, and Luke Zettlemoyer. 2018. Deep contextualized word representations. *arXiv preprint arXiv:1802.05365*.

Alec Radford, Karthik Narasimhan, Tim Salimans, and Ilya Sutskever. 2018. Improving language understanding by generative pre-training. *URL https://s3-us-west-2.amazonaws.com/openai-assets/researchcovers/languageunsupervised/language understanding paper.pdf*.

Pranav Rajpurkar, Jian Zhang, Konstantin Lopyrev, and Percy Liang. 2016. Squad: 100,000+ questions for machine comprehension of text. *arXiv preprint arXiv:1606.05250*.

Matthew Richardson, Christopher JC Burges, and Erin Renshaw. 2013. Mctest: A challenge dataset for the open-domain machine comprehension of text. In *Proceedings of the 2013 Conference on Empirical Methods in Natural Language Processing*, pages 193–203.

Amrita Saha, Rahul Aralikatte, Mitesh M Khapra, and Karthik Sankaranarayanan. 2018. Duorc: Towards complex language understanding with paraphrased reading comprehension. *arXiv preprint arXiv:1804.07927*.

Aju Thalappillil Scaria, Jonathan Berant, Mengqiu Wang, Peter Clark, Justin Lewis, Brittany Harding, and Christopher D Manning. 2013. Learning biological processes with global constraints. In *Proceedings of the 2013 Conference on Empirical Methods in Natural Language Processing*, pages 1710–1720.

Alon Talmor and Jonathan Berant. 2018. The web as a knowledge-base for answering complex questions. *arXiv preprint arXiv:1803.06643*.

Adam Trischler, Tong Wang, Xingdi Yuan, Justin Harris, Alessandro Sordoni, Philip Bachman, and Kaheer Suleman. 2016. Newsqa: A machine comprehension dataset. *arXiv preprint arXiv:1611.09830*.

George Tsatsaronis, Michael Schroeder, Georgios Paliouras, Yannis Almirantis, Ion Androutsopoulos, Eric Gaussier, Patrick Gallinari, Thierry Artieres, Michael R Alvers, Matthias Zschunke, et al. 2012. Bioasq: A challenge on large-scale biomedical semantic indexing and question answering. In *2012 AAAI Fall Symposium Series*.

Ashish Vaswani, Noam Shazeer, Niki Parmar, Jakob Uszkoreit, Llion Jones, Aidan N Gomez, Łukasz Kaiser, and Illia Polosukhin. 2017. Attention is all you need. In *Advances in neural information processing systems*, pages 5998–6008.

Ellen M Voorhees. 2001. The trec question answering track. *Natural Language Engineering*, 7(4):361–378.

Yi Wu, David Bamman, and Stuart Russell. 2017. Adversarial training for relation extraction. In *Proceedings of the 2017 Conference on Empirical Methods in Natural Language Processing*, pages 1778–1783, Copenhagen, Denmark. Association for Computational Linguistics.

Zheng Xu, Wen Li, Li Niu, and Dong Xu. 2014. Exploiting low-rank structure from latent domains for domain generalization. In *European Conference on Computer Vision*, pages 628–643. Springer.

Zhilin Yang, Peng Qi, Saizheng Zhang, Yoshua Bengio, William W Cohen, Ruslan Salakhutdinov, and Christopher D Manning. 2018. Hotpotqa: A dataset for diverse, explainable multi-hop question answering. *arXiv preprint arXiv:1809.09600*.

Dani Yogatama, Cyprien de Masson d'Autume, Jerome Connor, Tomas Kocisky, Mike Chrzanowski, Lingpeng Kong, Angeliki Lazaridou, Wang Ling, Lei Yu, Chris Dyer, et al. 2019. Learning and evaluating general linguistic intelligence. *arXiv preprint arXiv:1901.11373*.

Lantao Yu, Weinan Zhang, Jun Wang, and Yong Yu. 2017. Seqgan: Sequence generative adversarial nets with policy gradient. In *Thirty-First AAAI Conference on Artificial Intelligence*.

Meng Zhang, Yang Liu, Huanbo Luan, and Maosong Sun. 2017. Adversarial training for unsupervised bilingual lexicon induction. In *Proceedings of the 55th Annual Meeting of the Association for Computational Linguistics (Volume 1: Long Papers)*, pages 1959–1970, Vancouver, Canada. Association for Computational Linguistics.

Generalizing Question Answering System
with Pre-trained Language Model Fine-tuning

Dan Su[*], **Yan Xu**[*], **Genta Indra Winata, Peng Xu,**
Hyeondey Kim, Zihan Liu, Pascale Fung
Center for Artificial Intelligence Research (CAiRE)
Department of Electronic and Computer Engineering
The Hong Kong University of Science and Technology, Clear Water Bay, Hong Kong
{dsu, yxucb, giwinata, pxuab}@connect.ust.hk,
{hdkimaa, zliucr}@connect.ust.hk, pascale@ece.ust.hk

Abstract

With a large number of datasets being released and new techniques being proposed, Question answering (QA) systems have witnessed great breakthroughs in reading comprehension (RC) tasks. However, most existing methods focus on improving in-domain performance, leaving open the research question of how these models and techniques can generalize to out-of-domain and unseen RC tasks. To enhance the generalization ability, we propose a multi-task learning framework that learns the shared representation across different tasks. Our model is built on top of a large pre-trained language model, such as XLNet, and then fine-tuned on multiple RC datasets. Experimental results show the effectiveness of our methods, with an average Exact Match score of 56.59 and an average F1 score of 68.98, which significantly improves the BERT-Large baseline by 8.39 and 7.22, respectively.

1 Introduction

Reading comprehension (RC) is a fundamental human skills needed to answer questions that require knowledge of the world and understanding of natural language. This task is essential for intelligent dialogue systems to quickly respond in a search engine or a product recommendation system. Recently, we have witnessed several breakthroughs in question answering (QA) systems, such as bidirectional attention flow (BiDAF) (Seo et al., 2017), the attention over attention mechanism (AoA) (Cui et al., 2017), and a multi-hop architecture using gated-attention readers (Dhingra et al., 2017).

A large number of QA datasets have been proposed in recent years for single-hop and multi-hop reasoning applications (Rajpurkar et al., 2016; Lai et al., 2017; Saha et al., 2018; Trischler et al.,

2017; Joshi et al., 2017). However, each QA dataset is built for a particular domain and focus (Talmor and Berant, 2019). Dataset passages cover different topics, such as movies (Saha et al., 2018), news (Trischler et al., 2017), and biomedicine (Tsatsaronis et al., 2012). Also, the styles of questions (e.g., entity-centric, relational, other tasks reformulated as QA, etc.), the sources (e.g., crowd-workers, domain experts, exam writers, etc.), and the relationship of the question to the passage are different among datasets (e.g., collected as independent vs. dependent on evidence, multi-hop, etc). The availability of such datasets promotes the development of models that work well for only a specific domain. However, little attention (Chung et al., 2017; Sun et al., 2018) has been paid towards generalization, i.e., building QA systems that can generalize well on different datasets and transfer to new domains quickly.

One major factor that could contribute to generalization, is effective contextual representation (Talmor and Berant, 2019). Recently, models pre-trained on a large unlabeled corpus, by adding an extra final layer and fine-tuning on task-specific supervised data, obtained breakthrough performances on many language understanding tasks such as the GLUE benchmark and the SQuAD QA task (Radford et al., 2018; Devlin et al., 2019; Yang et al., 2019). This indicates the power of pre-trained language models in representing contextual information. Thus, we adopt XLNet (Yang et al., 2019), the state-of-the-art pre-trained language model as our language representation.

Another critical issue related to generalization is how to adapt to new QA tasks using few or even no prior training examples. McCann et al. (2018); Liu et al. (2019); Talmor and Berant (2019) show that promising results can be obtained in transferring to new domains by training models on multiple tasks simultaneously using multi-task learn-

---

[*] These two authors contributed equally.

Proceedings of the Second Workshop on Machine Reading for Question Answering, pages 203–211
Hong Kong, China, November 4, 2019. ©2019 Association for Computational Linguistics

ing. Multi-task learning explores the relationships between different tasks by capitalizing on relatedness while mitigating interference from dissimilarities, thus forcing models to learn useful representations more generally by unifying tasks under a single perspective. Thus, a model, which is trained on multiple source QA datasets, can achieve robust generalization and transferring ability.

To summarize, we present our work for the MRQA 2019 shared task on generalization. We propose to use multi-task learning on different source QA datasets and fine-tune XLNet (Yang et al., 2019), to build a QA system which has general linguistic intelligence.

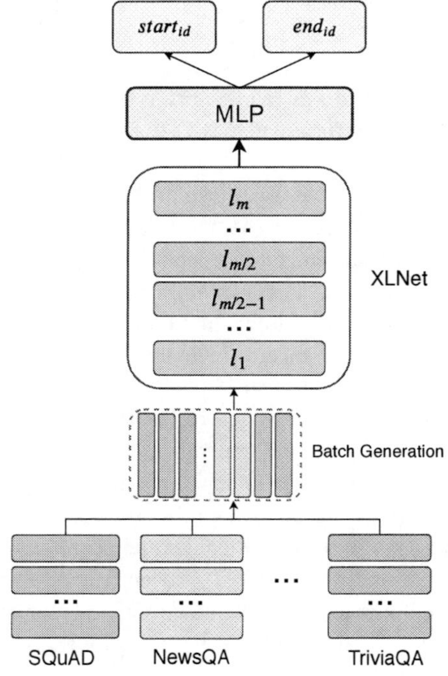

Figure 1: The model architecture. **GPU-version:** The blue boxes (first half) of XLNet layers remain unchanged during fine-tuning and only green boxes are updated due to the GPU's memory limitation. **TPU-version:** All layers of XLNet are fine-tuned.

2 Related Work

2.1 Pre-trained Language Models

Fine-tuning pre-trained language models via supervised learning has become the key to achieving state-of-the-art performance in various natural language processing (NLP) tasks. Among them, BERT (Devlin et al., 2019) extracts contextual meaning through bidirectional encoding with a masked language model and a next-sentence prediction objective. Recently, XLNet (Yang et al., 2019), a permutation language model, was introduced to leverage the bidirectional context and overcome the drawbacks of BERT due to its autoregressive nature. XLNet-based models have already achieved better performance than BERT-based models on many NLP tasks.

2.2 Question Answering

Unlike traditional knowledge-based QA (Kalyanpur et al., 2012), nowadays, many QA systems involve natural language understanding and knowledge of the world. Many datasets, such as SQuAD (Rajpurkar et al., 2016), NewsQA (Trischler et al., 2017), TriviaQA (Joshi et al., 2017), SearchQA (Dunn et al., 2017), HotpotQA (Yang et al., 2018), NaturalQuestions (Kwiatkowski et al., 2019), DROP (Dua et al., 2019), RACE (Lai et al., 2017), DueRC (Saha et al., 2018), BioASQ (Tsatsaronis et al., 2012), TextbookQA (Kembhavi et al., 2017), and RelationExtraction (Levy et al., 2017), have been published for specific QA tasks. Among all these tasks, one of the most widely studied one is extractive QA, which is to find a directly mentioned span in the article which answers the particular question. Although many studies on extractive QA have achieved significant improvements by leveraging attention-based models and pre-trained language representations, QA models might still perform poorly in unseen domains due to the data scarcity.

2.3 Multi-task Learning

Liu et al. (2019) proposed a multi-task learning framework-based pre-trained language model (MT-DNN) that leverages nine *natural language understanding* (NLU) datasets and outperforms BERT models. MT-DNN classifies NLU tasks into four classes and uses different loss functions for different task classes, which avoids the model overfitting on a single task by regularizing the language representation.

Meanwhile, Talmor and Berant (2019) proposed MultiQA, which leverages five large QA datasets and five small QA datasets. Merging various extractive QA datasets in training brings general improvement, and achieves the state-of-the-art performance on five QA datasets, which illustrates that training with multiple datasets improves both generalization and transferability.

Dataset	Source	Question	Multi-hop
In-Domain Datasets			
SQuAD	Wikipedia	Crowd	No
NewsQA	News	Crowd	No
TriviaQA	Snippets	Trivia	No
SearchQA	Snippets	Trivia	No
HotpotQA	Wikipedia	Crowd	Yes
NQ	Wikipedia	Query	No
Out-of-Domain Datasets			
DROP	Wikipedia	Crowd	Yes
RACE	Exam	Expert	Yes
DuoRC	Movie Plot	Crowd	No
BioASQ	Biomedical	Crowd	No
TQA	Textbook	Crowd	No
RE	Wikipedia	Crowd	No

Table 1: Characterization of the training and development datasets. *TQA*, *NQ* and *RE* are the abbreviations for *TextbookQA*, *NaturalQuestions* and *RelationExtraction*, respectively.

3 Methodology

3.1 Baseline

MRQA organizers have released the BERT-base and BERT-large models as baselines implemented using the AllenNLP (Gardner et al., 2018) platform. [1] The BERT transformer receives a passage and a question that is separated by an [SEP] token. On top of this, the baseline models deploys a linear layer to find the corresponding span which answers the question from the passage.

3.2 XLNet

Model XLNet (Yang et al., 2019) is a recently proposed generalized autoregressive pre-training model for language understanding which naively follows the Transformer(-XL) (Dai et al., 2019) architecture. Instead of the bidirectional encoding structure used in BERT (Devlin et al., 2019), XLNet leverages a permutation language modeling objective and target-aware representations with a two-stream attention mechanism to enable the model to capture the context on both sides. Besides the datasets which are also used in the pre-training procedure of BERT (Devlin et al., 2019), XLNet involves Giga5 (Parker et al., 2011), ClueWeb 2012-B (an extension version of Callan et al. (2009)) and Common Crawl (Buck et al.,

2014) for pre-training. XLNet captures general semantic meanings and produces effective representations to generalize language understanding. BERT is inferior to XLNet because it suffers significantly from the independence assumption and input noise, which prevent BERT from modeling the dependency between targets and result in a pre-training-finetune discrepancy.

Fine-tuning The common strategy in leveraging a pre-trained model is to fine-tune it with an additional linear layer or multilayer perceptron (MLP) on top and adapt it to specific tasks. Empirically, XLNet (Yang et al., 2019) achieves striking results when applied to other tasks through fine-tuning methods, and outperforms the previous state-of-the-art results on 18 tasks, including QA. The results shown in Yang et al. (2019) on the RACE and SQuAD datasets, showing that only an XLNet single model outperforms humans and the best ensemble by 7.6 and 2.5 points in EM, undoubtedly reveal the effectiveness of XLNet on QA tasks.

3.3 Attention-over-Attention

Attention-based neural networks have become a stereotype in most extractive QA systems and is well-known for its capability of learning the importance of distribution over the inputs. attention-over-attention (AoA) mechanism (Cui et al., 2017) is successful because it can generate an "attended attention" which considers the interactive information from both the query-to-document and document-to-query perspectives. Its effectiveness has been proved on public datasets such as the CNN, Children's Book Test, and SQuAD datasets.

4 Experiments

4.1 Preprocessing

The original setting of the sequence length is 512 in the XLNet-large model, but because of the constraint on the computational ability of a single GPU, a trade-off is made between the size of the context and the performance of the model. The sequence length is set as 340 when fine-tuning on the GPU but kept at 512 on the tensor processing unit (TPU). All the datasets are tokenized with SentencePiece (Kudo and Richardson, 2018) and uniformed in lower cases.

4.2 Data Analysis

Datasets Under the scenario of this task, the model should be trained on six training datasets.

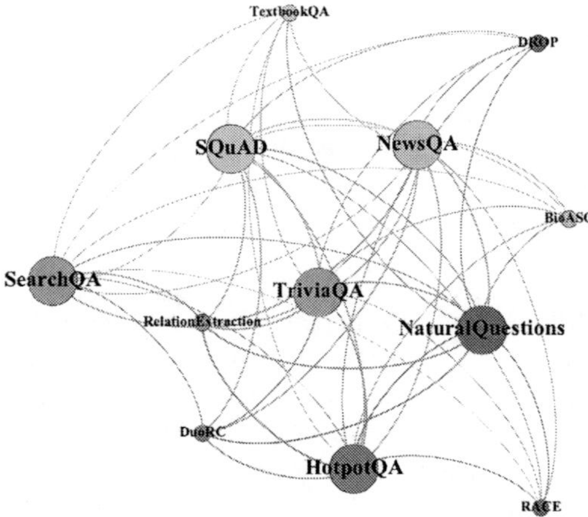

Figure 2: The visualization of the similarity between different datasets using the force-directed placement algorithm via the Gephi platform (Grandjean, 2015). We leverage the Louvain method (Blondel et al., 2008) to automatically cluster the node (datasets) into several communities and mark each community with different colors.

	GPU	TPU
Fine-tuned Layers	12 - 24 (13)	1 - 24 (24)
Floating Point	16	32
Training Batch Size	4	48
Sequence Length	340	512
MLP Layer Size	512, 384, 1	1024, 1

Table 2: Difference of hyper-parameters and the MLP structure when fine-tuning XLNet model on GPU and TPU.

Six in-domain datasets and six out-of-domain datasets are offered as development sets for evaluation. The characterization of the corresponding datasets is shown in Table 1. The twelve known datasets differ from each other in terms of the source of the data, the type of questions, and whether inference (multi-hop) is required during QA. Moreover, the sources of the data on the development datasets are more diverse and not fully covered by the training datasets, which indicates that the generalization ability of the representations produced by the model can significantly improve the performance on the development datasets.

Similarity Evaluation Following the similarity evaluation method utilized in Talmor and Berant (2019), we fine-tune XLNet with an additional MLP on a single GPU using the six training

datasets separately, and then evaluate the model on all the in-domain and out-of-domain development sets. More details about fine-tuning the XLNet model on the GPU are mentioned in §4.4. The evaluation results can be found in Table 3. When evaluating the in-domain datasets, the similarity can be computed as

$$Similarity = \frac{P_{ij}}{P_j} + \frac{P_{ji}}{P_i}, \qquad (1)$$

where P_{ij} refers to the F1 score when fine-tuning XLNet on dataset D_i and evaluating it on D_j, while P_i refers to the F1 score when fine-tuning and evaluating on D_i. When evaluating the similarity between the in-domain datasets and out-of-domain datasets,

$$Similarity = \frac{2 \cdot P_{ij}}{P_j}, \qquad (2)$$

where dataset D_j is one of the in-domain datasets, while D_i is among the out-of-domain datasets.

We visualize the datasets using the force-directed placement algorithm (Fruchterman and Reingold, 1991) for a more intuitive view, which is shown in Figure 2. Each node represents a dataset, and the in-domain datasets and out-of-domain datasets are distinguished by the size of the node. The nodes are linked by a set of edges acting as the springs, pulling nodes towards one another, while non-linked nodes are pushed apart. The weights of the edges act as the pulling force, influencing the distance and the relative position among nodes. In our case, we consider the similarities between nodes (datasets) as the pulling force. The nodes with higher similarity tend to be pulled closer and vise versa.

From Figure 2, the out-of-domain datasets tend to be pushed to the boundary of the figure, which indicates that they have lower similarity with the in-domain datasets. Except for the RelationExtraction dataset, all the out-of-domain datasets only have a strong relationship with one or two in-domain datasets but are positioned far from the others. This implies that to achieve consistently good performance on out-of-domain datasets, data samples from all the in-domain datasets are needed.

4.3 Data Feeding Methods

Empirically, the data feeding order when training and fine-tuning has a great impact on the performance of the model. In terms of the fine-tuning

Datasets	SQuAD	NewsQA	TriviaQA	SearchQA	HotpotQA	NQ
(I) SQuAD	**93.25**	84.99	67.67	43.42	83.48	83.52
(I) NewsQA	60.84	**72.43**	44.13	23.76	56.75	59.13
(I) TriviaQA	66.70	67.50	**76.24**	67.99	64.32	69.21
(I) SearchQA	35.43	43.70	60.16	**79.27**	40.21	54.11
(I) HotpotQA	69.28	64.65	54.12	34.07	**80.09**	64.78
(I) NQ	57.28	66.78	52.36	38.24	63.17	**80.60**
(O) DROP	51.07	33.62	30.04	16.20	48.07	49.54
(O) RACE	48.25	46.67	34.96	19.22	39.57	47.72
(O) DuoRC	61.73	61.45	48.66	29.49	54.24	59.18
(O) BioASQ	70.64	64.48	59.61	49.78	65.46	69.44
(O) TextbookQA	52.93	55.08	46.30	34.90	37.39	58.77
(O) RE	84.62	69.14	73.08	64.47	81.80	81.31

Table 3: Results for XLNet models that are only fine-tuned on a single training set but tested on all the in-domain and out-of-domain development sets. The models are fine-tuned on a single GPU following the GPU-version architecture that is further explained in §4.4. *NQ* and *RE* are the abbreviations for *NaturalQuestions* and *RelationExtraction*, respectively. All the results shown in the table are the corresponding F1 scores.

procedure with the six training sets, we propose two methods for data feeding.

The first method follows the idea of **multi-task learning**. In this task, because the six training sets differ in several aspects as explained in §4.2, we consider them different tasks and leverage the model to fully explore the general semantic representations of the samples in the training datasets. During multi-task learning, we combine all the training datasets and shuffle them to reduce the reliance on the model on the order of the data.

The second method is similar to curriculum learning (Bengio et al., 2009), but because of the sparse relation among the datasets, it's not practical to evaluate the difficulty and the degree of learning. So we simply propose to fine-tune the model using the training sets that are shuffled separately **one after another** with the same training steps.

4.4 Fine-tuning Methods

Various fine-tuning methods based on XLNet are tested to identify the most effective method to achieve better generalization performance. During the fine-tuning procedure, all the methods share a learning rate of 1×10^{-5}.

Fine-tuning on TPU The trend of the pre-trained models for language understanding (Yang et al., 2019; Devlin et al., 2019) is to achieve better performance with larger models, but this leads to their reliance on better computational resources. Even the fine-tuning procedure of XL-Net (Yang et al., 2019) is hard to handle in a normal GPU such as GTX 1080Ti, because of the memory size and the processing speed. To make it possible to fine-tune the XLNet model and adapt it to QA tasks on a single GPU, we make modifications to the MLP structure and the hyper-parameters, which are listed in Table 2. For the model on the GPU, only the last 13 layers are further tuned. Except for the reduction of the three hyper-parameters mentioned above, the MLP structure is also changed from a single large linear layer to a deeper but smaller structure.

To fulfill the fine-tuning procedure on the original structure of XLNet with a larger additional linear layer and achieve better performance on development sets and test sets, we take advantage of the TPU (Jouppi et al., 2017) from the Google cloud service. The TPU is a machine learning-oriented application-specific integrated circuit. It has a larger memory and faster computational speed than a GPU, since it consists of a large high bandwidth memory (HBM) and 32-bit floating-point multiply-accumulate systolic array matrix unit. In contrast to the computational power of a GTX 1080Ti (11.34 Tflops of 32-bit floating-point computation and 11 GB of memory), the TPU has 420 Tflops of a 32-bit floating-point computational speed and a 128 GB HBM, which allow us to train a deeper and larger model at a faster speed.

Fine-tuning with MLP Leveraging an MLP as the additional structure for fine-tuning a pre-

Dev Datasets	Multi-task XLNet-large		XLNet-large	
	EM	F1	EM	F1
DROP	40.45	48.93	38.79	48.78
RACE	34.12	49.23	**39.02**	**51.08**
DuoRC	54.63	64.64	50.50	60.62
BioASQ	54.79	70.12	52.06	70.67
TextbookQA	53.76	62.88	48.77	58.86
RelationExtraction	71.27	83.67	66.79	81.75
Average	51.50	63.25	49.32	61.96

Table 4: Results of models fine-tuned with different data feeding methods on development datasets. Both of the models are fine-tuned based on the off-the-shelf XLNet-large pre-trained model on a single GPU. We combine all the training datasets and shuffle the data to fine-tune the multi-task XLNet-large model, while for the other, we feed the data in the following order: SQuAD, NewsQA, TriviaQA, SearchQA, HotpotQA and NaturalQuestions.

Dev Datasets	MLP + GPU		AoA + GPU		MLP + TPU		BERT Large Baseline	
	EM	F1	EM	F1	EM	F1	EM	F1
DROP	40.45	48.93	34.20	43.59	41.04	51.11	33.91	43.50
RACE	34.12	49.23	33.83	48.47	37.22	50.46	28.96	41.42
DuoRC	54.63	64.64	53.03	62.47	51.70	63.14	43.38	55.14
BioASQ	54.79	70.12	56.32	71.58	59.62	74.02	49.74	66.57
TextbookQA	53.76	62.88	52.03	61.49	55.50	65.18	45.62	53.22
RelationExtraction	71.27	83.67	69.10	82.63	76.47	86.23	72.53	84.68
Average	51.50	63.25	49.75	61.71	53.59	65.02	45.69	57.42

Table 5: Results of multi-task models that are fine-tuned with the methods described in §4.4. Compared with the BERT-large baseline, XLNet shows its effectiveness and generalization ability on QA tasks and outperforms the BERT-large model, but the enormous amount of parameters in the XLNet model causes the performance of the model to be constrained by the access to better computational resources.

Test Datasets	Multi-task XLNet-large		BERT-large Baseline	
	EM	F1	EM	F1
BioProcess	56.16	72.91	46.12	63.63
ComplexWebQuestions	54.73	61.39	51.80	59.05
MCTest	64.56	78.72	59.49	72.20
QAMR	56.36	72.47	48.23	67.39
QAST	75.91	88.80	62.27	80.79
TREC	49.85	63.36	36.34	53.55
Dev Average	53.59	65.02	45.69	57.42
Test Average	59.59	72.94	50.71	66.10
Average	56.59	68.98	48.20	61.76

Table 6: Results on test datasets. The multi-task XLNet-large model is the final submission model that is fine-tuned on the TPU with 15k training steps.

trained model is a common strategy of task adaptation. In this task, we test the performance of XLNet with an MLP when fine-tuning on both the GPU and TPU. Because of the limitation of the memory size on the GPU, the MLP structure differs from that on the TPU. More details are shown in Table 2.

Fine-tuning with AoA Layer We also test the performance of the model when fine-tuning XLNet with an AoA layer on a single GPU. In this case, we add an additional AoA layer between the output layer of XLNet and MLP mentioned above. In the practical implementation of this method, the representations of the context and the query need to be split from the output of XLNet, while we can get the corresponding representation directly and separately when using BERT.

4.5 Results

Comparison between Data Feeding Methods

Table 4 shows the performance of the XLNet models fine-tuned with the two data feeding methods mentioned in §4.3 on the development sets. Both models are fine-tuned with an additional MLP on a single GPU based on XLNet-large. For the single-task XLNet model, we feed the data in the following order: SQuAD, NewsQA, TriviaQA, SearchQA, HotpotQA, and NaturalQuestions. In general, the multi-task data feeding method outperforms the method in which the datasets are fed one after another. On further observation, multi-task learning tends to enable the model to achieve uniform generalization performance on unseen datasets, while the single-task feeding method better benefits the tasks that are similar to the last task that is involved during fine-tuning. The fact that the single-task model achieves better performance on RACE than that using the multi-task learning method is related to the higher similarity between RACE and NaturalQuestions, which we can figure out from Figure 2.

Comparison between Fine-tuning Methods

The results of the experiments on different fine-tuning methods are shown in Table 5. All the experiments are evaluated on the development sets. Although the AoA layer improves the performance of BERT on the SQuAD dataset, which can be seen on the SQuAD leaderboard, it fails to improve generalization performance on XLNet. Moreover, while it takes 300k training steps to finish fine-tuning, we only need 100k training steps to fine-tune the XLNet model with an MLP (refer to §4.4) on this QA task. The XLNet model fine-tuned with an MLP on the TPU achieves the best performance, both on average and on each development dataset. It outperforms the baseline by a large margin, but only requires 15k training steps for fine-tuning. The TPU shows its effectiveness on training with its ability to afford a larger model, batch size, and sequence length.

Comparison with Baseline

The results on the test sets shown in Table 6 indicate that the multi-task XLNet-large model fine-tuned with a larger linear layer on the TPU con-sistently outperforms the BERT-large baseline by a huge margin. On the test set, our XLNet based model fine-tuned under the multi-task learning setting shows its robust generalization and transferring ability over the baseline.

5 Conclusion

In this paper, we propose a multi-task framework to improve the generalization ability of question answering systems by leveraging large pre-trained language models. Experimental results indicate the effectiveness of our methods on broader QA tasks, with an average Exact Match score of 56.59 and an average F1 score of 68.98, which are significantly higher than the BERT-large baseline results by 8.39 and 7.22, respectively.

References

Yoshua Bengio, Jérôme Louradour, Ronan Collobert, and Jason Weston. 2009. Curriculum learning. In *Proceedings of the 26th annual international conference on machine learning*, pages 41–48. ACM.

Vincent D Blondel, Jean-Loup Guillaume, Renaud Lambiotte, and Etienne Lefebvre. 2008. Fast unfolding of communities in large networks. *Journal of statistical mechanics: theory and experiment*, 2008(10):P10008.

Christian Buck, Kenneth Heafield, and Bas Van Ooyen. 2014. N-gram counts and language models from the common crawl. In *LREC*, volume 2, page 4. Citeseer.

Jamie Callan, Mark Hoy, Changkuk Yoo, and Le Zhao. 2009. Clueweb09 data set.

Yu-An Chung, Hung-Yi Lee, and James Glass. 2017. Supervised and unsupervised transfer learning for question answering. *arXiv preprint arXiv:1711.05345*.

Yiming Cui, Zhipeng Chen, Si Wei, Shijin Wang, Ting Liu, and Guoping Hu. 2017. Attention-over-attention neural networks for reading comprehension. In *Proceedings of the 55th Annual Meeting of the Association for Computational Linguistics (Volume 1: Long Papers)*, pages 593–602.

Zihang Dai, Zhilin Yang, Yiming Yang, William W Cohen, Jaime Carbonell, Quoc V Le, and Ruslan Salakhutdinov. 2019. Transformer-xl: Attentive language models beyond a fixed-length context. *arXiv preprint arXiv:1901.02860*.

Jacob Devlin, Ming-Wei Chang, Kenton Lee, and Kristina Toutanova. 2019. Bert: Pre-training of deep bidirectional transformers for language understanding. In *Proceedings of the 2019 Conference of the North American Chapter of the Association for Computational Linguistics: Human Language Technologies, Volume 1 (Long and Short Papers)*, pages 4171–4186.

Bhuwan Dhingra, Hanxiao Liu, Zhilin Yang, William Cohen, and Ruslan Salakhutdinov. 2017. Gated-attention readers for text comprehension. In *Proceedings of the 55th Annual Meeting of the Association for Computational Linguistics (Volume 1: Long Papers)*, pages 1832–1846.

Dheeru Dua, Yizhong Wang, Pradeep Dasigi, Gabriel Stanovsky, Sameer Singh, and Matt Gardner. 2019. DROP: A reading comprehension benchmark requiring discrete reasoning over paragraphs. In *Proc. of NAACL*.

Matthew Dunn, Levent Sagun, Mike Higgins, V Ugur Guney, Volkan Cirik, and Kyunghyun Cho. 2017. Searchqa: A new q&a dataset augmented with context from a search engine. *arXiv preprint arXiv:1704.05179*.

Thomas MJ Fruchterman and Edward M Reingold. 1991. Graph drawing by force-directed placement. *Software: Practice and experience*, 21(11):1129–1164.

Matt Gardner, Joel Grus, Mark Neumann, Oyvind Tafjord, Pradeep Dasigi, Nelson F Liu, Matthew Peters, Michael Schmitz, and Luke Zettlemoyer. 2018. Allennlp: A deep semantic natural language processing platform. In *Proceedings of Workshop for NLP Open Source Software (NLP-OSS)*, pages 1–6.

Martin Grandjean. 2015. GEPHI – Introduction to Network Analysis and Visualization. Http://www.martingrandjean.ch/gephi-introduction/.

Mandar Joshi, Eunsol Choi, Daniel Weld, and Luke Zettlemoyer. 2017. Triviaqa: A large scale distantly supervised challenge dataset for reading comprehension. *Proceedings of the 55th Annual Meeting of the Association for Computational Linguistics (Volume 1: Long Papers)*.

Norman P Jouppi, Cliff Young, Nishant Patil, David Patterson, Gaurav Agrawal, Raminder Bajwa, Sarah Bates, Suresh Bhatia, Nan Boden, Al Borchers, et al. 2017. In-datacenter performance analysis of a tensor processing unit. In *2017 ACM/IEEE 44th Annual International Symposium on Computer Architecture (ISCA)*, pages 1–12. IEEE.

Aditya Kalyanpur, Siddharth Patwardhan, BK Boguraev, Adam Lally, and Jennifer Chu-Carroll. 2012. Fact-based question decomposition in deepqa. *IBM Journal of Research and Development*, 56(3.4):13–1.

Aniruddha Kembhavi, Minjoon Seo, Dustin Schwenk, Jonghyun Choi, Ali Farhadi, and Hannaneh Hajishirzi. 2017. Are you smarter than a sixth grader? textbook question answering for multimodal machine comprehension. In *Proceedings of the IEEE Conference on Computer Vision and Pattern Recognition*, pages 4999–5007.

Taku Kudo and John Richardson. 2018. Sentencepiece: A simple and language independent subword tokenizer and detokenizer for neural text processing. In *Proceedings of the 2018 Conference on Empirical Methods in Natural Language Processing: System Demonstrations*, pages 66–71.

Tom Kwiatkowski, Jennimaria Palomaki, Olivia Redfield, Michael Collins, Ankur Parikh, Chris Alberti, Danielle Epstein, Illia Polosukhin, Matthew Kelcey, Jacob Devlin, Kenton Lee, Kristina N. Toutanova, Llion Jones, Ming-Wei Chang, Andrew Dai, Jakob Uszkoreit, Quoc Le, and Slav Petrov. 2019. Natural questions: a benchmark for question answering research. *Transactions of the Association of Computational Linguistics*.

Guokun Lai, Qizhe Xie, Hanxiao Liu, Yiming Yang, and Eduard Hovy. 2017. Race: Large-scale reading comprehension dataset from examinations. In *Proceedings of the 2017 Conference on Empirical Methods in Natural Language Processing*, pages 785–794.

Omer Levy, Minjoon Seo, Eunsol Choi, and Luke Zettlemoyer. 2017. Zero-shot relation extraction via reading comprehension. In *Proceedings of the 21st Conference on Computational Natural Language Learning (CoNLL 2017)*, pages 333–342.

Xiaodong Liu, Pengcheng He, Weizhu Chen, and Jianfeng Gao. 2019. Multi-task deep neural networks for natural language understanding. *arXiv preprint arXiv:1901.11504*.

Bryan McCann, Nitish Shirish Keskar, Caiming Xiong, and Richard Socher. 2018. The natural language decathlon: Multitask learning as question answering. *arXiv preprint arXiv:1806.08730*.

Robert Parker, David Graff, Junbo Kong, Ke Chen, and Kazuaki Maeda. 2011. English gigaword fifth edition, june. *Linguistic Data Consortium, LDC2011T07*, 12.

Alec Radford, Karthik Narasimhan, Tim Salimans, and Ilya Sutskever. 2018. Improving language understanding by generative pre-training. *URL https://s3-us-west-2. amazonaws. com/openai-assets/researchcovers/languageunsupervised/language understanding paper. pdf*.

Pranav Rajpurkar, Jian Zhang, Konstantin Lopyrev, and Percy Liang. 2016. Squad: 100,000+ questions for machine comprehension of text. In *Proceedings of the 2016 Conference on Empirical Methods in Natural Language Processing*, pages 2383–2392.

Amrita Saha, Rahul Aralikatte, Mitesh M Khapra, and Karthik Sankaranarayanan. 2018. Duorc: Towards complex language understanding with paraphrased reading comprehension. In *Proceedings of the 56th Annual Meeting of the Association for Computational Linguistics (Volume 1: Long Papers)*, pages 1683–1693.

Min Joon Seo, Aniruddha Kembhavi, Ali Farhadi, and Hannaneh Hajishirzi. 2017. Bidirectional attention flow for machine comprehension. In *5th International Conference on Learning Representations, ICLR 2017, Toulon, France, April 24-26, 2017, Conference Track Proceedings*.

Kai Sun, Dian Yu, Dong Yu, and Claire Cardie. 2018. Improving machine reading comprehension with general reading strategies. *arXiv preprint arXiv:1810.13441*.

Alon Talmor and Jonathan Berant. 2019. MultiQA: An empirical investigation of generalization and transfer in reading comprehension. In *Proceedings of the 57th Annual Meeting of the Association for Computational Linguistics*, Florence, Italy. Association for Computational Linguistics.

Adam Trischler, Tong Wang, Xingdi Yuan, Justin Harris, Alessandro Sordoni, Philip Bachman, and Kaheer Suleman. 2017. Newsqa: A machine comprehension dataset. In *Proceedings of the 2nd Workshop on Representation Learning for NLP*, pages 191–200.

George Tsatsaronis, Michael Schroeder, Georgios Paliouras, Yannis Almirantis, Ion Androutsopoulos, Eric Gaussier, Patrick Gallinari, Thierry Artieres, Michael R Alvers, Matthias Zschunke, et al. 2012. Bioasq: A challenge on large-scale biomedical semantic indexing and question answering. In *2012 AAAI Fall Symposium Series*.

Zhilin Yang, Zihang Dai, Yiming Yang, Jaime Carbonell, Ruslan Salakhutdinov, and Quoc V Le. 2019. Xlnet: Generalized autoregressive pretraining for language understanding. *arXiv preprint arXiv:1906.08237*.

Zhilin Yang, Peng Qi, Saizheng Zhang, Yoshua Bengio, William W Cohen, Ruslan Salakhutdinov, and Christopher D Manning. 2018. Hotpotqa: A dataset for diverse, explainable multi-hop question answering. *arXiv preprint arXiv:1809.09600*.

D-NET: A Simple Framework for Improving the Generalization of Machine Reading Comprehension

Hongyu Li, Xiyuan Zhang, Yibing Liu, Yiming Zhang,
Quan Wang, Xiangyang Zhou, Jing Liu, Hua Wu, Haifeng Wang
Baidu Inc., Beijing, China
{lihongyu04, zhangxiyuan01, liuyibing01, zhangyiming04,
wangquan05, zhouxiangyang, liujing46, wu_hua, wanghaifeng}@baidu.com

Abstract

In this paper, we introduce a simple system Baidu submitted for MRQA (Machine Reading for Question Answering) 2019 Shared Task that focused on generalization of machine reading comprehension (MRC) models. Our system is built on a framework of pre-training and fine-tuning, namely D-NET. The techniques of pre-trained language models and multi-task learning are explored to improve the generalization of MRC models and we conduct experiments to examine the effectiveness of these strategies. Our system is ranked at top 1 of all the participants in terms of averaged F1 score. Our codes and models will be released at PaddleNLP [1].

1 Introduction

Machine reading comprehension (MRC) requires machines to understand text and answer questions about the text, and it is an important task in natural language processing (NLP). With the increasing availability of large-scale datasets for MRC (Rajpurkar et al., 2016; Bajaj et al., 2016; Dunn et al., 2017; Joshi et al., 2017; He et al., 2018) and the development of deep learning techniques, MRC has achieved remarkable advancements in the last few years (Wang and Jiang, 2016; Seo et al., 2016; Xiong et al., 2016; Wang et al., 2017; Liu et al., 2018; Wang et al., 2018; Yu et al., 2018). Although a number of neural models obtain even human parity performance on several datasets, these models may generalize poorly on other datasets (Talmor and Berant, 2019).

We expect that a truly effective question answering system works well on both the examples drawn from the same distribution as the training data and the ones draw from different distributions. Nevertheless, there has been relatively little work that explores the generalization of MRC models.

This year, MRQA (Machine Reading for Question Answering) 2019 Shared Task tries to test whether the question answering systems can generalize well beyond the datasets on which they are trained. Specifically, participants will submit question answering systems trained on a training set pooled from six existing MRC datasets, and the systems will be evaluated on twelve different test datasets without any additional training examples in the target domain (i.e. generalization).

As shown in Table 1, the major challenge of the shared task is that the train and test datasets differ in the following ways:

- **Questions**: They come from different sources, e.g. crowdsourcing workers, examine writers, search logs, synthetics, etc.

- **Documents**: They involve passages from different sources, e.g. wikipedia, news, movies, textbook, etc.

- **Language Understanding Ability**: They might require different language understanding abilities, e.g. matching, reasoning and arithmetic.

To address the above challenge, we introduce a simple framework of pre-training and fine-tuning, namely D-NET, for improving the generalization of MRC models by exploring the following techniques:

- **Pre-trained Models**: We leverage multiple pre-trained models, e.g. BERT (Devlin et al., 2019), XLNET (Yang et al., 2019) and ERNIE 2.0 (Sun et al., 2019). Since different pre-trained models are trained on various

---

[1] `https://github.com/PaddlePaddle/`
`models/tree/develop/PaddleNLP/Research/`
`MRQA2019-D-NET`

Dataset	Question Sources	Document Sources	Language Understanding	Train	Dev	Test
SQuAD	Crowdsourced	Wiki.	Matching	✓	✓	
NewsQA	Crowdsourced	News	Matching	✓	✓	
TriviaQA	Trivia	Web Snippets	Matching	✓	✓	
SearchQA	Trivia	Web Snippets	Matching	✓	✓	
HotpotQA	Crowdsourced	Wiki.	Reasoning	✓	✓	
NaturalQuestions	Query Log	Wiki.	Matching	✓	✓	
BioASQ	Crowdsourced	Biomedical articles	Matching		✓	✓
DROP	Crowdsourced	Wiki.	Arithmetic		✓	✓
DuoRC	Crowdsourced	Movie	Reasoning		✓	✓
RACE	Teachers	Examination	Reasoning		✓	✓
RelationExtraction	Question Template	Wiki.	Matching		✓	✓
TextbookQA	Textbook	Textbook	Reasoning		✓	✓
BioProcess	Biologist	Biology Textbook	Reasoning			✓
ComplexWebQuestions	Synthetic & Rephrasing	Web Snippets	Reasoning			✓
MCTest	Crowdsourced	Story	Reasoning			✓
QAMR	Crowdsourced	Wiki.&News	Matching			✓
QAST	Crowdsourced	Speech Transcriptions	Matching			✓
TREC	Query Log	Web doc.	Matching			✓

Table 1: The datasets of MRQA 2019 Shared Task include 6 training sets and 12 testing sets. The train, dev and test datasets differ in the following ways (1) question sources; (2) document sources; (3) language understanding

corpus with different pre-training tasks (e.g. masked language model, discourse relations, etc.), they may capture different aspects of linguistics. Hence, we expect that the combination of these pre-trained models can improve the generalization capability of MRC models.

- **Multi-task Learning**: Since the pre-training is usually performed on corpus with restricted domains, it is expected that increasing the domain diversity by further pre-training on other corpus may improve the generalization capability. Hence, we incorporate masked language model by using corpus from various domains as an auxiliary task in the fine-tuning phase, along with MRC. The side effect of adding a language modeling objective to MRC is that it can avoid catastrophic forgetting and keep the most useful features learned from pre-training task (Chronopoulou et al., 2019). Additionally, we explore multi-task learning (Liu et al., 2019) by incorporating the supervised dataset from other NLP tasks (e.g. natural language inference and paragraph ranking) to learn better language representation.

Our system is ranked at top 1 of all the participants in terms of averaged F1 score. We also conduct the experiments to examine the effectiveness of multiple pre-trained models and multi-task learning. Our major observations are as follows:

- The pre-trained models are still the most important keys to improve the generalization of MRC models in our experiments. Moreover, the ensembles of MRC models based on different pre-trained models show better generalization on out-of-domain set than the ensembles of MRC models based on the same pre-trained models.

- The auxiliary task of masked language model can help improve the generalization of MRC models.

- We do not observe much improvements from the auxiliary tasks of natural language inference and paragraph ranking.

The remainder of this paper is structured as follows: Section 2 describes the detailed overview of our system. Section 3 shows the experimental settings and results. Finally, we conclude our work in Section 4.

2 System Overview

Figure 1 depicts D-NET, a simple framework of pre-training and fine-tuning to improve the generalization capability of MRC models. There are basically two stages in D-NET: (1) We incorporate multiple pre-trained language models. (2) We fine-tune MRC models with multi-task learning. In this section, we will introduce each stage in details.

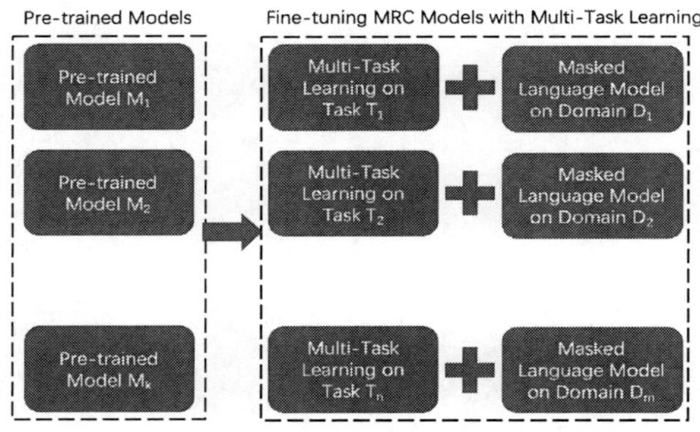

Figure 1: D-NET: A framework of pre-training and fine-tuning for MRC.

2.1 Pre-trained Models

Recently pre-trained language models present new state-of-the-art results in MRC. Since different pre-trained models are trained on various corpus with different pre-training tasks, they may capture different aspects of linguistics. Hence, we expect that the combination of these pre-trained models may generalize well on various corpus with different domains. The pre-trained models that are used in our experiments are listed below:

BERT (Devlin et al., 2019) uses multi-layer Transformer encoding blocks as its encoder. The pre-training tasks include masked language model and next sentence prediction, which enable the model to capture bidirectional and global information. In our system, we use the BERT large configuration that contains 24 Transformer encoding blocks, each with 16 self attention heads and 1024 hidden units.

Note that we use this pre-trained model for experimental purpose, and it is not included in the final submission. In our experiments, we initialize the parameters of the encoding layers from the checkpoint [2] of the model (Alberti et al., 2019) namely BERT + N-Gram Masking + Synthetic Self-Training. The model is initialized from Whole Word Masking BERT ($BERT_{wwm}$), further fine-tuned on the SQuAD 2.0 task with synthetic generated question answering corpora. In our experiments, we find that this model performs consistently better than the original $BERT_{large}$ and

$BERT_{wwm}$ without synthetic data augmentation, as officially released by Google [3].

XLNET (Yang et al., 2019) uses a novel pre-training task, i.e. permutation language modeling, by introducing two-stream self attention. Besides BooksCorpus and Wikipedia, on which the BERT is trained, XLNET uses more corpus in its pre-training, including Giga5, ClueWeb and Common Crawl. In our system, we use the 'large' configuration that contains 24 layers, each with 16 self attention heads and 1024 hidden units.

We initialize the parameters of XLNET encoding layers using the version that is released by the authors [4]. In our experiments, we find that XLNET shows superior performance on the datasets that require reasoning and arithmetic, e.g. DROP and RACE.

ERNIE 2.0 (Sun et al., 2019) is a continual pre-training framework for language understanding in which pre-training tasks can be incrementally built and learned through multi-task learning. It designs multiple pre-training tasks, including named entity prediction, discourse relation recognition, sentence order prediction, to learn language representations.

ERNIE uses the same Transformer encoder as BERT. In our system, we use the 'large' configuration that contains 24 Transformer encoding blocks, each with 16 self attention heads and 1024 hidden units. We initialize the parameters of ERNIE encoding layer using the official released

---

[2]The checkpoint can be downloaded from `https://worksheets.codalab.org/worksheets/0xd7b08560b5b24bd1874b9429d58e2df1`

[3] `https://github.com/google-research/bert`

[4] `https://github.com/zihangdai/xlnet/`

Model ID		M_0	M_1	M_2	M_3	M_4	M_5	M_6	M_7	M_8	M_9	M_{10}
Pre-trained Model	BERT	✓	✓	✓	✓	✓	✓					
	XLNET							✓	✓	✓	✓	
	ERNIE											✓
Masked LM	In-domain		✓	✓		✓	✓					
	Search Snippets		✓	✓	✓	✓	✓					
	Y!A				✓							
Supervised Task	MNLI			✓								
	ParaRank						✓					
Hyper Parameters	Max Seq Len	512	512	512	512	512	512	640	640	640	768	512
	Batch Size	48	48	48	48	32	48	128	24	24	24	64
	λ_{MLM}		2.0	0.4	0.4	0.4	0.4					
	λ_{MNLI}			0.4								
	λ_{PR}						0.8					

Table 2: The configurations and hyper-parameters of the eleven models used in our experiments. The configurations include the pre-trained models, the corpus for the masked language model task, the types of supervised NLP tasks. The hyper-parameters include the max sequence length, batch size and the mix ratio λ used the auxiliary tasks in multi-task learning.

version [5].

2.2 Fine-tuning MRC Models with Multi-Task Learning

To fine-tune MRC models, we simply use a linear output layer for each pre-trained model, followed by a standard softmax operation, to predict answer boundaries. We further introduce multi-tasking learning in the fine-tuning stage to learn more general language representations. Specifically, we have the following auxiliary tasks:

Masked Language Model Since the pre-training is usually preformed on the corpus with restricted domains, it is expected that further pre-training on more diverse domains may improve the generalization capability. Hence, we add an auxiliary task, masked language model (Chronopoulou et al., 2019), in the fine-tuning stage, along with the MRC task. Moreover, we use three corpus with different domains as the input for masked language model: (1) the passages in MRQA in-domain datasets that include wikipedia, news and search snippets; (2) the search snippets from Bing [6]. (3) the science questions in Yahoo! Answers.[7]. The side effect of adding a language modeling objective to MRC is that it can avoid catastrophic forgetting and keep the most useful features learned from pre-training

task (Chronopoulou et al., 2019).

Supervised Tasks Motivated by (Liu et al., 2019), we explore multi-task learning by incorporating the supervised datasets from other NLP tasks to learn more general language representation.

Specifically, we incorporate natural language inference and paragraph ranking as auxiliary tasks to MRC. (1) Previous work (Clark et al., 2019; Liu et al., 2019) show that MNLI (Williams et al., 2017) (a popular natural language inference dataset) can help improve the performance of the major task in a multi-task setting. In our system, we also leverage MNLI as an auxiliary task. (2) Previous work (Tan et al., 2017; Wang et al., 2018) examine the effectiveness of the joint learning of MRC and paragraph ranking. In our system, we also leverage paragraph ranking as an auxiliary task. We generate the datasets of paragraph ranking from MRQA in-domain datasets. The generated data and the details of data generation will be released at PaddleNLP.

3 Experiments and Results

3.1 Experimental Settings

In our experiments, we train eleven single models (M_0-M_{10}) under the framework of D-NET. Table 2 lists the detailed configurations and the hyper-parameters of these models. In the settings of multi-task leaning, we randomly sample

[5] https://github.com/PaddlePaddle/ERNIE
[6] http://www.msmarco.org/dataset.aspx
[7] http://goo.gl/JyCnZq

Systems	Dev In-domain F1	Dev Out-of-domain F1	Test F1
Official baseline	77.87	58.67	61.76
1 XLNET (M_6) + 1 ERNIE (M_{10}) (*submitted*)	**84.15**	**69.67**	**72.50**
4 BERTs (M_1-M_4)	84.25	68.33	-
4 XLNETs (M_6-M_9)	84.45	69.56	-
1 XLNET (M_6) + 1 BERT*	84.30	69.99	-
1 XLNET (M_6) + 1 ERNIE (M_{10}) + 1 BERT*	**84.82**	**70.42**	-

Table 3: System performance on the development and test set. Our submitted version for the shared task is marked as 'submitted'. Please refer to Table 2 with corresponding model ID for details about the model configurations. * We use the technique of knowledge distillation to learn a single BERT-based model from a teacher that is an ensemble of 4 BERTs(M_1-M_4).

batches from different tasks with 'mix ratio' 1 : $\lambda_{\text{MLM}} : \lambda_{\text{MNLI}} : \lambda_{\text{PR}}$.

When fine-tuning all pre-trained models, we use Adam optimizer with learning rate of 3×10^{-5}, learning rate warmup over the first 10% steps, and linear decay of the learning rate [8]. All the models are fine-tuned for two epochs. The experiments are conducted with PaddlePaddle framework on NVIDA TESLA V100 GPUs (with 32G RAM).

3.2 Experimental Results

3.2.1 The Main Results and the Effects of Pre-trained Models

Table 3 shows the main results and the results for the effects of pre-trained models. From Table 3, we have the following observations:

(1) Our submitted system significantly outperforms the official baseline by about 10 F1 score, and it is ranked at top 1 of all the participants in terms of averaged F1 score [9]. The technique of model ensemble can improve the generalization of MRC models. In the shared task, the participants are required to submit a question answering system which is able to run on a single GPU [10] with certain latency limit. Hence, we choose to submit a system that combines only one XLNET-based model with one ERNIE-based model.

(2) The pre-trained models are still the most important keys to improve the generalization of MRC models in our experiments. For example, pure XLNET-based models perform consistently better than BERT-based models with multi-task learning. Moreover, the ensembles of MRC models based on different pre-trained models show better generalization on out-of-domain set than the ensembles of MRC models based on the same pre-trained models. For example, the ensemble of one BERT-based model and one XLNET-based model has better generalization than the ensemble of one BERT-based models and the ensemble of four XLNET-based models. By incorporating one BERT-based model to our submitted system, the generalization capability of the system is further improved. One possible reason behind this observation is that different pre-trained models are trained on different corpus by designing different pre-training tasks (e.g. masked language model, discourse relations, etc.), and they may capture different aspects of linguistics.

3.2.2 The Effects of Multi-Task Learning

We conduct the experiments to examine the effects of multi-task learning on BERT. Table 4 shows the experimental results:

(1) From the first two rows in Table 4, we can observe that the auxiliary task of masked language model can improve the performance on both in-domain and out-of-domain development set, especially on the out-of-domain set. This means the task of masked language model can help improve the generalization of MRC models on out-of-domain data.

(2) From the last two rows in Table 4, we do not observe that the auxiliary tasks of natural language inference and paragraph ranking bring further benefits in terms of generalization. Although paragraph ranking brings better performance on the in-domain development set, it performs worse on the out-of-domain development set. This ob-

---

[8] When fine-tuning XLNET, we use layer-wise learning rate decay.

[9] Please refer to the official evaluation results on test set for the details: `https://docs.google.com/spreadsheets/d/1vE-uK4aUKqSnTyflwCrE9R9XP_J2Is2uN72tcGPKeSM`

[10] NVIDIA TITAN Xp

Models	Dev In-domain F1	Dev Out-of-domain F1
BERT (M_0)	82.40	66.35
BERT + MLM (M_1)	83.19	**67.45**
BERT + MLM, + MNLI (M_2)	83.15	66.92
BERT + MLM, + ParaRank (M_5)	**83.51**	66.83

Table 4: The experimental results on examining the effects of multi-task learning. Please refer to Table 2 with corresponding model ID for details about the model configurations.

servation is different from the previous work (Tan et al., 2017; Wang et al., 2018; Clark et al., 2019; Liu et al., 2019) that multi-task learning can improve the system performance. One possible reason might be the size of MRQA training data is large. Hence, the auxiliary tasks do not bring further advantages in terms of learning more robust language representations from more supervised data.

3.2.3 Summary

In a summary, we have the following major observations about generalization in our experiments: (1) The pre-trained models are still the most important keys to improve the generalization of MRC models in our experiments. The ensemble of MRC models based on different pre-trained models can improve the generalization of MRC models. (2) The auxiliary task of masked language model can help improve the generalization of MRC models. (3) We do not observe much improvements from the auxiliary tasks of natural language inference and paragraph ranking.

3.3 Analysis

In this section, we try to examine that what properties may affect the generalization capability of the submitted system. Specifically, we analyze the performance of the submitted system on different subsets of the testing set. Since the testing set differs from the training set in terms of document sources (see Table 1), we divide the testing set into two subsets: (1) Wiki & Web & News and (2) Other. Please refer to Table 5 for the detailed partition. The document source of the first subset is similar to the training set and we expect that the system works better on the first subset. However, we observe from Table 5 that the system performs similarly on two subsets. The difference on document sources does not bring too much difference on generalization.

We also divide the testing set into three sub-

Doc Source	Avg. F1
Wiki & Web & News	72.36
Other	72.60

Table 5: The performance of the submitted system on two subsets that contain different document sources. The two subsets are as follows: (1) Wiki & Web & News: DROP, RelationExtraction, ComplexWebQuestions, QAMR, TREC and (2) Other: BioASQ, DuoRC, RACE, Textbook, BioProcess, MCTest.

Language Understanding	Avg. F1
Matching	79.22
Reasoning	68.73
Arithmetic	61.53

Table 6: The performance of the submitted system on three subsets that require different language understanding ability. The three subsets are as follows: (1) Matching: BioASQ, RelationExtraction, QAMR, QAST, TREC; (2) Reasoning: DuoRC, RACE, Textbook, BioProcess, ComplexWebQuestions, MCTest and (3) Arithmetic: DROP.

sets by the requirement of language understanding ability: (1) Matching, (2) Reasoning and (3) Arithmetic. Please refer to Table 6 for the detailed partition. Since most of the questions in the training set (except HotpotQA) require only matching but less reasoning, we expect that the system performs better on the first subset. From Table 6, we observe that the system performs much worse on the the subsets of Reasoning and Arithmetic. Another reason might be that the current models are not well designed for reasoning or arithmetic. Hence, they perform worse on these subsets.

4 Conclusions

In this paper, we describe a simple baseline system that Baidu submitted for the MRQA 2019 Shared Task. Our system is built on a framework of pre-training and fine-tuning, namely D-NET. D-NET employs the techniques of pre-trained language models and multi-task learning to improve the generalization of MRC models and we conduct the experiments to examine the effectiveness of these strategies.

References

Chris Alberti, Daniel Andor, Emily Pitler, Jacob Devlin, and Michael Collins. 2019. Synthetic qa corpora generation with roundtrip consistency. In *arXiv preprint arXiv:1906.05416*.

Payal Bajaj, Daniel Campos, Nick Craswell, Li Deng, Jianfeng Gao, Xiaodong Liu, Rangan Majumder, Andrew McNamara, Bhaskar Mitra, Tri Nguyen, et al. 2016. Ms marco: A human generated machine reading comprehension dataset. In *arXiv preprint arXiv:1611.09268*.

Alexandra Chronopoulou, Christos Baziotis, and Alexandros Potamianos. 2019. An embarrassingly simple approach for transfer learning from pretrained language models. In *Proceedings of the 2019 Conference of the North American Chapter of the Association for Computational Linguistics: Human Language Technologies, Volume 1 (Long and Short Papers)*, pages 2089–2095.

Christopher Clark, Kenton Lee, Ming-Wei Chang, Tom Kwiatkowski, Michael Collins, and Kristina Toutanova. 2019. Boolq: Exploring the surprising difficulty of natural yes/no questions. In *arXiv preprint arXiv:1905.10044*.

Jacob Devlin, Ming-Wei Chang, Kenton Lee, and Kristina Toutanova. 2019. Bert: Pre-training of deep bidirectional transformers for language understanding. In *Proceedings of the 2019 Conference of the North American Chapter of the Association for Computational Linguistics: Human Language Technologies, Volume 1 (Long and Short Papers)*, pages 4171–4186.

Matthew Dunn, Levent Sagun, Mike Higgins, V Ugur Guney, Volkan Cirik, and Kyunghyun Cho. 2017. Searchqa: A new q&a dataset augmented with context from a search engine. In *arXiv preprint arXiv:1704.05179*.

Wei He, Kai Liu, Jing Liu, Yajuan Lyu, Shiqi Zhao, Xinyan Xiao, Yuan Liu, Yizhong Wang, Hua Wu, Qiaoqiao She, et al. 2018. Dureader: a chinese machine reading comprehension dataset from real-world applications. In *In Proceedings of Machine Reading for Question Answering (MRQA) Workshop at ACL. 2018.*, page 37.

Mandar Joshi, Eunsol Choi, Daniel S Weld, and Luke Zettlemoyer. 2017. Triviaqa: A large scale distantly supervised challenge dataset for reading comprehension. In *arXiv preprint arXiv:1705.03551*.

Xiaodong Liu, Pengcheng He, Weizhu Chen, and Jianfeng Gao. 2019. Multi-task deep neural networks for natural language understanding. In *Proceedings of the 57th Annual Meeting of the Association for Computational Linguistics*, pages 4487–4496, Florence, Italy. Association for Computational Linguistics.

Xiaodong Liu, Yelong Shen, Kevin Duh, and Jianfeng Gao. 2018. Stochastic answer networks for machine reading comprehension. In *Proceedings of the 56th Annual Meeting of the Association for Computational Linguistics (Volume 1: Long Papers)*, pages 1694–1704.

Pranav Rajpurkar, Jian Zhang, Konstantin Lopyrev, and Percy Liang. 2016. Squad: 100,000+ questions for machine comprehension of text. In *Proceedings of the 2016 Conference on Empirical Methods in Natural Language Processing*, pages 2383–2392.

Minjoon Seo, Aniruddha Kembhavi, Ali Farhadi, and Hannaneh Hajishirzi. 2016. Bidirectional attention flow for machine comprehension. In *arXiv preprint arXiv:1611.01603*.

Yu Sun, Shuohuan Wang, Yukun Li, Shikun Feng, Hao Tian, Hua Wu, and Haifeng Wang. 2019. Ernie 2.0: A continual pre-training framework for language understanding. In *arXiv preprint arXiv:1907.12412*.

Alon Talmor and Jonathan Berant. 2019. Multiqa: An empirical investigation of generalization and transfer in reading comprehension. In *arXiv preprint arXiv:1905.13453*.

Chuanqi Tan, Furu Wei, Nan Yang, Bowen Du, Weifeng Lv, and Ming Zhou. 2017. S-net: From answer extraction to answer generation for machine reading comprehension. In *arXiv preprint arXiv:1706.04815*.

Shuohang Wang and Jing Jiang. 2016. Machine comprehension using match-lstm and answer pointer. In *arXiv preprint arXiv:1608.07905*.

Wenhui Wang, Nan Yang, Furu Wei, Baobao Chang, and Ming Zhou. 2017. Gated self-matching networks for reading comprehension and question answering. In *Proceedings of the 55th Annual Meeting of the Association for Computational Linguistics (Volume 1: Long Papers)*, pages 189–198.

Yizhong Wang, Kai Liu, Jing Liu, Wei He, Yajuan Lyu, Hua Wu, Sujian Li, and Haifeng Wang. 2018. Multi-passage machine reading comprehension with cross-passage answer verification. In *Proceedings of the 56th Annual Meeting of the Association for Computational Linguistics (Volume 1: Long Papers)*, pages 1918–1927.

Adina Williams, Nikita Nangia, and Samuel R Bowman. 2017. A broad-coverage challenge corpus for sentence understanding through inference. In *arXiv preprint arXiv:1704.05426*.

Caiming Xiong, Victor Zhong, and Richard Socher. 2016. Dynamic coattention networks for question answering. In *arXiv preprint arXiv:1611.01604*.

Zhilin Yang, Zihang Dai, Yiming Yang, Jaime Carbonell, Ruslan Salakhutdinov, and Quoc V Le. 2019. Xlnet: Generalized autoregressive pretraining for language understanding. In *arXiv preprint arXiv:1906.08237*.

Adams Wei Yu, David Dohan, Minh-Thang Luong, Rui Zhao, Kai Chen, Mohammad Norouzi, and Quoc V Le. 2018. Qanet: Combining local convolution with global self-attention for reading comprehension. In *arXiv preprint arXiv:1804.09541*.

An Exploration of Data Augmentation and Sampling Techniques for Domain-Agnostic Question Answering

Shayne Longpre,[*] Yi Lu,[*] Zhucheng Tu,[*] Chris DuBois

Apple Inc.

{slongpre, ylu7, zhucheng_tu, cdubois}@apple.com

Abstract

To produce a domain-agnostic question answering model for the Machine Reading Question Answering (MRQA) 2019 Shared Task, we investigate the relative benefits of large pre-trained language models, various data sampling strategies, as well as query and context paraphrases generated by back-translation. We find a simple negative sampling technique to be particularly effective, even though it is typically used for datasets that include unanswerable questions, such as SQuAD 2.0. When applied in conjunction with per-domain sampling, our XLNet (Yang et al., 2019)-based submission achieved the second best Exact Match and F1 in the MRQA leaderboard competition.

1 Introduction

Recent work has demonstrated that generalization remains a salient challenge in extractive question answering (Talmor and Berant, 2019; Yogatama et al., 2019). It is especially difficult to generalize to a target domain without similar training data, or worse, any knowledge of the domain's distribution. This is the case for the MRQA Shared Task.[1] Together, these two factors demand a representation that generalizes broadly, and rules out the usual assumption that more data in the training domain will necessarily improve performance on the target domain. Consequently, we adopt the overall approach of curating our input data and learning regime to encourage representations that are not biased by any one domain or distribution.

As a requisite first step to a representation that generalizes, transfer learning (in the form of large pre-trained language models such as Peters et al. (2018); Howard and Ruder (2018); Devlin et al. (2019); Yang et al. (2019)), offers a solid foundation. We compare BERT and XLNet, leveraging

Transformer based models (Vaswani et al., 2017) pre-trained on significant quantities of unlabelled text. Secondly, we identify how the domains of our training data correlate with the performance of "out-domain" development sets. This serves as a proxy for the impact these different sets may have on a held-out test set, as well as evidence of a representation that generalizes. Next we explore data sampling and augmentation strategies to better leverage our available supervised data.

To our surprise, the more sophisticated techniques including back-translated augmentations (even sampled with active learning strategies) yield no noticeable improvement. In contrast, much simpler techniques offer significant improvements. In particular, negative samples designed to teach the model when to abstain from predictions prove highly effective out-domain. We hope our analysis and results, both positive and negative, inform the challenge of generalization in multi-domain question answering.

We begin with an overview of the data and techniques used in our system, before discussing experiments and results.

2 Data

We provide select details of the MRQA data as they pertain to our sampling strategies delineated later. For greater detail refer to the MRQA task description.

Our training data consists of six separately collected QA datasets. We refer to these and their associated development sets as "in-domain" (ID). We are also provided with six "out-domain" (OD) development sets sourced from other QA datasets. In Table 1 we tabulate the number of "examples" (question-context pairs), "segments" (the question combined with a portion of the context), and "no-answer" (NA) segments (those without a valid answer span).

To clarify these definitions, consider examples

---

[*] equal contribution

[1] https://mrqa.github.io/shared

Proceedings of the Second Workshop on Machine Reading for Question Answering, pages 220–227
Hong Kong, China, November 4, 2019. ©2019 Association for Computational Linguistics

Dataset	Examples	Segments	NA (%)
SQuAD (Rajpurkar et al., 2016)	87K	87K	0.1
SearchQA (Dunn et al., 2017)	117K	657K	56.3
NaturalQuestions (Kwiatkowski et al., 2019)	104K	189K	36.3
TriviaQA (Joshi et al., 2017)	62K	337K	57.3
HotpotQA (Yang et al., 2018)	73K	73K	0.3
NewsQA (Trischler et al., 2017)	74K	214K	49.0
Total	**517K**	**1557K**	**47.3**

Table 1: Number of examples (question-context pairs), segments (question-context chunks), and the percentage of No Answer (NA) segments within each dataset.

with long context sequences. We found it necessary to break these examples' contexts into multiple segments in order to satisfy computational memory constraints. Each of these segments may or may not contain the gold answer span. A segment without an answer span we term "no-answer". To illustrate this pre-processing, consider question, context pair (q, c) where we impose a maximum sequence length of M tokens. If $len(c) > M$ then we create multiple overlapping input segments $(q, c_1), (q, c_2), ..., (q, c_k)$ where each c_i contains only a portion of the larger context c. The sliding window that generates these chunks is parameterized by the document stride D, and the maximum sequence length M, shown below in Equation 1.

$$(q, c) \rightarrow \left\{ (q, c_{i \cdot D : M + i \cdot D}), \forall i \in [0, k] \right\} \quad (1)$$

The frequencies presented in Table 1 are based on our settings of $M = 512$ and $D = 128$.

3 System Overview

3.1 XLNet

While we used BERT Base (Devlin et al., 2019) for most of our experimentation, we used XLNet Large (Yang et al., 2019) for our final submission. At the time of submission this model held state-of-the-art results on several NLP benchmarks including GLUE (Wang et al., 2018). Leveraging the Transformer-XL architecture (Dai et al., 2019), a "generalized autoregressive pretraining" method, and much more training data than BERT, its representation provided a strong source of transfer learning. In keeping with XLNet's question answering module, we also computed the end logits based on the ground truth of the start position during training time, and used beam search over the end logits at inference time. We based our code

on the HuggingFace implementation.[2] of BERT and XLNet, and used the pre-trained models in the GitHub repository.

3.2 Domain Sampling

For the problem of generalizing to an unseen and out-domain test set, it's important not to overfit to the training distribution. Given the selection of diverse training sources, domains, and distributions within MRQA we posed the following questions. Are all training sources useful to the target domains? Will multi-domain training partially mitigate overfitting to any given training set? Is it always appropriate to sample equally from each?

To answer these questions, we fine-tuned a variety of specialized models on the BERT Base Cased (BBC) pre-trained model. Six models were each fine-tuned once on their respective in-domain training set. A multi-domain model was trained on the union of these six in-domain training sets. Lastly, we used this multi-domain model as the starting point for fine-tuning six more models, one for each in-domain training set. In total we produced six dataset-specialized models each fine-tuned once, one multi-domain model, and six dataset-specialized models each fine-tuned twice.

There are a few evident trends. The set of models which were first fine-tuned on the multi-domain dataset achieved higher Exact Match (EM) almost universally than those which weren't. This improvement extends not just to in-domain datasets, but also to out-domain development sets. In Figure 1 we observe these models on the Y-axis, and their Exact Match (EM) scores on each in-domain and out-domain development set. This confirms the observations from Talmor and Berant (2019) that multi-domain training improves robustness and generalization broadly, and suggests that a variety of question answering domains is significant across domains. Interestingly, the second round of fine-tuning, this time on a specific domain, did not cause models to significantly, or catastrophically forget what they learned in the initial, multi-domain fine-tuning. This is clear

---

[2] https://github.com/huggingface/ pytorch-transformers Our implementation modifies elements of the tokenization, modeling, and training procedure. Specifically, we remove whitespace tokenization and other pre-processing features that are not necessary for MRQA-tokenized data. We also add subepoch checkpoints and validation, per dataset sampling, and improved post-processing to select predicted text without special tokens or unusual spacing.

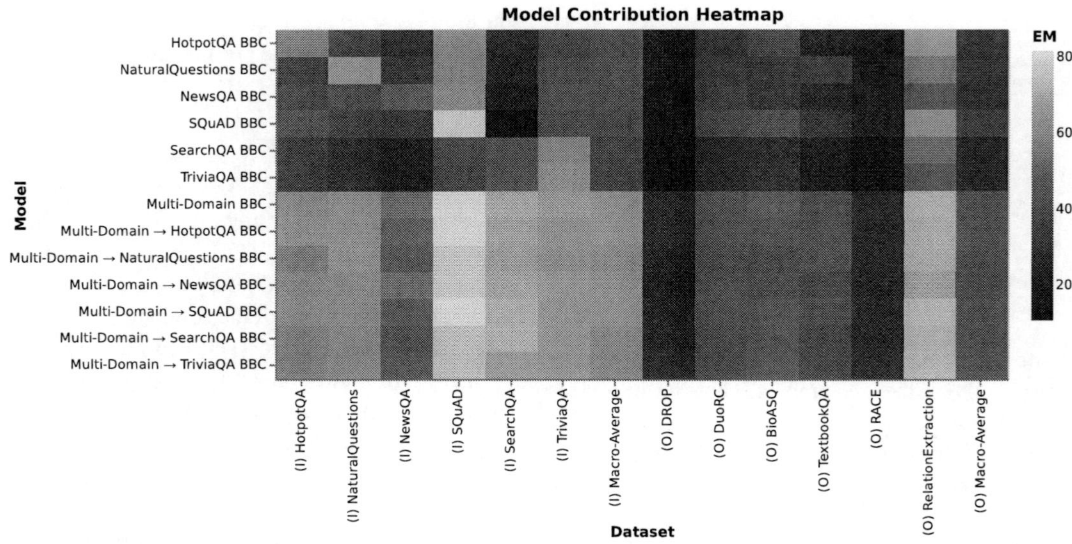

Figure 1: Heatmap of Exact Match (EM) for BERT Base Cased (BBC) models, the top six fine-tuned directly on each training dataset, and the bottom six fine-tuned on multi-domain before being fine-tuned on each training dataset.

from comparing the generic "Multi-Domain BBC" to those models fine-tuned on top of it, such as "Multi-Domain → SQuAD FT BBC".

Secondly, we observe that the models we fine-tune on SearchQA (Dunn et al., 2017) and TriviaQA (Joshi et al., 2017) achieve relatively poor results across all sets (in-domain and out-domain) aside from themselves. The latter datasets are both Jeopardy-sourced, distantly supervised, long context datasets. In contrast, the SQuAD (Rajpurkar et al., 2016) fine-tuned model achieves the best results on both in and out-domain "Macro-Average" Exact Match. Of the models with multi-domain pre-fine-tuning NewsQA, SearchQA, and TriviaQA performed the worst on the out-domain (O) Macro-Average. As such we modified our sampling distribution to avoid oversampling them and risk degrading generalization performance. This risk is particularly prevalent for SearchQA, the largest dataset by number of examples. Additionally, its long contexts generate 657K segments, double that of the next largest dataset (Table 1). This was exacerbated further when we initially included the nearly 10 occurrences of each detected answer. TriviaQA shares this characteristic, though not quite as drastically. Accordingly, for our later experiments we chose not to use all instances of a detected answer, as this would further skew our multi-domain samples towards SearchQA and TriviaQA, and increase the num-

			In-Domain		Out-Domain	
NA	Model	MSL	EM	F1	EM	F1
No	BBC	200	65.70	75.98	45.80	56.78
	BBC	512	65.29	76.01	45.59	57.40
	XBC	200	43.78	65.24	43.78	52.12
	XBC	512	65.91	74.93	49.59	59.61
Yes	BBC	200	66.11	76.41	46.19	57.51
	BBC	512	66.20	76.77	46.28	58.00
	XBC	200	68.67	77.69	50.04	59.68
	XBC	512	**70.04**	**79.15**	**50.71**	**61.16**

Table 2: Model performance including or excluding No-Answer (NA) segments in training. We examine how these results vary with the max sequence length (MSL). BBC refers to BERT Base Cased and XBC refers to XLNet Base Cased.

ber of times contexts from these sets are repeated as segments. We also chose, for many experiments, to sample fewer examples of SearchQA than our other datasets, and found this to improve F1 marginally across configurations.

3.3 Negative Sampling

While recent datasets such as SQuAD 2.0 (Rajpurkar et al., 2018) and Natural Questions (Kwiatkowski et al., 2019) have extended extractive question answering to include a No Answer option, in the traditional formulation of the problem there is no notion of a negative class. Formulated as such, the MRQA Shared Task guarantees the presence of an answer span within each example. However, this is not guaranteed within each segment, producing NA segments.

At inference time we compute the most probable answer span for each segment separately and then select the best span across all segments of that $(\mathbf{q}, \mathbf{c})$ example to be the one with the highest probability. This is computed as the sum of the start and end span probabilities. At training time, typically the NA segments are discarded altogether. However, this causes a discrepancy between train and inference time, as "Negative" segments are only observed in the latter.

To address this, we include naturally occurring "Negative" segments, and add an abstention option for the model. For each Negative segment, we set the indices for both the start and end span labels to point to the [CLS] token. This gives our model the option to abstain from selecting a span in a given segment. Lastly, at inference time we select the highest probability answer across all segments, excluding the No Answer [CLS] option.

Given that 47.3% of all input segments are NA, as shown in Table 1, its unsurprising their inclusion significantly impacted training time and results. We find that this simple form of Negative Sampling yields non-trivial improvements on MRQA (see Table 2). We hypothesize this is primarily because a vaguely relevant span of tokens amid a completely irrelevant NA segment would monopolize the predicted probabilities. Meanwhile the actual answer span likely appears in a segment that may contain many competing spans of relevant text, each attracting some probability mass. As we would expect, the improvement this technique offers is magnified where the context is much longer than M. To our knowledge this technique is still not prevalent in purely extractive question answering, though Alberti et al. (2019) cite it as a key contributor to their strong baseline on Google's Natural Questions.

3.4 Paraphrasing by Back-Translation

Yu et al. (2018) showed that generating context paraphrases via back-translation provides significant improvements for reading comprehension on the competitive SQuAD 1.1 benchmark. We emulate this approach to add further quantity and variety to our data distribution, with the hope that it would produce similarly strong results for out-domain generalization. To extend their work,

we experiment with both query and context paraphrases generated by back-translation. Leveraging the same open-sourced TensorFlow NMT codebase,[3] we train an 8-layer `seq2seq` model with attention on the WMT16 News English-German task, obtaining a BLEU score of 28.0 for translating from English to German and 25.7 for German to English, when evaluated on the `newstest2015` dataset. We selected German as our back-translation language due to ease of reproducibility, given the public benchmarks published in the `nmt` repository.

For generating query paraphrases, we directly feed each query into the NMT model after performing tokenization and byte pair encoding. For generating context paraphrases, we first use SpaCy to segment each context into sentences,[4] using the `en_core_web_sm` model. Then, we translate each sentence independently, following the same procedure as we do for each query. In the course of generating paraphrases, we find decoded sequences are occasionally empty for a given context or query input. For these cases we keep the original sentence.

We attempt to retrieve the new answer span using string matching, and where that fails we employed the the same heuristic described in Yu et al. (2018) to obtain a new, estimated answer. Specifically, this involves finding the character-level 2-gram overlap of every token in the paraphrase sentence with the start and end token of the original answer. The score is computed as the Jaccard similarity between the sets of character-level 2-grams in the original answer token and new sentence token. The span of text between the two tokens that has the highest combined score, passing a minimum threshold, is selected as the new answer. In cases where there is no score above the threshold, no answer is generated. Any question in each context without an answer is omitted, and any paraphrased example without at least one question-answer pair is discarded.

3.4.1 Augmentation Strategy

For every query and context pair (q, c), we used our back-translation model to generate a query paraphrase q' and a context paraphrase c'. We then create a new pair that includes the paraphrase q' instead of q with probability $P_q(x)$, and independently we choose the paraphrase c' over c with

---

[3]`https://github.com/tensorflow/nmt`
[4]`https://spacy.io/`

probability $P_c(x)$. If either q' or c' is sampled, we add this augmented example to the training data. This sampling strategy allowed us flexibility in how often we include query or context augmentations.

3.4.2 Active Learning

Another method of sampling our data augmentations was motivated by principles in active learning (Settles, 2009). Rather than sampling uniformly, might we prioritize the more challenging examples for augmentation? This is motivated by the idea that many augmentations may not be radically different from the original data points, and may consequently carry less useful, repetitive signals.

To quantify the difficulty of an example we used $1 - F1$ score computed for our best model. We chose F1 as it provides a continuous rather than binary value, and is robust to a model that may select the wrong span, but contains the correct answer text. Other metrics, such as loss or Exact Match do not provide both these benefits.

For each example we derived its probability weighting from its F1 score. This weight replaces the uniform probability previously used to draw samples for query and context augmentations. We devised three weighting strategies, to experiment with different distributions. We refer to these as the hard, moderate and soft distributions. Each distribution employs its own scoring function S_x (Equation 2), which is normalized across all examples to determine the probability of drawing that sample (Equation 3).

$$S(x) = \begin{cases} 1 - F1(x) + \epsilon & \text{Hard Score} \\ 2 - F1(x) & \text{Moderate Score} \\ 3 - F1(x) & \text{Soft Score} \end{cases} \quad (2)$$

$$P(x) = \frac{S(x)}{\Sigma_{i=1..n}S(i)} \quad (3)$$

The hard scoring function allocates negligible probability to examples with $F1 = 1$, emphasizing the hardest examples the most of the three distributions. We used an ϵ value of 0.01 to prevent any example from having a zero sample probability. The moderate and soft scoring functions penalize correct predictions less aggressively, smoothing the distribution closer to uniform.

4 Experiments and Discussion

During our experimentation process we used our smallest model BERT Base Cased (BBC) for the most expensive sampling explorations (Figure 1), XLNet Base Cased (XBC) to confirm our findings extended to XLNet (Table 2), and XLNet Large Cased (XLC) as the initial basis for our final submission contenders (Table 3).

Our training procedure for each model involved fine-tuning the Transformer over two epochs, each with three validation checkpoints. The checkpoint with the highest Out-Domain Macro-Average (estimated from a $2,000$ dev-set subsample) was selected as the best for that training run. Our multi-domain dataset originally consisted of 75k examples from every training set, and using every detected answer. We modified this to a maximum of 120k samples from each dataset, 100k from SearchQA, and using only one detected answer per example; given our findings in Section 3.2.

We trained every model on 8 NVIDIA Tesla V100 GPUs. For BBC and XBC we used a learning rate of $5e - 5$, single-GPU batch size of 25, and gradient accumulation of 1, yielding an effective batch size of 200. For XLC we used a learning rate of $2e - 5$, single-GPU batch size of 6, and gradient accumulation of 3, yielding an effective batch size of $6 \cdot 8 \cdot 3 = 144$. We found the gradient accumulation and lower learning rate critical to achieve training stability.

We conduct several experiments to evaluate the various sampling and augmentation strategies discussed in Section 3. In Table 2 we examine the impact of including No Answer segments in our training set. We found this drastically outperformed the typical practice of excluding these segments. This effect was particularly noticeable on datasets with longer sequences. As expected, the improvement is exaggerated at the shorter max sequence length (MSL) of 200, where including NA segments increases Out-Domain EM from 43.78 to 50.04 on the XBC model.

Next, we evaluate our back-translated query and context augmentations using the sampling strategies described in Section 3.4.2. To select the best $P_q(x)$, $P_c(x)$ and sampling strategy we conducted the following search. First we explored sampling probabilities 0.2, 0.4, 0.6, 0.8, 1.0 for query and context separately, using random sampling, and subsequently we combined them using values informed from the previous exploration, this time

Mode	$P_q(x)$	$P_c(x)$	In-Domain F1							Out-Domain F1						
			HotpotQA	Natural Questions	NewsQA	SearchQA	SQuAD	TriviaQA	Macro-Average	BioASQ	DROP	DuoRC	RACE	Relation Extraction	TextbookQA	Macro-Average
–	0	0	82.62	82.15	72.52	82.80	**94.50**	78.28	82.14	**73.00**	63.52	**65.68**	**53.25**	88.49	64.38	**68.07**
R	0.2	0.2	82.42	82.29	72.45	83.20	94.09	**79.44**	82.32	70.45	63.97	62.75	52.66	88.09	63.28	66.87
	0.2	0.4	82.59	**82.51**	72.30	84.50	94.35	79.09	**82.56**	72.02	**64.29**	63.61	52.32	**88.85**	64.12	67.54
	0.4	0.4	82.58	82.28	71.72	83.80	94.02	77.78	82.03	69.60	63.45	63.56	52.74	88.22	63.67	66.87
S	0.2	0.2	82.44	82.10	72.06	83.67	94.32	76.58	81.86	70.47	64.14	63.15	52.61	88.37	63.60	67.06
	0.2	0.4	82.50	81.69	72.43	84.46	93.98	76.80	81.98	70.79	60.62	63.48	52.38	87.38	62.07	66.12
	0.4	0.4	82.07	82.15	72.07	84.20	93.99	77.20	81.95	71.34	62.64	62.81	50.65	87.60	63.12	66.36
M	0.2	0.2	**82.72**	82.26	72.22	83.45	94.12	76.55	81.89	71.46	63.89	63.29	51.67	87.98	**64.85**	67.19
	0.2	0.4	82.41	82.15	**72.60**	**84.88**	93.85	77.34	82.20	71.66	63.89	62.12	52.67	88.03	64.05	67.07
	0.4	0.4	82.55	82.09	72.57	84.30	94.19	76.97	82.11	71.13	63.03	62.58	51.65	87.76	64.67	66.80
H	0.2	0.2	81.68	81.15	70.55	80.51	94.05	74.80	80.46	70.60	62.55	61.96	52.23	87.87	61.16	66.06
	0.2	0.4	82.05	81.45	70.84	81.92	94.18	75.49	80.99	72.89	62.29	63.30	51.66	87.63	62.00	66.63
	0.4	0.4	81.93	81.45	71.67	81.71	93.92	75.96	81.11	71.26	61.52	62.06	51.36	86.91	60.18	65.55

Table 3: F1 scores for data augmentation using different proportions of query and context paraphrasing and different sampling distributions on XLNet Large Cased, on individual datasets. R, S, M, H refer to random, soft, moderate, and hard modes from Section 3.4.2 respectively.

Dataset	Out-Domain EM	F1
BioASQ (Tsatsaronis et al., 2015)	60.28	71.98
DROP (Dua et al., 2019)	48.50	58.90
DuoRC (Saha et al., 2018)	53.29	63.36
RACE (Lai et al., 2017)	39.35	53.87
RelationExtraction (Levy et al., 2017)	79.20	87.85
TextbookQA (Kembhavi et al., 2017)	56.50	65.54
Macro-Average	56.19	66.92

Table 4: Breakdown of hidden development set results by dataset using our best XLNet Large model.

Submission	EM	F1
D-NET (Baidu)	**60.39**	**72.55**
Ours (Apple)	59.47	70.75
FT_XLNet (HIT)	58.37	70.54
HLTC (HKUST)	56.59	68.98
BERT-cased-whole-word (Aristo@AI2)	53.52	66.27
XERO (Fuji Xerox)	52.41	66.11
BERT-large + Adv. Training (Team 42-alpha)	48.91	62.19
BERT large baseline (MRQA Organizers)	48.20	61.76
BERT base baseline (MRQA Organizers)	45.54	58.50

Table 5: Macro-Average EM and F1 on the held-out leaderboard test sets.

searching over sampling strategies: random, soft, moderate and hard. We present the best results in Table 3 and conclude that these data augmentations did not help in-domain or out-domain performance. While we observed small boosts to metrics on BBC using this technique, no such gains were found on XLC. We suspect this is because (a) large pre-trained language models such as XLC already capture the linguistic variations in language introduced by paraphrased examples quite well, and (b) we already have a plethora of diverse training data from the distributions these augmentations are derived from. It is not clear if the boosts QANet Yu et al. (2018) observed on SQuAD 1.1 would still apply with the additional diversity provided by the five additional QA datasets for training. We notice that SearchQA and TriviaQA benefit the most from some form of data augmentation, both by more than one F1 point. Both of these are distantly supervised, and have relatively long contexts.

Our final submission leverages our fine-tuned XLC configuration, with domain and negative sampling. We omit the data augmentation and active sampling techniques which we did not find to aid out-domain performance. The results of the leaderboard Out-Domain Development set and final test set results are shown in Table 4 and Table 5 respectively.

5 Conclusion

This paper describes experiments on various competitive pre-trained models (BERT, XLNet), domain sampling strategies, negative sampling, data augmentation via back-translation, and active learning. We determine which of these strategies help and hurt multi-domain generalization, finding ultimately that some of the simplest techniques offer surprising improvements. The most significant benefits came from sampling No Answer segments, which proved to be particularly important for training extractive models on long sequences. In combination these findings culminated in the second ranked submission on the MRQA-19 Shared Task.

References

Chris Alberti, Kenton Lee, and Michael Collins. 2019. A BERT baseline for the Natural Questions. *arXiv preprint arXiv:1901.08634.*

Zihang Dai, Zhilin Yang, Yiming Yang, William W Cohen, Jaime Carbonell, Quoc V Le, and Ruslan Salakhutdinov. 2019. Transformer-XL: Attentive language models beyond a fixed-length context. *arXiv preprint arXiv:1901.02860*.

Jacob Devlin, Ming-Wei Chang, Kenton Lee, and Kristina Toutanova. 2019. BERT: Pre-training of deep bidirectional transformers for language understanding. In *Proceedings of the 2019 Conference of the North American Chapter of the Association for Computational Linguistics: Human Language Technologies, Volume 1 (Long and Short Papers)*, pages 4171–4186.

Dheeru Dua, Yizhong Wang, Pradeep Dasigi, Gabriel Stanovsky, Sameer Singh, and Matt Gardner. 2019. DROP: A reading comprehension benchmark requiring discrete reasoning over paragraphs. In *Proceedings of the 2019 Conference of the North American Chapter of the Association for Computational Linguistics: Human Language Technologies, Volume 1 (Long and Short Papers)*, pages 2368–2378.

Matthew Dunn, Levent Sagun, Mike Higgins, V Ugur Guney, Volkan Cirik, and Kyunghyun Cho. 2017. SearchQA: A new Q&A dataset augmented with context from a search engine. *arXiv preprint arXiv:1704.05179*.

Jeremy Howard and Sebastian Ruder. 2018. Universal language model fine-tuning for text classification. In *Proceedings of the 56th Annual Meeting of the Association for Computational Linguistics (Volume 1: Long Papers)*, pages 328–339.

Mandar Joshi, Eunsol Choi, Daniel Weld, and Luke Zettlemoyer. 2017. TriviaQA: A large scale distantly supervised challenge dataset for reading comprehension. In *Proceedings of the 55th Annual Meeting of the Association for Computational Linguistics (Volume 1: Long Papers)*, pages 1601–1611.

Aniruddha Kembhavi, Minjoon Seo, Dustin Schwenk, Jonghyun Choi, Ali Farhadi, and Hannaneh Hajishirzi. 2017. Are you smarter than a sixth grader? textbook question answering for multimodal machine comprehension. In *2017 IEEE Conference on Computer Vision and Pattern Recognition (CVPR)*, pages 5376–5384. IEEE.

Tom Kwiatkowski, Jennimaria Palomaki, Olivia Redfield, Michael Collins, Ankur Parikh, Chris Alberti, Danielle Epstein, Illia Polosukhin, Matthew Kelcey, Jacob Devlin, Kenton Lee, Kristina N. Toutanova, Llion Jones, Ming-Wei Chang, Andrew Dai, Jakob Uszkoreit, Quoc Le, and Slav Petrov. 2019. Natural questions: a benchmark for question answering research. *Transactions of the Association of Computational Linguistics*.

Guokun Lai, Qizhe Xie, Hanxiao Liu, Yiming Yang, and Eduard Hovy. 2017. RACE: Large-scale reading comprehension dataset from examinations. In

Proceedings of the 2017 Conference on Empirical Methods in Natural Language Processing, pages 785–794.

Omer Levy, Minjoon Seo, Eunsol Choi, and Luke Zettlemoyer. 2017. Zero-shot relation extraction via reading comprehension. In *Proceedings of the 21st Conference on Computational Natural Language Learning (CoNLL 2017)*, pages 333–342.

Matthew Peters, Mark Neumann, Mohit Iyyer, Matt Gardner, Christopher Clark, Kenton Lee, and Luke Zettlemoyer. 2018. Deep contextualized word representations. In *Proceedings of the 2018 Conference of the North American Chapter of the Association for Computational Linguistics: Human Language Technologies, Volume 1 (Long Papers)*, pages 2227–2237.

Pranav Rajpurkar, Robin Jia, and Percy Liang. 2018. Know what you don't know: Unanswerable questions for SQuAD. In *Proceedings of the 56th Annual Meeting of the Association for Computational Linguistics (Volume 2: Short Papers)*, pages 784–789.

Pranav Rajpurkar, Jian Zhang, Konstantin Lopyrev, and Percy Liang. 2016. SQuAD: 100,000+ questions for machine comprehension of text. In *Proceedings of the 2016 Conference on Empirical Methods in Natural Language Processing*, pages 2383–2392.

Amrita Saha, Rahul Aralikatte, Mitesh M Khapra, and Karthik Sankaranarayanan. 2018. DuoRC: Towards complex language understanding with paraphrased reading comprehension. In *Proceedings of the 56th Annual Meeting of the Association for Computational Linguistics (Volume 1: Long Papers)*, pages 1683–1693.

Burr Settles. 2009. Active learning literature survey. Technical report, University of Wisconsin-Madison Department of Computer Sciences.

Alon Talmor and Jonathan Berant. 2019. MultiQA: An empirical investigation of generalization and transfer in reading comprehension. *arXiv preprint arXiv:1905.13453*.

Adam Trischler, Tong Wang, Xingdi Yuan, Justin Harris, Alessandro Sordoni, Philip Bachman, and Kaheer Suleman. 2017. NewsQA: A machine comprehension dataset. *ACL 2017*, page 191.

George Tsatsaronis, Georgios Balikas, Prodromos Malakasiotis, Ioannis Partalas, Matthias Zschunke, Michael R Alvers, Dirk Weissenborn, Anastasia Krithara, Sergios Petridis, Dimitris Polychronopoulos, et al. 2015. An overview of the BIOASQ large-scale biomedical semantic indexing and question answering competition. *BMC bioinformatics*, 16(1):138.

Ashish Vaswani, Noam Shazeer, Niki Parmar, Jakob Uszkoreit, Llion Jones, Aidan N Gomez, Łukasz Kaiser, and Illia Polosukhin. 2017. Attention is all you need. In *Advances in neural information processing systems*, pages 5998–6008.

Alex Wang, Amanpreet Singh, Julian Michael, Felix Hill, Omer Levy, and Samuel R Bowman. 2018. GLUE: A multi-task benchmark and analysis platform for natural language understanding. *EMNLP 2018*, page 353.

Zhilin Yang, Zihang Dai, Yiming Yang, Jaime Carbonell, Ruslan Salakhutdinov, and Quoc V Le. 2019. XLNet: Generalized autoregressive pretraining for language understanding. *arXiv preprint arXiv:1906.08237*.

Zhilin Yang, Peng Qi, Saizheng Zhang, Yoshua Bengio, William Cohen, Ruslan Salakhutdinov, and Christopher D Manning. 2018. HotpotQA: A dataset for diverse, explainable multi-hop question answering. In *Proceedings of the 2018 Conference on Empirical Methods in Natural Language Processing*, pages 2369–2380.

Dani Yogatama, Cyprien de Masson d'Autume, Jerome Connor, Tomas Kocisky, Mike Chrzanowski, Lingpeng Kong, Angeliki Lazaridou, Wang Ling, Lei Yu, Chris Dyer, et al. 2019. Learning and evaluating general linguistic intelligence. *arXiv preprint arXiv:1901.11373*.

Adams Wei Yu, David Dohan, Minh-Thang Luong, Rui Zhao, Kai Chen, Mohammad Norouzi, and Quoc V Le. 2018. QANet: Combining local convolution with global self-attention for reading comprehension. *arXiv preprint arXiv:1804.09541*.

Author Index